MONEY IN A FREE SOCIETY

MONEY IN A FREE SOCIETY

*Keynes, Friedman,
and the New Crisis
in Capitalism*

TIM CONGDON

ENCOUNTER BOOKS
New York · London

Portions of this book were originally published by Edward Elgar Publishing in 2007 under the title *Keynes, the Keynesians, and Monetarism.*

First American edition published in 2011 by Encounter Books, an activity of Encounter for Culture and Education, Inc., a nonprofit, tax exempt corporation.
Encounter Books website address: *www.encounterbooks.com*

Manufactured in the United States and printed on acid-free paper. The paper used in this publication meets the minimum requirements of ANSI/NISO Z39.48-1992 (R 1997) (*Permanence of Paper*).

FIRST AMERICAN EDITION

LIBRARY OF CONGRESS CATALOGING-IN-PUBLICATION DATA
Congdon, Tim.
Money in a free society : Keynes, Friedman, and the new crisis in capitalism / by Tim Congdon.
p.   cm.
Includes bibliographical references and index.
ISBN-13: 978-1-59403-524-1 (hardcover : alk. paper)
ISBN-10: 1-59403-524-5 (hardcover : alk. paper)
1. Money. 2. Quantity theory of money. 3. Fiscal policy.
4. Banks and banking. 5. Macroeconomics. 6. Keynesian economics.
7. Friedman, Milton, 1912–2006. I. Title.
HG221.C74126 2011
339.5'2—dc22
2010046197

10 9 8 7 6 5 4 3 2 1

CONTENTS

LIST OF FIGURES

LIST OF TABLES

Foreword

IN MID-2007 I brought out a collection of essays titled *Keynes, the Keynesians, and Monetarism*, which enjoyed some esteem but could hardly claim to be a best-seller. As the book was being published, the world economic situation changed radically. The benign outcomes of the twenty years up to mid-2007, the so-called "Great Moderation," were replaced in late 2007 and 2008 by financial crisis, and in 2009 by the worst plunge in demand, output, and employment since the 1930s, or, in a phrase, by the "Great Recession." I was therefore most grateful to Roger Kimball when he suggested that Encounter Books might like to publish another collection, using some of the material from *Keynes, the Keynesians, and Monetarism*, but adding some of my more recent pieces, particularly those prompted by the dramatic slide in the world economy. This book is about the same length as the 2007 collection, but roughly half of it is new.

Money in a Free Society is intended for both the general reader and professional economists, particularly economists who are involved in the formulation and criticism of actual policy. (As will be clear from the rather sharp comments I make in the introduction, I am less interested in the views of economists in the universities, who – in my opinion – should be ashamed of the mess their subject is in.) Most of the essays should not be too technical for readers of *The Wall Street Journal* or *BusinessWeek*. However, five of them are a bit hard (essays 4, 6, 10, 15, and 16), particularly essay 4. I have to apologize for this, but essay 4 is in fact the crucial one in debunking much current nonsense about the exhaustion of monetary policy at the so-called "zero bound."

I am known as the U.K.'s leading monetarist economist, a position I have occupied for over thirty years. Milton Friedman, the intellectual leader of monetarism, is indeed one of the two heroes of this book. One aim of *Money in a Free Society* is to argue that Friedman's work needs to be recovered and re-emphasized. However, I do not agree with all of Friedman's analytical approach, and one essay here is in fact about the differences between American and British monetarism. The other hero is Keynes, for reasons which may become clearer when the reader reaches the last few essays.

Both Keynes and Friedman were very transatlantic figures. They traveled on several occasions between the U.K. and the U.S., and their influence in both countries was enormous. In economics there is still a "special relationship" between America and Britain. Unfortunately, this book is sometimes straddled somewhat awkwardly over the ocean, and I expect some American readers to complain that it is nearer to Devon than to Cape Cod. Well, you must take it or leave it.

I have no illusions that – in the current era of information overload, and media and Internet bombardment – readers are going to absorb every word. I therefore follow this foreword with a summary of the main points. If the summary serves as an appetizer, so much the better.

I have decided not to clutter this foreword with the usual thanks to the people who have influenced me and helped me in my work. They know who they are and that I am grateful to them. That is enough.*

TIM CONGDON
December 13, 2010

POSTSCRIPT: The bulk of this book was completed in August 2010, but revisions were made until the end of 2010. In early November, the Federal Reserve announced that over the next six months it would purchase $600 billion of long-dated Treasuries in a set of operations called "QE2" – i.e., the second round of "quantitative easing." In my view, operations of this kind should have been announced in early 2009. I approve of them wholeheartedly. The key essay 4 in this collection explains why they are a Good Thing in depressed economic conditions. It remains to be seen whether these operations do in fact boost the growth rate of the quantity of money, broadly defined, but that does appear to have been their initial effect, and wider signs of economic improvement have started to appear.

---

* I am most grateful to the production team at Encounter Books, particularly Linda Bridges, for their work on the original typescript.

SUMMARY OF KEY MESSAGES

Part	Argument
1. Did His Disciples Betray Keynes?	Yes. They dropped the monetary side of Keynes's work, misrepresented his message as anti-market and pro-state-intervention, and oversimplified his views on the merits of fiscal policy. Specifically, Paul Krugman has misinterpreted Keynes's "liquidity trap" in order to establish his case for more public spending and large budget deficits in the U.S. and Japan.
2. Is "the Keynesian Revolution" a Factoid?	Yes. The notion that in the first thirty years after 1945 governments used fiscal policy to manage demand and so maintain "full employment" cannot be sustained even in the U.K., the supposed heartland of "the Keynesian revolution." Widespread belief that there was a "Keynesian revolution" stems from the constant repetition of an untruth and is a factoid. The good macroeconomic outcomes of the Great Moderation in the twenty years up to 2007 were largely due to the incorporation of monetarist ideas in policy thinking and practice.
3. Does Fiscal Policy Work?	No. As Friedman noted on many occasions, the historical record shows that fiscal policy is ineffective. It is invariably smothered by the

effects of the quantity of money on the economy. The U.K.'s 1981 Budget was a crushing refutation of Keynesian fiscalism.

4. Was There a "Monetarist Counterrevolution"?

Yes. The monetarist counterrevolution led by Milton Friedman was a central element in the resurgence of conservatism in the 1980s. Despite some difficulties in applying monetarist ideas to policy-making and many important continuing debates between monetarists, their main messages remain of great relevance to policy-making today.

5. How Does the Economy Work?

As both Keynes and Friedman said, the levels of national income *and wealth* are a function of the quantity of money. The concept of money at work here must be broadly defined to include all, or nearly all, of banks' deposit liabilities. When the quantity of broad money rises sharply, the first effects are likely to be seen in asset markets (common stocks and real estate), before they spread around the economy.

ACKNOWLEDGMENTS

ESSAY 1: Revised and updated version of an article, "Are We Really All Keynesians Now?" in the April 1975 issue of *Encounter*, originally republished with the permission of the editor of *Encounter* in the author's *Reflections on Monetarism* (Aldershot, U.K., and Brookfield, Vt.: Edward Elgar, 1992).

ESSAY 2: Revised and expanded version of a review of the second volume of Skidelsky's biography of Keynes, which appeared in *The Spectator* (November 7, 1992), by kind permission of the publisher of *The Spectator*.

ESSAY 3: Revised and updated version of a lecture given at Cardiff Business School in November 1990, and first published in the author's *Reflections on Monetarism*.

ESSAY 4: Revised and expanded version of a paper, "Monetary Policy at the Zero Bound," in the January–March 2010 issue of *World Economics* (Henley-on-Thames: Economic and Financial Publishing), by kind permission of the editorial board and publisher of *World Economics*.

ESSAY 5: Reprinted, with minor changes, from the author's "Did Britain Have a Keynesian Revolution? Fiscal Policy since 1941," in John Maloney, ed., *Debt and Deficits: An Historical Perspective* (Cheltenham, U.K., and Lyme, N.H.: Edward Elgar, 1998), with the copyright held by the author.

ESSAY 6: Slightly revised version of a paper, "Two Concepts of the Output Gap," in the January–March 2008 issue of *World Economics*, by kind permission of the editorial board and publisher of *World Economics*.

ESSAY 7: Revised and updated version of a paper, "The U.K.'s Achievement of Economic Stability: How and Why Did It Happen?" in the October–December 2002 issue of *World Economics*, by kind permission of the editorial board and publisher of *World Economics*.

ESSAY 8: Reprinted, with minor changes, from the March 2011

issue of *Economic Affairs* (London: Institute of Economic Affairs), by kind permission of the Institute of Economic Affairs.

ESSAY 9: Revised version of an article, "The Futility of Deficit Financing as a Cure for Recession," in *The Times* (October 23, 1975), by kind permission of *The Times*.

ESSAY 10: Reprinted, with minor changes and some updating, from a paper, "Why the 1981 Budget Mattered: The End of Naïve Keynesianism," in Philip Booth, ed., *Were 364 Economists All Wrong?* (London: Institute of Economic Affairs, 2006), by kind permission of the Institute of Economic Affairs.

ESSAY 11: Revised and expanded version of a paper, "On the Ineffectiveness of Fiscal Policy as an Instrument of Macroeconomic Policy," in the March 2009 issue of *Economic Affairs*, by kind permission of the Institute of Economic Affairs.

ESSAY 12: Revised and updated version of chapter 4, titled "The Philosophical Implications," of the author's *Monetarism: An Essay in Definition* (London: Centre for Policy Studies, 1978), by kind permission of the Centre for Policy Studies.

ESSAY 13: Revised and updated version of a paper, "British and American Monetarism Compared," given at the eighth Keynes seminar at the University of Kent and published in Roger Hill, ed., *Keynes, Money, and Monetarism* (London: Macmillan, 1989), by kind permission of Palgrave Macmillan.

ESSAY 14: Revised and updated version of a paper, "Monetarism: A Rejoinder," in the July–September 2004 issue of *World Economics*, by kind permission of the editorial board and publisher of *World Economics*.

ESSAY 15: Abbreviated and updated version of the author's paper "Money, Asset Prices, and the Boom-Bust Cycles in the U.K.," in Kent Matthews and Philip Booth, eds., *Issues in Monetary Policy: The Relationship between Money and Financial Markets* (Chichester: John Wiley and Sons, 2006).

ESSAY 16: Revised and updated version of a special report, "Broad Money vs. Narrow Money: Their Respective Roles in the Determination of Asset Prices and National Income," published in April 2007 by Lombard Street Research, based on the author's Special Paper no. 166 for the London School of Economics' Financial Markets Group, by kind permission of Lombard Street Research and the LSE's Financial Markets Group.

ESSAY 17: This paper began as a weekly note for an Internet-based research business, International Monetary Research Ltd., which the author founded in February 2009. An earlier version was published in the first issue of *Central Banking* in 2010, and the current version, which is slightly different, is reprinted with the usual permission.

ESSAY 18: Revised and expanded version of a paper, "The Unnecessary Recession," in the June 2009 issue of *Standpoint* (London: Social Affairs Unit Magazines), by kind permission of Social Affairs Unit Magazines. The paper was republished, with minor changes, as "Did Bernanke's 'Creditism' Aggravate the Financial Crisis of 2008?" in Steven Kates, ed., *Macroeconomic Theory and Its Failings* (Cheltenham, U.K., and Northampton, Mass.: Edward Elgar, 2010), pp. 26–39.

INTRODUCTION

HAS FREE-MARKET CAPITALISM been caught with its pants down? In the two decades up to mid-2007 the world's leading nations – including the United States – enjoyed a remarkable period of macro-economic stability, known as the "Great Moderation." Inflation was low and output grew steadily, year after year. Supporters of the free-market system gushed about its efficiency and success, not least because its most conspicuous alternative and rival for most of the twentieth century – Soviet Communism – had collapsed in the early 1990s. But the three years starting in mid-2007 were a disaster, with the largest fall in output since the Great Depression of the 1930s. At the time of writing (December 2010) the unemployment rate in the United States has been at or above 9.5 percent for over a year, the longest period of such high unemployment since the data were first prepared in their current form in 1948. The Great Moderation has been followed by the Great Recession. Quite suddenly, free-market capitalism is widely seen as a failure. The critics point fingers at it, as if it were an ideological emperor with no clothes.

The argument of this collection of essays is that there is nothing much the matter with the economies of the capitalist West, but that there is a great deal wrong with its economics and economists. Economics as an intellectual discipline is in chaos, with an obvious lack of an agreed-upon toolkit to deal with the problems thrown up by recent events. The debates relate particularly to those branches of the subject concerned with the determination of output and employment for the economy as a whole or, in a word, to "macroeconomics"; they also revolve around the intellectual legacy of John Maynard Keynes, a remarkable Englishman who could be portrayed as the Churchill of economics.[1] Keynes's 1936 book, *The General Theory of Employment, Interest, and Money*, now approaching its seventy-fifth anniversary, continues to be widely quoted and discussed, and is regarded almost as holy scripture by his disciples. (Those disciples also propound the notion of "the Keynesian revolution," arguing that their hero's ideas were directly responsible for the improvement in macroeconomic performance in the first twenty-five years after the Second World War. The three essays in the second section of this book suggest that "the Keynesian revolution" is a factoid.)

Policy responses to the Great Recession have varied sharply among nations. In the immediate aftermath of the financial breakdown of late 2008, measures of so-called "fiscal stimulus" were adopted, with more or less enthusiasm, across the advanced world. Keynes – often seen as the originator of the idea that fiscal action (meaning an increase in the budget deficit) can boost output and employment – was invoked as newly relevant and important. It was almost as if the Messiah had risen from the dead. Indeed, Keynes's biographer, Lord Skidelsky, penned a best-selling book under the title *The Return of the Master*. But by late 2010 the policies of the United States under the Obama administration had diverged from those being pursued in the rest of the world. Whereas the Obama administration adhered to the fiscal expansionism and large budget deficits associated with Keynes, most European governments had decided that their budget deficits must be curbed and their public finances put on a path to medium-term sustainability. Are the American Keynesians right or wrong in the advice they have given to President Obama? Will the American policy answer to the Great Recession prove better or worse than the European?

The essays in this book have been written over a period of more than thirty years. Nevertheless, they all have a bearing, to a greater or lesser extent, on the central macroeconomic issues raised by the Great Recession. Is Keynesian fiscal activism the best antidote to high unemployment, or not? What does the answer to this question tell us about the determination of national income, output, and employment? How does money fit into the story? Does monetarism – the belief that "money matters" to macroeconomic developments – offer a better interpretation of the Great Recession than Keynesianism? And should policymakers pay more attention to the recommendations given by Milton Friedman, the acknowledged leader of monetarist thought, and less to those attributed to Keynes by his followers?

I.

As the first two essays in this book make clear, Keynes was an economist interested – above all – in the relationship between money and the economy. One of the early provisional titles of *The General Theory* was *The Monetary Theory of Production*.[2] Further, his interest was not in a theoretical, abstract notion of money, but in its real-world, institutional embodiment in the form of bank deposits. (See essay 4, especially pp. 83–86.) Indeed, for Keynes the quantity of money was virtually synonymous with the quantity of bank deposits. The interaction between the banking system and the rest of the economy mattered vitally to his vision of how economies worked. (This was perhaps less obvious in *The General Theory* than in his 1930 *Treatise on Money*, which essay 2 suggests was in fact a better book.) The same remark could equally well be made of Friedman. The great work he co-authored with Anna Schwartz, *A Monetary History of the United States 1867–1960*, highlighted the disintegration of the banking system and a collapse in the quantity of money in the early 1930s as the causes of the Great Depression.[3]

To the extent that the Great Recession was "a crisis of capitalism," it was a crisis about the definition of the banking system's function in a capitalist economy. Given Keynes's specialist knowledge of banking institutions, it might be expected that these aspects would receive the most emphasis in the current revival of interest in his work. But that has not been the pattern of the recent intellectual response. Instead the prevalent tendency in modern macroeconomics is either to disparage banks and bankers, or to ignore them altogether. More generally, the focus of macroeconomics nowadays is on variables – any variables – other than the quantity of money. At academic conferences, use of the phrase "the quantity of money" causes attendees to cough and splutter, as if they suffered from an allergic condition.[4] (By "the quantity of money" I mean – like Keynes and Friedman – a concept dominated by bank deposits.)

To demonstrate my point, I will briefly distinguish among and review four schools of thought that have had a role in recent policy thinking. They are extraordinarily diverse and often in conflict, but they share one common feature. As we shall see, they all say very little, or even nothing at all, about money and banking. If Keynes and Friedman are in their different ways the heroes of *Money in a Free Society*, these schools of thought and their votaries are its anti-heroes.

OLD KEYNESIANISM

The first might be characterized as "Keynesianism as it is usually understood," or "Old Keynesianism." Old Keynesianism certainly originates in Keynes's work, particularly in a theory of national-income determination propounded in *The General Theory*. (I call it "*a* theory of national-income determination" because I don't regard it as in any way canonical. But for many economists it is "*the* theory of national-income determination." It does in fact provide the rationale for the fiscal stimulus program now being carried out by the Obama administration.) The underlying framework of thought views aggregate expenditure as the sum of consumption (which depends on income) and investment (which is influenced by the rate of interest as well as "animal spirits," and so does not depend directly on income and can be regarded as "autonomous"). A few lines of algebra show that – with a constant ratio of consumption to income – national income and expenditure are a multiple of investment. Indeed, they can be seen as a multiple of a wider notion of "autonomous spending," or of investment and government spending combined. So, if aggregate demand is too weak and unemployment too high, the state has merely to increase its own spending, and total demand and output will expand by some multiple of that extra spending. All being well, the dosage of fiscal boost can be adjusted to deliver a desired level of "full employment."[5]

This doctrine is simple and beguiling. The word "Keynes" has been reduced to a marketing jingle for public-works expenditures and a large budget deficit. Stated baldly, Old Keynesianism contains no reference to the quantity of money or the banking sector, and appears to be able to proceed regardless of financial constraints. ("You can spend yourself rich.") When the leading American champions of the Keynesian argument at present – notably Paul Krugman of Princeton University and *The New York Times*, and Joseph Stiglitz of Columbia University – set out the justification for a big budget deficit, they do not dilute it by also recommending a stance on monetary policy.[6]

Regrettably, Keynesian fiscal activism has a major defect: it does not work. The third section of this book has four essays on the various weaknesses of fiscal policy. The first is on Milton Friedman's changing attitudes towards the subject. As a young economist in his thirties, Friedman was friendly towards fiscal analysis, seeing cyclical variations in the budget deficit as a means of facilitating countercyclical changes in the rate of money-supply growth. Later he came to despise fiscal policy. His examination of the evidence persuaded him that no clear link existed in practice between changes in the budget position and concurrent or subsequent changes in aggregate demand. More data are now available, as discussed in essay 11 (and to some extent in essays 10 and 18), and they confirm Friedman's doubts.

The inadequacy of fiscal policy in macroeconomic management was widely accepted in Europe in the 1970s and 1980s. So there is something of a puzzle about the Obama administration's enthusiasm for it.[7] A particularly important turning point in the U.K. was the 1981 Budget, when, in open defiance of the Keynesians' thinking, the Thatcher government raised taxes in the middle of a recession. Despite protests from 364 Keynesian economists in a letter to *The Times*, the economy soon returned to growth and in the late 1980s entered another boom period. (The letter from the 364 Keynesians was organized by two Cambridge economics dons, Frank Hahn and Robert Neild.) Essay 10 explains that the 364 were not just wrong, but came to look ridiculous. As American Keynesians have never suffered the intellectual humiliation of their British counterparts, they may retain more confidence in the efficacy of fiscal therapy. That may be why Krugman's and Stiglitz's nostrums are still influencing policy. Nevertheless, as of December 2010, the Obama fiscal boost is undoubtedly failing.

NEW KEYNESIANISM

Given the disillusionment with fiscal activism that became widespread more than thirty years ago, the dominant style of policy-making across the advanced world from the 1980s to the Great Recession gave greater prominence to monetary policy. A new approach developed, associated with a distinctive set of ideas that passed under the label "New Keynes-ianism." It is the second of the four schools of thought under review here. The incorporation of "Keynes" in the brand name was a tribute to the continuing power and resilience of his reputation. Indeed, the use of "Keynes" in the labeling exercise was remarkable, in that the new approach had no obvious connection with Keynes's own work.[8] (See p. 157 and p. 160 in essay 6 for the origins and original justification of this label.) The fiscal aspect so prominent in Old Keynesianism was dropped almost entirely. The main elements in the New Keynesian model were instead threefold. The change in inflation was attributed to the amount of slack in the economy, measured by a concept known as "the output gap"; the change in the output gap was taken to reflect the growth in demand and output relative to the trend rate of output growth, with the level of the interest rate set by the central bank a key influence on demand growth; and, finally, the central bank set the interest rate in accordance with the level of the output gap and the deviation of inflation from its desired level. An implication was that the central bank's interest rate was much more than a key policy instrument. In the New Keynesian schema, it became in effect the *only* policy instrument, the factotum of macroeconomics. (New Keynesianism also depended on a particular meaning of "the output gap," a concept which is far more ambiguous than many economists realize. Essay 6 discusses the evolution of the "gap" concept from Keynesian roots in the early 1960s to the monetarist present-day version. Ironically, it is the *monetarist* version that figures in New *Keynesianism*.)

The three bits to New Keynesianism could be translated into three equations.[9] To distill the millions of prices, quantities, and behaviors in a modern economy into a mere three equations was, on the face of it, an astonishing intellectual achievement. The parsimony of the construction was noteworthy for another reason as well: it enabled economists to talk about demand, inflation, and central-bank action without any reference to money and commercial banking. New Keynesianism – like Old Keynesianism – dispensed with the quantity of money as an analytical category. Since three-equation New Keynesianism seemed to be working well for most of the Great Moderation, economists patted themselves on the back that they had a small and successful model of "how the economy works." Moreover, this model's omission of money and commercial banking had a professional advantage. It meant that economists – including economists in central banks – did not have to waste time trying to understand how banks and the financial system operated, and how they interacted with the rest of the economy. Like the teaching of macroeconomics in certain universities, monetary policy could be conducted without any mention of the quantity of money.[10]

But New Keynesianism had a major flaw. This was hidden during the Great Moderation, but glaringly exposed in the Great Recession. One of its three equations was the Taylor rule, so named after John Taylor of Stanford University, who was undersecretary of the Treasury in the George W. Bush administration. The rule stipulated how much the central bank should change the short-term interest rate in response to deviations of inflation and the output gap from desired levels. It was derived from data in a period (1983–1992) when the economy was prosperous, output was never much beneath its trend level, and the central-bank interest rate was consistently positive. (See footnote 33 to essay 6 for a full reference to the Taylor paper.) But the Great Recession was utterly different from the Great Moderation, with such extensive changes in behavior that key relationships were invalidated. The plunge in demand was so severe that it forced output a long way beneath its trend level. Indeed, the output gap took such a high negative value that the application of the Taylor rule would have required the central-bank interest rate to go negative. But, because the central bank cannot charge us interest on the legal-tender bank notes that we hold, a negative central-bank interest rate is a practical impossibility. So the Taylor rule could not tell policy-makers how to respond to the Great Recession. In its heyday the New Keynesians' three-equation model was sometimes described as the "workhorse" of modern central banking. In the Great Recession this workhorse had to be sent to the knackers' yard.

NEW CLASSICAL ECONOMICS

The neglect of commercial banking in New Keynesianism could be justified by an argument that was also central to our third school of thought, New Classical Economics. New Classical Economics is usually seen as the logical elaboration of a core message of Milton Friedman's monetary economics. In his celebrated 1967 presidential address to the American Economic Association, Friedman proposed a simple but revolutionary idea. This was that in an inflationary era pay bargainers would adjust their demands for today's wage increases in the light of their expectations that the price level would be higher a year or two from now. Such "rational expectations" would prevent the inflation rate from eroding the real value of the pay increase agreed upon.

The idea of rational expectations – that households and companies behave so as not to be fooled by economic developments around them, and as if economic theory were correct – was and remains the bedrock of New Classical Economics. Unfortunately, the whole line of thought ran amok. The common-sense insight that people adjust their actions in line with their beliefs about the future, particularly their inflation expectations, was transformed into a range of utterly implausible intellectual confections. These were presented in academic papers of extreme complexity, where the author's aim all too often was to display mathematical prowess rather than to reach a closer approximation to the truth. With some reason, Skidelsky said in *The Return of the Master* that, although the leaders of New Classical Economics had won Nobel Prizes, "to the non-economist they will seem mad."[11]

One argument was that because the two sides of a balance sheet are always equal, and because banks therefore do not represent net wealth to anyone, the levels and rates of change of banks' liabilities – including their deposit liabilities – do not matter to other macroeconomic variables. Since bank deposits constitute the bulk of the quantity of money as usually defined, the implication was that neither the quantity of money nor its rate of change had any bearing on inflation, asset prices, the exchange rate, and so on.[12] True enough, the main statement of these propositions – in a 1980 article by the University of Chicago professor Eugene Fama – included a list of assumptions needed to make them work. It was at least implied that, if the assumptions did not hold in the real world, then neither did the conclusions. (See footnote 10 to essay 4 for further discussion of these assumptions.)

But Fama did not think that the possible unrealism of the assumptions undermined the relevance of his paper. Meanwhile other economists thought that Fama's work justified eliminating from their analytical purview both commercial banks and broadly defined money aggregates dominated by bank deposits. In the U.K. this position was taken by Patrick Minford, then at Liverpool University, during a boom in the late 1980s. A salient feature of this boom, as of a similar episode in the early 1970s, was that bank balance sheets were growing at an extraordinarily rapid speed, sometimes of more than 20 percent a year. That was also the rate of growth of the bank deposits that constituted the quantity of money, as traditionally defined. Minford denied that the 20-percent-a-year growth of the quantity of money contained any message about future inflation.[13] (He was wrong. When double-digit inflation returned briefly in 1990 after a long period of much lower inflation, the reputation for economic competence of the Conservative government then in power declined sharply.)

If bank deposits did not matter, were all monetary assets unimportant in New Classical Economics? Since over 99 percent of payments in a modern economy are settled across bank accounts, that might logically have been the conclusion. But it was not. The devotees of New Classical Economics managed to persuade themselves that one kind of money – the monetary base issued by the central bank (i.e., notes and coins, and commercial banks' own cash reserves at the central bank) – was net wealth in non-banks' hands. So changes in the monetary base were deemed to have huge significance for the economy's future path, even though the total value of cash transactions is less than 0.75 percent of the value of total transactions in a modern economy.[14] Indeed, because New Classical theorists emphasized the role of expectations in people's behavior, some academic papers ascribed a major macroeconomic role to expectations about the growth of the monetary base.[15]

Does one have to suggest that this was bizarre? A brief glance at reality ought to have been sufficient to verify that hardly any households or businesses took the trouble to acquire meaningful information about the monetary base, even if they knew what the phrase meant. If they didn't have much information about it, or indeed if they did not even know the meaning of the phrase, how could they form sophisticated expectations about its future path? And, if they didn't form such expectations, how were these supposed expectations able to matter vitally to the economy? Given the exiguous role of the monetary base in modern transactions and its smallness relative to other monetary assets and especially relative to total wealth, the emphasis on the base in New Classical Economics has to be described as perplexing. At any rate, New Classical Economics dismisses the banking industry, and money in the form of bank deposits, as of no independent interest in macro-economic analysis.[16]

CREDITISM

It is obvious from the historical record, first, that phases of serious financial upheaval tend be characterized by instability in output and employment, and, second, that serious financial upheaval is particularly marked in the banking industry. Given this record, there has to be a very high likelihood of a systematic connection between banking trauma and macroeconomic dislocation. Nevertheless, many economists are not persuaded by arguments in which money and banks' deposit liabilities are the key operative terms. Instead they prefer to talk in terms of "credit" and, more specifically, bank lending to the private sector. They think it is the *asset* side of banks' balance sheets, not the *liability* side, that "really matters." Indeed, loose and informal accounts of how "credit" affects the business cycle were two-a-penny in the nineteenth century and remained so in the early part of the twentieth century.

Credit-based theories became implausible in the middle of the twentieth century, when – because of the two world wars – banks' assets were dominated by government securities. It made little sense to talk about bank credit to the private sector as a driver of macroeconomic instability, when bank credit to the private sector was modest relative to bank balance sheets and national income. But the long boom starting in 1945 was accompanied, remorselessly, by bank lending to the private sector growing faster than national income. Credit to the private sector edged out government securities as banks' main assets. By the late 1980s, across the industrial world, claims on the private sector were over 80 percent of banks' assets. Economists at the United States' East Coast universities – such as Ben Friedman at Harvard (not to be confused with the redoubtable Milton Friedman of the University of Chicago), Mark Gertler at New York University, and, in particular, Ben Bernanke at Princeton – began to assemble theories in which bank lending was judged to have an effect on the economy separate from that of "the quantity of money" (i.e., bank deposits). In one of these articles, Bernanke and Gertler coined the word "creditism," envisaging a new set of ideas as an alternative to the more familiar money-oriented macroeconomics.

Unlike New Classical Economics and the two kinds of Keynesianism, Creditism does put the banking system in the center of the macroeconomic stage. But it shares with these other schools of thought an aversion to "money" as a key variable. Indeed, its origins are to be sought partly in the long-standing dissatisfaction with money and monetarism at the East Coast universities. Over thirty years ago an amusing distinction was drawn between the United States' coastal "saltwater" economics departments (at places like Harvard, Princeton, and Yale), which regarded government action as the answer to economic problems, and the inland "freshwater" economics departments (Chicago, Minneapolis, Rochester), which tended to see government as itself the problem.[17] Creditism is definitely a product of the saltwater departments. In the Great Recession, with Bernanke as chairman of the Fed, it became hugely important in providing the intellectual rationale for key decisions, including the bank-recapitalization exercises of autumn 2008. Creditism is heavily criticized in essays 17 and 18 as the "particular line of thought" that must carry "a large share of the blame" for what went wrong in this period.

To summarize, modern macroeconomics is dominated by schools of thought in which the banking system plays little or no role. In Old Keynesianism, New Keynesianism, and New Classical Economics, the exclusion of banks is conscious and deliberate, and well-known academic papers defend it. This is surely weird. How can any observer of economic developments in the last few years overlook the centrality of the banking system in the turmoil and instability? Such issues as banks' asset composition and capital adequacy have become commonplaces of political debate, about which every member of Congress and every media pundit must have an opinion. Whereas academic economists deny that banks matter to macroeconomic outcomes, a constant succession of events sends the clear and overwhelming message that banks matter hugely to spending, output, and employment. True enough, the Creditism associated with Ben Bernanke does acknowledge the macroeconomic significance of the banking system, but it pays the most attention to banks' assets, not the deposit liabilities that dominate the quantity of money.

Keynes and Friedman would have been astonished by this shift in intellectual fashion.[18] Both wrote repeatedly about the importance of integrating money into a full understanding of how the economy works. Friedman once said that a book about macroeconomics without a reference to money was like a book on love without a mention of sex.[19] The sexlessness and sterility of modern macroeconomics has been all too obvious in the Great Recession.

II.

Does this book have any answers to current policy dilemmas? Essays 15 and 16 argue that national income and wealth are determined, in nominal terms, by the quantity of money, where the quantity of money includes all relevant bank deposits, including deposits that cannot immediately be used for transactions. Much economic theorizing is about how changes in the quantity of money affect the value of one particular type of asset, the fixed-interest bonds issued by governments and companies. Keynes said that increases in the quantity of money normally raised the price of bonds and lowered their yields or, in his terminology, "the rate of interest." In essay 4, I argue against Krugman's interpretation of Keynes, in that he equates "the rate of interest" with the money-market rate set by the central bank, not the bond yield. I also explain that increases in the quantity of money affect the price not just of fixed-interest bonds, but also of equities and real estate, and the impact of changes in the quantity of money on the economy is largely felt through these asset-price movements. The state – either the government or the central bank – can always create new money by borrowing from the banking system and using the loan proceeds to make purchases of any kind from the private sector. Such purchases add to bank deposits, and therefore increase both the quantity of money and the equilibrium values of national income and wealth.

Keynes was a strong advocate of increases in the quantity of money to end deep recessions, as am I. In the mid-1930s he conjectured that sometimes action on these lines would fail to raise bond prices or reduce "the rate of interest," a state of affairs labeled "the liquidity trap" by his Cambridge colleague Dennis Robertson. Krugman has made a great hullabaloo about Japan and the U.S. being in "the liquidity trap" today, so that – in his view – monetary policy is useless and fiscal policy becomes the one remaining weapon to end recessions. In essay 4, I argue that Krugman's misunderstanding of Keynes has led him to underestimate seriously both the ability of the monetary authorities to increase the quantity of money and the power of such increases to boost macroeconomic outcomes. In real-world economies with equities and real estate (unlike Keynes's caricature of the real world in *The General Theory*, where bonds are the only asset), Keynes's liquidity trap will never be observed. The liquidity trap is a sort of Loch Ness monster of macroeconomics. No one – not even Paul Krugman – has seen it, even if it has spawned a large number of amusing myths and anecdotes, and provoked much highbrow conceptual tourism.

American public debt is on an unsustainable trajectory, mainly because President Obama has listened to his Keynesian advisers and accepted their claims that extra public spending will boost employment. The growth of public debt must be halted, while – if the money stagnation of 2009 and 2010 persists – action must be taken to restore a positive rate of money-supply growth. It seems possible that – under international regulatory pressure – banks will continue to shrink their risk assets (mostly their claims on the private sector) for several quarters, perhaps even for a few years. In these circumstances, the right policy approach is for the state to create money. (Of course, not too much money should be created, because that would cause high inflation; but stimulatory measures can be calibrated so that just enough money growth occurs to get the economy moving.)

Further, the government does not need to run a budget deficit for the state to create money. Either the federal government or the Federal Reserve can borrow from the banking system and use the loan proceeds to buy back long-dated debt in the hands of the non-bank public. Expansionary monetary policy of this kind can be conducted even if the budget is in balance or surplus. On a big enough scale, a monetary boost will overwhelm the supposedly deflationary consequences of a deficit-reduction package. In essay 4, I describe the official transactions necessary for these outcomes as "debt-market operations," to distinguish them from the "money-market operations" that are a more familiar part of central banks' routine. To revive an economy in a severe downturn, debt-market operations, conducted with sufficient aggression (or *à outrance* – "to the uttermost" – as Keynes put it), are far more powerful and effective than money-market operations. If stimulatory money-market operations were compared to a cup of espresso to wake up an economy in a cyclical doze, then debt-market operations would resemble an injection of adrenalin in response to anaphylactic shock.

The Great Recession and the persistence of weak demand in recent quarters are not due to inherent weaknesses in the capitalist system. They are instead to be attributed to bad economic policies and poor economic advice, and these bad policies and poor advice stem from the failures of contemporary economics as an intellectual discipline. In particular, this volume argues that the neglect of banking and the quantity of money in fashionable academic journals and the East Coast's saltwater universities has done much harm to the American economy.

In the long run, Friedman's prescription is correct. As he said on countless occasions, stable growth of the quantity of money is a condition of wider macroeconomic stability (that is, the stability of demand, output, and employment), while a low rate of growth of the quantity of money is needed to deliver low inflation or, better still, price stability. Because the Federal Reserve under Bernanke has not paid enough attention to the behavior of money, it has presided over extreme volatility in the rate of money-supply change and severe macroeconomic instability. In essays 12, 13, and 14, I contend that the monetarist counterrevolution was pivotal to the revival of free-market thinking in the 1970s and 1980s. The ideas in that counterrevolution need to be recovered and revitalized, as part of a broader defense of the free-market economy and a free society.

PART ONE

DID HIS DISCIPLES

BETRAY KEYNES?

PREFACE

KEYNES'S INTRODUCTION to economics came in the opening years of the twentieth century at Cambridge University, where the dominant figure was Alfred Marshall. Marshall's most famous work was his *Principles of Economics*, which Keynes started to read in 1905, at the age of twenty-two. However, his first real enthusiasm was not for Marshall's solid if rather dreary work, but rather for William Stanley Jevons's *Investigations in Currency and Finance*. In a letter of July 8, 1905, to Lytton Strachey, Keynes described Jevons's *Investigations* as a "most thrilling volume."[1] Like all his contemporaries, Jevons believed in the importance of money and banking to the workings of the economy as a whole. Not surprisingly, the economics books that Keynes read in his twenties were predominantly in the monetary area. In 1911 the United States' foremost economist, Irving Fisher of Yale, brought out a big book called *The Purchasing Power of Money*. When Keynes reviewed it for *The Economic Journal*, he did not dispute Fisher's main point. This was to affirm the validity of the quantity theory of money, in which changes in the price level were heavily influenced by changes in the quantity of money.

At the start of the twenty-first century, the quantity theory of money is usually bracketed with monetarism and placed at the conservative end of the political spectrum. As we shall see later (in essay 12), there are good reasons for this tendency. But a hundred years ago the ideological landscape was very different. The conservative position was to favor "sound money," where money was "sound" if it either was a precious metal or had a definite, unbreakable link with a precious metal. When *The Purchasing Power of Money* was published, most of the leading nations had been on the gold standard for at least a generation. In Britain almost no one opposed the fixed link between the pound and gold, which had been maintained since 1821; £3 17s. 10½d. of sterling

3

coin was taken to be fully convertible into an ounce of gold, in the same way that 1,760 yards made up a mile and 14 pounds were equivalent to a stone. One of Fisher's key findings in his 1911 book was that the sharp increase in the availability of gold since the 1890s had been responsible for a major inflation in the United States.[2] This helped to convince him to favor and advocate a different monetary regime, in which the focus would be the discretionary management of the currency in order to achieve price stability. Fisher's position was radical and avant garde, even perhaps a little left of center.

Essay 3 suggests that Fisher's argument had been anticipated more than a century earlier by Henry Thornton in his 1802 *An Inquiry into the Nature and Effects of the Paper Credit of Great Britain*. Both Thornton and Fisher saw that, because the price level of goods depended on the quantity of money relative to the quantity of goods, the state could try to achieve price stability by managing the quantity of money. In Thornton's words, the Bank of England should allow "a slow and cautious extension" of the sum of paper money in circulation, "as the general trade of the kingdom enlarges itself"; or, as Fisher put it in 1911, the price level could be "kept almost absolutely stable" by "the issue of inconvertible paper money in quantities ... proportioned to [the] increase of business."[3]

The financial exigencies of the First World War caused Britain to leave the gold standard. A key public-policy issue in the early 1920s became: Should the pound be restored to the gold standard at the price that had prevailed for almost a century until 1914? Unfortunately, a return to the gold standard at the pre-war parity would make British products uncompetitive in world markets. Keynes was therefore opposed to it. In a series of newspaper articles, brought together in his 1923 pamphlet, *A Tract on Monetary Reform*, he instead proposed "a managed currency" on Fisher's lines. Essay 3 discusses the tensions between the exchange rate and the quantity of money as nominal "anchors" in the conduct of British monetary policy from 1700 to today. Ironically, in the late 1980s it was the so-called "Keynesians" who vilified a discretionary policy based on domestic monetary trends and wanted a fixed exchange system in the form of the European Exchange Rate Mechanism. Did they not see that – like the return to the gold standard in the 1920s – the ERM would leave British output and employment at the mercy of a foreign central bank, in this case the German Bundesbank? Did they not understand that, if they wanted to be loyal to their intellectual hero, they should have supported a policy based on domestic monetary conditions? Or had they perhaps read rather less of Keynes's work than they liked to pretend?

Essays 1, 2, and 4 are also about continuities and discontinuities in economic thought, but they are more directly relevant to current policy perplexities in North America and elsewhere. Keynes continued through the 1920s to believe that monetary policy could have powerful effects on macroeconomic conditions. His 1930 two-volume *Treatise on Money* looked in some detail into how monetary-policy instruments might be deployed to affect employment, output, and the domestic price level. This may have shocked defenders of the external discipline imposed by the gold standard, but it had a neutral or even conservative message for social organization. The conduct of monetary policy by the central bank – or even by the central bank in cooperation with the government – needed neither extra public expenditure nor official powers to control investment and "plan" the economy. If monetary policy could stabilize an economy in which private property and market forces were dominant, there was – of course – no case for an upheaval in property relationships or state direction of employment and production.

But in the early 1930s Keynes pioneered a new approach to the determination of national income. Its core was that national income was a multiple of "autonomous demand," which can be loosely equated with investment and government spending. His 1936 book, *The General Theory of Employment, Interest, and Money*, developed these ideas in more depth and implied that an increase in government spending could be used to generate an increase in output that would be severalfold (perhaps two or three times, perhaps five times) higher than itself.[4] Fiscal policy was upgraded and monetary policy downgraded. Keynes conjectured that, in extreme conditions, additions to "the quantity of money" would not lead to a drop in "the rate of interest." Yet, without a fall in the rate of interest, Keynes thought that extra money could not boost aggregate demand. One of Keynes's Cambridge colleagues, Dennis Robertson, gave this vexed state of affairs the memorable sobriquet of "the liquidity trap." While Keynes admitted that he had never seen a real-world "liquidity trap," he wanted people to believe that its possible future appearance was a major flaw in free-market capitalism.

As noted in the introduction, in the late 1990s Paul Krugman made the challenging claim that Japan was in a real-world liquidity trap, and he used that claim to recommend that the Japanese government increase public spending and run a large budget deficit. In the Great Recession of 2008–2010, he repeated his claim and recommendation, but now in the context of the United States itself. Essay 4 argues that Krugman has misinterpreted Keynes. The phrases "the quantity of money" and "the rate of interest" are ambiguous, and Krugman in his newspaper articles and popular books has used them in a different way from Keynes in *The General Theory*. If "the quantity of money" is given Keynes's meaning, then monetary policy contains a much larger toolkit than Krugman appreciates, and the scope of expansionary monetary operations has not been exhausted in either Japan or the United States. It follows that Krugman has not established a case for extra public spending and a large budget deficit in either country.

Krugman's writings demonstrate one point beyond contradiction: that interest in Keynes remains lively and intense more than sixty years after his death in 1946. *The General Theory* continues to sell in significant numbers, despite being an extraordinarily difficult book to read. Essay 2 considers the relative merits of *The General Theory* and Keynes's other writings, many of which not only are comprehensible to the non-economist, but are even a joy to read. That essay concludes that *A Treatise on Money* is in many ways superior to *The General Theory*. Remarkably, one of the earliest and most avid readers of *A Treatise on Money* was Milton Friedman, as a student at the University of Chicago in 1932.[5]

The first version of essay 1 was written in the 1970s, when inflation was the world's principal economic problem. In both the U.S. and the U.K., the self-styled "Keynesians" of that era were articulate protagonists of direct intervention in the price mechanism by means of prices and incomes policies (or wage and price controls, as they are known in the U.S.). Essay 1 shows that Keynes himself always believed that control of the quantity of money was the correct method to combat inflation. In that sense he was a monetarist before it became fashionable.

The larger lesson is to be suspicious of economists who invoke the name of Keynes as a debating point, particularly if they do not support what they say with a verifiable reference to his work. Too many people try to buttress their own flimsy intellectual positions by asserting that "Keynes said this" or "Keynes would have recommended that," where Keynes's views are claimed to be similar to theirs. Don't trust them.

ESSAY 1

WERE THE KEYNESIANS LOYAL FOLLOWERS OF KEYNES?

TRIBAL WARFARE is not the most attractive feature of contemporary economics, even if it is much the most exciting. But the vigor of debate occasionally makes it less careful and precise than it should be. Distinguished economists are misled by their own slogans and tend to assert glibly what they know should be argued cautiously. One particular vice is the habit of attaching a brand name to a school of thought, not with the intention of designating a common theme, but with that of heightening rhetorical impact. It is right to be suspicious of this tendency because it conveys a possibly spurious impression of unanimity, of a confederation of intellects, which can persuade non-participants in the debate by sheer force of numbers. But there can be a still more serious reason for distrust. When the confederation becomes known by a special name there is a danger that the name can give a distorted idea of the quality of its intellectual weaponry. The danger is greatest when the name used is that of a much revered warrior, now dead, who achieved a number of famous victories in his lifetime.

In economics, the revered warrior in all confrontations is still John Maynard Keynes. A quote from Keynes, no matter how slight and trivial, appears to silence opposition. It has the same force as an appendix of mathematical reasoning or a half-dozen learned articles. It can be a powerful blow in debate, and, indeed, it can sometimes serve as a substitute for thought. It is important, therefore, to examine carefully the credentials of any group that calls itself "Keynesian." In the 1960s and 1970s the Keynesian label was attached to a body of economists in England, principally from Cambridge University, who held distinctive views on the problem of inflation control. (Keynesians were even more numerous in American universities, but the focus here is on the U.K. After all, Britain was Keynes's home and the country in which he had the most direct influence.)

In choosing this label, the Keynesians had – or believed they had – a great advantage. It was then – and remains today – a commonplace that Keynes was worried above all by the depression of the 1930s and the attendant unemployment, and that his work on inflation was insubstantial and can be neglected. The Keynesians therefore had the freedom to propound their own views as those of Keynes. This freedom amounted to a license to counterfeit his intellectual coinage.[1]

In fact, it is not true that Keynes was uninterested in inflation. He had lived through the most rapid inflation of the twentieth century: that between 1914 and 1920, which ravaged the British financial system and devastated the currencies of most European countries. His writings on inflation are extensive. The post-war British Keynesians' views on inflation can be compared with, and checked against, Keynes's own position. It emerges that several leading strands in Keynesian thought cannot be said to have their origins in Keynes's work. The claim of a close correspondence between the two was based on a myth – a myth that was carefully nurtured by a number of economists who collaborated with Keynes in the 1930s, but who outlived him and propagated an influential, but spurious, oral tradition. Tribes, even tribes of economists, need myths. They serve as both emotional support and a sort of shared intellectual cuisine. This particular myth must be exploded. A summary of the Keynesians' position is of course needed to define the debate. The account here tries to do justice to Keynesian thought, despite the obvious and unavoidable danger that, if one highlights its central elements, its variety and subtlety may not be sufficiently acknowledged.

I.

The British Keynesians of the 1960s and 1970s saw the inflationary process as almost exclusively a question of "cost push." A number of forces were identified as responsible for rising costs of production throughout the economy, and prices were seen as being raised in response to higher costs, in order to preserve profit markups. This cost–push process was contrasted with "excess demand" explanations of inflation, in which the causes were said to be too much demand for labor (which, then, raised wages and costs) and for goods (which enabled firms to raise prices without fearing loss of business). Of the forces driving up costs trade-union bargaining pressure (or "pushfulness") was usually given priority, although rising import costs might also be mentioned. The Keynesians were ambivalent in their attitude to the union movement, because it was regarded as both the cause of a self-defeating jostling among different groups for a larger share of the national cake (which they deplored) and the agent of income redistribution in favor of the lower classes (which they applauded). Nevertheless, they made numerous criticisms of the trade unions, and some of them were scathing. At one extreme Lord Balogh – who served as an economic adviser to Harold Wilson, the prime minister from 1964 to 1970 – was outspoken and unhesitating in his condemnation. Others were more circumspect. In his contribution to a book titled *Keynes: Aspects of the Man and His Work* (based on the first Keynes seminar, which had been held at the University of Kent in 1972), Dr. Roger Opie – a don at New College, Oxford – attributed their behavior to the economic context in which they operated. It was, he said, the experience of past high employment which had let the unions taste power, while the combination of organized labor and oligopolized industry had given them the opportunity to exercise it without limit.[2] Professor Joan Robinson recognized the conflict between the public aims of the labor movement as a whole and the private, self-interested objectives of the individual unions. In her view, although the vicious inflationary spiral caused by wage bargaining did "no good to the workers," nevertheless it remained "the duty of each trade union individually to look after the interests of its own members individually."[3]

Accompanying this hostility, open or disguised, to the trade unions was a set of beliefs about the operation of the labor market. Wages were deemed to be set not by demand and supply, but by bargaining and power. According to the Keynesians, workers did not move quickly and easily from industry to industry and from firm to firm in response to the incentives of better pay and prospects. The labor market was instead characterized by rigidities and imperfections, and wage determination took place in an environment of "countervailing power," without respect for fairness or for social justice. ("Countervailing power" was a phrase coined by the American Keynesian, Professor John Kenneth Galbraith.) Moreover, the imperfections in the labor market were matched by imperfections in the production and supply of goods. Opie's reference to "oligopolized industry" was typical. Occasionally even the retailers took their share of the blame. As Sir Roy Harrod put it, the distributors were "sometimes up to a little mischief."

In short, the core of cost-push inflation was the conflict among managers, trade unionists, and the non-unionized as they struggled endlessly to increase, or at least preserve, their share of the national product. The timing and size of the demands placed on the economy were not thought to have a primarily economic explanation. The principal influences were instead social and psychological, and they operated continuously. The outcome of the distributional struggle was determined not by productivity but by bargaining strength, with the strike threat being a crucial determinant.

What, then, was the Keynesians' answer to cost-push inflation? It was direct intervention by the government in the form of prices and incomes policies. The Keynesians were united in this, and in the 1970s they probably convinced a majority of the academic economics profession in the U.K.[4] Few clearer statements of support can be found than that from Sir Roy Harrod in *Keynes: Aspects of the Man and His Work*, where he wrote, "I am myself a definite advocate of what we call an 'incomes policy.' I believe there must be direct interference." To the Keynesians a prices and incomes policy served many functions. It was, first and foremost, a weapon to fight inflation. But it was more than that. By enabling a central authority to monitor price movements, it superseded – or, at least, overrode – the monopoly bargaining power of large firms and the trade unions. It could thereby contribute to attempts to distribute economic rewards more fairly. Indeed, it could become a means of attaining social justice.[5]

What of the uses of monetary correctives? These were scorned. To quote Harrod again: "I do not think it is any good saying that banks can stop inflation – saying, let them reduce the money supply. How can the poor banks reduce the money supply? What actually happens is that wage-earners get a demand granted which must raise costs."[6]

If monetary methods had been adopted they would have caused

unemployment, and this was thought to be unacceptable. It would have been the negation of Keynesianism if unemployment were the best method of fighting rising prices.

The Keynesian position had the merit of internal consistency. If economists believed that "greed" and "envy" were the causes of inflation, they were logical to doubt the efficacy of such indirect methods of control as changes in taxation and interest rates. It was much easier to legislate against greed and envy directly, by laying down statutory limitations on their effects. Keynesianism was also consistent with a particular perception of reality and an associated approach to policymaking. If monopoly power were pervasive, and if markets were stunted by imperfections and rigidities, there was an evident futility in applying remedies that worked on the assumptions of ubiquitous competition and the responsiveness of supply to incentives. But – as we shall see – the Keynesians' position was not consistent with that of Keynes. Their policy prescriptions had no foundation in his written work and were incompatible with fundamental aspects of his economic philosophy.

But surely, it might be said, the Keynesians must have been basing their case on some element of Keynes's thinking. Was there any kinship between their arguments and his? In fact, there was an assumption common to both their way of thinking and the most important part of Keynes's work. It was a technical assumption, slipped into the interstices of the theoretical structure and, for that reason, one whose significance was easily overlooked. It was the assumption in books III and IV of *The General Theory of Employment, Interest, and Money* that the analysis was to be conducted in terms of "wage-units."

Keynes was not concerned in his investigation of unemployment with the relationship between capital inputs and output. The vital relationships for him were those between employment, output, and demand. The function of the wage-unit assumption was that it enabled his analysis to focus on these relationships "provided we assume that a given volume of effective demand has a particular distribution of this demand between different products uniquely associated with it." The wage-unit was defined as the sum of money paid to each "labor-unit" or, in effect, each worker.[7] This was a very useful assumption. Keynes could proceed to the determination of output and employment without needing a prior theory of the determination of the money wage and without troubling himself too much over microeconomic details. It might seem to follow that Keynes considered money wages to be given exogenously, perhaps as a result of bargaining.

The subtle effect of the wage-unit assumption on later thinking was noticed by Sir John Hicks in his 1974 volume, *The Crisis in Keynesian Economics*. The validity of analysis conducted in wage-units turned on what Sir John called "the wage theorem," that "when there is a general (proportional) rise in money wages, the normal effect is that all prices rise in the same proportion."[8] Given the wage theorem, it was immaterial what the particular money wage might be. The relationships between liquidity preference, the investment function, and the rest – the hub of Keynes's economics – were unaffected. Consequently, it became a convenient and innocuous simplification to assume a fixed money wage. Further, the relationship between aggregate demand and the money wage could be neglected.

This chain of thought – or, rather, this compound of faulty thought habits and pseudo-empirical hunches – was the source of all the trouble. Keynes made the wage-unit assumption because it facilitated his theoretical task. He could grapple more quickly with the issues of demand and employment once the awkward problem of money-wage determination had been sidelined. But this did not mean that he thought money wages were determined exogenously in the real world. Unfortunately, the Keynesians came to think just that. It is almost comical to picture Sir Roy Harrod indulging in an elaborate exegetical hunt – just before an academic conference in the 1970s – to find some justification for his conjecture:

> I have searched through his writings very carefully, not long ago – for the purpose of discovering anything he had to say about what we call "cost-push inflation." I could find only one short passage in Keynes, just a couple of sentences, where he said, . . . Of course the wage-earners might demand more than corresponding to their rise in productivity, might demand more and get more. . . . You can find those words if you search; I ought to give you chapter and verse, but I have not put down the page reference; they are there all right.[9]

The fact is that Keynes wrote almost nothing about "what we call 'cost-push inflation.'" The "one short passage" may or may not be a figment of Sir Roy's imagination. The many thousands of words written by Keynes on inflation as an excess-demand phenomenon are palpable and, to anyone who "searches through his writings very carefully," rather obtrusive.

There are, however, many echoes between the Keynesians' and Keynes's views on social fairness. His writings at times resemble a roll-call of the class structure of a late industrial society, with references to profiteers, rentiers, and unions scattered throughout their pages. The passages on income distribution in *How to Pay for the War* describe the upward swirl of the wage-price spiral particularly well. Here, indeed, it might be said, is the endless social struggle for a higher proportion of the national income.[10] But it is difficult to infer Keynes's attitude to the labor movement from his writings. He was certainly alerted to its potential impact on the organization of the employment market. In one of his public speeches he described trade unionists as, "once the oppressed, now the tyrants, whose selfish and sectional pretensions need to be bravely opposed."[11] But the harshness of that observation was unusual. Perhaps it was an isolated piece of bravura intended more for public-relations purposes than as an expression of an inner conviction. In *The General Theory* (and elsewhere) the unions are a fact of life; they are not the subject of a favorable or adverse judgment.

II.

But, if there are some reasons for attributing Keynesian views to Keynes's intellectual legacy, there are many more reasons for denying a strong connection between the two. Before moving on to an examination of Keynes's theory of inflation, it is essential to challenge a widespread misapprehension: that Keynes knew nothing about, and was uninterested in, the price mechanism or, more generally, in what we would now call microeconomics. This is simply untrue.[12] His awareness of the virtues (within limits) of the price mechanism saved him from the common assumption among the Keynesians that official interference to restrain rises in the absolute price level – or, more explicitly, prices and incomes policies – had no damaging repercussions on the configuration of relative prices. He doubted the effectiveness of price controls, with his skepticism based on first-hand knowledge of conditions in the inflation-ridden European economies after the First World War. (He visited both Germany and Russia in the early 1920s.) In *The Economic Consequences of the Peace* (1919), he wrote, "The preservation of a spurious value of the currency, by the force of law expressed in the regulation of prices, contains in itself, however, the seeds of final economic decay, and soon dries up the sources of ultimate supply." A page later he added, "The effect on foreign trade of price-regulation and profiteer-hunting as cures for inflation is even worse."[13] He derided the "bread subsidies" which were common at the time.

Similarly, he regarded centralized control of the wage level as problematic in a democracy. There are recurrent passages in Keynes – particularly when Britain returned to the gold standard in 1925 – where the need to bring down the level of wages is stressed (if the exchange rate had to be unnecessarily raised). But it was precisely the impracticality of efforts to depress the general wage level that made adjustments of the exchange rate expedient. In 1931, just before Britain left the gold standard, Keynes wrote that the reduction of all money wages in the economy "if it were to be adequate would involve so drastic a reduction of wages and such appallingly difficult, probably insoluble, problems, both of social justice and practical method, that it would be crazy not to try [the alternative of import restrictions]."[14]

Of course, the Keynesians could argue in the 1970s – and like-minded economists might argue today – that people have become habituated to regulation and control. The improvement in communications has made it that much easier to administer and police a prices and incomes policy. It might be contended that in these altered circumstances Keynes would revise his views, acknowledging some merits in legally imposed limitations on wage and price rises. It is impossible to argue with this. The conjecture might be true, but surely no one can give a definite answer one way or the other. What is clear is that there is nothing in Keynes's writings which explicitly envisages and endorses a prices and incomes policy, and there is much in their mood and tenor which is contemptuous of its makeshift predecessors in the 1920s.

What, then of Keynes's views of the inflationary process? The first point is that Keynes regarded inflation as an excess-demand phenomenon. There is very little, if anything, in his writings to suggest that he regarded it as something else. Perhaps the most lucid and consecutive discussion to be found in his work is in chapter 21 of *The General Theory* on "The Theory of Prices" (especially pp. 295 to 303). Paradoxically, however, it is rather hard to use this section for our purposes. The difficulty is that Keynes thought the proposition that inflation was due to excess demand so self-evident that he did not bother to argue it. The discussion consists of permutations of assumptions, all of which derive from a theoretical position of extreme orthodoxy. No alternative to excess-demand inflation is contemplated, let alone explored.

The form of the discussion is to put forward, as a pivot for further argument, the principle that "So long as there is unemployment, employment will change in the same proportion as the quantity of money; and when there is full employment, prices will change in the same proportion as the quantity of money."[15] The validity of this principle is shown to depend on five conditions. Only one of the five conditions is concerned with the institutional context of wage bargaining. It is the tendency for the wage-unit – or, in effect, money wages – to rise before full employment has been reached. Let me quote the relevant passage in full:

> In actual experience the wage-unit does not change continuously in terms of money in response to every small change in effective demand; but discontinuously. These points of discontinuity are determined by the psychology of the workers and by the policies of employers and trade unions.[16]

In other words, the significance of the union movement is recognized. But the exercise of bargaining power depends on prior changes in "effective demand."

This was plainly thought to be the normal run of events. These "discontinuities" represented "semi-inflations," which "have, moreover, a good deal of historical importance." It is not surprising that Keynes saw unions as susceptible to the same economic pressures as firms or individuals. In his lifetime, the membership of the union movement was substantially reduced on two distinct occasions – between 1921 and 1924, and between 1929 and 1932. In both instances the cause was the downturn in demand. To summarize, Keynes believed there to be an interplay between institutions and economic forces. He did not believe, as the Keynesians of the 1970s sometimes appeared to do, that institutions dictate to or overwhelm these forces, and that politics always trumps economics.[17]

Whereas Keynes hardly ever attributed to trade unions a causal role in inflation, there are in *The General Theory* and other places an abundance of passages in which inflation is seen as "a monetary phenomenon." Indeed, on one occasion Keynes gave a definition of inflation which was stated in terms of the money supply. He did not dither between two competing modern definitions, of "rising prices" and "aggregate demand in excess of aggregate supply." Instead, in his words, "From 1914 to 1920 all countries experienced an expansion in the supply of money relative to the supply of things to purchase, that is to say Inflation."[18]

Moreover, the emphasis on money in the inflations of the First World War is consonant with the dominant themes of Keynes's depression economics. The more simple-minded explanations of Keynes's theory often concentrate unduly on the need for public works to raise spending. But this neglects the cause of inadequate private investment, which was too much liquidity preference or, roughly speaking, the behavior of the demand for money.[19] When savings take the form of liquid holdings (such as bank deposits) rather than illiquid holdings (like plant and machinery), the demand for goods declines and unemployment rises. The traditional answer was to lower the rate of return on liquid holdings, until savers shifted back into illiquid. But Keynes saw that, in certain extreme circumstances, there might be psychological and institutional barriers to a sufficient reduction in the rate of interest. It followed from this that monetary policy, intended to engineer changes in interest rates, could not by itself cause a recovery of demand. The potential impotence of monetary policy had to be remedied, in his words, by "a somewhat comprehensive socialisation of investment." If investment were in state hands, it could be undertaken with larger ambitions than mere profit maximization. In particular, it could be stepped up in order to promote higher employment.

However, if the risk that monetary policy might become impotent in a depression is one of the principal conclusions of Keynes's economics, there is no foundation for the widespread Keynesian attitude that "money does not matter." Keynes's writings are replete with references to the banking system and financial assets. It would be remarkable if he thought them irrelevant to problems of economic policy in normal circumstances. (Of course, the 1930s were not normal circumstances. But it should be remembered that three out of the eight historical illustrations in chapter 30 of *A Treatise on Money*, the book that preceded *The General Theory*, were analyses of inflations. Keynes did think about the longer time span.[20])

In Keynes's works, the monetary variable under discussion was usually the rate of interest (the price of money) rather than the money supply (its quantity). This has subsequently been a fertile and persistent source of disagreement between the Keynesians and others. The Keynesians say that no support is to be found in *The General Theory* or elsewhere for the mechanistic rules advocated by, for example, Milton Friedman of the Chicago School, in which the monetary variable emphasized is the quantity of money. It is true that nowhere in Keynes is there a forthright recommendation for stable growth of a monetary aggregate. But there are sections of *A Tract on Monetary Reform* that come remarkably close to this standard monetarist position.[21] (Keynes's proposal for "a managed currency" is discussed in more detail in essay 3, on pp. 40–41.)

Of course, Keynes was in no position to talk with confidence about fluctuations in money-supply growth, because he lived in an age before full statistics were available. The rate of interest, on the other hand, was something known and observable. There are extensive passages in *A Treatise on Money* (1930) where Keynes was examining such measures of the money supply as he could find, and trying to identify relationships between them on the one hand and nominal asset prices and national income on the other. The two most interesting cases were in Britain in the decade after the First World War and in the U.S. between 1925 and 1930.[22] There were mismatches between changes in the money supply and changes in nominal national income, which he attributed to "lags" between "profit" and "income inflations." The discussion in these pages is a fascinating attempt to understand the transmission mechanism of monetary policy.

Keynes's tendency to focus on the price of money, rather than its quantity, may also have reflected his involvement in life insurance and fund management. He was active in City finance and speculation throughout the 1920s and 1930s, and to some extent he looked at the monetary situation in the same way as bankers and brokers do. Bankers, who have to arrange loans from day to day, think of the demand for credit as fickle and volatile, while economists, who look at a range of monetary aggregates as measured by long-run time series, regard it as continuous and stable. Bankers see interest rates, which give signals of credit availability, as the determining variable, while monetary economists have a greater tendency to watch the money supply. Keynes mostly thought in terms of interest rates. But this does not mean that, in the general run of events, he distrusted the effectiveness of monetary policy as a method of changing demand, output, and employment. A clear statement of his position is again to be found in *A Treatise on Money*. The authorities have, he said, no control over individual prices (like those of cars or meat) in the economic system. Nor do they have *direct* control over the money supply, because the central bank must act as lender of last resort. But they do determine one price, "the rate of discount," or the rate of interest. It is this which gives them leverage over the system as a whole.[23]

III.

One final point, which is perhaps decisive in refuting the Keynesians, needs to be made: it is that when Britain was confronted with nasty outbreaks of inflation during his lifetime, Keynes supported policies of a traditional, demand-restrictive nature. It has been too readily assumed that the years from 1914 to 1945 were of prolonged and unremitting depression, characterized by falling or stable prices, and that Keynes was therefore never called upon to offer advice on the control of inflation. This is quite wrong. In early 1920, Britain was in the midst of an inflationary boom of proportions that have never been paralleled before or since (though conditions in 1973–74 were, in some respects, rather similar). In 1918 and 1919 money wages soared by nearly 30 percent a year, and even by February 1920 there seemed no sign of an imminent release from the grip of the price explosion that had inevitably followed.

The chancellor of the exchequer, Austen Chamberlain, asked for an interview with Keynes to obtain his opinion on the right course of action. Chamberlain later summarized his impression of the interview as, "K. would go for a financial crisis (doesn't believe it would lead to unemployment). Would go to whatever rate is necessary – perhaps 10 percent – and would keep it at that for three years."[24]

Shortly afterwards Keynes prepared a fifteen-point memorandum in which he amplified his advice. Perhaps its most startling feature is the similarity between the economic issues of early 1920 and those of late 1974, and only a little less startling is Keynes's set of recommendations to deal with the problems. He wanted stiff and harsh deflation.

Is this document an aberration? Would Keynes have retracted it with the benefit of hindsight and of the breakthroughs in economic thought he pioneered in the 1930s? In 1942 he was shown his 1920 memorandum. He was not in the least repentant. Far from thinking his position too iconoclastic, he acknowledged that other economists at the time had thought exactly the same and that they had been equally right. To quote:

> As usual the economists were found to be unanimous and the common charge to the contrary without foundation! I feel myself that I should give today exactly the same advice that I gave then, namely a swift and severe dose of dear money, sufficient to break the market, and quick enough to prevent at least some of the disastrous consequences that would then ensue. In fact, the remedies of the economists were taken, but too timidly.[25]

There is no need to go any further. The argument could be reinforced by an analysis of Keynes's views of war finance, but there is already enough evidence to validate the main contentions of this essay. There was almost nothing in Keynes's writings, philosophy, or work that coincided with the views on inflation policy held by the British Keynesians of the 1960s and 1970s. They favored direct government interference to keep prices down; he scorned price regulation as ineffective and harmful. They considered inflation to be a cost-push phenomenon; he never envisaged it as anything but a phenomenon of excess demand. They dismissed monetary policy; he thought the one sure answer to inflationary excess was "a swift and severe dose of dear money."

The Keynesians of the 1970s were critics of free-market capitalism and advocates of direct government intervention in the price mechanism. But they were not loyal followers of Keynes. The self-styled Keynesians of the early twenty-first century are still critics of free-market capitalism and advocates of direct government intervention in the price mechanism. Are these Keynesians any more to be trusted than their predecessors over thirty years ago?

ESSAY 2

WHAT WAS KEYNES'S BEST BOOK?

LARGE NUMBERS of books and papers are still being written about Keynes in the opening years of the twenty-first century. As the introduction to the current volume shows, the name "Keynes" continues to have enormous brand value in economics and has been appropriated by diverse bodies of thought, some of which have only a loose connection with Keynes's own teaching. How should Keynes's work now be viewed? What was its purpose, and does it remain relevant? From the perspective of the early twenty-first century, what was his most interesting and durable contribution? What was his best book?

I.

Keynes can be seen as an analyst and defender of managed capitalism. He explained – or at any rate is supposed to have explained – how harmful fluctuations in business activity could be smoothed out by well-judged government action, and he therefore made the market economy work more efficiently. As such, he might be represented as a hero of the Right. Alternatively, he can be interpreted as the champion of the public sector, the foremost advocate of the large-scale nationalization of the British economy which occurred in the late 1940s. If so, he is one of the great thinkers of the Left. The diversity of appreciations of Keynes stems from the difficulty of locating his work in the complex political spectra of the modern world.

Born in 1883, he grew up in the ordered and stable milieu of late-Victorian and Edwardian England. He was the son of a Cambridge don and was himself to become a fellow of King's College. One aspect of the order and stability of British society in his youth and early adulthood was its currency, the pound sterling. It had been tied to gold since the late seventeenth century and had much the same value (in terms of the things it would buy) in 1910 as it had had two hundred years earlier. When Keynes first started to think about the theory of credit and money, most people believed that the value of money would be roughly the same when they died as when they were born.

Britain's currency stability was ruptured by the First World War. The government resorted to the printing presses to finance military spending. The result was a severe inflation, which led to a large gap between labor costs in Britain and competitor nations, the suspension of the gold standard, and a devaluation of sterling against the dollar. The central question for economic policy in 1919 was, Should Britain return to the gold standard and, if so, at what exchange rate? The consensus of the great, the good, and the orthodox was that Britain should return to gold as soon as possible, with the gold price (in terms of sterling) the same as it had been in 1914. There was much to be said in favor of the orthodox view, not least that it had been the traditional response in previous post-war contexts. Britain's rulers had refused to accept a permanent devaluation of the pound (against bullion) after the wars of William III and the Napoleonic Wars.

Keynes's most important insight in the early 1920s was that the gold standard was obsolete. As is well known, he opposed the particular exchange rate against the dollar ($4.86 to the pound) implied by the restoration of the pre-war gold price. He thought, correctly, that the British and American price levels were out of line at the $4.86 exchange rate and that the attempt to bring the price levels into balance (that is, to reduce British prices) would be deflationary, and would lead to unnecessary declines in output and employment. When the chancellor of the exchequer, Winston Churchill, decided to return to gold, Keynes brought his criticisms together in a celebrated pamphlet, *The Economic Consequences of Mr. Churchill*. Keynes's analysis was fully vindicated by events. Britain suffered a general strike in 1926 and a few years of industrial semi-stagnation, whereas other nations enjoyed the prosperity of the Roaring Twenties. Keynes's reputation as an economic analyst, commentator, and adviser was hugely enhanced.

But his attack on the gold standard was over a much wider front than the criticism of one particular gold price. Keynes saw that the growth of banking systems in the century of peace before 1914 had dramatically reduced the use of gold in transactions. By the beginning of the twentieth century virtually all significant payments, including international payments, were in paper money. In a formal sense gold remained the ultimate bedrock of the system, and people appeared justified in believing that their paper was "as good as gold." But, in truth, changes in the quantity of paper money (i.e., bank notes and deposits) had become both the principal regulator of the business cycle and the main determinant of the price level. In this new world, fluctuations in the quantity of gold were accidental, their impact on monetary policy was capricious, and their relevance to meaningful policy goals (the stability of output and prices) was highly debatable. What was the point of the gold link? Surely, gold's continuing prestige relied on superstition and tradition, and had no rational, scientific basis. As Keynes remarked in his 1923 *Tract on Monetary Reform*, gold had become "a barbarous relic."

Both *A Tract on Monetary Reform* and *The Economic Consequences of Mr. Churchill* were based on newspaper articles. Neither pretended to be serious academic tomes. Keynes's journalistic activity was frantic at this stage of his career and seems to have been motivated by the desire to have a big income. (He received £4,000 for organizing some supplements to the *Manchester Guardian Commercial* in 1922, a sum equivalent to about £135,000 [or over $200,000] in the money of 2011.) However, the two short books identified the vital monetary question of the twentieth century. If governments could no longer rely on the gold standard, how should the task of monetary management be performed? Even if the British government had restored the gold link at a more sensible exchange rate than $4.86 to the pound, would it really have been advisable to make interest rates depend on the fluctuating moods of the foreign-exchange markets and the accidents of gold-mining technology?

Keynes wanted to replace the gold standard with a managed currency, where the essence of the management task was to control the level of bank credit (and of bank deposits, which constituted most of the quantity of money) by a number of instruments that were just beginning to be understood. Bank rate – the rate of interest set by the Bank of England in its money-market activities – was a traditional weapon of considerable power. But Keynes was also attracted to the practice of influencing banks' reserves by open-market operations, which were being developed in the United States by the newly created Federal Reserve System under the leadership of Benjamin Strong. (The Federal Reserve had been founded in 1914 and was a much younger institution than the Bank of England.) Keynes had no doubt that currency stabilization was vital to the preservation of the market economy. As he remarked in the *Tract*, "The individualistic capitalism of today presumes a stable measuring rod of value, and cannot be efficient – perhaps cannot survive – without one." (Keynes's views in the *Tract* are discussed further on pp. 40–42 in essay 3. His admiration for Benjamin Strong – which was shared by Milton Friedman – is also noted in essay 13, on the differences between American and British monetarism.)

Keynes took his analysis further in a two-volume work, *A Treatise on Money*, published in 1930. It was a remarkable production, combining abstract analysis with detailed descriptions of monetary institutions and particular historical episodes. It expressed Keynes's considerable interest in international currency matters and theorized on the role that banking arrangements might play in macroeconomic instability. It went much further than the *Tract* and the miscellaneous pamphlets in setting out an agenda for monetary reform in a world that had outgrown gold. But its publication coincided with the worst collapses in demand and output ever inflicted on the international economy, and the most humiliating setback for the capitalist system. American industrial production fell by 45 percent between 1929 and 1932. Even worse, in some countries (although not Britain) the recovery from the slump was gradual and reluctant. Political extremism took hold in leading industrial nations, notably Germany, Italy, and the Soviet Union, and many intellectuals thought that the serious political debate had been polarized between Communism and Fascism. Keynes decided that yet more analysis and explanation were needed. In 1936 he published his *General Theory of Employment, Interest, and Money*, a book that is usually regarded as the start of modern macroeconomics. Indeed, it is often described as the greatest book on economics written in the twentieth century.

Its emphasis was rather different from the *Tract* and the *Treatise*. Like its predecessors, it contained ample discussion of interest rates and money, and of their relationships with other variables and their impact on the economy. But its main innovation was a new theory of the determination of national income. National income could be seen, according to Keynes, as a multiple of the level of investment. Unfortunately, investment undertaken by private agents was highly variable from year to year, because it was susceptible to volatile influences from financial markets and erratic swings in business sentiment.

In an extreme case – later given the sobriquet "the liquidity trap" by another Cambridge economist, Dennis Robertson – investors might be so afraid of future capital losses that, even if the central bank injected new money into the economy, they would not buy bonds at a higher price and force down the rate of interest. In other words, the lack of confidence might be so severe that monetary policy had become ineffective in boosting demand. The answer, so Keynes told the world, was for investment to be undertaken to a much greater extent by the public sector. In his words, there should be a "somewhat comprehensive socialisation of investment." Moreover, fiscal policy should be used actively to stimulate spending in recessions and to restrain spending in booms. (Krugman believes his own advocacy of fiscal policy in the United States today has the same rationale as Keynes's in *The General Theory*. Essay 4 disputes this interpretation.)

The message of *The General Theory* was political dynamite. By implication governments were right to nationalize important industries, because this would make it easier for them to prevent economic instability and to reduce unemployment. Further, they were wrong to rely exclusively on the old technique of Bank rate (and even some of the new American techniques of monetary policy), which had seemed adequate in the predominantly private-enterprise economy of the Victorian era (and of the United States in the Roaring Twenties). Indeed, a careless reader of *The General Theory* might conclude that monetary policy was of little interest in understanding macroeconomic fluctuations.

II.

The author of *A Tract on Monetary Reform* in 1923 had seemed concerned to preserve "individualistic capitalism." The author of *The General Theory* in 1936 celebrated the imminent prospect of a "somewhat

comprehensive socialisation of investment." Which was the authentic
Keynes? What did he really say? Or were there several contradictory
spirits in the same man, and did his work have many meanings? In the
second volume of his magnificent biography of Keynes, published in
1992, Skidelsky made the controversial suggestion that "the *Treatise*
and not *The General Theory* was Keynes's classic achievement."[1] For at
least four reasons, that verdict looks far more persuasive from the
standpoint of the early twenty-first century than it would have done in,
say, 1952 or 1962.

First, *The General Theory* is distressingly hard to read. While its subject matter is inescapably complex, Keynes did not make it accessible to
the general reader. The first sentence of the preface warned that the
book was "chiefly addressed to my fellow economists," but the second
expressed a hope that it would be "intelligible to others." But the truth
is that the book's contents were unintelligible even to economists until
they were further clarified by Keynes in short subsequent papers, and
translated into diagrams and equations by disciples and critics. Paul
Samuelson – who in due course became one of Keynes's vocal admirers
– admitted *The General Theory* "is a badly written book." It was "poorly
organized" and abounded in "mares' nests of confusions." Indeed, "I
think I am giving away no secrets when I solemnly aver – upon the
basis of vivid personal recollection – that no one else in Cambridge,
Massachusetts, really knew what it was all about for twelve or eighteen
months after publication."[2]

Part of the trouble was that Keynes, keen to emphasize the original-
ity of his contribution, used familiar terms in unfamiliar ways and concocted new labels for well-known analytical categories. He had to devote
several pages to explaining what he was about.[3] This would have inter-
rupted the flow of the argument in any circumstances, but the problem
was compounded by both repetition and digression. (*The General Theory* contained an appendix on the accountancy of depreciation and a
chapter on mercantilism and various contemporary monetary cranks.
Neither had much to do with the main argument.) *A Treatise on Money*
was also a rather unwieldy book, and it had its fair share of esoteric
terms, but it was more direct in its message and easier to read.

Second, *The General Theory* has little to say about banks and credit
creation, and almost nothing about international finance. But, as the

author of the *Tract* and the *Treatise* was fully aware, any attempt to understand the real-world problems of monetary management is also necessarily an attempt to understand the behavior of banking systems and internationally traded currencies. As Hicks noted, ". . . the *General Theory* is the theory of the closed economy. If we want to read what Keynes said on the theory of international money . . . we have to go to the *Treatise*."[4]

True enough, *The General Theory* makes countless references to money and interest rates. But – unlike the *Treatise* – it does not distinguish clearly between the central bank and the commercial banks, and between legal-tender monetary-base assets (always worth their nominal value, by law) and the deposits issued by commercial banks (which might not be repaid in full if banks went bust). When Keynes was writing, the collapse of hundreds of American banks, because of loan losses and the banks' inability to meet deposit obligations, was a central fact about the American economic scene. Deposits were not as good as notes, and the notion of "money" was heterogeneous and difficult to define. But in *The General Theory* Keynes treated all money assets identically, as a single homogeneous mass, in the apparent belief that the potential insolvency of private commercial banks was not an important element in financial and economic instability. To quote Hicks again, "Money, in the *General Theory*, is stripped to its bare bones; we get no more of the monetary system than is necessary for a particular purpose. The *Treatise* is a Treatise on Money, in a way that the other is not."[5]

Further, by identifying certain special and unusual conditions in which the interest rate could not be reduced by central-bank policy (i.e., in the conditions Robertson labeled "the liquidity trap"), *The General Theory* misled two generations of British economic policy-makers into thinking that monetary policy-making was trivial in normal times. They thought that they could neglect banking, money, and monetary policy, with disastrous results in two boom-bust episodes and the Great Recession. (The two earlier episodes – the Heath-Barber boom of the early 1970s and the Thatcher-Lawson boom of the late 1980s – are discussed further from a monetary perspective in essay 14.)

Third, in a significant sense *The General Theory* was a less general book than the *Treatise*. The *Treatise* was an attempt to produce a comprehensive text covering everything of importance in the monetary field. In addition to describing a range of banking institutions, the *Treatise* was clear that the problem of maintaining balance in an investment portfolio involved money and a variety of other securities, including bonds *and equities*.[6] Implicitly, the level of the equity market (and indeed of other asset prices) was influenced by the quantity of money. But – apart from one or two exceptional passages – in *The General Theory*, portfolio balance is reduced to the choice between money *and fixed-interest bonds alone*.[7] With fixed-interest bonds taken as representative of capital assets as a whole, this truncation of the problem of portfolio balance might appear harmless. But Keynes's narrowly restricted approach to portfolio balance in *The General Theory* was essential to a critical part of the book's argument.

By taking "bonds" as the alternative to money, Keynes could make statements about the relationship between the quantity of money and the yield on bonds, and by regarding the yield on bonds as synonymous with the "rate of interest," he could make grand claims to be propounding a new theory of the monetary determination of interest rates. In this theory, a change in the quantity of money would usually alter the equilibrium rate of interest, with the rate of interest adjusting until the demand to hold money balances was equal to the actual quantity of money in existence. Keynes was not shy about the virtues of this theory, which he opposed to an alternative "classical" view, in which changes in the rate of interest were responses to differences between savings and investment. By denying the validity of the classical view, he was able to cast aspersions on the efficiency of market mechanisms and the self-adjusting properties of a capitalist economy dominated by private property. But these aspersions were legitimate only if the monetary theory of interest-rate determination were correct, while its correctness depended on the assumption that bonds were the only non-money assets in the economy.

An obvious question needs to be asked. If the range of non-money assets were widened to include equities and real estate, would Keynes's monetary theory of "the rate of interest" still hold water? The answer must be: Not necessarily, because so much would depend on investors' expectations and the scope for substitution between bonds and other assets. If – starting from equilibrium – the quantity of money were increased in an economy that included equities and real estate, logically the equilibrium values of both equities and real estate would advance, at least in the short run. The dividend yield on equities and the rental yield on real estate would fall, on just the same lines as – according to Keynes – the price of bonds ought to rise and the "rate of interest" on bonds to decline.

However, in the medium and long runs, the result of the money injection, and the drop in asset yields and surge in asset prices, might well be a boom in the economy and inflation. If so, holders of fixed-interest bonds would see the real value of their investment fall. It follows that the initial reaction of alert, forward-looking investors to an increase in the quantity of money might be to sell bonds in the search for a yield high enough to compensate for future inflation. An increase in the quantity of money would lead to a *rise*, not a fall, in the equilibrium "rate of interest." In short, if the analysis of *The General Theory* were made more general (and closer in fact to that of the *Treatise*) by adding extra assets, the monetary theory of "the rate of interest" would crumble into incoherence.[8] One of Keynes's difficulties was that he wanted his "rate of interest" (i.e., his bond yields) to be susceptible to central-bank action in normal conditions, but – as he well knew – central banks did not typically deal in long-dated bonds. Sometimes he wrote as if the central bank's task was the setting of the "rate of interest" at the short end, which would affect the much more important long-dated-bond yields almost by sympathetic magic. But in the real world long-dated-bond yields do not move mechanically with the money-market rate. As Keynes admitted, he had "slurred over" problems of definition.[9] The *Treatise* – which did not make extravagant boasts about a new theory of interest-rate determination – was less ambitious, but also more satisfactory.

Finally, the practical results of Keynes's recommendations in and after *The General Theory* have become tarnished. In Britain the "somewhat comprehensive socialisation of investment" of the late 1940s led to mismanagement and inefficiency in nationalized industries on a scale that became fully recognized only following privatization under the Conservatives in the 1980s. It speaks volumes that the Labour Government elected in 1997 left the transport and energy utilities in private hands, with the problematic exception of the railways. Fiscal activism failed to stabilize output and employment in the late twentieth century, and in most European countries it has been replaced by fiscal rules, typically with a medium-term orientation. In the 1980s and early 1990s, the very large budget deficits endorsed by some Keynesians threatened financial ruin for Italy and other significant countries. Again in the 2010s, the immense budget deficits in the U.S., the U.K., and many other countries are increasingly being interpreted not as a boost to aggregate demand, but as a burden to future generations because of their runaway interest costs. By contrast, the issues raised by the *Tract* and the *Treatise* are very much alive, and the conclusions drawn by the early Keynes are still surprisingly viable. The *Tract*'s argument became particularly pertinent when the United States ended the convertibility of the dollar into gold in 1971 and thereby broke the last remnant of a gold-based currency system. The method of currency management proposed by Keynes in 1923 – to stabilize the growth of bank credit and the money stock – has clear affinities with the behavior – or at least the behavior intended at its foundation – of one of the great modern central banks, the European Central Bank. (The ECB's first chief economist, Otmar Issing, certainly saw the analysis of money-growth trends as basic to the central-bank research effort. However, the ECB did little to boost money growth in 2010, despite a severe recession in its peripheral members, such as Greece and Ireland.)[10] Money targeting has also been adopted – if more reluctantly – by other central banks, such as the American Federal Reserve and the Bank of England, at various times in the last thirty years.

III.

Keynes's contribution is far more substantial than his overrated *General Theory*. *The General Theory* represents only a fraction of all the words he wrote on economics, while the range of his work includes a major book on probability theory, essays in biography, and dozens of topical articles on politics and culture. It must be conceded that – despite its faults – *The General Theory* did stimulate a revolution in macroeconomic thinking. But *The General Theory* can be more easily understood if it is seen as a sequel to *A Treatise on Money*, which is in many ways a superior piece of work. Schumpeter commented that "There cannot be any doubt that [*The General Theory*] owed its victorious career to the fact that its argument implemented some of the strongest political preferences of a large number of modern economists."[11] In other words, the success of *The General Theory* owed more to its left-of-center political message than to its technical content.

ESSAY 3

KEYNES, THE KEYNESIANS, AND THE EXCHANGE RATE

ONE OF THE most-quoted remarks in economics comes in the final chapter of *The General Theory of Employment, Interest, and Money,* where Keynes wrote:

> . . . the ideas of economists, both when they are right and when they are wrong, are more powerful than is commonly understood. Indeed the world is ruled by little else. Practical men, who believe themselves to be quite exempt from any intellectual influences, are usually the slaves of some defunct economist. Madmen in authority, who hear voices in the air, are distilling their frenzy from some academic scribbler of a few years back.[1]

Keynes believed that his book would be a particularly powerful "intellectual influence" on such "practical men." He wanted to harness the fiscal powers of the state to make the trade cycle obsolete. For about twenty-five years after the Second World War, British economists thought that Keynes's ambition had been largely fulfilled. The improvement in macroeconomic conditions was taken to be the triumph of modern economic theory, the so-called "Keynesian revolution," over a number of ancient financial prejudices. The most salient of these prejudices was one that appealed to conventional morality and common sense, the traditional doctrine that the government should balance its budget and keep its finances in good order.

In the late 1960s no British economist expected the next twenty-five years to see large cyclical fluctuations in economic activity. The trade cycle may not yet have become obsolete, but it was thought to have depreciated to the point of insignificance. These expectations were to prove wrong. The next twenty-five years were to see three major cyclical episodes, commonly identified with the chancellor of the exchequer under whom they began. The first was the Barber boom of 1971 to 1973, followed by the severe downturn of 1974 and 1975; the second, from early 1978 to mid-1979, could be called the Healey boomlet, and it gave way to the recession of 1980 and early 1981; and the third was the Lawson boom of mid-1986 to mid-1988, which preceded the recession of 1990 to 1992. These episodes were not as extreme as the slump of the early 1930s, but they were comparable – in the amplitude of the fluctuations and other characteristics – to the trade cycles of the nineteenth century. More recently, the Great Recession of 2008 to 2010 came as a shocking reminder that economic stability has still not been secured.

Three questions arise: Why did these large cyclical fluctuations return? What mistakes were governments and central banks making? And, Were their mistakes tactical and accidental in nature, or the result of a strategic misunderstanding of how the economy works? More pointedly, why did the madmen in authority behave as they did? And to which defunct economists were they listening? In attempting to answer these questions the approach here will be largely historical. The reference to "defunct economists" will be far from rhetorical. Why were British economists, and hence the British government, so unprepared for the problems of the 1970s and 1980s? And why did they flunk the examination to which they were subjected in the Great Recession? The essay will be mostly an exercise in the history of ideas, particularly ideas about macroeconomic policy.

I.

The notion of "macroeconomic policy" is very modern. In the eighteenth century no one believed that the government had either the ability or the responsibility to manage the economy. Cyclical fluctuations in economic activity were sometimes pronounced, but they were regarded as Acts of God, like the weather or earthquakes. Theorizing about the role of money in the trade cycle was rudimentary. In previous centuries the money stock had consisted entirely of metals, particularly gold and silver, and the quantity of money had therefore been determined by the past production of gold and silver mines. There had been little opportunity to substitute paper for these metals, because of the lack of trust in paper alternatives. However, as the eighteenth century wore on, Britain's political stability and the development of a satisfactory legal framework encouraged people to carry out an increasing proportion of their transactions in bank notes and bills of exchange. These paper instruments – whose validity depended on credit – came increasingly to perform the monetary functions of the precious metals.

But the growth of paper credit introduced a new risk. This was that the individuals and organizations issuing the paper alternatives to the precious metals might not be able to redeem them at their face value. A goldsmith banker might issue a note recognizing an obligation to repay the bearer on demand a particular weight of gold or silver, and the note might circulate widely and with perfect creditworthiness for many months or even years. But, if one of its holders presented it to the goldsmith banker and he was unable – for any reason – to pay over the stated quantity of precious metal, his entire note issue would fall into disrepute, and this part of the money stock would no longer be able to circulate. Sudden collapses in the creditworthiness of paper lay behind some of the most severe cyclical fluctuations of the eighteenth century, even though precious metals continued to be the most important monetary asset. London bankers tried to anticipate the dangers by opening accounts and establishing a good relationship with the Bank of England, on the understanding that the Bank would act as a source of precious metals in an emergency. Country bankers in turn opened accounts and established good relationships with the London bankers.

The legislative response to these developments was twofold. First, restrictions were placed on the ability of private banks to issue notes, although these restrictions were surprisingly late in coming; they were more a feature of the nineteenth than the eighteenth century. Secondly, the Bank of England – which was seen as the core institution from an early stage – was required in successive Bank Charter Acts to redeem its note liabilities at a fixed price in terms of the precious metals. The price of gold was fixed at £3 17s. 10½d. an ounce by Sir Isaac Newton in 1717, and the first denominationalized notes were printed in 1725.[2] In other words, the Bank of England was mandated to protect a fixed exchange rate between its paper liabilities and the precious metals. After the Napoleonic Wars, Parliament deprived silver of much of its former monetary role and established gold monometalism as the basis of Britain's money in 1821. Thereafter the essential features of Britain's monetary arrangements, and indeed the defining characteristics of the classical gold standard under its aegis, were the fixed gold price of £3 17s. 10½d. an ounce, and the ready convertibility of notes into gold and vice versa.

The logic of this system is easy to analyze and defend. Let us take it for granted that the public at large wants a money that is fairly reliable in terms of its ability to purchase non-monetary things. In this context precious metals have one key advantage as a monetary asset. Because they are highly durable, virtually all of the last period's stock of metals survives into the current and next periods. Further, as long as mining technology changes only slowly and there are no new discoveries, the production of new gold and silver in any one period should be only a small fraction of the stock of these metals accumulated over past centuries. As a result the stock of precious metals is very stable over time. Since it is therefore unlikely to increase more rapidly than world output, the price of commodities in general should be roughly stable in terms of the precious metals.

From this point of view, the introduction of paper alternatives to precious metals is potentially dangerous. The production of paper money requires almost no resources. The quantity of paper money – unlike the quantity of precious metals – can be easily multiplied tenfold or a hundredfold. If this multiplication of the quantity of money occurs in a short period with no matching increase in output, the value of money is certain to collapse. Public policy could anticipate this problem by insisting that paper be convertible into gold at a fixed price. If the fixed exchange rate between paper and gold is maintained, and if the value of gold remains reasonably stable in terms of commodities, then the value of paper should also remain reasonably stable in terms of commodities. Here was the rationale for the gold standard in the nineteenth century. With paper anchored to gold at a fixed exchange rate, the growth of paper money could not have systematic inflationary consequences.

The gold standard was a success. Although the economy was subject to occasional cyclical disturbances, and the price level varied both within these cycles and over longer periods, nineteenth-century Britain was a model of financial stability. Such was the admiration for Britain's achievement that by the 1880s most other major industrial countries had also adopted gold as the basis for their monetary systems, creating the international gold standard of the late nineteenth century. The "rules of the game" were well known. The central bank of every participating country had to preserve the convertibility of its note liabilities into gold at the agreed fixed exchange rate. The paper/gold exchange rate within each country implied certain exchange rates between the paper currencies of the participant countries. If an exchange rate came under pressure, the consequent external drain on the central bank's gold reserve had to be countered by raising interest rates. On the other hand, when a central bank's gold reserve was ample, it could cut interest rates. In the case of the Bank of England, its interest-rate decisions were determined fairly mechanically by watching the Proportion between its gold holdings and its deposit liabilities.[3] By the late nineteenth century its gold holdings varied mainly because of international pressures, rather than domestic changes in financial confidence. The practice of relating interest-rate decisions to gold holdings and the exchange rate became deeply entrenched. The dependence of interest rates on international financial developments increased, even as the U.K.'s weight in the world economy – and hence its share of the total world gold stock – diminished.

But another and quite different approach to monetary policy would have been possible, and had indeed been intimated by some economists many years before. It would have relied on two revolutionary ideas which emerged in the debates on British financial policy during the Napoleonic Wars, debates which in their complexity and sophistication can fairly be described as the matrix of modern monetary theory. The urgency of those controversies arose because, under the strains of war, the Bank of England had been forced to suspend the convertibility of its notes into gold in 1797. There was widespread public concern that the value of the notes, which continued to circulate as currency, would decline steadily. The vital question was how to stabilize the real value of the notes in the absence of the fixed anchor to gold.

The first of the two revolutionary ideas was that of the "general price level." Nowadays the concepts of an overall price level, of a price index that quantifies it, and of an inflation rate measured by changes in the index are generally accepted. Indeed, they are so commonplace that we rarely stop to think about them. That was not so in the 1790s. People were aware of the need to have a reliable monetary unit and standard of value, but they were not sure how best to formalize this need in precise numerical terms. Thus, when David Ricardo wrote about the depreciation of the currency in a famous pamphlet of 1810 he gave it the title *The High Price of Bullion, a Proof of the Depreciation of Bank Notes.* He thought of currency depreciation in terms of the price of gold, not in terms of a general price level. However, there had already been innovators who had seen the potential for applying index numbers to the problem. According to Schumpeter, "A great step toward full realization of the importance of the method was made in 1798, when Sir George Shuckburgh-Evelyn presented a paper to the Royal Society in which, with apologies for treating a subject so much below the dignity of that august body, he used an index number – of a primitive kind, no doubt – for measuring the 'depreciation of money.'"[4] The approach became progressively more refined in the course of the nineteenth century. In 1922 the American economist Irving Fisher, professor of political economy at Yale from 1898 to 1935, published a monumental work on *The Making of Index Numbers.* One of the motives of this work – and, in fact, one of Fisher's strongest professional interests – was to define a price index whose stability would be the prime objective of monetary policy.

The second revolutionary idea, and perhaps an even more fundamental one, was to recognize that the nature of the inflationary process was radically changed by the introduction of paper money. With the functions of money increasingly being performed by paper instruments, the quantity of such instruments could affect the prices of goods and services. The link between the quantity of gold and its price had been the central interest of earlier monetary commentators. But, as more notes and bills of exchange entered into circulation, economists began to surmise that the connection might be between the quantity of all forms of money, both gold and paper, and the price level. The starting point for their analyses was the crude but serviceable principle that the greater the quantity of paper credit, the higher the price level. By extension, the higher the rate of increase in paper credit, the faster the rate of inflation.

The most impressive early work on these ideas was *An Inquiry into the Nature and Effects of the Paper Credit of Great Britain* by Henry Thornton, published in 1802. The timing of this great book, five years after the Bank of England's suspension of gold convertibility, was not an accident. Thornton was acutely aware of the dangers inherent in a system of paper credit. He emphasized that an excessive issue of bank notes would lead to rises in the price level, while warning, on the other hand, that sharp contractions of the note issue could cause downturns in economic activity. His advice to the Bank of England was therefore to "limit the amount of paper issued, and to resort for this purpose, whenever the temptation to borrow is strong, to some effectual principle of restriction; in no case, however, materially to diminish the sum in circulation, but to let it vibrate only within certain limits" and "to afford a slow and cautious extension of it, as the general trade of the kingdom enlarges itself."[5]

Here is the kernel of a new approach, the beginnings of the idea of "monetary policy" or even "macroeconomic policy." Decisions on monetary management are no longer motivated by the gold price or an exchange rate between paper and a metal. Instead the central bank is understood to have fairly deliberate goals: to stabilize the price level and, as far as possible, to avoid large fluctuations in economic activity. Moreover, it is to achieve these goals by trying to control "the sum in circulation" or, as we would now say, by regulating the money supply. This way of conducting monetary policy – where the quantity of paper money is the target of central-bank action – is clearly quite different from the earlier approach, with its focus on a particular gold price or exchange rate.[6]

II.

Thornton's hint of a new style of monetary regulation was not taken up in his lifetime. On the contrary, the gold standard became established, gained increasing credibility, and flourished until the First World War. But after 1918 another phase of intense monetary controversy began. The problem was – just as it had been after the Napoleonic Wars – whether Britain should restore the gold standard at the pre-war parity. The majority of bankers, politicians, and so-called "practical men" associated the gold standard with the stability and prosperity of the Victorian period. Perhaps without thinking very hard about the issues, they wanted to return to the gold standard. This point of view was expressed officially in the reports of the Cunliffe Committee, in 1918 and 1919, which said that restoration should occur as soon as possible. However, a small group of economists were skeptical, believing that the success of the gold standard in the nineteenth century had been largely a fluke and preferring a more deliberate and (as they described it) scientific approach to monetary policy.

The foremost skeptic about the gold standard was John Maynard Keynes. In his *Tract on Monetary Reform*, published in 1923, he identified the risk that gold could be kept in line with output only through chance discoveries of the metal. In any case, since Britain held only a small part of the world's gold stock, a return to the pre-war standard would leave it vulnerable to changes in other countries' demand for gold. There was no alternative to managing the currency:

> If providence watched over gold, or if Nature had provided us with a stable standard ready-made, I would not, in an attempt after some slight improvement, hand over the management to the possible weakness or ignorance of boards and governments. But this is not the situation. We have no ready-made standard. Experience has shown that in emergencies ministers of finance cannot be strapped down. And – most important of all – in the modern world of paper currency and bank credit there is no escape from a "managed" currency, whether we wish it or not; convertibility into gold will not alter the fact that the value of gold itself depends on the policy of the central banks.[7]

The answer, then, was not to go back to a fixed gold price, but to have a "managed currency." But how, in more specific terms, should a managed currency work? What objectives should policy-makers have, and how should these objectives be achieved?

Keynes was clear about what he wanted. He was against not only the gold standard, but also a fixed exchange rate between the pound and the dollar, since this would leave Britain too much at the mercy of the American Federal Reserve. Although he recognized that "an internal standard, so regulated as to maintain stability in an index number of prices, is a difficult scientific innovation never yet put into practice," that was nevertheless the ideal he favored: "I regard the stability of prices, credit and employment as of paramount importance."[8] He referred with enthusiasm to the champion of index-number computation, Irving Fisher, for his pioneering advocacy of price stability as against exchange stability.

The *Tract* also devoted much space to the principles and practice of monetary management. In Keynes's view, "The internal price level is mainly determined by the amount of credit created by the banks, chiefly the Big Five," and "The amount of credit . . . is in its turn roughly measured by the volume of the banks' deposits."[9] There is a certain lack of clarity in these remarks, since it is not obvious whether it is the asset or liability side of banks' balance sheets that Keynes wanted to emphasize. But, if we agree that new lending creates deposits, this would be no great problem. The discussion of the mechanics of monetary control was also rather confusing. Keynes seemed to oscillate between two views, one that the size of banks' balance sheets is a multiple of their cash reserves, which can be determined by open-market operations, and another that "adequate control" over an important part of banks' assets (i.e., their advances and bills) "can be obtained by varying the price charged, that is to say the bank rate."[10]

These technical complications were to become of huge importance in later controversies, but they should not be allowed to hide the essence of the "managed currency" as Keynes envisaged it. The ultimate target should be the stability of the domestic price level, not the gold price or the exchange rate; and that target should be attained by managing the growth rate of banks' balance sheets, through interest-rate variations if appropriate. It might not add much to say that Keynes's managed currency had a certain amount in common with latter-day "monetarism," since that begs the question of how monetarism should be defined.[11] But there cannot be much doubt that – for most of his career – Keynes disliked having a fixed exchange rate as a policy target and paid close attention to credit and monetary variables when assessing economic prospects. That, on a careful reading of the texts, should be uncontroversial.

At first, Keynes's proposals for a managed currency got nowhere.

Britain returned to the gold standard in 1925, with unhappy consequences for economic activity and employment, just as Keynes had
expected. But after the departure from the gold standard in 1931, and
the subsequent disintegration of international monetary order, Britain
willy-nilly had the managed currency that Keynes advocated. Domestic
objectives, not the gold price or the exchange rate, dominated
policy-making in the 1930s. Until late in his career Keynes insisted that
domestic objectives, not external, should come first. In a speech on the
proposed International Monetary Fund in the House of Lords in May
1943, he reiterated his priorities. In his words,

> We are determined that, in future, the external value of sterling
> shall conform to its internal value, as set by our own domestic
> policies, and not the other way round . . . [W]e abjure the instru-
> ments of bank rate and credit contraction operating through an
> increase in unemployment as a means of forcing our domestic
> economy into line with external factors. I hope your Lordships
> will trust me not to have turned my back on all I have fought for.[12]

It would be natural to assume that the post-war "Keynesian revolution" would reflect the implementation of a macroeconomic policy
directed at domestic priorities. That, indeed, is how some of the hagiog-
raphers have seen it. They have claimed that official policy in the first
thirty years after 1945 was dominated by the aim of maintaining the
domestic goal of full employment. Since a much closer approximation to
full employment was achieved in these years than in the inter-war
period, that may seem a reasonable assertion. However, monetary policy
was certainly not organized in the way that Keynes had recommended in
A Tract on Monetary Reform or in his speech to the House of Lords.

On the contrary, the lodestar for interest-rate decisions was the
pound's exchange rate against the dollar. For twenty-two years, from
1945 to 1967, the pound was constrained by the Bretton Woods regime
of fixed exchange rates and kept close to its central parity. (Admittedly,
a big devaluation occurred in 1949, but the $2.80 rate was then main-
tained until 1967.) It was true that sterling's explicit link with gold had
been broken and that the Bank of England did not redeem its note liabilities with any precious metal, as it had done before 1914. But the

pound was tied to the dollar, and the dollar was fixed to gold at the official price of $35 an ounce. Britain may no longer have been on a formal gold standard, but sterling maintained a constant, if indirect and perhaps rather clandestine, relationship with gold for many years after Keynes's death.

III.

In these years of fixed exchange rates, academic and official interest in monetary policy dwindled steadily. Indeed, it could be argued that Keynes's *General Theory* was both the climax and the terminus of the nineteenth-century tradition of trade-cycle theorizing, in which credit and money had been so important. Afterwards the overwhelming majority of British economists downplayed the significance of credit and money in macroeconomic fluctuations and inflation. There were at least three reasons for the new neglect of monetary analysis.

The first was that Keynes himself had been moving in this direction late in his career. At the time of the *Tract* he believed, with few qualifications, in the ability of interest-rate changes to manage the currency and so to achieve desired macroeconomic outcomes. But in the 1930s very low interest rates were unable to prevent the persistence of high unemployment. One task of *The General Theory* was therefore to identify those circumstances in which low interest rates would be ineffective in stimulating investment and encouraging employment. Keynes suggested that there could be a situation, a so-called "liquidity trap," where people were so shell-shocked by the deflationary environment around them that they could not be induced to move out of cash into other assets. It seemed that the deflation could not be countered by central-bank action to cut interest rates. As noted elsewhere in this volume, Keynes went on to advocate that the government take direct responsibility for investment in order to offset the possible impotence of interest rates. In his words, "it seems unlikely that the influence of banking policy on the rate of interest will be sufficient by itself to determine an optimum rate of investment. I conceive, therefore, that a somewhat comprehensive socialisation of investment will prove the only means of securing an approximation to full employment."[13]

The second reason for the growing indifference towards monetary policy was that for almost twenty years, from 1932 to 1951, interest rates were virtually constant. Bank rate was held at 2 percent throughout the period, apart from a brief (and insignificant) interruption at the beginning of the Second World War. Since hardly any interest-rate changes occurred, there seemed little practical benefit in analyzing the results of such changes. As interest rates had clearly not been much of an influence on business conditions for such a long period, economists thought they could ignore the possibility that interest rates might become important in the future. Even in the 1950s and 1960s interest-rate variations were small for most of the time. In British universities, theorizing about the effect of interest rates on the economy – and so about monetary policy overall – became moribund.

Thirdly, during the war, and for many years afterwards, the British economy was subject to a wide variety of administrative controls of one sort or another. Rationing, conscription, and the requisitioning of resources for the armed forces had a clear military function and could not be accepted for long in peacetime. But other restrictions – such as exchange controls, tight planning controls on building materials, controls on new issues, and so on – survived long after the war had ended. Many civil servants and politicians thought that the economy could be run better by relaxing or tightening these controls than by relaxing or tightening monetary policy. Their ideal was not Keynes's "managed currency," which would have been fully compatible with market capitalism, but a semi-socialist mixed economy with extensive economic planning. In the late 1940s and 1950s a large number of British economists undoubtedly welcomed the retention of controls and a commitment to planning.

If this seems a strong statement, it needs to be emphasized that 1963 saw the publication of an official document on *Conditions for Faster Growth*, which enjoined a more active government role in industry, with the full blessing of the Conservative government of Harold Macmillan. In 1964 the Department of Economic Affairs, with even more interventionist objectives, was established by the newly elected Labour government of Harold Wilson. Wilson had previously been an economics don at Oxford University, and his government introduced large numbers of academic economists into Whitehall. It is a fair comment that none of these economists was much interested in monetary policy, but all of them were fascinated – in one way or another – by the potential of "economic planning."

By the late 1960s hardly any British economist thought that interest rates could or should be varied to influence domestic economic variables. The immensely influential National Institute of Economic and Social Research never mentioned the money supply, in any of its definitions, in its *Reviews*. It only occasionally referred to credit variables, and even then the focus was on hire purchase rather than mortgage lending. Whole volumes were written on macroeconomic policy with hardly any comment on money. For example, in a book on *The Labour Government's Economic Record: 1964–70*, edited by Wilfred Beckerman and published in 1972, there was only one index reference to "the money supply," whereas there were seventeen to the National Economic Development Council, twenty-one to the National Board for Prices and Incomes, and no less than forty-one to the National Plan and "Planning."[14] In the late 1940s, shortly after Keynes's death, the Department of Applied Economics had been founded at Cambridge, but it never sustained his interest in money and banking. In the early 1970s the Cambridge Economic Policy Group was established with the support of such well-known figures as Lord Kaldor and Professor Robert Neild, and its personnel overlapped with those of the longer-established DAE. The much-publicized recommendations in its *Economic Policy Review* almost never contained remarks on monetary policy, unless they were dismissive. According to one article in its March 1977 issue, "In our view there is no justification at all for incorporating a target for domestic credit expansion in official economic policy."[15] (As mentioned in the introduction to this book, Neild was one of the organizers of the letter to *The Times* from the 364 economists protesting the 1981 Budget. See also pp. 49–50 in this essay.)

An extraordinary somersault had been accomplished. Whereas in 1923 the managed currency favored by Keynes had seen the restraint over credit growth as central to monetary regulation, in the 1970s Cambridge economists and, indeed, most economists in British universities saw no merit in targets for credit and monetary growth. Many of them saw no point in analyzing credit or monetary trends at all. Inflation was better understood, in their view, by watching the behavior of wages and the exchange rate. The readiness of staff at the National Institute and the

Department of Applied Economics to adopt the label of "Keynesian" was the more remarkable in that it overlooked huge chunks of Keynes's own writing. These economists did not seem to appreciate that their ways of thinking were a betrayal of Keynes's ideas. Instead their loyalty was to second-rate textbooks that regurgitated, for decades after they had lost any practical relevance, the dangers of the liquidity trap and interest-inelastic investment. (The next essay will review claims made by the American Keynesian Paul Krugman that in recent years the U.S. and Japanese economies have succumbed to the liquidity trap.)

The questions arise, How then was the Keynesian revolution accomplished? and, What were the techniques of economic policy that gave the British economy its stability in the first twenty-five years after the war? If Keynes's managed currency was forgotten by most British economists, who or what should be awarded the medals for the relative financial tranquillity of the immediate post-war decades? It is here that we come to yet another paradox. There can be hardly any doubt that the key economic constraint on British governments in those years was the avoidance of sterling devaluation. Whenever policy-makers embarked on unduly stimulatory policies, the pound would come under downward pressure on the foreign exchanges and the resulting "sterling crisis" would oblige the government to think again. It was the succession of sterling crises, and the need to check them by credit restrictions and/or higher interest rates, that kept inflation under control.

Since the pound/dollar rate was the linchpin of the system, American monetary policy determined British monetary policy. Fortunately, American monetary policy in the first twenty-five years after the war was a model of anti-inflationary prudence and countercyclical stability. As Keynes had noted in his May 1943 speech to the House of Lords, in a fixed-exchange-rate system, "the instruments of bank rate and credit contraction" would be dictated from outside Britain. But it was precisely these instruments that not only kept the U.K. price level in line with the world price level (of traded goods, expressed in terms of a common currency), but also delivered the full employment, low inflation, and cyclical moderation of the post-war period. The exchange rate played a benign, indeed a positive, role in British macroeconomic management. Keynes's suspicion of international financial influences on monetary policy-making proved misplaced.

Before we discuss what happened after the pound/dollar link was broken, another irony needs to be mentioned. American monetary policy in the first two decades after the Second World War was unquestionably a success compared with other periods, both before and after. But why? Many of the good decisions can be attributed, of course, to the professionalism of the Federal Reserve staff and the budgetary restraint of Presidents Truman and Eisenhower. But there was another factor at work. One of the reasons for the Federal Reserve's tightening of monetary policy in the late 1950s was to protect the dollar on the foreign exchanges and, in particular, to preserve the $35-an-ounce gold price. Gold was still the bedrock of the Bretton Woods system. Does it follow from this argument that the Keynesian revolution was not the result of the discretionary demand management and fiscal fine-tuning so much praised in the textbooks? Can the happy stability of the 1950s and 1960s instead be seen to rest on two fixed exchange rates, the $2.80 rate between the pound and the dollar, and the $35-an-ounce official price of gold? Was the prosperity of that period due not to the final abandonment of the "barbarous relic," but rather to the U.K.'s membership in the Bretton Woods system and the world's last inarticulate clinging to a gold anchor?

IV.

The two exchange rates were scrapped in the early 1970s. In August 1971, because of the rapid decline in America's gold reserve, President Nixon suspended the dollar's convertibility into gold, and in June 1972 the pound left the embryonic European "currency snake," after belonging for less than two months. Sterling's exit from the snake was to inaugurate a period of deliberate floating. We have already seen that one of the key preconditions for wise domestic monetary management – namely, a deep and extensive understanding of monetary economics among professional economists – no longer existed in Britain. Very few academic economists were interested in the pre-Keynesian tradition of trade-cycle analysis, the acknowledged classics of monetary theory, or contemporary monetary institutions. As a result there was no longer any heavyweight intellectual obstacle to rapid expansion of domestic credit and the money supply. The external barrier to inflationary policies, which had been imposed by a fixed exchange rate for over twenty years, was now also removed.

The scene had been set for the Barber boom of the early 1970s. Credit and money growth were extraordinarily fast by any previous standards. But most British economists were unconcerned about the potential inflationary repercussions and instead celebrated the very rapid output growth from mid-1972 to mid-1973. (The level of GDP was 8.6 percent higher in real terms in the middle two quarters of 1973 than in the middle two quarters of 1972. Domestic demand grew even faster.) On May 7, 1973, Peter Jay, the economics editor of *The Times*, wrote an article entitled, "The Boom That Must Go Bust." In the same month, the *National Institute Economic Review* judged that "there is no reason why the present boom should either bust or have to be busted." The *Review* was undoubtedly representative of professional economic opinion.

Later it became uncontroversial that something had gone horribly wrong. The current-account deficit on the balance of payments was a post-war record in 1974, and in mid-1975 the inflation rate hit 25 percent. In 1976 Denis Healey, the chancellor of the exchequer, introduced money-supply targets in order to establish a monetary framework for reducing inflation. These targets opened up the possibility that interest-rate changes might be determined by the behavior of monetary growth rather than by the exchange rate. The targets were expressed in terms of broad money, which is dominated by bank deposits. Broad-money targets were to survive for almost a decade, until they were dropped in late 1985. Although the need for some kind of money target, or a so-called "nominal framework," was widely accepted, it would be wrong to think that academic economists were much involved in its introduction. On the contrary, the case for money targets was urged most vigorously by City economists and in the financial press, notably *The Times*.[16]

The heyday of broad-money targets was in early 1980, only a few months after the Thatcher government had come to power. At about the same time as the announcement of the Medium-Term Financial Strategy in the Budget of that year, the government published a Green Paper titled *Monetary Control*. It set out the rationale and the method of operation of broad-money targets. In its words, "The government's policy is . . . to sustain downward pressure on prices by a progressive reduction of the rate of growth of the money supply over a period of years." (This statement clearly implied that monetary growth caused inflation.) The reduction in monetary growth was to be accomplished partly by curbing public-sector borrowing from the banks (which depended on the total amount of public-sector borrowing minus sales of public-sector debt to non-banks) and partly by discouraging bank lending to the private sector. Although the authors of the Green Paper were skeptical that the private sector's demand for bank finance was responsive to interest rates in the short run, their aversion to quantitative credit restrictions left interest rates as the only instrument available to regulate credit expansion. It followed that interest rates were to be raised if monetary growth was ahead of target, but lowered if it was behind target.

In effect, the Green Paper *Monetary Control* set out an approach to monetary policy that – in its emphasis on the credit counterparts to deposit growth and its focus on domestic rather than external objectives – had clear similarities to Keynes's scheme for a "managed currency" in *A Tract on Monetary Reform*. Moreover, in a number of speeches, Sir Geoffrey Howe, the chancellor of the exchequer, argued that the exchange rate had to be allowed to float if the government was to have the freedom over interest rates required to achieve its money-supply targets. Interest rates were to be governed by domestic criteria, with a view to attaining price stability, rather than by the exchange rate.

The question of what happened to broad-money targets, and the system of financial control associated with them, is not much debated now. There is hardly space here to provide a detailed history of British economic policy in the early 1980s.[17] However, certain salient points are essential to the argument. In late 1980 monetary growth ran far ahead of target, obliging the government to keep interest rates high despite a deepening industrial recession. The exchange rate rose to remarkable levels, and by early 1981 the pound was clearly overvalued. Most economists, appalled by this turn of events, urged the government to ease the deflationary pressures. They wanted it to pay more attention to the exchange rate and less (or none at all) to domestic monetary trends.

But in the Budget of March 1981, the government raised taxes in order to keep public-sector borrowing within the targets stated in the Medium-Term Financial Strategy. Two professors of economics at

Cambridge – Frank Hahn and Robert Neild – organized a letter to *The Times* from 364 economists at British universities, which claimed that the government's policies "will deepen the depression, erode the industrial base of the economy and threaten its social and political stability." The 364 economists were wrong. The British economy began to recover only a few months after the letter was written, and above-trend growth was maintained from late 1983 to 1989. (For further discussion of the 1981 Budget and its sequel, see essay 10.)

But to assume therefore that the letter from the 364 had no influence would be a very serious mistake. It accurately reflected the overwhelming consensus of British academic opinion. Whenever officials from the Treasury or the Bank of England took part in academic conferences, both in these years and later, they were subjected to a barrage of scorn for obeying their political masters and implementing money-supply targets. The constant sniping took its toll. Perhaps even more important, there was only limited academic interest in the technical operation of the system of monetary management actually at work in the early 1980s. A substantial literature developed on the merits of an alternative system of monetary-base control, but this was not strictly relevant to the day-to-day problems facing the Treasury and the Bank of England.

For example, whereas City newsletters and circulars discussed the problem of "overfunding" in some detail in 1984 and 1985, it received hardly any comment in academic journals. The reason was simple. There were very few university economists who respected what the government was trying to do, namely, to combat inflation by reducing the rate of broad-money growth. (Overfunding was the practice of selling public-sector debt to the non-bank private sector in an amount greater than the budget deficit, in order that the excess proceeds could be used to reduce the banks' claims on the public sector, and hence reduce both banks' assets and their deposit liabilities. The opposite practice of "underfunding" – the deliberate incurring by the government of liabilities to the banks in order to create money – is related to the "quantitative easing" discussed in the next essay. Both overfunding and underfunding are examples of "debt-market operations," as they are termed there.)

So when broad-money targets were scrapped in late 1985, there was general relief in university economics departments that, at long last, the government had returned to sanity. "Sanity" was to be understood, in their view, as the former style of macroeconomic management, with interest-rate changes determined largely by the pound's fortunes on the foreign exchanges. The government nevertheless retained monetary targets, at least in form. Few people outside the Treasury took these targets, which came to be expressed in terms of narrow money rather than broad money, all that seriously. City commentators noted that the quantity of notes and coin, which is the main constituent of the officially favored narrow-money measure, M0, was determined by the current economic situation, rather than being a determinant of the future behavior of demand and output. It followed from this that narrow money could not have any causal role in the inflationary process.

Keynes had, in fact, made precisely the same point in the *Tract* over sixty years earlier. He remarked that, in the circumstances of the early 1920s, "Cash, in the form of bank and currency notes, is supplied *ad libitum*, i.e. in such quantities as are called for by the amount of credit created and the internal price level established." It followed that ". . . the tendency of today – rightly I think – is to watch and control the creation of credit and to let the creation of currency follow suit, rather than, as formerly, to watch and control the creation of currency and to let the creation of credit follow suit."[18]

Keynes's preference for watching bank credit and deposits rather than currency (in the form of coin and notes) was partly a by-product of his aversion to gold. Under the Bank Charter Act of 1844 the Bank of England had been required to restrict the fiduciary-note issue (i.e., that part of the note issue not backed by gold holdings in its Issue Department). Gold had therefore remained, in principle, the ultimate regulator of the quantity of notes. But Keynes wanted "the volume of paper money" (i.e., notes) to be "consequential . . . on the state of trade and employment, bank rate policy and Treasury bill policy," so that the "governors of the system would be bank rate and Treasury bill policy." He therefore made "the proposal – which may seem, but should not be, shocking – of separating entirely the gold reserve from the note issue." If this were done, monetary policy would be free to serve the government's proper objectives, which in his view were, of course, the "stability of trade, prices and employment."[19]

The Treasury's adherence to M0 in the mid- and late 1980s was half-hearted, as well as half-baked. Nevertheless, as Keynes would have expected, it had unfortunate consequences. Because M0 is an indicator rather than a cause of inflation, it failed abjectly to give advance warning of future inflationary trouble. The role of two self-styled "monetarist" advisers to the government, Sir Alan Walters and Patrick Minford, in this failure needs to be mentioned. In the early 1980s they were both critical of the importance attached to credit and broad money, and advocated that narrow money be given a more prominent role. Conservative politicians did not trust the great mass of left-leaning British academic economists, but they did consult the ideologically sound Walters and Minford. The advice of these two economists was therefore instrumental in undermining the framework of monetary management which was in existence before Mrs. Thatcher and her Treasury ministers started listening to them. (Minford is also mentioned in essay 14.)

In his book *Britain's Economic Renaissance*, Walters observed that it is money in the "transactions sense that plays the central role in the theoretical structure and the propositions of monetarism." He gave paying a bus fare as an example of the kind of transaction he had in mind, and he distinguished this sharply from "credit." (To quote, "You pay your bus fare with money; you do not offer the fare collector a promissory note."[20]) But, whatever the role of money in this "transactions sense" in either Walters's or the British government's understanding of monetary economics during the 1980s, it had actually been superseded several decades earlier by the leaders of economic thought.

The whole point of Keynes's critique of classical monetary theory was that it overlooked the position of money in a portfolio of assets. If the demand to hold money rose for reasons of increased liquidity preference, the demand to buy goods and services would fall. In Keynes's extreme case of the liquidity trap, the ability of money's non-transactions role to expand indefinitely could become the jinx of the capitalist system. Hicks also saw the need to locate money in a framework of portfolio choice, proposing that the principle of marginal maximization should be borrowed from microeconomics.[21] Friedman's attempt to restate the quantity theory related the demand for money to wealth, as well as to income and other variables.[22] Walters's silence on these basic ideas, and their many implications, is further testimony to British economists' lack of insight into the role of credit and money in macro-economic fluctuations.

V.

The sequence of events after the scrapping of broad-money targets in 1985 had clear similarities to that after the abandonment of a fixed exchange rate in 1971 and 1972, except that the boom evolved somewhat more slowly. The focus of monetary policy again became the exchange rate. In late 1985 and early 1986, with the dollar falling rapidly on the foreign exchanges, the exchange rate did not signal a need for higher interest rates. The pound itself fell heavily in late 1986, particularly against the deutschemark, but this was interpreted as a necessary and welcome result of lower oil prices. (In 1984 exports of oil had amounted to almost £15 billion, equivalent to almost 20 percent of total exports of goods. The pound was widely seen as a "petro-currency.")

From March 1987 to March 1988 sterling was deliberately kept in a band of 2.95 to 3 against the deutschemark. However, with German interest rates so much beneath those in Britain, this external factor argued for an easing, rather than a tightening, of domestic monetary policy. In effect, from late 1985 to early 1988 there was no meaningful external constraint on domestic monetary policy. The external environment allowed rapid growth of domestic credit and fast monetary expansion, just as it had after the ending of the dollar's convertibility into gold in August 1971 and the pound's exit from the European snake in June 1972. Interest rates fell, credit growth accelerated, and the growth rate of broad money – no longer dampened by overfunding – also increased. By late 1986 the economy was undoubtedly growing at an above-trend rate. By mid-1987 it was in a full-scale boom. The mood of businessmen, particularly get-rich-quick property speculators, was an almost exact replica of that in the Barber boom fifteen years earlier. Indeed, the bank-lending and broad-money numbers themselves were remarkably similar.

Did British economists, of either the Keynesian or narrow-money schools, object? Did they warn that the boom would inevitably end in a worse balance-of-payments deficit, a rising inflation rate, and a need for a sharp cyclical downturn to offset the excesses of the boom? Sadly, the short answer is, No. The clear majority of them – in the universities, in the official policy-making machine, and in the City – raised no objections and issued no warnings. On the contrary, the consensus macroeconomic forecast in 1986, 1987, and early 1988 was that the economy was about to slow down to a trend rate of output growth without any rise in interest rates. (This tendency to predict a slowdown two or three quarters from the current quarter was so widespread and persistent that it became known as "forecasters' droop.") All of the so-called lending forecasting bodies – the London Business School, the National Institute, the Treasury, and their many imitators – believed that the inflation rate in the late 1980s would be similar to, or lower than, that in the mid-1980s.[23]

Without an appropriately valued fixed exchange rate to guide interest-rate decisions, academic economists were slaphappy about the medium-term implications of grossly unsustainable domestic monetary trends. The indifference of academic opinion gave economic advisers in the civil service and the Bank of England a pretext for not alerting their political masters to the foolishness of their policies.[24] The Lawson boom of the late 1980s – like the Barber boom of the early 1970s – was the result of British economists' lack of recognition of how credit and money affect demand, output, employment, and inflation. It was due, above all, to a great vacuum in intellectual understanding. The Lawson boom was followed, like the Barber boom, by a sharp rise in inflation and a recession. It therefore wrecked the greatest asset the Thatcher government had in the general elections of 1983 and 1987, a high reputation for managerial competence in running the economy and controlling inflation. These consequences can be fairly described as the revenge of the 364.

However, there was no excuse for the vacuum in intellectual understanding. Keynes had set out over sixty years earlier, in his *Tract on Monetary Reform*, how a system of monetary policy focused on domestic objectives should work. The key intermediate indicators in the *Tract* were the growth rates of credit and bank deposits (or, as we would now say, broad money), just as they were in the original Medium-Term Financial Strategy declared in 1980. Keynes's agenda in the *Tract* should be seen as the logical culmination of many decades of analysis and theorizing about the trade cycle. This tradition of British monetary economics began with Thornton and Ricardo, and proceeded through (among others) John Stuart Mill, Walter Bagehot, and Alfred Marshall, to Keynes's contemporaries, Dennis Robertson and Ralph Hawtrey. But it withered and died in the 1950s and 1960s. It suffered, most of all, from the deliberate and ideologically motivated neglect of an economics profession far more interested in planning how a semi-socialist economy might work in the future than in understanding how a free-market economy had operated in the past (and does now operate and will indeed continue to operate in the future).

The closing phase of the Lawson boom saw a vigorous debate between those economists who favored membership of the European Monetary System and those who wanted to maintain policy independence. The dominant position in the U.K. economics establishment – with its strong Keynesian leanings – was to support EMS membership. This was a bizarre twist, in two ways. The fixing of the exchange rate was not the currency regime endorsed in the great mass of Keynes's writings on the topic, and the effect of linking the pound with the deutschemark was to subordinate U.K. interest rates to decisions taken by the avowedly monetarist Bundesbank.[25] Indeed, if the U.K. had turned out to be a long-term participant in European monetary unification, it would have lost control of both monetary and fiscal policy. It is fair to ask, Was this how "the Keynesian revolution" was supposed to end? And, if one wants to find the "defunct economists" to blame for the muddles and disasters of the 1970s and 1980s, is it not justified to suggest that the academic Keynesians – most of whom never paid much attention to Keynes's early work in the *Tract* and were not prepared to plow through the detailed institutional material in the *Treatise* – should be identified as the culprits?

In the event, the pound joined the Exchange Rate Mechanism, a necessary period of apprenticeship before joining the full EMS, in October 1990. But it stayed inside the ERM for less than two years, enduring a recession far worse than the EMS advocates had envisaged. Comparisons were drawn between the decision to accept the exchange-rate discipline of the ERM in 1990 and the decision to accept the exchange-rate discipline of the gold standard in 1925, to which Keynes had so eloquently objected. The pound was expelled from the

ERM on September 16, 1992, in circumstances of extreme international humiliation. The U.K. has subsequently both eschewed a fixed-exchange-rate link with any other currency and declined to participate in European monetary union. Somehow it was also able to run its own currency and economy with an impressive degree of stability from 1992 to 2007, before sliding into the Great Recession in 2008.

Arguably, macroeconomic policy in the early phase of the fifteen years of stability had some similarities to the scheme for a "managed currency" adumbrated by Keynes in 1923 in *A Tract on Monetary Reform*. Indeed, from 1992 to 1997 a guideline for broad-money growth was in existence, even if its bearing on actual decision-making was murky. (The guideline was dropped in 1997, when the Bank of England received operational independence. The story of how the stability of the 1992–2007 period should be interpreted is taken up in essay 7.)

ESSAY 4

KEYNES, BERNANKE, AND KRUGMAN, AND THE PATHOLOGIES OF CAPITALISM

WHAT CAN policy-makers do to stimulate an under-employed economy when the budget deficit is large and cannot be further increased (because of worries about long-run government solvency), and when interest rates have fallen to zero and cannot be reduced? As the recognized "textbook approaches" to both monetary and fiscal expansion appear to be at their limits, is policy impotent?

These questions have seemed irrelevant over most of the three-quarters of a century since the publication of Keynes's *General Theory* in 1936. In the 1970s and 1980s economists knew that their subject had trouble finding politically acceptable prescriptions for inflation, but Keynesian economics was supposed to have made the opposite problem – of depression and deflation – easy to remedy. According to a widely shared consensus, policy-makers had to expand the budget deficit and slash interest rates, and sooner or later the economy would revive. Over the last fifteen years Japan has shown that a large budget deficit and zero, or virtually zero, interest rates may not be sufficient for macroeconomic recovery. In several widely quoted papers written in 1998 and 1999 Professor Paul Krugman of Princeton University claimed that Japan was suffering from "the liquidity trap," a malady originally diagnosed in the *General Theory*.[1] The usual understanding of this idea is that in a liquidity trap monetary policy is ineffective because increases in "the quantity of money" cannot reduce "the rate of interest" beyond a certain point. (As will emerge in the next few pages, the notions of "the quantity of money" and "the rate of interest" are so ambiguous and awkward that they must be adorned with quotation marks.)

In late 2002 and early 2003 concern was expressed that even the United States could face the same dilemma. The Fed funds rate had fallen from over 6 percent in late 2000 to 1¼ percent two years later in response to a mild recession. But by mid-2003 the American economy had not achieved a convincing return to above-trend growth and seemed no longer to be responsive to cheap money. In remarks to the National Economists Club in Washington on November 21, 2002, Professor Ben Bernanke of Princeton, then a recently appointed governor of the Federal Reserve System, outlined possible responses to a chronic deflation in the United States. He noted that "some observers have concluded that when the key rate stands at or near zero, the central bank has 'run out of ammunition'" – that is, it "no longer has the power to expand aggregate demand and hence economic activity." There seemed to be a risk that monetary policy would be ineffective at the so-called "zero bound."

I.

Bernanke rejected this pessimism. In his words, "a central bank, either alone or in cooperation with other parts of the government, retains considerable power to expand aggregate demand . . . even when its accustomed policy rate is at zero."[2] According to Bernanke, the problem of the alleged ineffectiveness of monetary policy at the "zero bound" was not insuperable. The essence of Bernanke's answer to deflation was the purchase of government securities, and perhaps other assets, by "the monetary authorities" (i.e., the government and the central bank working together) in order to alter macroeconomic conditions. He referred without embarrassment both to the printing presses and to an academic paper by Milton Friedman which opined that money could be added to any economy by a "helicopter drop." The November 2002 speech caused Bernanke subsequently to be lampooned as "helicopter Ben."[3] (In the present essay the implementation of monetary policy by state-sector asset purchases and sales is called "debt management." However, Bernanke's own preference may be a phrase that includes the word "credit," in line with his 1988 proposal of "creditism" as an alternative to "monetarism."[4])

In the event, the American economy did recover in 2004 and 2005, with the housing market proving – if anything – *too* sensitive to the low level of interest rates. The Fed funds rate remained at under 1¼ percent until mid-2004, with house prices surging over the next two years, at least partly because of the boom in sub-prime financing. But Bernanke's November 2002 presentation acquired new and reinforced topicality after he became Fed chairman in 2006. The financial crisis of 2007–2008 was followed by the so-called "Great Recession" of 2008–2010, the United States' worst cyclical setback since the 1930s. Many commentators felt that the U.S. had succumbed to the same sort of deflationary *malaise* as Japan a few years earlier. Bernanke was seen as having a particular responsibility for ensuring that the U.S. did not repeat Japan's mistakes.

The purpose of this essay is to endorse Bernanke's main conclusion that policy options have not been exhausted when the interest rate has fallen to zero, but to elaborate one of his provisos. The proviso is that in certain special circumstances the Federal Reserve, or any similarly situated central bank, retains the power to conduct a meaningful expansionary policy only when it acts in concert with the government. These special circumstances are called here "the *narrow* liquidity trap." The remarkable feature of this trap is that the central bank – when acting by itself in transactions with its usual customers, the commercial banks – cannot increase the quantity of money and thereby boost demand. Further, these malign special circumstances do seem to have arisen in Japan in the early years of the twenty-first century and more recently in the United States.

In Japan it was therefore essential that the Ministry of Finance co-operate with the Bank of Japan to overcome deflation. An argument is made below that, if the Ministry of Finance had worked with the Bank of Japan in an appropriate way, they could together have raised the quantity of money (or its rate of growth) to whatever figure they wished. The quantity of money in this context is taken to mean a broadly defined money measure including bank deposits. Assuming that the money injection was sufficient in amount, it should have resulted in a large-scale macroeconomic recovery. Admittedly, "should have" is not the same as "would have." Even with a big increase in the quantity of money, the possibility remained that demand in the Japanese economy would not have been revitalized. Later in this essay the relevant passages in *The General Theory* will be quoted to show that, when Keynes concocted the liquidity trap in the 1930s, his main concern was that the increases in a *broadly* defined money measure would fail to lower the yield on long-dated bonds and so to spur a recovery. His liquidity trap might therefore be termed "the *broad* liquidity trap." If the Japanese economy were wholly resistant to stimulus from an increase in the quantity of money, Keynes's warning in 1936 would have been validated.

But in fact a range of policy options to raise the broadly defined quantity of money (and/or the rate of money growth) was not tried in Japan. So no one knows for certain whether this policy would have succeeded or failed. Krugman was therefore premature in saying that Japan was in a Keynes liquidity trap. He has also been misguided in more recent commentary on the American economic scene. He has made two claims. The first is that American monetary policy has lost "traction" and can do nothing further once the Fed funds rate is close to nil (i.e., when the American economy is in "the zero bound" and allegedly suffers from a liquidity trap).[5] Second, in several columns in *The New York Times*, he has identified fiscal stimulus as the only remaining method of boosting demand. Both these claims are false.

II.

Some diagramatic analysis is needed before differentiating between the narrow and broad liquidity traps. Crucial is a distinction between two types of open-market operations. The first type is money-market operations, where the central bank transacts with the commercial banking system, and influences both the banks' cash reserves and the very-short-term interest rate. The second type is debt-market operations, where the government (and/or the central bank) transacts with all other agents in the economy, and can change the quantity of bank deposits held by non-bank private-sector agents. In order to help the discussion, a simplified economy is assumed. As the simplifications are not supposed to make the economy unrealistic, comments will be made as necessary to link the figures to real-world categories.

The economy has four types of agent: the non-bank private sector, the government, the central bank, and the commercial banks. The last three of these are assumed to have both assets and liabilities, whereas the non-bank private sector is a pure creditor. The government and the central bank together constitute the state sector, and can be understood to have a joint interest in macroeconomic stability. The government is the only net debtor in the economy. Its debts can be both short-term and long-term, and can be held by any of the three other types of agent. However, non-banks' demand function for government bonds is different from that of both the central bank and the commercial banks. This difference between non-banks' and banks' demand function for government bonds is important, since it has a critical bearing on the monetary consequences of official decisions on the maturity profile and instrument composition of the public debt.[6]

Although the government is the only net debtor, it can hold assets. In particular, it can hold a deposit with either the central bank or the commercial banking system. The size of this deposit does not affect its expenditure, which is determined by much broader political and macroeconomic considerations. In accordance with internationally recognized practice, the government's deposit is therefore not included in the quantity of money. The government's behavioral indifference to the size of its money balance contrasts dramatically with the attitude of the private sector. In accordance with standard theory, the private sector's demand to hold money can be represented by a well-defined function of a small number of independent variables, including income. If the independent variables other than income are taken as given, the function can be understood to have the property that the private sector's desired ratio of money to income is constant. There is an obvious asymmetry between the government's indifference to its money/income ratio and the private sector's desire to maintain a particular money/income ratio. This asymmetry is fundamental to the whole subject, because it is one of the key characteristics of the economy that enable the state sector to exert leverage over aggregate demand by the management of its own balance sheet. (For further discussion of the asymmetry, see footnote 10.)

The central bank's assets and liabilities are always identical. The central bank can hold claims on any of the three other agents. The usual assumption is that it is publicly owned, although the Federal Reserve is in fact owned by the member banks of the Federal Reserve System. Whatever its ownership structure, the central bank does not seek profits and is risk-averse. As the central bank traditionally had the role of "the banker to the government" in most countries, a natural conjecture is that its assets include claims on government. In most countries, government securities are indeed one element in central-bank assets, although typically the central bank does not hold long-dated government bonds. The central bank's aversion to long-dated bonds stems from one of their well-known properties, namely, that their price fluctuates sharply with the bond yield. If the central bank's bond holdings had to be "marked to market," these fluctuations might cause large and unwelcome profits and losses. In most countries, the central bank's portfolio is therefore dominated by short-dated government bonds, very-short-dated government securities, or short-dated claims on the non-bank private sector where the risk of default has been transferred to other private-sector entities. (Very-short-dated government securities are known as Treasury bills in the U.S. and the U.K., and as Financing bills [from the Ministry of Finance] in Japan. Central banks may also lend to the commercial banks to bolster the banks' cash reserves, and they may hold high-quality claims on non-banks. Loans to commercial banks and holdings of securities issued by the non-bank private sector are hugely important in the real world, but are not mentioned in the rest of this essay, as their inclusion would add nothing of direct significance to the matters under discussion.)

In most countries, central-bank liabilities are of three main kinds: the central bank's capital, the note issue, and the deposits (or "cash reserves") maintained by the commercial banks. Central-bank capital is ignored in the next few pages, but remarks are made later – particularly in the Japanese context – about the possible implications of central-bank losses. The note issue is also ignored in the main text of this essay, but of course in the real world it is the most basic form of money. (The consequences of attempts to expand the quantity of money by uninhibited expansion of the note issue are interesting and important, but not immediately central to the subject under discussion. They are mentioned towards the end of the essay.)

Nowadays nearly all countries have legislation ("legal-tender laws") which says that notes are worth their stated nominal value by law. It is the ability of the monetary authorities to manufacture notes at negligible cost that gives them "the power of the printing press." The principal holders of the note issue are non-bank private-sector agents, but banks also keep some notes in their tills and vaults ("till money" or "vault cash") to meet deposit withdrawals. Commercial banks maintain deposits at the central bank and can convert any sum in their deposits into notes. This would enable them to meet withdrawals from their customers if their vault cash had run out. In practice, banks manage their balance sheets to ensure that their vault cash and central-bank deposits are never depleted. However, vault cash pays no interest, and deposits at the central bank have traditionally not done so.[7] Because of the resulting poor return on their cash assets, commercial banks try to keep the ratio of these assets to total assets as low as possible, subject to the constraint that the cash must never run out altogether. Textbooks sometimes say that banks' deposit liabilities (and so the quantity of money) are a stable multiple of their cash reserves. This may well be true in most countries for much of the time, but it is important to remember that banks' *desired* ratio of cash reserves to their total assets and liabilities is actively determined by banks' management. It is not fixed by custom or statute at a constant value for all time.

Banks' managements have to seek a balance between the loss of profits from too high a cash ratio and the risk of illiquidity (of being forced "to close their doors") from too low a cash ratio. As will emerge in due course, this point is vital in understanding the origins of the special circumstances in which the central bank has trouble stimulating the economy. Banks' *actual* cash-to-assets ratio may be more stable than the *desired* ratio, because a minimum ratio is mandated by the central bank or by legislation. If the minimum ratio is above the level that would be freely chosen by banks' managements were they left to themselves, then the observed cash-to-assets ratio is likely to be relatively stable. Monetary economists may then be under the impression that banks' deposit liabilities change more or less exactly in line with their cash reserves. With a further assumption about a constant ratio between banks' cash reserves and the public's note holdings, they may conclude that "the quantity of money is a stable multiple of the monetary base." But, as will soon emerge, this conclusion may not be empirically robust outside settled macroeconomic conditions. The stability of banks' cash-to-assets ratio can be an artefact of official regulation, not of maximizing behavior.

As with the central bank, the commercial banks' assets and liabilities are always identical. Since most industrial nations have now enjoyed over sixty years of uninterrupted peace, the asset sides of banks' balance sheets are dominated by loans to the private sector. However, this was not always so. During the Second World War, banks were obliged to lend almost exclusively to government. In the immediate post-war decade, claims on government constituted over two-thirds of banks' assets in the U.K. and many other nations. In order to keep matters simple, it is assumed in the figures below that banks have no claims on the non-bank private sector.

Banks therefore have only two kinds of assets: their cash reserves, which have already been discussed, and claims on government. Unlike the central bank, commercial banks are usually privately owned and profit-seeking. They therefore want to make a profit on their holdings of government securities and may be tempted to move further down the yield curve than the central bank. However, banks are unlike non-bank companies in a fundamental respect. Their ratios of assets and liabilities to capital are much higher than is normal for non-bank companies. Under the Basel rules as originally enforced, equity capital was not to be less than 4 percent of assets. More typically, equity capital is 5 to 8 percent of assets, giving an assets-to-capital multiple of roughly twelve to twenty times. (Note that at the time of writing [December 2010], the Basel capital rules have been quite recently renegotiated, with some details yet to be tidied up.) In the non-financial corporate sector of most modern economies, the multiple is rarely more than three times. The extremely high gearing found in the banking industry necessitates a strong aversion to risky assets characterized by price volatility, such as long-dated government bonds. Instead, banks prefer short-dated government bonds, even if the return appears minuscule. Indeed, because of their high gearing, banks can earn a satisfactory return on capital from very-low-yielding assets. An asset with a mere 1 percent margin over a bank's cost of funds delivers a 20 percent return on capital to a bank with a capital-to-assets ratio of 5 percent. It follows that banks are usually willing to hold low-yielding short-dated government bonds, which are unattractive to non-bank investors.

The commercial banks have two kinds of liability, their capital and their deposits. In the current financial crisis, the role of banks' capital in their balance-sheet management has become a topic of huge interest, both within officialdom and to the media. Indeed, there is an increasing tendency to view banks' capital – and not their cash reserves – as the key driver of their asset-acquisition strategies. The dependence of banks' balance-sheet size on their capital adequacy will be noted at the relevant stages in the discussion, but perhaps it should receive even greater emphasis. Deposits could be obligations to either the government or the non-bank private sector. In practice, governments only rarely hold large deposits with commercial banks.[8]

What, finally, is to be said about the non-bank private sector? In the real world, private-sector agents own a vast assortment of assets and incur a range of liabilities. In the current exercise their financial position is drastically simplified, and they are the only net creditors. They hold claims on the government, in the form of the long-dated government bonds that are usually too risky for the banks, and claims on the commercial banks, in the form of deposits, which constitute the whole of the quantity of money. In order to highlight the economic essence of the transactions under consideration, non-banks are assumed not to hold the other main type of money asset, namely notes (or indeed coin).

One final definitional point is needed. In the simplified economy about to be discussed, the quantity of money consists entirely of deposits held by non-banks with commercial banks. This is realistic and appropriate, for three reasons. First, across the industrial world measures of the quantity of money (on the broad definitions) are dominated by bank deposits. Second, non-banks do not keep deposits with the central bank. In modern conditions the central bank is a specialized non-profit-seeking institution whose tasks are to act as banker to the government and to the commercial banking system, but not to the rest of the economy. The central bank therefore does not offer banking facilities to non-banks. The point is hardly esoteric, but it has an interesting consequence. The macroeconomic impotence of the central bank's operations could be readily overcome, in the special circumstances soon to be outlined, if the economy did not have this institutional characteristic. If non-banks maintained accounts at the central bank, the central bank could increase their deposits (i.e., the quantity of money) by the simple expedient of lending directly to them. Third, it is reasonable to exclude commercial banks' cash reserves from the definition of

66

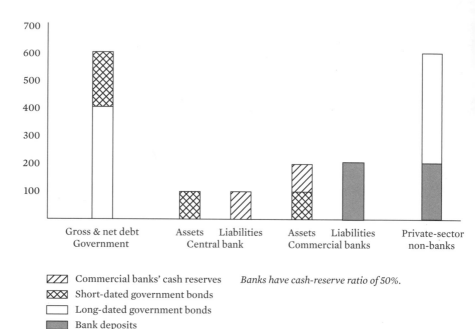

FIGURE 4.1
THE INITIAL SITUATION

Gross & net debt
Government

Assets   Liabilities
Central bank

Assets   Liabilities
Commercial banks

Private-sector
non-banks

▨ Commercial banks' cash reserves   *Banks have cash-reserve ratio of 50%.*
▨ Short-dated government bonds
☐ Long-dated government bonds
▨ Bank deposits

money, because this deposit has no direct bearing on either non-banks' or banks' purchases of goods and services.[9]

The assumed economy can now be portrayed in figures. The first figure describes "the initial situation" for all three types of open-market operations. The first type is money-market operations, in which only the central bank and the commercial banks participate; the second and third are debt-market operations involving all four of the types of agent found in the economy. Both the money-market operations and the debt-market operations are represented in further figures by simultaneous additions or subtractions to both sides of either the central bank's or the commercial banking system's balance sheet. The operations can affect the composition of the government's debt and – except in a special case – the quantity of money. However, the government's net debt and the non-bank private sector's net wealth are unchanged throughout.[10] (As is clear, because the operations are about the management of a public debt that exists and is assumed constant, the effects – or supposed effects – of fiscal policy on aggregate demand can be ignored. Debt management is an annex of monetary policy; it is not a by-product of fiscal policy.)

The numbers in the figures are for purposes of illustration only. In the initial situation government debt is equal to 600 units, and consists of 400 units of long-dated government bonds and 200 units of short-dated government bonds. The central bank's assets are represented entirely by 100 units of short-dated government bonds, while its liabilities are 100 units of deposits ("cash reserves") held by the commercial banks. The commercial banks hold 100 units of short-dated government bonds and the 100 units of cash reserves, and their liabilities are 200 units of bank deposits owed to the non-bank private sector. The non-bank private sector's assets amount to 400 units of long-dated government bonds and 200 units of bank deposits ("the quantity of money").

III.

We may now describe "money-market operations" more specifically. In these operations the central bank changes the level of the deposits – the cash reserves, the holdings of monetary base – that the commercial banks maintain with it. As the concern here is to stimulate a depressed economy, the central bank's first step is to increase the deposit. In the example, it purchases the 100 units of short-dated government bonds held by the commercial banks and credits 100 units to their deposit. (See figure 4.2.)

Evidently, the central bank's assets and liabilities have both doubled, and they remain identical to each other. The commercial banks' assets and liabilities are the same size as before, but the composition of their assets has changed. Their assets now consist entirely of cash reserves. (As is familiar, the central bank could also expand the commercial banks' deposit with it by lending to them. In that case 100 units would be added to both sides of the central bank's balance sheet, which would again double in size, but its extra asset would be a loan to the commercial banks instead of a government bond. The commercial banks' assets and liabilities would increase by 100, to a total of 300 units, but the quantity of money would be unchanged. The additional liability would be a borrowing from the central bank, not deposits from non-banks.)

Because the cash reserves are not remunerative, the commercial

FIGURE 4.2
MONEY-MARKET OPERATION
First Step

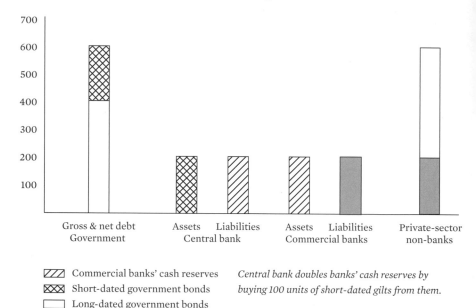

FIGURE 4.2
MONEY-MARKET OPERATION
First Step

banks appear to have an incentive to undertake further transactions to restore their profitability. As their cash reserves have doubled, it ought to be safe for them to double their balance-sheet size, either by lending to the non-bank private sector, by lending to the government, or by purchasing securities from non-banks. In the example, they might, for instance, purchase 200 units of long-dated government bonds from non-banks. (See figure 4.3.) They would finance this purchase by issuing claims against themselves in the form of deposits. If so, a doubling of banks' cash reserves would have led to a doubling of the quantity of money. The standard textbook account – in which a given percentage increase in the monetary base leads to an identical percentage increase in the quantity of money – would be right.

However, the discussion earlier emphasized that banks' managements have to make a decision to expand their earning assets in response to the increase in their cash reserves. Suppose that loans to the private sector are likely to earn a poor return compared with the risks involved. Suppose also that yields on bonds are so low that the most probable

FIGURE 4.3
MONEY-MARKET OPERATION
Second Step

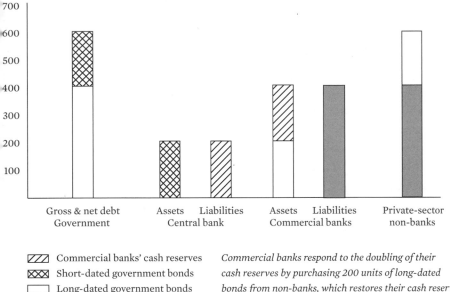

	Commercial banks' cash reserves
	Short-dated government bonds
	Long-dated government bonds
	Bank deposits

Commercial banks respond to the doubling of their cash reserves by purchasing 200 units of long-dated bonds from non-banks, which restores their cash reserve ratio of 50% and doubles the quantity of money.

next move is an upward yield movement that will reduce the bonds' capital value. The severity of the capital loss will of course be greater if only long-dated bonds can be purchased from non-banks, as is the case in the example being discussed here. In these special circumstances – when any acquisition of non-cash assets by the commercial banks is unattractive – the banks' managements may become indifferent between cash and other assets. The reluctance to purchase non-cash assets impedes balance-sheet expansion even if the interest rate in the short-term money markets, and so banks' marginal cost of funds, is zero. Indeed, the banks may want to fix or even to reduce the size of their balance sheets because they are constrained by inadequate capital.

As the central bank purchases short-dated government bonds from them, the banks shed non-cash assets, and their cash ratio rises indefinitely. In the extreme, banks' balance sheets fail to expand even if the central bank's purchases of bonds are on a massive scale running into tens of billions of dollars or euros or pounds sterling, or trillions of yen. Crucially, banks' deposit liabilities to non-banks – which make up the quantity of money – do not increase. Thus the supposedly stimulatory open-market operations are ineffective, because the commercial banks are in a liquidity trap. Note that this liquidity trap relates to banks' cash reserves (also known, of course, as part of "the monetary base," "high-powered money," and "outside money"), not to the quantity of money as such. Because it relates to a narrow concept of monetary assets, it might be termed the narrow liquidity trap. When this trap holds, the short-term interest rate is zero and the central bank cannot drive interest rates lower or increase the quantity of money by increasing its own liabilities.

These are the special circumstances in which the central bank – acting by itself in transactions with commercial banks – cannot resuscitate the economy. The Bank of Japan, the Japanese banking system, and the Japanese economy were in a narrow liquidity trap in the early years of the present century and may still be so today (December 2010). In 2001 and 2002 the Bank of Japan made outright purchases of government bonds of over 19 trillion yen (over $150 billion, at the exchange rate then prevailing). On the liabilities side of the balance sheet, commercial banks' reserve balances jumped from 4.6 trillion yen at the end of 2000 to 14.7 trillion yen at the end of 2002, or by 217.1 percent. Over the same two years, the monetary base as a whole soared from 64.5 trillion yen to 87.1 trillion yen, or by 35.0 percent. Yet M2 plus certificates of deposit – then the most widely followed measure of broad money – increased only from 629.3 trillion yen at the end of 2000 to 668.5 trillion yen at the end of 2002, or by 6.2 percent. The slowness of broad-money growth reflected a contraction in banks' claims on the private sector. In the credit-counterpart arithmetic for M2 plus CDs, domestic credit to the private sector declined by 49.0 trillion yen in the two years to the end of 2002. The banks' claims on the private sector fell from 559.4 trillion yen at the end of 2000 to 510.4 trillion yen at the end of 2002, or by 8.8 percent.[11] The divergence between the trebling of banks' cash reserves and an almost 10 percent decline in their loan portfolios is remarkable. These developments plainly contradict two familiar textbook ideas, that the quantity of money is a stable and predictable multiple of the monetary base, and that banks automatically respond to injections of cash reserves by expanding their earning assets.

The United States was not in a narrow liquidity trap in late 2002 and early 2003, when Bernanke's original thoughts on the zero bound were being formulated and debated. The ratio between banks' cash assets and total assets fluctuated in 2002 and 2003, but there was nothing unusual to report. Even then, the American banking system had its problems, but on the whole it was profitable and well capitalized. In that context, if banks' managements found their cash rising sharply relative to their earning assets, they would seek new lending opportunities or purchase additional securities. They would try to expand their balance sheets, resulting in new money creation. In the two years up to February 2003 the U.S. monetary base grew by 17.2 percent, M2 by 16.8 percent, and M3 by 17.7 percent.[12] (For the definitions of M2 and M3, see the table on p. 347 below.) However, the sound position of American banks in late 2002 and early 2003 did not preclude the United States' succumbing to a Japanese-style narrow liquidity trap at some later date. At that time some observers worried that, if the U.S. banks were to incur heavy losses on some of their assets and have a high proportion of their capital wiped out, they might come to operate in a macroeconomic environment so grim that they would view all non-cash earning assets as unappealing. If so, the Federal Reserve would not be able to stimulate the economy by money-market operations even at a zero Fed-funds rate. An argument can be made that this is exactly what happened in the crisis of 2007–09, with some banks seeing much of their capital eliminated by losses on sub-prime mortgages.

Had it then become true that the Fed could not revive the economy purely by transactions between itself and the commercial banks? In late 2008 the Fed embarked on aggressively expansionary open-market operations, leading to a multiplication of banks' cash reserves. But in the nine months starting in November 2008, banks were shedding loan assets at a rate of about ½ percent a month. The conjunction of excess cash reserves and shrinking loan assets implied that the American economy was in a narrow liquidity trap. The suggestion mooted in Bernanke's November 2002 talk – that to stimulate demand the Federal Reserve would have to act in concert with the U.S. government – was no longer hypothetical. The Fed and the Treasury might have to coordinate their actions, and undertake the transactions that are here called "debt-market operations," if they wanted to boost aggregate demand.

* * *

IV.

The essence of debt-market operations is that the monetary authorities (i.e., the government or the central bank, or possibly even both operating at the same time) transact with non-banks in order to change their bank deposits. When, for example, the government purchases assets from non-banks, its own deposit (which is *not* part of the quantity of money) goes down and the non-banks' deposits (which *are* included in the quantity of money) go up; and vice versa when it sells assets to them. (Central-bank purchases of assets from non-banks are not discussed in depth in the main body of this essay, as they raise distinct policy issues, particularly as regards "exiting" from a monetary stimulus.)[13]

A particularly simple case arises when the government finances its asset purchase by borrowing from the commercial banking system. The government sells 100 units of newly issued short-dated government bonds to the commercial banks, and they pay for the bonds by crediting 100 units to a newly created government deposit. *This deposit is not money.* (See figure 4.4. It may look like "money," as the term is popularly used, but – to repeat – there is an asymmetry here, and public-sector deposits are excluded from officially defined money measures in most countries.) The government then uses its bank deposit to purchase 100 units of long-dated government bonds from the non-bank private sector. The government's deposit drops to nothing, and the non-bank private sector's deposits increase by 100 units. *These deposits are money.* The quantity of money therefore rises by 100 units, while the stock of long-dated government bonds contracts by 100 units. (See figure 4.5.) The non-bank private sector's wealth is unchanged, but – because the quantity of money has risen – the equilibrium value of nominal national income ought also to have risen.[14]

Note that – starting from a severely depressed economy – this benign outcome has been achieved merely by a change in the composition and ownership of the national debt. The average life of the debt has shortened, and a higher proportion of it is held by the banking system. What does the government do in the final situation with the long-dated government bonds? The answer is that it cancels them. If the certificates establishing ownership are made of paper, they are pulped; they

FIGURE 4.4
DEBT-MARKET OPERATION
First Type – First Step

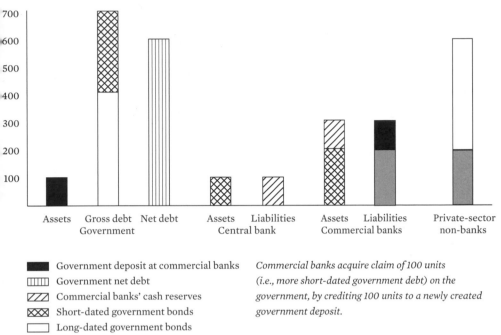

Assets	Gross debt	Net debt	Assets	Liabilities	Assets	Liabilities	Private-sector
	Government		Central bank		Commercial banks		non-banks

■ Government deposit at commercial banks

▥ Government net debt

▨ Commercial banks' cash reserves

▩ Short-dated government bonds

☐ Long-dated government bonds

▦ Bank deposits

Commercial banks acquire claim of 100 units (i.e., more short-dated government debt) on the government, by crediting 100 units to a newly created government deposit.

disappear from the economy. Of course, it is pointless for the government to hold claims on itself.

A slightly more complicated story has to be told if the government finances its asset purchase by borrowing from the central bank rather than from commercial banks. In the second sequence of transactions outlined in the figures, the first step is for the government to sell 100 units of newly issued short-dated government bonds to the central bank. The central bank pays for these bonds by crediting 100 units to a newly created government deposit. (See figure 4.6.) As in the previous case, the government uses the deposit to buy 100 units of long-dated government bonds from non-banks and instructs the central bank to pay the non-banks 100 units of claims on itself. The non-banks expand their deposits by leaving these claims on the central bank (i.e., cash reserves) with the commercial banks. (See figure 4.7.) So the commercial banks have 100 units of extra deposit liabilities and 100 units of

FIGURE 4.5
DEBT-MARKET OPERATION
First Type – Second Step

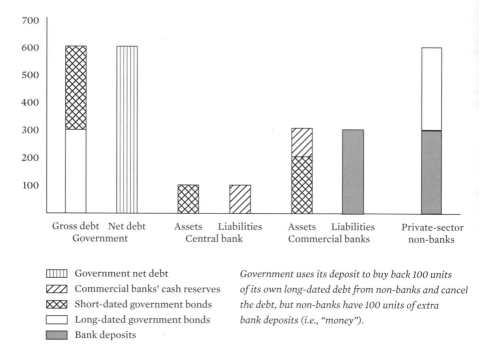

	Government net debt
	Commercial banks' cash reserves
	Short-dated government bonds
	Long-dated government bonds
	Bank deposits

Government uses its deposit to buy back 100 units of its own long-dated debt from non-banks and cancel the debt, but non-banks have 100 units of extra bank deposits (i.e., "money").

extra cash reserves on the asset side of the balance sheet. The quantity of money has already increased by 100 units, but – as the commercial banks have a higher cash ratio than before – they may want to acquire further earning assets. The central bank may or may not want additional monetary expansion. If it does not want such expansion, it sells 100 units of short-dated government debt to the commercial banks. (See figure 4.8.) This sale of short-dated government bonds to mop up the banks' cash reserves is, of course, a money-market operation – which, by itself, has no effect on the quantity of money.[15] In the final situation, the commercial banks have – compared with the initial situation – 100 units of extra deposit liabilities and 100 units of extra short-dated government bonds.

Plainly, the final situation is the same whether the government borrows from the commercial banks or the central bank. (Compare figures 4.5 and 4.8.) The ability of expansionary debt-market operations to increase the quantity of money does not depend on how the govern-

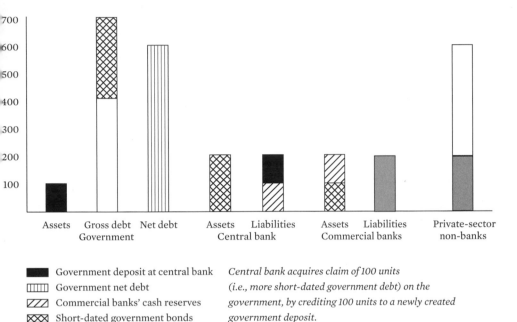

FIGURE 4.6
DEBT-MARKET OPERATION
Second Type – First Step

■ Government deposit at central bank
▥ Government net debt
▨ Commercial banks' cash reserves
▧ Short-dated government bonds
▭ Long-dated government bonds
▒ Bank deposits

*Central bank acquires claim of 100 units
(i.e., more short-dated government debt) on the
government, by crediting 100 units to a newly created
government deposit.*

ment finances the operation, as long as the finance is from a banking institution. The crucial step is the purchase of an asset from the non-bank private sector and the settlement of that purchase with money. In the economy assumed in this essay, which has much the same institutions as real-world modern economies, the finance ministry can always arrange for the government to make such purchases. The mechanism of debt-management operations is available at any particular moment to expand the quantity of money without limit. (There is a caveat here: that – realistically – debt-market operations are taking place over time. Other forces, such as the repayment of bank loans by the private sector, may reduce the quantity of money during the period in which the expansionary debt-market operations are being conducted. These other forces may, partly or even wholly, offset the positive effect of such operations on the quantity of money.)[16]

* * *

FIGURE 4.7
DEBT-MARKET OPERATION
Second Type – Second Step

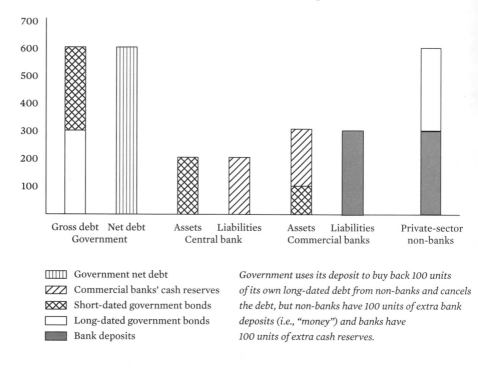

	Government net debt
	Commercial banks' cash reserves
	Short-dated government bonds
	Long-dated government bonds
	Bank deposits

Government uses its deposit to buy back 100 units of its own long-dated debt from non-banks and cancels the debt, but non-banks have 100 units of extra bank deposits (i.e., "money") and banks have 100 units of extra cash reserves.

V.

The analysis has shown that the monetary authorities can expand the quantity of money – without limit and at any time – by debt-market operations. Two questions now arise. The advantages and disadvantages of debt-market operations are compared with those of money-market operations in this section, while in the next the possibility is entertained that – because of one or a number of liquidity traps – increases in the quantity of money may fail to stimulate demand and output.

The ideas developed so far have a vital message for the structure of policy-making. In principle the government can completely by-pass the central bank and conduct monetary policy on its own. This is obvious from the hypothetical sequences of transactions that are here called "debt-market operations."[17] The point matters critically to the allocation of blame for policy failures. If the present argument is correct, one reason for the apparent inefficiency of Japanese policy over the last fif-

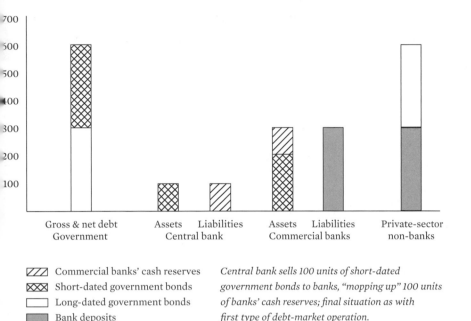

FIGURE 4.8
DEBT-MARKET OPERATION
Second Type – Third Step

	Commercial banks' cash reserves
	Short-dated government bonds
	Long-dated government bonds
	Bank deposits

Central bank sells 100 units of short-dated government bonds to banks, "mopping up" 100 units of banks' cash reserves; final situation as with first type of debt-market operation.

teen years has been that the Japanese authorities have regarded the Bank of Japan as omni-competent and all-powerful in monetary policy. In fact, responsibility for good and bad decisions has rested not with the Bank of Japan alone, but with the Bank of Japan and the Ministry of Finance together. Indeed, because the central bank's scope to affect macroeconomic outcomes has been compromised in a narrow liquidity trap, arguably the Ministry of Finance should have taken the initiative in easing monetary policy. In particular, it should have concentrated sales of new debt at the short end of the yield curve (where they would have been bought by the banks) and undertaken deliberate purchases of long-dated government bonds from non-banks.[18]

Clearly, an advantage of debt-market operations over money-market operations is that they allow the monetary authorities to influence the quantity of money directly, rather than indirectly by expanding the monetary base and hoping that the commercial banks will want to increase their earning assets. In this sense, debt-market operations are more certain in effect than money-market operations.

But debt-market operations have another merit, particularly given the rather fraught political debate about the banking industry in modern conditions. Since expansionary debt-market operations replace long-dated debt with short-dated debt, and so alter the composition but not the size of the public sector's debt, they have little significance for the amount of risk in the public sector's balance sheet.[19] By contrast, aggressive attempts by the central bank to stimulate the economy by money-market operations can leave its balance sheet exposed to interest-rate movements.

The central bank's vulnerability to loss is readily illustrated by Japanese experience. At various stages in the last fifteen years, the Bank of Japan – responding to international criticism – bought government bonds on a massive scale and increased its balance sheet to a remarkable extent. As noted above, by the end of 2002 its balance sheet was in fact equal to about a quarter of gross domestic product, a ratio far higher than in any other industrial country at that time. At least superficially, the result was an alarming concentration of risk in the Bank of Japan's balance sheet. For several years it held between 80 and 100 trillion yen (between $800 billion and $1 trillion, at an exchange rate of 100 yen to the dollar) of government securities, including substantial amounts with a residual maturity of over ten years. According to some observers (such as Krugman), the return of a meaningfully positive rate of inflation in Japan would have been a success because it would have lowered real interest rates and stimulated more investment. Unfortunately, bond yields would almost certainly also have risen. The capital value of bonds – including the bonds in the Bank of Japan's vast portfolio – would therefore have declined.[20] One possibility – that the decline in the bonds' capital value would have led to losses large enough to wipe out the Bank of Japan's capital – could not be excluded.

Would this matter? The Bank of Japan is government-owned, and the bonds are government liabilities. The incurrence of heavy losses on government bond holdings by the Bank of Japan would be a transfer from one account in the state sector to another account in the state sector, a case of Peter robbing Peter to pay Peter, with no net effect on Japan's wealth. Most fundamentally, no resource losses would correspond to the apparent accounting losses. These arguments are analytically correct. Indeed, it might make political sense for the government to offer the Bank of Japan an immediate indemnity for potential losses on its bond portfolio.[21] The trouble is that many members of Japan's political elite may not see it that way. Insofar as the Bank of Japan were condemned for the losses due to its excessive bond holdings, the stigma of inefficiency and waste would probably attach to the banking system as a whole. It would therefore be more difficult to organize capital injections from the state into insolvent commercial banks or to induce foreign banks and non-bank companies to invest much-needed new capital in the banking sector.

By contrast, when government buys in its own bonds with the help of debt-market operations, they can be removed from the economy altogether by the cancellation of the debt. The tiresome – and essentially trivial – problem of central-bank "insolvency" would not arise. Such operations avoid the duplication and opacity in the public sector's accounts when the central bank takes too much risk onto its balance sheet. A key implication is that close cooperation between the central bank and the finance ministry is beneficial for monetary policy at all times. The two institutions need together to prepare a joint strategy for money-market operations and debt-market operations, in order to influence the quantity of money and the long-term bond yield, as well as the monetary base and the short-term interest rate. This conclusion is not new. In the context of the U.K.'s problems in managing the large debt it had incurred in the Second World War, the Radcliffe Report said in 1959, "Throughout our review of the problems of debt management we have been aware of the monetary repercussions of every action taken or proposed. It is not merely that monetary action and debt management interact so that they ought to be under one control: they are one and indivisible; debt management lies at the heart of monetary control, and it is essential that this unity should be adequately reflected in our institutional arrangements."[22] In his 1963 essay on "The Principles of Debt Management," James Tobin asserted, "There is no neat way to distinguish monetary policy from debt management, the province of the Federal Reserve from that of the Treasury. Both agencies are engaged in debt management in the broadest sense, and both have powers to influence the whole spectrum of debt." He also emphasized the essential "indivisibility of the problem." Fiscal policy and debt management have monetary effects, whatever the institutional apparatus.[23]

TABLE 4.1
TYPES OF OPEN-MARKET OPERATION

Money-market operations

The central bank makes loans (in its own liabilities) to commercial banks and/or conducts transactions (purchases and sales of securities), again with commercial banks.

These loan operations and securities transactions affect the quantity of central-bank liabilities (i.e., the monetary base) held by the commercial banks and the wider economy, and also influence the short-term policy rate, which often is taken to describe monetary policy.

Debt-market operations

The "monetary authorities" (i.e., the government as well as the central bank) conduct transactions (purchases and sales of securities, or even of real assets) with non-banks.

Purchases of assets increase the quantity of money (i.e., bank deposits) directly without necessarily affecting the monetary base. They may affect the base, although the change in the base may not be of great macroeconomic importance.

When purchases are made by the government, the government can finance them by borrowing from the commercial banks or the central bank.

Government debt-market operations, type 1	When the borrowing is from commercial banks, new bank deposits are created, and in the first instance these are held by the government. When they are used to purchase securities from non-banks, the new deposits are credited to the non-banks' accounts, increasing the quantity of money.
Government debt-market operations, type 2	When the borrowing is from the central bank, a new deposit is created at the central bank. When it is used to purchase securities from non-banks, both the monetary base and the quantity of money increase. An offsetting money-market operation can "mop up" newly

created base, if monetary-base holdings are regarded as excessive.

| Central-bank debt-market operations | Debt-market operations can be conducted by the central bank acting by itself. In order to stimulate the economy, it finances its purchases by issuing liabilities to the commercial banks. The result is simultaneous expansion of both the base and the quantity of money, as in the Bank of England's "quantitative easing" exercise. |

Note that the above is not an exhaustive list of all possible transactions between the government, the central bank, the commercial banks, and the non-bank private sector. A wide range of other transactions – including, for example, central-bank lending to the non-bank private sector and government purchases of private-sector assets financed by central-bank or commercial-bank borrowing – can be imagined.

One way of denigrating debt-market operations is to classify them as "unconventional" techniques of monetary policy. On the contrary, the epithet "unconventional" should be attached to the unfortunate modern habit of regarding the setting of short-term interest rates as the alpha and omega of monetary policy.[24] The tendency to see the setting of short-term interest rates as, by itself, a complete description of monetary policy results in a grotesque underestimation of the monetary authorities' ability to influence macroeconomic outcomes.

VI.

So, by means of debt-management operations, the monetary authorities can expand the quantity of money without limit. Debt-management operations conducted with the support of the finance ministry can increase the quantity of money even if the banking system is in a narrow liquidity trap. The traditional view among macroeconomists has been that an increase in the quantity of money would boost the equilibrium level of national income. Nevertheless, it remains possible that the economy will not respond positively to an increase in the quantity of money. As contemporary economists – including Krugman – continue to invoke Keynes's notion of a liquidity trap, it is necessary to check what Keynes actually said.

Detailed exegesis will now establish that Keynes's trap was a broad liquidity trap, in which increases in *the quantity of money* (not increases in *the monetary base*) failed to lower the yield on long-dated bonds. It will also be shown that Professor Krugman – whose writings in the late 1990s made strong claims that Japan suffered from a liquidity trap – was not in fact talking about Keynes's trap. Instead he invented three new liquidity traps. All of them are interesting and add to macroeconomic understanding. However, Krugman's failure to distinguish between the narrow and broad traps made him too pessimistic about the ability of Japanese policy-makers to escape from their macroeconomic *malaise*.

As Leijonhufvud pointed out, the outcome of any macroeconomic theorizing depends on the type of economy assumed, notably the system of aggregation chosen. According to Leijonhufvud, the standard "Keynesian macromodel" uses five aggregates: consumer goods, capital goods, labor services, money, and government debt ("bonds"). But a model could have three aggregates, or five, or a hundred and five. In Leijonhufvud's words, choosing "a particular mode of aggregation is a rather mechanical task – merely a matter of stripping down the model to a manageable, simplified form."[25] There are debates about the system of aggregation in *The General Theory*, but there should not be all that much disagreement about the definition of the liquidity trap. Keynes's emphases are so definite and repetitive as to make the underlying meaning clear enough, even if his use of words could have been more exact. The trouble arises in applying Keynes to the conditions of the early twenty-first century. Modern followers of Keynes – including Krugman – sometimes have different systems of aggregation. As a result, they claim to be talking about a liquidity trap originating in the 1930s when they are in fact talking about their own.

Keynes's liquidity trap arose when indefinitely large increases in the quantity of money were unable to raise the price of bonds (and so reduce bond yields). Because of the downward rigidity of bond yields, investment would not respond to monetary policy. Further, since in a crude Keynesian schema national income was a multiple of investment, increases in the quantity of money could not increase national income.

These simple statements give the correct definition of Keynes's liquidity trap. But a little exegesis is needed to pin down more precisely the meaning of the two phrases, "the quantity of money" and "the price of bonds."

The quantity of money may be taken first. Keynes – who had been introduced to the old controversy between the Currency and Banking Schools at an early stage in his career as an economist – was well aware of the phrase's slipperiness.[26] In the 1920s he and Dennis Robertson had collaborated on a book called *The Banking System and the Price Level*, with the aim of seeing how the emergence of a modern banking system would affect the business cycle. Keynes's own *Treatise on Money* had noted on p. 5 that "we thus have side by side State money or money proper and bank money."[27] Keynes's theorizing was almost exclusively about bank money, the kind of money that had become dominant by the early twentieth century. In a footnote to chapter 13 of *The General Theory* Keynes acknowledged that "we can draw the line between 'money' and 'debts' at whatever point is most convenient for handling a particular problem." Nevertheless, "It is often convenient in practice to include in money time-deposits with banks and, occasionally, even such instruments as (e.g.) treasury bills. As a rule, I shall, as in my *Treatise on Money*, assume that money is co-extensive with bank deposits."[28] In other words, Keynes's concept of money was a broad one *that even included time-deposits*. The purpose of this definition was inherent in the "particular problem" that Keynes was handling, as we shall soon see.

What about "the price of bonds"? There are two operative words, "price" and "bonds," and both need amplification. Keynes meant by "bonds" liabilities of the government or companies with a given nominal redemption value and a fixed coupon or interest payment. (The best example of the sort of bond he had in mind was one issued by the British government, also known as a gilt-edged security.) He was not very precise about the length of the period to redemption, which varied at different stages of his discussion. Indeed, at one point in *The General Theory* Keynes admitted that he had "slurred over" problems of definition. But he undoubtedly thought that long-dated debt was more significant macroeconomically than short-dated debt. This was the clear message of an extended discussion about the formation of bond prices in chapter 15 of *The General Theory*.

In Keynes's words, "it is by playing on the speculative motive [to hold money balances] that monetary management (or, in the absence of management, chance changes in the quantity of money) is brought to bear on the economic system." The lesson of experience had been that "the aggregate demand for money to satisfy the speculative motive usually shows a continuous response to gradual changes in the rate of interest, i.e., there is a continuous curve relating changes in the demand for money to satisfy the speculative motive and changes in the rate of interest as given by changes in the prices of bonds and debts of various maturities." This long and technical sentence was followed by the dramatic pronouncement that, if there were no such continuous curve, " 'open-market operations' would be impracticable." The reason was that "in normal circumstances the banking system is in fact able to purchase (or sell) bonds in exchange for cash by bidding the price of bonds up (or down) in the market by a modest amount; and the larger the quantity of cash which they seek to create (or cancel) by purchasing (or selling) bonds and debts, the greater must be the fall (or rise) in the rate of interest."[29]

Keynes's use of the phrase "the banking system" here is troublesome, as it is ambiguous. Did he mean the central banking "system" (such as the Federal Reserve System in the United States) or the commercial banking "system"?[30] (An argument could be made that, if Keynes meant "the central banking system," his work contained both the narrow and the broad liquidity traps, even if he did not make a clear distinction between them.) At any rate, Keynes did spell out his views about the relative importance of the different types of bonds being bought and sold in open-market operations. "Where . . . (as in the United States, 1933–34) open-market operations have been limited to the purchase of very-short-dated securities, the effect may, of course, be mainly confined to the very-short-term rate of interest and have but little reaction on the much more important long-term rates of interest." To summarize, "bonds" in Keynes were bonds of any maturity, and "the rate of interest" might be one of a large number of "rates of interest" corresponding to bonds' residual maturity. But the vital interest rate was the long-term rate of interest, which fluctuated with the price of long-dated bonds.

The conclusion is reinforced by references to monetary policy in chapter 19 of *The General Theory*, ostensibly about "Changes in Money-Wage." The chapter showed that reductions in money wages might not lead to more employment, if they were accompanied by offsetting contractions in labor's spending power. So, ". . . wage reductions, as a method of securing full employment, are also subject to the same limitations as the method of increasing the quantity of money." An adverse change in business expectations might "limit the efficacy of increases in the quantity of money as a means of increasing investment," while "a moderate increase in the quantity of money may exert an inadequate influence over the long-term rate of interest." Keynes accepted that "A change in the quantity of money . . . is already within the power of most governments by open-market policy or analogous measures." But "there is no ground for the belief that a flexible wage policy is capable of maintaining a state of continuous full employment . . . any more than for the belief that an open-market policy is capable, unaided, of achieving this result."[31] So chapter 19 had the same message as chapter 15. It was the long-term rate of interest that mattered, while changes in the quantity of money could be effected by the government through open-market operations. The trouble was that increases in the quantity of money might not always lead to reductions in the long-term rate of interest.

So – in the special circumstances that bothered Keynes – stimulatory open-market operations are ineffective, because the non-bank private sector is in a liquidity trap. This liquidity trap arises from the quantity of money (i.e., the bank deposits held by the non-bank private sector), not from banks' cash reserves or the monetary base. Because it relates to a broad concept of monetary assets, it might be termed "the broad liquidity trap." When this trap holds, the price of long-dated bonds does not decline when the quantity of money is increased. So the long-term rate of interest cannot be reduced by monetary policy.

Two final points conclude this section. First, the explanation for Keynes's adoption of a broad measure of money should now be evident. Keynes was concerned with the decisions taken by private-sector agents to balance their holdings of money against their holdings of bonds. He therefore had to have an all-inclusive measure of money, as the nearest alternative asset would be a non-money asset (i.e., a bond). If he had focused instead on a narrow measure of money, he could have made no definite statement about the relationship with bond prices. The nearest alternative to a narrow money balance is a money balance in a broader measure of money.

By the same token, the nearest alternative to coin is a bank note; the nearest alternative to a bank note is a demand deposit; the nearest alternative to a demand deposit is a time deposit or deposit account. Switches between notes and coin, or between notes and current accounts, or between demand and time deposits, are money-into-money transactions and could be termed "money transfers." Such money transfers have by themselves no effect on bond prices or indeed on anything relevant to macroeconomic outcomes.[32] This point – which provides the analytical justification for focusing on an all-inclusive, broadly defined money aggregate – is developed at greater length in essays 15 and 16.

Second, Keynes of course knew that central banks tended to concentrate their operations at the short end. But one very consistent theme in all his writing was that he wanted monetary policy to affect the long rate. Logically, he advocated that monetary operations should be at all points on the yield curve. Towards the end of *A Treatise on Money* the proposal was for a "monetary policy *à outrance.*" (The *Treatise* was published in 1930, after the crash on Wall Street. Concern about the deterioration in world economic activity had already made the design of stimulatory monetary policy a live topic.) Monetary policy *à outrance* was to include the purchase of debt of all maturities, as well as money-market operations to lower the very-short-term interest rate.[33] In *The General Theory* he said, "Perhaps a complex offer by the central bank to buy and sell at stated prices gilt-edged bonds of all maturities, in place of the single bank rate for short-term bills, is the most important practical improvement which can be made in the technique of monetary management."[34]

Unfortunately, the argument in *The General Theory* was abstract. Its relationship to the institutional structure of a modern economy was loose and imprecise. In chapter 15 – the *locus classicus* of Keynes's liquidity trap – he referred to "the banking system" and "the monetary authority," but he did not differentiate between "the government," "the central bank," and "the commercial banks," as has been done in this essay. He complained that the type of monetary policy he favored was unpopular with "the monetary authority," which was not, "as a rule, an equally willing dealer in debts of all maturities." He objected to the concentration of open-market operations on the short end and to the practice of leaving "the price of long-term debts to be influenced by belated and imperfect reactions from the price of short-term debts." In his view, "there is no reason why they need be so."[35]

But was Keynes being naïve? There was a simple and rather obvious reason why *the central bank* would not conduct operations at the long end. As explained earlier, any central bank has to worry about the losses and profits of its operations, and holding long-dated paper is liable to generate large losses and profits. (Note that in the 1930s the Bank of England was still privately owned. It could not have tolerated the profit swings implied by the sort of operations Keynes had in mind. The shareholders of the Federal Reserve System have always been its member banks, and in this sense the Fed also has been and remains privately owned.) But – as has been explained here – *the government* need suffer from no such inhibitions. If Keynes had seen that the government, the central bank, and the commercial banks have different roles and different constraints on their behavior, he might have made the distinction between money-market operations and debt-market operations, and the related distinction between a narrow liquidity trap and a broad liquidity trap. Surprisingly, macroeconomic theory has failed to bring the subject into good order since he wrote in the 1930s.

VII.

Krugman's observations on Japan and the liquidity trap pay homage to the great works of the 1930s, notably to the IS/LM model proposed by Hicks as a distillation of *The General Theory*. (See essay 10, p. 221, and essay 11, pp. 234–235, for an explanation of the IS/LM model.) However, a careful reading of Krugman's extensive and widely quoted writings on these matters raises questions about the ancestry of his ideas and, in particular, about the legitimacy of his appeal to the classics. So far it has been shown that Keynes's liquidity trap involved two aggregates, money (broadly defined to include all bank deposits) and bonds, and that its main concern was the relationship between the quantity of money and the long-term bond yield. The next step is to identify the rationale of the liquidity trap. Why did Keynes propose that, under certain conditions, an increase in the quantity of money might not reduce the long-term bond yield?

His key remarks on the matter appeared in chapters 13 and 15 of *The General Theory*. Chapter 13 tried to answer the question why someone should hold money for any purpose other than the transactions and precautionary motives. After all, by holding bonds rather than money, someone obtains an income, the rate of interest, which "is the reward for parting with liquidity for a specified period."[36] Keynes found the necessary condition for such speculative money holding in "the existence of *uncertainty* as to the future rate of interest." If the rates of interest ruling in future could be foreseen with certainty, "it must always be more advantageous to purchase a debt than to hold cash as a store of wealth." However, if the future rates of interest were uncertain, the outcome could be quite different. It needs to be remembered that the price of bonds moves inversely with their yields. So, if interest rates and bond yields rise, a capital loss is suffered, with the loss being higher the more long-dated is the bond. Keynes warned that, for an investor thinking of acquiring a bond with a life of n years, ". . . if a need for liquid cash may conceivably arise before the expiry of n years, there is a risk of loss being incurred in purchasing a long-term debt and subsequently turning it into cash, as compared with holding cash."

Chapter 15 covered somewhat different ground from chapter 13, but on the question of the motive for holding money on speculative grounds it merely reiterated what was said in chapter 13. ". . . [U]ncertainty as to the future course of the rate of interest is the sole intelligible explanation" of the speculative demand for money.[37] Keynes's conclusion was that investors who expected the next move in interest rates to be upwards would hold at least part of their wealth in the form of money rather than bonds. They would do this even though they would be forgoing income in the immediate future. An extreme situation could arise when bond yields had fallen so low that the only sensible expectation was a future rise in yields (i.e., the only sensible expectation was a capital loss). In that eventuality investors would keep idle any extra money balances injected into their portfolios. The economy would be in a liquidity trap. Open-market operations – even debt-market operations of the kind described in this essay – could not rescue it. In short, Keynes's liquidity trap was the result of an unhappy relationship between the quantity of money and the long-term yield on bonds, where, once this yield had fallen to a low level, expectations about its future behavior (i.e., expectations of capital losses on the bonds) caused people to accumulate money balances without limit. Beneath a certain interest rate, the demand for money became infinitely interest-elastic.

How, then, does Krugman see the liquidity trap? In particular, does the infinite interest-elasticity of the demand for money have the same explanation in his work as that proposed by Keynes in *The General Theory*? Putting together answers to these questions is not made any easier by the multiplicity and variety of Krugman's writings, and the mutability of his views over time and between papers. His work has come in two phases, in commentary on Japan in the late 1990s and the opening years of the present century, and more recently in commentary on the global financial crisis that started in mid-2007. In the first phase, his central proposition was that Japan suffered from a liquidity trap; in the second phase, it was that even the American economy had become blighted in this way. In the discussion on Japan, Krugman had two official websites, one created while he was at the Massachusetts Institute of Technology and the second established after his move to Princeton.[38] (There was also an unofficial website devoted to Krugman, set up by an admirer.) To take just one snapshot from this intellectual kaleidoscope, in early 2003 the MIT website had twenty pieces on Japan, twelve of which were "models" and eight "diatribes," while the Princeton website had ten pieces directly relating to Japan, with seven categorized as "models" and three as "diatribes." Virtually all of the thirty pieces were published in 1998 and 1999.

It was not clear – and perhaps never will be clear – which was meant as the Authorized Version. The MIT website included a long and relatively early paper – from May 1998 – entitled "Japan's Trap." Krugman's book *The Return of Depression Economics*, published in 1999, had a chapter on Japan, but did not refer to any of his models or diatribes apart from the May 1998 paper.[39] So this one seems to deserve special attention and is the focus of discussion here. (In 2009 Krugman published *The Return of Depression Economics and the Crisis of 2008*, which has a substantial overlap of content with the 1999 volume. However, chapter 9, "The Sum of All Fears," was entirely new and included the observations that after the collapse of the United States' shadow banking system, "the Fed found itself presiding over a Japanese-style liquidity trap, in which conventional monetary policy had lost all traction over the real economy" [p. 175], and that the United States' "policy helplessness is reminiscent of Japan in the 1990s" [p. 180]. So Krugman appears – at a quite recent date – to have seen the latest American problem in much the same terms as Japan's ongoing trauma, which justifies the continued analysis here of the original pieces on Japan.)

Krugman was notably critical of the Bank of Japan for its commitment to long-run price stability. In the May 1998 paper this commitment was said to have perverse effects. In his words, "when the central bank increases the current money supply," the commitment to long-run stability implied that this increase would be retracted at a later stage. So – paradoxically – a monetary injection *then* would lower "the expected rate of money growth . . . and the expected rate of inflation" (i.e., the inflation prevailing *in subsequent periods*). But a lowering of the expected rate of inflation implied an increase in the real interest rate. Moreover, in the extreme, the expected rate of inflation might become an expected rate of deflation. Of course, once expectations of deflation have become embedded in the system, real interest rates would be positive even with a zero nominal interest rate. Indeed, with interest rates at zero and bonds paying no interest, and with the central bank committed to long-run price stability, holding bonds would give no better return than holding money. (They would both have a positive real return equal to the expected rate of deflation.) If the central bank were to expand the quantity of money in these conditions, it would pile up uselessly in bank accounts and have no stimulatory effect on the economy. In Krugman's words, ". . . [S]ince the nominal interest rate cannot go negative, any increase in money beyond the level that drives the rate to zero will simply be substituted for bonds, with no effect on spending. And therefore no open-market operation, no matter how large, can get the economy to full employment. In short, the economy is in a classic liquidity trap."[40]

This may be a liquidity trap, but is it "a classic liquidity trap"? And is it Keynes's liquidity trap? The answer has to be, No. It has been shown that Keynes's trap turned on *expectations about bond yields*. Although Krugman's discussion was conceptually rich (and, perhaps as a result, not easy to follow), one point about the proposed trap was clear. It relied on *expectations about the price level of goods and services*. More precisely, it worked because price deflation led to a positive real interest rate on financial assets, and so made the holding of such assets attractive relative to the purchase of goods and services. Krugman's first liquidity trap may have thrown new light on Japan's current dilemma and added insights to the theoretical debate, but it is not "a classic liquidity trap." It is a new trap that he has invented.

Later in the May 1998 paper Krugman introduced another idea. "Moving outside the formal model, the prospects for a liquidity trap also depend on investment demand. Here demography . . . comes into play: the prospective decline in the labor force reduces the expected return on investments." A few sentences later the suggestion was made more definite. ". . . [W]hile it is quite easy to make the case that Japan really is in a liquidity trap, it is much harder to give a convincing explanation of why. Demography seems to be the leading candidate. . . ." This notion was again provocative. The thought was that, if the quantity of money were increased, economic agents would let the money accumulate in idle balances, and would not build more factories and office buildings, purchase new capital equipment, and so on. In jargon, the demand price for tangible capital assets would not increase. The reason would be adverse expectations about returns on these tangible capital assets, stemming from a bleak demographic situation.[41]

Like the first Krugman trap, this one looked plausible and may have been a major part of the Japanese problem. But did it have anything to do with Keynes's trap, which – to repeat – arose because of *expectations about bond yields*? The answer once more has to be, No. Although *The General Theory* did make some remarks about demographics and the connection with asset returns, they were not integrated into the discussion of the liquidity trap. This is not to reject the possibility that the interest-elasticity of the demand for money might become infinite because of poor prospective returns on tangible capital assets. But the trap is not Keynes's; it is another of Krugman's inventions.

There is one more liquidity trap in Krugman's work. In an influential paper published in 1999 Allan Meltzer said that the Bank of Japan had not exhausted the scope for monetary policy action because it could have been far more aggressive in purchasing foreign currency and so driving down the yen's exchange rate.[42] A fall in the exchange rate should have led to the return of inflation and, hence, to the benign effects on expected real asset returns required to stimulate the economy. A related, but more general, argument was that, as long as investments expected to provide a healthy positive return exist somewhere in the world, a nation with low-return (or zero- or negative-return) assets ought still not to be in a liquidity trap. Instead of letting wealth accumulate in ever-larger bank deposits in the local currency, people would want to convert their local currency into foreign currency and so acquire the means to purchase the positive-return assets available in other countries. In the process the exchange rate should fall, again leading to the return of inflation.

Krugman's objection was that exchange-rate expectations could be perverse. Suppose that a central bank – such as the Bank of Japan – is a doughty inflation fighter committed to a strong currency. Domestic demand is weak and does not respond to an easing of monetary policy, even with interest rates at zero. Total demand might still be boosted to a full-employment level if foreign demand (i.e., a current-account surplus, with exports above imports) could fill the gap. But a weak exchange rate is needed to promote buoyant exports and to generate a current-account surplus. The trouble – according to Krugman – stemmed from a central bank pledged to long-run price stability. Because the financial markets would know about the central bank's pledge, currency depreciation *now or in the near future* would generate expectations of an offsetting appreciation *in the more distant future*. If the central bank were to purchase large quantities of foreign currency to drive down the exchange rate, it would have to pay for them by creating extra local-currency deposits. Unfortunately, expectations of a bounce-back in the exchange rate would cause the extra money balances to accumulate endlessly, as in other liquidity traps, with no effect on the economy. According to Krugman in a November 1998 website paper, the culprit was "expectations that the real exchange rate" would "revert to its 'normal' level," since these would "limit the extent of real depreciation, even at a zero . . . rate [of interest]."[43]

The essence of this final Krugman liquidity trap was therefore that the demand for local-currency money became infinitely elastic with respect to the exchange rate (not the interest rate), because of *expectations about the exchange rate*. If the demand for money were at the same time infinitely elastic with respect to the interest rate, intervention on the foreign exchanges – like domestic open-market operations – could not rescue the economy. The open economy, like the closed economy, would be caught in a liquidity trap. This again is an interesting idea which enriches the debate about monetary policy. But – as with the two previous traps – it is not found in *The General Theory* or any other of Keynes's writings. In fact, *The General Theory* is almost exclusively about a closed economy. There are some passages about how adhesion to the gold standard might constrain reductions in interest rates, but there is nothing whatever about the effect of exchange-rate expectations on the demand to hold local-currency money. So the third trap is yet another of Krugman's inventions.

Earlier, this essay proposed a much simplified, but not unrealistic, economy, and used it as the context for distinguishing between money-market operations, which could directly change the monetary base (but could change the quantity of money only indirectly and with some uncertainty), and debt-market operations, which could directly change the quantity of money. With this distinction in mind, it further identified two kinds of situation in which monetary policy might become ineffective: a narrow and a broad liquidity trap. It showed, through quotations from *The General Theory*, that the trap that really bothered Keynes was the broad liquidity trap. A review of Krugman's writings in the late 1990s has shown that he had three liquidity traps, which – despite his description of them as "classic" – were all different from the liquidity trap in *The General Theory* and in Hicks's celebrated paper on the IS/LM model. Whereas Keynes's trap stemmed from malignant expectations about *the yield on long-dated bonds*, Krugman's traps were due to malignant expectations about *the price behavior of other aggregates*. His first was about *the price level of goods and services*, his second about *the rate of return on tangible capital assets*, and his third about *the exchange rate between local and foreign currencies*. None of Krugman's traps are the trap that worried Keynes.

VIII.

To say that Krugman's traps are different from Keynes's trap is not to deny their relevance to current policy problems or the contribution that their further analysis might make to macroeconomic theory. But have modern macroeconomists made too much of a fuss about "the" liquidity trap? The definition of a liquidity trap depends on the system of aggregation assumed in the economy under discussion. A vast number of liquidity traps can be devised between money and another aggregate, where the source of the problem is that expectations about the aggregate's price (in terms of money) cause agents to have an infinitely elastic demand for money. A narrow liquidity trap can be distinguished from Keynes's broad liquidity trap when the monetary base is differentiated from the quantity of money and, as a result, the banking system's demand for earning assets is differentiated from non-bank private-sector agents' demand for long-dated bonds. The narrow liquidity trap becomes possible, in other words, when the system of aggregation is extended from an economy with money and bonds to an economy with monetary-base assets, bank deposits, and bonds. Krugman's traps are different from either the broad or the narrow liquidity trap because he has brought more aggregates into his economy. In his first trap the aggregates concerned are money (or perhaps "financial assets" encompassing both money and very-low-interest short-dated bonds) on the one hand, and goods and services on the other; in his second trap the aggregates are money and tangible physical assets; and in his final trap the aggregates are local-currency and foreign-currency money. Additional traps would be possible were the economy to take on yet more aggregates.

In short, the number of liquidity traps can be multiplied by assuming an ever-greater variety of economies with different systems of aggregation. When the point has been grasped, another thought soon follows. What was so revolutionary about the liquidity trap in *The General Theory*? The title of Keynes's book – emphasizing the comprehensiveness of his new theory and belittling the narrowness of "the classical school" (as he called it) – was a brilliant piece of intellectual marketing. But his liquidity trap highlighted only one of the pathologies of a modern capitalist economy. Dozens of other traps, with the same basic structure (i.e., an infinitely elastic demand for money, in a context where agents are balancing their wealth between money and another aggregate), can be concocted. All that economists have to do is to add more aggregates against which agents have to balance their money holdings and propose sufficient perversity in the aggregates' price expectations.[44]

The ability of modern economists to multiply liquidity traps, and to

Table 4.2
Different Kinds of "Liquidity Trap"

Liquidity Traps Arising from Expectations about Financial-Asset Yields

Narrow liquidity trap – Commercial banks' demand for monetary base is infinitely elastic, even at zero money-market rates, so that cash constitutes an ever-rising share of their assets as the central bank tries to stimulate the economy by "money-market operations."

Broad liquidity trap – The non-bank private sector's demand to hold money (i.e., bank deposits) is infinitely elastic at prevailing long bond yield, because of perverse expectations about future bond yields. The ratio of money to national income rises without limit, as the quantity of money rises because of bank balance-sheet expansion due to lending to the private sector and/or debt-market operations.

Krugman's Three Liquidity Traps

First trap – The non-bank private sector's demand to hold money (i.e., bank deposits, presumably) is infinitely elastic because of perverse expectations about the price level of goods and services.

Second trap – The non-bank private sector's demand to hold money is infinitely elastic because of perverse, highly pessimistic expectations about the rate of return on tangible capital assets.

Third trap – The non-bank private sector's demand to hold money is infinitely elastic because of perverse expectations about the exchange rate between local and foreign currencies.

Keynes's trap in *The General Theory* was the "broad liquidity trap." It related to the "bond yield" and a broadly defined money measure; it did not relate to "the short-term interest rate" (i.e., the central-bank policy rate) and the monetary base, although much of the discussion in *The General Theory* was confusing because of a "slurring" (Keynes's own word) of definitions.

None of Krugman's three traps can be identified in Keynes's *General Theory*.

identify a wide variety of other potential causes of depression and deflation, does not mean that the liquidity-trap idea is unimportant for policy-making. However, Keynes did not believe – at the time he was writing – that any economy had suffered from a liquidity trap. He was quite explicit about this point. Chapter 15 of *The General Theory* noted "the possibility" that liquidity preference "may become virtually absolute in the sense that everyone prefers cash to holding a debt which yields so low a rate of interest." But he noted that, "whilst this limiting case might become practically important in future, I know of no example of it hitherto."[45] That is why Krugman's claims about modern Japan in the late 1990s and the opening years of the twenty-first century – that it genuinely did suffer from a liquidity trap – were so challenging. If they were true, even more disturbing would be his recent claims that monetary policy cannot be used to tackle the Great Recession in the United States. But Krugman's analysis was (and remains) flawed, and his critique misdirected. His analysis was flawed in that he seemed not to understand that his traps were original intellectual constructs different from those proposed by Keynes and Hicks in the 1930s. His critique was (and remains) misdirected because – despite the proliferation of traps in his work – he did not make the vital distinction between the narrow and broad liquidity traps.

This essay has argued that monetary policy consists of both money-market operations (which fix the quantity of the monetary base and the short-term interest rate) and debt-market operations (which have a direct effect on the quantity of money and affect long-term bond yields, as well as other asset prices). When defined widely in this way, monetary policy in Japan was not exhausted in the late 1990s, when Krugman wrote his seminal pieces, and it has not been exhausted subsequently in Japan, the United States, or anywhere else. It is true that the use of money-market operations to reduce the short-term interest rate had gone as far as it could in Japan in the late 1990s, and it has gone as far as it can in the U.S. in the present Great Recession. The short-term rate cannot go negative. When an economy is in a narrow liquidity trap, its central bank can usefully do nothing more if it restricts its transactions to the rest of the banking system. But the Japanese authorities in the late 1990s – and even in a phase of so-called "quantitative easing" between March 2001 and March 2006 – did not consciously try debt-market operations. The Ministry of Finance continued, very mistakenly, to sell vast quantities of long-dated government bonds to non-banks.

The ministry should instead have concentrated new issues at the short end, where they ought to have been attractive to the banks; it might even have considered outright purchases of long-dated government bonds financed by overdraft borrowing from the banks or the Bank of Japan. Crucially, these operations are best carried out in the government's name, and ought to have been undertaken jointly by the Bank of Japan and the Ministry of Finance. By such operations they could have increased the quantity of money to any figure that they chose. Japan may or may not have been in a broad liquidity trap. It is possible – although surely not very plausible – that a 10, 20, or 30 percent increase in broad money would have had no effect on the prices of financial assets, the price level of goods and services, the demand price of tangible physical assets, and the yen exchange rate. Since aggressively expansionary debt-market operations were not implemented to achieve a money-supply jump on this scale, no one – including Professor Krugman – can know.

Debt-market options are also available in the U.S. today and, if used without inhibition, could expand a broadly defined quantity of money by any amount that the monetary authorities wished. Admittedly, American policy-makers seem baffled about the relationship between the quantity of money as usually defined (i.e., inclusive of most bank deposits) and expenditure.[46] However, the large facts about M2 and nominal GDP over the last fifty years are obvious enough (see table 4.3 on p. 99) and have a compelling message for policy-making. They establish at least a presumption that an increase of 10, 20, or 30 percent in M2 would raise equilibrium national income, if not by exactly 10, 20, or 30 percent, at least by a number that would be within striking distance of those figures. Krugman's appeal to fiscal policy is therefore unnecessary.[47] Indeed, given that the United States' public debt is rising dramatically, and that this rise threatens a huge increase in debt interest costs and the future tax burden, so-called "expansionary fiscal policy" is surely misguided.

IX.

The distinction between the narrow and broad liquidity traps also helps inform the discussion of Bernanke's November 2002 remarks about deflation risks in the United States. A more detailed review of his proposals may now be helpful, to see what precise role he envisaged for the Treasury.

He was in fact refreshingly radical and open-minded about the potential range of the Federal Reserve's operations, outlining four types of special transactions. The first was the pre-commitment of future money-market rates. In Bernanke's words, by promising to keep the "overnight rate" at zero for a stipulated period of time (perhaps running into months or quarters), the Fed might "induce a decline in longer-term rates." Second, the Fed might purchase securities further down the yield curve. Ceilings might be announced "for yields on longer-dated Treasury debt" (such as two-year paper), with the Fed enforcing the ceilings "by committing to make unlimited purchases of securities up to two years from maturity at prices consistent with targeted yields." If necessary, it could take the policy out to "still longer maturities, say three to six years." Third, although in principle the Fed was restricted by its mandate from buying private-sector assets, it might achieve much the same effect by purchasing "agency debt" (such as mortgage-backed securities issued by the General National Mortgage Association) or by making long-term loans (up to 180 days) to the banks, taking commercial paper as security. Finally, it could operate in the foreign-exchange market, selling dollars and buying foreign government debt.[48]

In Bernanke's 2002 talk all these special operations would help to raise the prices of certain assets in more direct and certain ways than would be possible with conventional money-market operations at the very short end. But why, if such operations are so effective when administered in significant doses in emergencies, are they not administered in smaller doses all the time? Part of the answer has already been discussed, that the Federal Reserve is a bank, even if a very unusual sort of bank, and it does have to report profits and losses.[49] If the Federal Reserve were to hold large amounts of six-year government bonds and agency securities, it might incur heavy losses if the prices of these securities were to fall. Bernanke's support for operations a long way "down the curve" was reminiscent of suggestions made by Keynes in the 1930s. But Bernanke's proposals suffered from the same weakness as Keynes's, namely, that central banks are not "as a rule an equally

TABLE 4.3
MONEY AND NOMINAL GDP IN THE U.S.,
1959–2009
% compound annual increase

	Nominal GDP	M2
1960s*	6.9	7.0
1970s	10.2	9.6
1980s	7.8	7.9
1990s	5.5	3.9
2000s	4.3	6.5
Whole period**	7.0	7.0

* I.e., Q4 1959–Q1 1969, and so on for the other decades

** I.e., Q4 1959–Q1 2009

Sources: St. Louis Federal Reserve Economic Data; for nominal GDP, quarterly data originally from Department of Commerce; for M2, data originally from Federal Reserve, with last month in quarter taken to define quarter's value

willing dealer in debts of all maturities" because they face a budget constraint.

The same drawback would apply to central-bank acquisition of claims on the private sector and of foreign exchange. Moreover, central-bank purchases both of securities issued by the private sector and of large amounts of foreign exchange are highly political acts. Domestically, the Fed would no doubt limit itself to purchases of highly rated corporate bonds, but companies whose bonds were not purchased might complain of favoritism. On the external front, Bernanke himself noted that heavy foreign-exchange operations would have implications for foreign policy and could not be unconstrained. The Federal Reserve would need to coordinate its activities not just with the Treasury, but also with the State Department. Bernanke frequently acknowledged the need for the Fed to cooperate with the U.S. government, but his comments would have been more precise if he had made a sharp and clear distinction between money-market and debt-market operations. His remarks did in fact contain an implicit reference to debt-market operations. In the section on "Fiscal Policy," he recognized that, even without tax cuts or increases in public expenditure, the government "could acquire existing real or financial assets." He continued, "If the Treasury issued debt to purchase private assets and the Fed then purchased an equal amount of Treasury debt with newly created money, the whole operation would be the economic equivalent of direct open-market operations in private assets."

This suggestion has some similarities to the second category of debt-market operations outlined above, where the government borrows from the central bank. However, in the present essay the funds raised by such borrowing are used to buy back existing long-dated government bonds from non-banks, not privately issued securities and certainly not "existing real assets."[50] Buy-backs of existing government bonds would be far less politically controversial than the asset purchases discussed by Bernanke, while the monetary effect – the effect that would significantly alter the equilibrium values of key macro variables – would be the same.

Towards the end of his remarks Bernanke adverted to the Japanese situation. His verdict was that Japan suffered from "political constraints" on the appropriate actions rather than "a lack of policy instruments." In his words, "In the resulting political deadlock, strong policy actions are discouraged, and cooperation among policy-makers is difficult to achieve." The analysis in this essay supports the view that the trouble in Japan has been institutional and political rather than economic in character, but it tightens the critique of Japanese policy-making. To repeat, the Bank of Japan was expected to reflate the economy single-handedly by money-market operations, when the correct response would have been for the Bank of Japan and the Ministry of Finance to collaborate on expansionary debt-market operations. The same observation now applies in the United States, given that it too – at the time of writing (December 2010) – has slid into a narrow liquidity trap. The Fed and the Treasury have to work together, with expansionary debt-market operations supplementing, or even superseding, money-market operations, which have already cut the Fed funds rate to zero.

Economists have been puzzled by policy-makers' inability to revive demand in Japan. Bernanke's appeal to "the printing presses" in 2002 was and remains compelling. We know both that governments can print money and that economic agents have a finite demand for real money balances. We therefore believe that policy-makers can engineer whatever inflation rate they choose. The generation of inflation, and the prevention of inflation, seem extremely easy: just print the right amount of money.[51]

X.

And it is easy. The sentence "the government can print money without limit" is correct, but the key word is *government*. The problem of the ineffectiveness of monetary policy arises only because the task of creating legal-tender money – the key monetary-base asset – has been delegated to a central bank. A central bank is distinct from the government, even if it is government-owned and subject to specific legislation. Because it is a bank, it has assets and liabilities, and it also has to report profits and losses. Its ability to run accounting losses and the range of assets it can buy have to be restricted. (Note that the accounting losses may have only a tenuous connection with resource costs to society.) Further, because it is a unique kind of institution (which serves only the government and the banking system, and perhaps some foreign governments), it does not in the normal course of events have a business relationship with non-bank private-sector agents. Crucially, it does not take deposits from non-banks.

These institutional features of a central bank – the limitations on the range of assets it can sensibly purchase and on its incurrence of deposit liabilities to non-banks – constrain its ability to conduct aggressively expansionary open-market operations. They are part of the syndrome that has been called here "the narrow liquidity trap." Until 2007 Japan was the most prominent example of this trap and, if there had been good management in other countries, it ought to have proved the only one. As it happens, in the most stressful period the Bank of Japan had been extraordinarily flexible in the range of assets that it would purchase, and it continues today (December 2010) to run a risk of reporting losses in excess of its capital if and when the Japanese economy recovers. However, the vast expansion of its liabilities to the banking system has not led to an increase in the quantity of money (on the broad definitions), because the banks' demand for cash reserves has been – for all practical purposes – infinitely elastic. This infinite elasticity of the demand for this monetary-base asset can be attributed to both the banks' shortage of capital and the unattractiveness to them of possible earning assets.

But the government can print money and/or borrow without limit from commercial banks, and it can purchase any asset from non-banks. One answer to the Japanese *malaise* would have been for the government to pass legislation giving the Ministry of Finance the right to issue legal tender and then to print massive quantities of yen notes. There are precedents for this sort of monetary policy aggressiveness – even, one might say, monetary adventurism – in supposedly stable and well-governed industrial nations. The U.S. federal government embarked on a large-scale issue of "greenbacks" during the Civil War, and during the First World War the British government issued "Bradburys" (notes that were liabilities of the Treasury, not the Bank of England).[52] In the extreme, the Japanese government today could follow those examples. If the result were very fast growth of a broadly defined money measure (i.e., one inclusive of notes *and deposits*), inflation would surely ensue.

Constitutional structures matter. One reason why legislatures around the world have delegated the issue of legal-tender money to central banks is that they are likely to be more reluctant to over-issue than politicians. If Japan's Ministry of Finance had been given the power to issue bank notes in 2003, the political problem might have become the need to take it away in 2005 and 2006 after a colossal inflationary boom. Fortunately, there is a means of expanding the quantity of money without a constitutional outrage. That is for *the government* (repeat: *the government*) to borrow from "the banking system" (either the central bank or the commercial banks) on a large scale and to purchase assets from the non-bank private sector with the loan proceeds. Contrary to some of the more daring passages in Bernanke's 2002 remarks, the government does not need to engage in politically contentious purchases of securities issued by the private sector. It need only buy back its own long-dated debt. In summary, the key to solving a deflation arising from a narrow liquidity trap is for *the government* to work with the central bank and to conduct expansionary debt-market operations, preferably in its own name. Just as there is no constraint on the size of the note issue when the finance ministry seizes the right to issue legal tender (as it often does in wartime), so there is no constraint on the size of the monetary injection (i.e., the increase in bank deposits) that can be engineered by debt-market operations.

The purpose of this essay has been to clarify some fundamental issues in macroeconomic policy-making. There is much unnecessary confusion about the respective roles of fiscal policy, debt management, and monetary policy. Some well-respected macroeconomists say that debt management is not part of monetary policy; they claim that, no matter how it is conducted, it cannot alter macroeconomic outcomes. Other equally well-respected macroeconomists regard debt management as an integral part of monetary policy and believe that it can alter macroeconomic outcomes profoundly.[53] The confusion stems partly from a failure to define the categories in theoretical models. This essay has shown how "the liquidity trap," supposedly a unique theoretical construct which revolutionized monetary economics, can be bent like a piece of intellectual plasticine by changing the system of aggregation in an assumed hypothetical economy.

But all the conclusions of macroeconomic theory depend on the components of the models under discussion. It was unfortunate that in *The General Theory* Keynes used two imprecise phrases, "the monetary authority" and "the banking system." He took "the monetary authority" to be the agent in open-market operations, and he failed to differentiate between the government and the central bank; and he regarded "the banking system" as the set of organizations that issued "the quantity of money," instead of differentiating between "the central bank" and "the commercial banks," and between "the monetary base" and "deposits held by the non-bank private sector." These weaknesses of *The General Theory* are the more curious when contrasted with the detailed discussion of institutions in *A Treatise on Money*. Today's economists need to develop theories in which the monetary base and the quantity of bank deposits have their own supply and demand functions, and to stop talking about the "the supply of *money*" and "the demand for *money*." Monetary-base assets and bank deposits have very different characteristics, and the word "money" – when used without qualification – has multiple meanings. A more careful use of words may lead to a better understanding of how monetary policy and debt management interact. That better understanding may help policy-makers to inoculate their economies against the deflationary disease that has long afflicted Japan and that in 2009 threatened almost universal macroeconomic trauma.

PART TWO

IS "THE KEYNESIAN REVOLUTION" A FACTOID?

PREFACE

THE WORD "factoid" was coined by Norman Mailer in his 1973 biography of Marilyn Monroe. A factoid is a statement, often a large and ambitious generalization, that is "valid" only because of its constant and prominent repetition, and the credence then paid to it by a large number of people. As defined by the *Compact Oxford English Dictionary*, it is "an item of unreliable information that is repeated so often that it becomes accepted as fact."[1]

The notion of "the Keynesian revolution" is well known. Numerous books and papers have asserted that the activation of fiscal policy in accordance with the Keynesian blueprint was responsible for macro-economic performance being markedly better in the first twenty-five years after the Second World War than in the twenty-five years before it. Across the industrial world, employment was much closer to being "full" in the 1950s and '60s than it had been in the 1920s and '30s, while politicians certainly made a lot of noise in the later period about how government action could and should manage demand. Sir John Hicks, the author of the IS/LM interpretation of *The General Theory*, once said that the decades immediately after 1945 were "the Age of Keynes."

But is "the Keynesian revolution" a factoid? The first essay in this section examines the reality of fiscal policy in the U.K. in the key period, as opposed to the pattern of conduct attributed to politicians and officials in the relevant government department (the Treasury) by outside Keynesian economists. It turns out that many officials did not like Keynes or his ideas, and until the mid-1960s they gave policy advice and persuaded politicians to act on largely non-Keynesian lines. (Keynes's style was not always endearing. He told one senior official to his face that he was "intellectually contemptible.") To be sure, there may have been a few years in the late 1960s and early 1970s when policy-making was substantially Keynesian, but the results were disastrous. In any case, by the late 1970s monetarism had made so much progress that Keynesian ideas were peripheral in decision-making. My conclusion in essay 5 is: "The U.K. is the homeland of Keynesian thought, but in the actual conduct of British fiscal policy 'the Keynesian revolution' is and always has been an illusion." (The original version of the essay was written in 1997. In retrospect, I would gladly replace the word "illusion" with "factoid.")

In the United States also, actual fiscal experience was far from the Keynesian textbook theories. As Herbert Stein explained in his 1969 book, *The Fiscal Revolution in America*, the historical record was full of twists and turns, and indeed upsets and confusions. On October 8, 1953, when American employment was as "full" as it was ever to be in the putative "Age of Keynes," President Eisenhower addressed a press conference with the message, "Balancing the budget will always remain a goal of any administration that believes as much as we do that the soundness of our money must be assured, and that the unbalanced budget has a very bad effect on it."[2] Nevertheless, it is true that in the early 1960s Keynesians came to occupy the main policy-making and policy-influencing positions in the Kennedy administration, and that fiscal policy in the 1960s was organized deliberately to influence demand and output. Arthur Okun, appointed to the Council of Economic Advisers in late 1964, was one of the most influential members of the Kennedy-era Keynesians. He devised the idea of "a GNP gap," to be understood as the shortfall of output from its full-employment level.

The second essay here shows how the Okun "gap" concept, undoubtedly a brainchild of Keynesian macroeconomics, was challenged and eventually replaced over the next the twenty-five years by a very different "gap" notion. This was based on the concept of a natural rate of unemployment advanced in Friedman's 1967 presidential address to the American Economic Association, and it might be called the "monetarist output gap." Whereas the Okun-originated, Keynesian output gap was an affiliate of fiscal expansionism (intended to boost output and "close the gap"), the natural-rate-based, monetarist concept was part of a framework of thought in which unduly stimulatory fiscal *and monetary* policies would cause ever-accelerating inflation. Further, whereas the Keynesian output gap went along with the political determination of government spending and the budget deficit to promote full employment, the monetarist output gap was associated with a more technical and apolitical style of policy-making geared to the attainment of low inflation. Ideally, the de-politicization of decisions would allow policy – principally monetary policy – to be delegated to a specialist committee in an "independent" central bank. (The central bank could be independent in the sense that the government had no power to censure the committee's decisions on interest rates, but it remained subject to review by the legislature.)

What have been the results of applying the two different gap concepts and their competing visions of the policy-making process? In the U.S. of the 1960s the Keynesians' emphasis on fiscal policy and neglect of monetary policy led to a rise in the budget deficit and an upturn in money growth. The upturn in money growth was followed by an increase in inflation, which reached double-digit levels in the 1970s. By common consent, the Great Inflation was a failure of economic expertise and a setback for economics as "a science." Economists – unlike physicists – did not seem much good at saying how particular effects resulted from particular causes. The central task in the late 1970s and early 1980s was to stop inflation. The monetarists' solution – deliberate action by the state to curb money growth – was adopted in virtually all the leading nations, although with large variations in response due to local conditions. The Great Inflation gave way after a few years to the Great Moderation, a period of about fifteen to twenty years (with its length again varying from country to country) of benign macroeconomic outcomes, with low or even negligible inflation, impressive steadiness in output growth, and high employment.

How was the Great Moderation to be explained in intellectual terms? The third essay in this section tries to answer this question from a U.K. perspective, although the Great Moderation was more or less universal. The essay denies that either old-style fiscalist Keynesianism or money-target-focused monetarism could take the credit for the dramatically improved numbers. (Nevertheless, it was true that in the U.S. and elsewhere money growth was lower and more stable in the twenty years up to 2006 than in the previous twenty years.) Instead, the key to the success of those years was a distinctive style of policy-making ("the New Consensus Macroeconomics" or "output-gap monetarism"), in which independent central banks varied the short-term interest rate in order to keep the natural-rate-based output gap as close to zero as possible. In that sense monetarism – with its rejection of a long-run trade-off between inflation and unemployment and its prioritizing of monetary policy over fiscal policy – had triumphed, while the concept of the natural-rate-based output gap had played a vital analytical role. Moreover, the macroeconomic numbers delivered in the Great Moderation were better not only than those during the Great Inflation, but also than those during the heyday of the supposed "Keynesian revolution" in the 1950s and '60s. (See pp. 168–172 for the U.K. and, particularly, pp. 179–182 for the U.S.)

Yes, the notion of "the Keynesian revolution" is a factoid.

ESSAY 5

DID BRITAIN HAVE
A "KEYNESIAN REVOLUTION"?

THE COMMON understanding of the phrase "the Keynesian revolution" is a reappraisal of the theory of fiscal policy after the publication of Keynes's *The General Theory of Employment, Interest, and Money* in 1936, followed by the practical adoption of the new ideas by the major industrial countries in the 1940s and '50s. Specifically, whereas before the Keynesian revolution governments' priority in fiscal policy was to maintain a balanced budget, afterwards the budgetary balance was varied countercyclically in order to reduce fluctuations in economic activity. Britain is often regarded as the home of the Keynesian revolution. For example, the opening sentence of chapter 7 of Christopher Dow's *The Management of the British Economy 1945–60* asserts, "There is probably no country in the world that has made a fuller use than the U.K. of budgetary policy as a means of stabilizing the economy."[1]

A detailed narrative account of the evolution of fiscal policy in the Keynesian direction in the United States has been provided by Herbert Stein in *The Fiscal Revolution in America*. Stein describes the immense initial enthusiasm of young American economists, such as Paul Samuelson and Kenneth Boulding, for *The General Theory* in the late 1930s. As a result, "By 1940 Keynes had largely swept the field of the younger economists, those who were soon to be 'back-room boys' in Washington and who, when they reached the age of forty-five or so, would be ready to come into the front room when John F. Kennedy became President in 1961."[2] No similarly organized story has been told about the U.K., perhaps because the policy revolution is deemed to be so self-evident that an analysis of personalities and events is unnecessary. (As discussed in the four essays in the first part of this book, Keynes himself had rather different attitudes and emphases from the Keynesians.[3])

The purpose of this essay is to suggest that, between the 1940s and the 1970s, both the thinking behind British macroeconomic policy-making and the actual conduct of policy were far from the Keynesian model. As there is little question that between the mid-1970s and the Great Recession of 2008–2010 fiscal policy ceased to be Keynesian in either form or substance, this essay raises doubts about whether Britain ever had a Keynesian revolution. To throw more light on the issue, statistical tests are conducted on the relationship between changes in the budget position and the level of economic activity. The results of these tests are reported in the appendix to this essay. They show that the level of economic activity was not a significant influence on the changes in the cyclically adjusted budget position in the supposedly Keynesian period between 1948 and 1974. (Less surprisingly, it was also not a significant influence between 1975 and 1994). On this basis, the answer to the question, Did Britain have a Keynesian revolution? is, No. However, the absence of a Keynesian revolution in fact does not exclude the possibility that there was a Keynesian revolution in intention. This essay's first task has to be a review of the structure of macroeconomic policy-making, and the ideas held by policy-makers, from the 1930s onwards.

I.

Keynes was appointed to the Economic Advisory Council, a high-level body set up to advise the government on economic matters, at its formation in 1930. It was the successor to a similar committee, created in 1925, to advise the Cabinet. The importance of this appointment should not be exaggerated, because – in the words of Lord Bridges – both the 1925 committee and the Economic Advisory Council were throughout the 1930s "rather remote from the active centre of things."[4] In particular, Keynes failed in 1931 and 1932 to halt the public-expenditure cuts advocated by the May Committee, despite his ferocious and well-known attack on them in the *New Statesman*.[5] These cuts were a classic example of government expenditure being dominated by budget-balancing principles, instead of by the requirements of the business cycle. They were also an important part of the provocation for the new theories to be expressed in *The General Theory*.

Despite Keynes's apparent ineffectiveness in the policy debate of the early 1930s, the Economic Advisory Council set the precedent for professional economists to supplement civil-service advice on key issues in economic policy. Because of the imperative to reach the best possible decisions in wartime, the Economic Advisory Council was followed in 1939 by a Central Economic Information Service in the Cabinet Office. With a full-time staff of economists and statisticians, it was given the job of assembling in one place information about production that had previously been available only from a wide variety of sources. This had obvious significance for the organization of military output, but it also made possible the first estimates of national income and expenditure. Early in 1941 the Central Economic Information Service was split into two, with the economists becoming the Economic Section of the Cabinet Office and the statisticians the Central Statistical Office. The service's work made possible the publication of the first National Income White Paper, which informed the tax decisions made by Sir Kingsley Wood, the chancellor of the exchequer, in the Budget of April 7, 1941.

According to B. E. V. Sabine, "1941 . . . was the watershed year when the Budget could at last be seen to be performing its correct dual function of raising the taxation required and restricting purchasing power."[6] The connection between tax decisions and consumer spending power – and so, by extension, between the government's financial position and aggregate demand – had been emphasized by Keynes in articles in *The Times* on "Paying for the War," where he developed the idea of an "inflationary gap." (These articles are discussed in more detail in essay 10.) The gap, the excess of the nation's *ex ante* propensity to spend over its *ex ante* ability to supply, made sense conceptually only in the context of Keynes's theory of national-income determination. "It is impossible to divorce the practice of the Kingsley Wood regime from the theories of Keynes," particularly "in the recasting of Budget mathematics to highlight the gap."[7] Dow agrees that 1941 was the turning point. "Since 1941 almost all adjustments to the total level of taxation have been made with the object of reducing excess demand or of repairing a deficiency."[8]

Keynes is also credited with a role in the authorship of the 1944 White Paper on Employment Policy. The Employment Policy White Paper is widely regarded as the charter for demand-management policies in the postwar period, largely because of its reference to "a high and stable level of employment" as an objective of official policy. However, the actual wording of the White Paper is far from enthusiastic in its endorsement of a Keynesian purpose for fiscal policy. One passage reads, "To the extent that the policies proposed in this Paper affect the balancing of the Budget in a particular year, they certainly do not contemplate any departure from the principle that the Budget must be balanced over a longer period." Further, "An undue growth in national indebtedness will have a quick result on confidence. But no less serious would be a budgetary deficit arising from a fall in revenues due to depressed industrial and commercial conditions."[9] It is plainly implied that depressed conditions might not justify discretionary action to expand the budget deficit.

At any rate, by the late 1940s Cabinet ministers and many civil servants recognized that the annual Budget ought to be framed with a view to influencing the level of economic activity. In 1948 Sir Stafford Cripps combined the functions of chancellor of the exchequer with those of minister for co-ordination of economic affairs. In his Budget speech of 1950, he said, "Excessive demand produces inflation and inadequate demand results in deflation. The fiscal policy of the Government is the most important single instrument for maintaining that balance."[10] This is clear and straightforward, and it undoubtedly represents an official stamp of approval for Keynesianism.

There is also no question that, when that statement was made, it was uncontroversial and commanded support from all parts of the political spectrum. The Conservative Party came to power in 1951 and made more deliberate use of monetary policy than its predecessor. Most notably, it allowed Bank rate to rise from 2 percent (where it had been stuck, apart from a brief period at the start of the Second World War, since 1932) to 2½ percent in November 1951 and 4 percent in March 1952. Thereafter, the Bank rate was varied mostly in response to the vicissitudes of the exchange rate. But monetary policy was not thought to have a major part to play in influencing demand. Because it was assigned to the task of stabilizing foreign-exchange sentiment towards the pound, fiscal policy could instead be used for the vital aim of managing the domestic economy and trying to secure, on average, a high level of employment. The 1941 and other wartime Budgets had set a precedent for the use of fiscal policy in peacetime. Fiscal policy was taken as being more or less equivalent to discretionary changes in taxation, since public expenditure was judged too inflexible for short-run demand management.[11] In the words of Ian Little, commenting on fiscal policy in the 1950s, "in almost all respects, taxation (and, more generally, fiscal policy) is superior to monetary policy."[12]

By the start of the 1960s economists had begun to feel more confident about quantifying the effect of tax changes on demand. As they could estimate the link between tax changes and consumption, and since consumption was the largest component of aggregate demand, they believed they had leverage over the economy as a whole. As Dow put it, "[T]he procedure of official forecasting is designed to fit in with the procedure of budget-making."[13] To quote Little again, writing in 1961, "Mr. Heathcoat-Amory was the first Chancellor to predict demand in percentages in his 1960 Budget speech. More recently, Mr. Selwyn Lloyd has said, 'I believe it will be within our power to expand at the rate of 3 percent per annum over the next five years, but to do this our exports will have to rise at approximately double this rate.'" Little welcomed the shift to forecasts of demand constituents in percentage terms, concluding his references to Heathcoat-Amory and Selwyn Lloyd with the remark, "Let us hope these are straws in the wind of change."[14]

II.

Superficially, informed views on fiscal-policy theory and the actual conduct of fiscal policy had made a comprehensive shift from primitive pre-Keynesian budget balancing in the early 1930s to sophisticated Keynesian demand management in the early 1960s. However, even at the level of ideas, the Keynesian triumph was far from complete. Influential writers in the Keynesian camp themselves conceded that official thinking was more muddled and ambivalent in this period than was commonly thought. In particular, the conventions for measuring the various categories of public expenditure and taxation, and the differences between them, harked back to the budget-balancing orthodoxies of the pre-Keynesian era. For example, in *The Management of the British Economy*, Dow protested against the survival of accounting practices that had originated in the Exchequer and Audit Departments Act of 1866 or even earlier. To those well versed in the precepts of modern macroeconomics, "The traditional Exchequer accounts have constantly to be explained away as misleading." Indeed, in a footnote Dow admitted that the references to fiscal policy in the 1944 White Paper on Employment Policy were "highly confused," because of tensions between economists working in Whitehall and "the guardians of the older Treasury tradition."[15]

Moreover, these guardians of the older tradition did write, quite extensively, about how they thought the public finances should be organized. In 1959 Sir Herbert Brittain, a recently retired senior Treasury official, published a book titled *The British Budgetary System*, to serve as "a new and comprehensive account of our budgetary system and of the parliamentary and administrative arrangements that are part of it." He saw his book as following in the wake of *The System of National Finance* by Lord Kennet and Mr. Norman Young, which had previously "filled that role." The book contained not a single reference to Keynes. Indeed, it is not going too far to say that, in certain respects, Brittain's description of budgetary arrangements appeared to be deliberately anti-Keynesian. Chapter III, on "The General Design of the Budget," placed a section on "Prudent Finance" before sections on "Social and Political Questions" and "Broad Economic and Financial Policy."

The comments on budget deficits under the "Broad Economic and Financial Policy" heading were highly traditional. Not only must the deficit be as low as possible in the interests of control, but also "regard must be had to the fact that any deficit inevitably means an increase in the national debt." Brittain noted the doctrine that "an indefinite increase in the national debt does not matter so long as the rate of increase is less than the rate of increase in national income," but he rejected it on the grounds that the tax burden depended on the size of all transfer payments and not on the debt-interest charge alone. "[I]t may be dangerous to mortgage in advance any given part of the increase in revenue for the debt charge, irrespective of other possible claims."[16] The section's verdict was that "dangerous results" might

proceed from a lack of confidence in the public finances. Finally, a footnote was attached, claiming that most of the 1944 Employment Policy
White Paper, and in particular the passage in paragraphs 74 to 79 "dealing with Central Finance," had stood up "to the test of post-war expenditure."[17] Paragraphs 74 to 79 were exactly those which had reiterated
the virtues of balancing the budget over the business cycle.

How should this balancing of the budget be defined? The central
principle of the Treasury's fiscal conservatism was that the budget
should be balanced "above the line." The distinction between items
above and below the line was related, but not identical, to the distinction between income and capital. The crucial difference was that recurrent items of capital expenditure were regarded as above the line, "as
there is no case for spreading it over a period, and to borrow every year
would only increase the cost over the years by unnecessary payments of
interest."[18] So borrowing was legitimate to cover the cost of exceptional, non-recurrent capital expenditure, but that was all.

Which set of ideas – the Keynesian countercyclical activism
described by Dow and Little or the fiscal conservatism defended by the
Treasury knights – was in fact the predominant influence in the late
1940s, the 1950s, and the early 1960s? On some interpretations the
data give a clear-cut answer. As noted by Robin Matthews, writing in
1968, "throughout the post-war period the Government, so far from
injecting demand into the system, has persistently had a large current
account surplus . . . [G]overnment saving has averaged about 3 percent
of the national income."[19] A surplus of this kind would be the likely
outcome of applying the above-the-line/below-the-line methodology
favored by Brittain and the other traditional Treasury knights, since it
would correspond to the recurrent capital costs covered by revenue.
The ratio of the U.K.'s national debt to its gross domestic product fell
sharply from 1945 to the mid-1970s, despite the charter for permissive
deficit financing that Keynes was supposed to have given policy-makers
in *The General Theory*.

Matthews continued, provocatively, to assert that fiscal policy
appears "to have been deflationary in the post-war period." However,
there is an important theoretical objection to this conclusion. The characterization of fiscal policy is beset with ambiguities. Quite apart from
all the uncertainties about specifying the appropriate concept of the

budget balance, fiscal policy can be measured and described in terms of either the *level* or the *change* in the budget balance. Matthews's conclusion depends on the premise that fiscal policy is best described in terms of the level of the budget balance. A counterargument could be made that the change in the balance, appropriately defined, is the government's discretionary response to the economic situation and is therefore a better way of thinking about "policy."

Fortunately, several studies have been made of the relationship between the economy and changes in the budget balance in the first twenty-five years after 1945. B. Hansen, conducting a statistical review of *Fiscal Policy in Seven Countries 1955–65* for the Organization for Economic Cooperation and Development, judged that fiscal policy in the U.K., measured in terms of changes in the cyclically adjusted deficit, had been destabilizing over the period.[20] (In other words, action had been taken to increase the deficit when the economy was operating at an above-normal level and to reduce it when the economy was below normal.) In his narrative account *The Treasury under the Tories 1951–64*, Samuel Brittan was also highly critical. In 1971 he published *Steering the Economy*, a revised and updated version of *The Treasury under the Tories*. In it he suggested that "Chancellors behaved like simple Pavlovian dogs responding to two main stimuli: one was 'a run on the reserves' and the other was '500,000 unemployed' – a figure which was later increased to above 600,000."[21] Even Dow – who made such strong claims for the historical reality of the Keynesian revolution in the early chapters of *The Management of the British Economy 1945–60* – acknowledged in later chapters that practice and results had been very different from theory and plan. In the event, many "adjustments of policy were occasioned by the balance of payments," not the level of unemployment relative to a desired figure. The external interference had the result that, "[a]s far as internal conditions are concerned . . . , budgetary and monetary policy failed to be stabilizing and must on the contrary be regarded as having been positively destabilizing. Had tax changes been more gradual, and credit regulations less variable, demand and output would probably have grown much more steadily."[22]

The conclusion must be that, over at least the first two-thirds of the period from 1945 to the mid-1970s, fiscal policy was not Keynesian in the normally understood sense. The trend level of the budget deficit was determined by "the older Treasury tradition," with its emphasis on the sustainability of government debt relative both to national income and to the size of the public sector's stock of capital assets. Policy-determined variations in the deficit around this trend level were largely motivated by the balance of payments and the state of the pound, not by the countercyclical requirements of the domestic economy and unemployment.

The election of the Labour government in October 1964, with Harold Wilson as prime minister, was accompanied by a large influx of professional economists into Whitehall. Many of them thought fiscal policy could and should be used to manage the economy. But economic policy in the years from 1964 to 1970 was again dominated by the balance of payments. The government sought financial help from the International Monetary Fund after the pound's devaluation in November 1967. The Budget of 1968 contained the largest tax increases since 1945, with fiscal policy specifically designed to curb the current-account deficit. Unhappily, the current account's initial response to devaluation was slow. In June 1969 the government and the IMF reached agreement on further measures, with the Letter of Intent referring to a target for domestic credit expansion of £400 million in the 1969–70 fiscal year. In the U.K. context, domestic-credit expansion (DCE) was a new policy indicator, essentially equal to all new bank credit extended to the public and private sectors; DCE to the public sector was equal to the public-sector borrowing requirement (PSBR) minus net sales of public-sector debt to non-banks. A target for DCE implied some sort of limit on the budget deficit and so precluded countercyclical action to lower unemployment.

One result of the IMF's involvement in British macroeconomic policy was to make the PSBR – a cash measure of borrowing, which integrated readily with monetary analysis – the most prominent measure of the budgetary position. This led to a substantial modernization of the lexicon of fiscal policy, but policy itself was certainly not Keynesian. Most Keynesians were scornful of the IMF medicine, on the grounds that it was merely a refurbishment of old sound-finance doctrines. But the current account of the balance of payments was converted, after adoption of the IMF's prescription, from deficit in 1968 to large surplus in 1970. Indeed, a common refrain in 1970 and 1971 was that the fiscal contraction of 1968 had not turned the balance of payments round, whereas the monetary squeeze of 1969 had worked. The effectiveness of fiscal policy was compared unfavorably with that of monetary policy.

Another theme in policy-making circles in the early 1970s was that the U.K.'s poor long-term record on economic growth could be largely blamed on undue anxiety about the balance of payments and the exchange rate. For example, Samuel Brittan argued that a balance-of-payments deficit was a non-problem, since the drain on the U.K.'s foreign-exchange reserves could be halted simply by allowing the exchange rate to float.[23] The editor of an important collection of essays, *The Labour Government's Economic Record 1964–70*, judged in 1972 that, because of the reluctance to devalue the pound earlier, "the Government never achieved any room for manœuvre . . . It is little wonder that they were eventually blown off course."[24]

The intellectual groundwork had been laid for the aggressive expansionism of macroeconomic policy in the two years to mid-1973. Policy-makers were determined that the exchange rate would not be allowed to hold back economic growth. Credit restrictions were relaxed in late 1971, and a highly stimulatory budget was introduced by the chancellor of the exchequer, Mr. Anthony (later Lord) Barber, in March 1972. In response to the inevitable resulting weakness of the pound, the exchange rate was floated in June 1972. In 1973 gross domestic product rose by over 7 percent. But the trend growth rate of the U.K. economy remained much as before, and the "Barber boom" led to severe overheating. Inflation (as measured by the twelve-month increase in the retail-price index) rose to double-digit rates in 1974 and peaked at 26.9 percent in August 1975, while the current account of the balance of payments incurred the heaviest-ever deficits (relative to GDP) in the post-war period.

In the subsequent debates the policy thinking behind the expansionism of the early 1970s was often labeled "Keynesianism." Two years in the early 1970s (from mid-1971 to mid-1973) may indeed have been the only phase in the first three post-war decades – the supposed "Age of Keynes" – when policy was properly Keynesian, uncluttered by the constraints of the fixed exchange rate (as before 1971) or by an entirely different framework of thought (as after the mid-1970s). At the time, the Barber boom was regarded as Keynesian in intention by those who decided policy and as Keynesian in form by the majority of commentators. It was also an unmitigated disaster. The euphoria of 1973 was followed over the next two years by the worst recession, the highest inflation, and the widest payments gap in the second half of the twentieth century.

III.

After some point in the mid-1970s, it no longer makes any sense to describe British macroeconomic policy as "Keynesian." Textual and narrative analysis has to admit that there is scope for debate about whether fiscal policy was Keynesian between 1945 and 1974, but there is no doubt about the period starting in 1979. Policy-makers, official advisers to Treasury ministers, and commentators are all agreed that, after the election of the Conservative government under Mrs. (later Lady) Thatcher, fiscal policy was determined by non-Keynesian considerations.

But that leaves undetermined the precise moment between 1974 and 1979 when fiscal policy-makers consciously and deliberately abandoned Keynesian thinking. Of course, the notion of a "precise moment" is misleading. The attitudes of the key politicians, advisers, and academics were in constant flux. They changed at different times to different degrees and in different ways from one person to another. Mr. Denis (later Lord) Healey, who was chancellor of the exchequer from 1974 to 1979 and took a closer interest in the niceties of economic theory than most chancellors, made a fascinating appraisal in his autobiography, *The Time of My Life*. He found the PSBR so vulnerable to the economic cycle that it was "impossible to get [it] right," which – in his opinion – undermined the heavy emphasis on the PSBR in "the so-called 'budget judgement,' which in turn determined the extent to which taxes or spending should be raised or lowered."[25] But he was also suspicious of dependence on the money supply, as "the monetary statistics are as unreliable as all the others." His response was to become "an eclectic pragmatist."[26] This may sound like a fudge, but it had an important consequence. After noting that when he arrived at the Treasury in 1974 it was still Keynes's intellectual "slave,"

Healey ventured the comment, "I abandoned Keynesianism in 1975."[27]

But the private and retrospective reflections of a chancellor of the exchequer are not the same as the public and transparent passage of events. For most observers 1976 was the crucial turning point. Heavy selling pressure on the foreign exchanges hit the pound in the spring, obliging the government to introduce a package of expenditure cuts and other policy changes. On July 22, Healey announced a target for the growth of the money supply, on the M3 measure (which includes bank deposits), of 12 percent during the 1976–77 fiscal year. It was the first time that a target for monetary growth had been included in an official statement on macroeconomic policy. As the pound remained under pressure in the next few months, the government again sought help from the IMF in late September. The IMF made a loan, but it attached the condition that DCE should not exceed £9 billion in 1976–77, £7.7 billion in 1977–78, and £6 billion in 1978–79. As in the late 1960s, this implied a constraint on the amount of bank credit extended to the public sector and so on the size of the budget deficit. Fiscal policy could not be focused on the management of domestic demand and the maintenance of high employment, because it had to give priority to an externally imposed target.

In the event, the government easily met the IMF's targets, and the pound staged a spectacular recovery in 1977. However, the inflationary trauma and exchange-rate crises of the mid-1970s stimulated drastic rethinking about both the theory and the practice of macroeconomic policy-making. This rethinking has been given the generic brand name of "monetarism." Arguably "monetarism" was – and remains – an even more disparate body of thought than Keynesianism, but the label cannot now be shaken off. In the mid-1970s two central tenets of monetarism were that high inflation was caused by high monetary growth and that targets to restrict monetary growth were therefore the key to controlling inflation. A large budget deficit undermines the task of monetary restraint, because there is a risk that the government will have to finance its deficit from the banking system. In that case the banks add claims on the government to their assets and incur deposit liabilities to the private sector on the other side of the balance sheet. These deposits are money. A target for monetary growth therefore implies some limit on the budget deficit. It needs to be emphasized that the limit is determined by the logic of monetary targeting. The limit applies whether or not the government is borrowing from the IMF, and irrespective of the exchange-rate regime it has adopted (that is, irrespective of whether the exchange rate is fixed or floating).

The potential monetary consequences of excessive budget deficits demonstrate the interdependence of fiscal and monetary policy. If a decline in monetary growth is necessary in order to lower inflation, then cuts in the PSBR are also an essential element in the program. It follows that policy should be expressed in terms of both monetary growth and the fiscal position, and that these should be seen as two sides of the same coin of "financial policy." (In effect, financial policy comprises both monetary and fiscal policy.) Moreover, the U.K.'s inflationary plight in the mid-1970s was such that a rapid deceleration in monetary growth would inevitably cause a severe recession and soaring unemployment. So – for those persuaded by the broad thrust of the monetarist case – it was generally accepted that the reductions in monetary growth and the PSBR should be phased in over a number of years. Official policy should not just look to the next budget and the next year ("the short run"); it should be framed within a three- to five-year context of financial rehabilitation. Here lay the justification for medium-term macroeconomic planning, with the budget deficit geared to restoring medium- and long-run financial stability. Policy should not try to manipulate demand and employment from year to year in a Keynesian manner.[28]

Ideas of this kind were developed particularly among London-based policy-making and policy-advising circles in the crises of the mid-1970s. These circles included the Treasury, the Bank of England, some brokerage firms in the City, and what might be termed "higher economic journalism."[29] The intellectual input from economists in universities outside London was minimal. In fact, most academic economists remained wedded to Keynesianism, a preference that led to sharp debates between the university-based profession and policy-makers in the 1980s. The London Business School played a vital role in promoting the new ideas. James Ball, who joined the staff as professor of economics at its foundation in 1965, had in the previous year published *Inflation and the Theory of Money*. While eclectic in its approach, this book did recognize the relevance of money to inflation outcomes. In a later work, *Money and Employment*, Ball saw many virtues in what he termed "pragmatic monetarism."[30]

In 1977 two of Ball's colleagues, Mr. Terry (later Lord) Burns and Mr. Alan (later Sir Alan) Budd, proposed the adoption of a medium-term financial plan in the London Business School's *Economic Outlook*. In 1979 the same two authors wrote an article in the same publication on "The Role of the PSBR in Controlling the Money Supply." In 1981 a book of *Essays in Fiscal and Monetary Policy* contained a paper by them on "The Relationship between Fiscal and Monetary Policy in the London Business School Model." It made strong claims that "The relationship between fiscal and monetary policy is a very close one, and under a floating exchange rate the prime determinant of monetary variations is changes in fiscal policy" and – even more ambitiously – that "Changes in the monetary aggregates are an 'efficient' estimate of overall policy stance."[31] The paper had originally been given at seminars organized by the Institute for Fiscal Studies in 1977 and 1978.

This emphasis on monetary variables as the best indicators of policy, combined with the coordination of fiscal and monetary policy in a medium-term context, set the scene for the introduction of the Medium-Term Financial Strategy (MTFS). The Thatcher government made clear soon after its election in June 1979 that it saw control of the money supply as necessary and sufficient to curb inflation. It was forthright in its rejection of Keynesian prescriptions. On October 5, 1979, a meeting to discuss medium-term financial planning was held at the Treasury, with Sir Geoffrey (later Lord) Howe, his officials, and a number of outside economists known to be monetarist in their doctrinal affiliations. Sir Frederick Atkinson, of Keynesian leanings, retired in late 1979 and was replaced as head of the Government Economic Service by Terry Burns on January 1, 1980. In the Budget of March 26, 1980, the first version of the MTFS was announced. It set out targets to reduce the PSBR from 3¼ percent of GDP in the 1980–81 fiscal year to 3 percent in 1981–82, 2¼ percent in 1982–83, and 1½ percent in 1983–84, and in parallel gradually to lower the rate of increase in the sterling M3 measure of money.

Two points need to be made about the original MTFS. First, it did not envisage a return to a balanced budget at any date, and its supporters did not appeal to old-fashioned balanced-budget rhetoric to defend their position.[32] Second, the rationale for targeting the PSBR was to support monetary control, which had increasingly been seen in the late 1970s as more fundamental to the macroeconomic outlook than fiscal policy.

The existence of the fiscal targets in the MTFS is crucial to understanding the 1981 Budget, which was the final nail in the coffin of Keynesianism at the policy-making level. The year 1980 had seen the deepest recession in the post-war period, with GDP dropping by almost 2½ percent. In early 1981 output was undoubtedly well beneath its trend level. Meanwhile the pound had been a strong currency for over eighteen months, and there was no external constraint on fiscal relaxation. But the government decided to increase taxes by over £4 billion, equivalent to almost 2 percent of GDP. In the event, the economy began to recover in the middle of 1981, which gave encouragement to the beleaguered policy-makers in Whitehall that they were on the right lines. Despite setbacks in other branches of macroeconomic policy, the government persevered with the fiscal component of the MTFS.

By the mid-1980s the PSBR as a percentage of GDP was down to the levels envisaged in the original MTFS. However, the official rationale for PSBR targeting had changed markedly. In 1980 sterling M3 had grown well above the top of its target range, greatly embarrassing the government, which had at first placed heavy emphasis on this measure of money as the keystone of macroeconomic policy. In response, the target was "quickly abandoned (although not formally) as the government came to recognize [sterling M3's] apparent misleading behaviour."[33] (Given the drastic nature of the *volte-face* on sterling M3, it may be worth mentioning that the DCE target contained in the IMF's Letter of Intent in 1976 was broadly defined. It was equal to the increase in sterling M3 and the banking system's external liabilities; it therefore related to commercial-bank credit and not merely to credit extended by the central bank. Whatever the government's view by 1981, the IMF had certainly thought five years earlier that the behavior of sterling M3 was important.)

With the money supply dethroned, there was no longer any sense in justifying PSBR targets by their contribution to monetary control. Instead the emphasis shifted to such considerations as the need to prevent debt from rising too fast relative to GDP and, more specifically, to avoid an excessive burden of debt interest. The downfall of the monetary argument for fiscal restraint was also attributable in part to evidence from Professor Milton Friedman to the Treasury and Civil Service Committee of the House of Commons. Friedman, universally acknowledged as one of the intellectual founders of monetarism, told the committee that the concern with the PSBR was "unwise," partly "because there is no necessary relation between the size of the PSBR and monetary growth."[34]

The defense of PSBR targeting instead relied increasingly on the need to secure long-run fiscal solvency. An illustration of the new approach was the publication of a Green Paper titled *The Next Ten Years: Public Expenditure and Taxation into the 1990s*, in conjunction with the 1984 Budget. This was the first Budget presented by Mr. Nigel (later Lord) Lawson, who was to remain chancellor until 1989. Paragraph 56 of the Green Paper projected the PSBR/GDP ratio into future years and noted that, "net of debt interest, little or no change in the PSBR is assumed." It continued, "on this basis the tax burden for the non–North Sea sector can be reduced to the extent that public expenditure falls more than North Sea tax revenues as a share of GDP."[35]

This sounds complicated, but the essential message was that any success in controlling non-interest public expenditure would in future be translated into tax cuts. The PSBR/GDP ratio might decline, but only as a consequence of lowering the ratio of debt interest to GDP. The PSBR was intended to drop to 1 percent of GDP by 1993–94, helped by the projection of a sufficiently large decline in the ratio of debt interest to GDP. Separately, Lawson described a situation in which the PSBR was 1 percent of GDP as "the modern equivalent of a balanced Budget."[36] That ratio of the PSBR to GDP had earlier been judged compatible with long-run price stability in a paper published in the London Business School's *Economic Outlook* in 1983.[37]

The 1984 Green Paper was a theoretical document. The results in practice were very different. In the late 1980s the economy experienced a strong and unforeseen boom in activity, which gave the usual cyclical boost to the public finances. The PSBR declined to less than 2 percent of GDP in the 1986–87 fiscal year and turned into a small surplus in 1987–88. In 1988–89 the surplus widened to £14.7 billion, or 3 percent of GDP. The attainment of a surplus in 1987–88 and the extent of the surplus in 1988–89 were not predicted by the Treasury. In the 1988 Budget, Lawson took the unusually benign fiscal performance as an opportunity to reinstate the doctrine of a balanced budget. In his words, "henceforth a zero PSBR will be the norm. This provides a clear and simple rule, with a good historical pedigree."[38]

The aim of balancing the budget (in the sense of keeping the PSBR at zero) over the cycle remained the cornerstone of fiscal policy from the 1988 Budget until the 1997 general election. It was reiterated during the early 1990s, when in a deep recession the government once again incurred heavy deficits. As in the similar circumstances of 1981, the two budgets of 1993 raised taxes sharply in order to restore a satisfactory fiscal position over the medium term. But the official argument for a balanced budget was less strident and ideological, and far more pragmatic, than the case for medium-term PSBR reductions in the early 1980s. As in the Lawson period, it continued to rely on broad notions of stability and solvency. It eschewed Keynesian demand-management considerations and was rather casual about the interdependence of fiscal and monetary restraint. As Burns put it in 1995, now as permanent secretary to the Treasury delivering the South Bank Business School annual lecture,

> Essentially we have two objectives, low inflation and stable public finances. We have two instruments, interest rates and fiscal policy. Both instruments can have an impact on inflation but only fiscal policy can ensure stable public finances on a sustained basis. Intuitively, therefore, it seems clear that monetary policy will bear the main burden of delivering low inflation with fiscal policy taking the burden of delivering sound public finances.

This formulation was rather vague, and later in the lecture Burns conceded that there were "no hard and fast rules" for fiscal policy. But he made one exception: the need to contain "debt service costs and the level of total debt outstanding in a way that avoids being caught in a debt trap where it is only possible to finance debt interest charges by higher levels of borrowing."[39]

No official statement on fiscal policy in the 1980s and 1990s was expressed in terms of the old distinction between above-the-line and below-the-line items. In this respect the principles of sound finance, as they were understood in the closing years of the 1979–97 Conservative government, departed significantly from their counterparts in the inter-war period and, indeed, from more distant Gladstonian precursors. Instead of the aim to achieve balance or surplus above the line, the PSBR was the main benchmark of fiscal policy.

The PSBR had initially been formulated inside the Treasury in the early 1960s, to help in the presentation of financial statistics. Its first major policy applications were in support of the IMF's balance-of-payments objectives in the late 1960s, and again in 1976 and 1977. In the early phase of the Thatcher government, the announcement of a PSBR limit had been intended to buttress monetary restraint. To focus on the PSBR as a means of preventing excessive growth of debt was therefore a significant shift in its pattern of deployment.

These points did not – and do not now – invalidate the PSBR's legitimacy as a target or control variable. The alternatives also have their weaknesses. However, it is interesting to note that, if the old above-the-line/below-the-line distinction had survived, the U.K.'s public finances would have appeared to be in some disarray by the mid-1990s. The PSBR was held down during the Thatcher and Major Conservative administrations not by curbing current spending relative to revenues, but by restricting capital expenditure and taking in money from privatization. While the Treasury and its Conservative political masters acknowledged a long-run solvency constraint on fiscal policy, they defined it in a quite different manner from their predecessors before the supposed "Keynesian revolution."

At any rate, there is little doubt that – certainly since 1979, and perhaps since 1975 or 1976 – fiscal policy was not regarded as "Keynesian" by policy-makers or their key advisers. There was a brief phase in 1979 and 1980 when fiscal policy could be characterized as "monetarist" more than anything else. Later it became subordinate to "sound finance," dressed up in modern terminology but with a rather incoherent rationale. Arguably the Conservatives' zero-PSBR-over-the-cycle maxim was less restrictive of debt than the Treasury's old orthodoxies of the 1930s and 1940s. There were some similarities between the formulations of the 1990s and those earlier orthodoxies, but they were not consciously intended by their proponents. Policy-makers sometimes admitted that they remembered what they were taught at university, namely, that changes in the budget deficit could have significant effects on the level of demand in the economy.[40] But such considerations were secondary, or even tertiary, in actual policy decisions.

IV.

The record of official statements, positions, and speeches is therefore very far from unanimous that fiscal policy was conducted on Keynesian lines even in the period from 1945 to the early 1970s, while it is clear-cut that a marked shift away from Keynesianism occurred in the mid-1970s. But the analysis so far has been literary and textual. Like all such analysis, it has required selection from a wide mass of statements, and it has involved judgments about different actors' tone of voice and their balance of priorities. An alternative approach is to review policy actions in statistical terms, which should put the analysis and conclusions on a more objective plane.

The broad meaning of the phrase "Keynesian fiscal policy" is well known. If fiscal policy is on Keynesian lines, the budget deficit is increased when unemployment is "high" and reduced when it is "low." The statistical test should therefore be designed to answer the question, Did policy-makers vary the deficit directly with the level of unemployment? But a number of different statistical series could be deployed to handle this question. What are the right concepts of "the budget deficit" and "the level of unemployment"?

Several competing notions of the budget deficit are candidates. As already demonstrated, for much of the 1950s and 1960s the Treasury continued to frame budgetary decisions in accordance with the principle that the budget should be balanced "above the line." The above-the-line central-government position is, however, too narrow to serve as a valid indicator of the underlying thrust of fiscal policy. It excludes many capital items and the effect of public corporations' transactions, yet some Keynesians insist that capital spending, particularly capital spending by the nationalized industries, ought to be a prime instrument of countercyclical fiscal policy.[41] On the other hand, the public-sector borrowing requirement, which came to dominate public discussion of fiscal policy from the mid-1970s onwards, is too broad. It is affected by "financial transactions," such as nationalization, privatization, and government lending to industry and for house purchasing. Such transactions do not constitute net injections into or withdrawal from aggregate demand.

According to most authorities, the best compromise between narrow and broad measures of the budgetary position is "the public sector's financial deficit."[42] This covers the entire public sector, but excludes the effect of purely financial transactions. It approximates to the difference between the flow of the public sector's receipts and expenditures, and this difference is usually taken to mean the addition to or subtraction from the circular flow of income which lies at the heart of the Keynesian theory of income determination. A complication is that the public sector's financial deficit both is an influence on and is influenced by the cyclical course of the economy. (Social-security spending rises and falls with unemployment, while tax receipts vary inversely with it.) Discretionary policy action is therefore best understood as and measured by its effect on the cyclically adjusted estimate of the deficit, not on the unadjusted deficit. In the statistical work in the appendix to this essay, fiscal policy decisions are therefore measured by the change in the cyclically adjusted public-sector financial deficit. (Various methods of cyclical adjustment are possible. See the appendix for the method adopted in this essay. Two sets of assumptions are used to obtain two separate estimates of the cyclically adjusted fiscal policy. The estimation of two such series helps in checking whether the conclusions are special and depend on the assumptions, or are more general and robust.)

The identification of the appropriate unemployment variable is also difficult. In the 1950s, "full employment" was widely thought to mean an unemployment rate, measured by the count of benefit claimants as a proportion of the workforce, of under 2 percent.[43] But in the 1970s and 1980s economists stopped thinking about full employment as a single number, while various institutional changes to the structure of the labor market caused an increase in the level of unemployment consistent with a stable rate of price change (the so-called "natural rate of unemployment"). In the late 1980s and the 1990s, the Conservative government's measures to increase labor-market flexibility may have reduced the natural rate. These ambiguities suggest that no long-run series for unemployment is altogether reliable as a guide to the state of the labor market.

A more general measure of activity in the economy is provided by "the output gap," defined as the upwards or downwards deviation of output from its trend and usually expressed as a percentage of that trend.[44] Like assessments of the "fullness" of full employment, calculations of the output gap depend partly on the analyst's methods. But the temptation and opportunity to manipulate the numbers is less with politically neutral GDP figures than with politically charged unemployment statistics. Further, cross-checks can be made among several different techniques for calculating output gaps, which limits the scope for the analyst to impose his own hunches and prejudices. Comparison is also possible with calculations made by, for example, the Organization for Economic Cooperation and Development. (The method of calculating the output gap in this essay is explained in the appendix.)

The discussion so far has pinned down the statistical test more exactly as an attempt to answer the question, Did the cyclically adjusted public-sector financial deficit (PSFD) vary inversely with the output gap? If fiscal policy was Keynesian, the deficit ought to have increased when the level of output was beneath trend and declined when it was above trend. Table 5.1 in the appendix shows the output gap, the unadjusted PSFD/GDP ratio, and both the level and change in the cyclically adjusted PSFD/GDP ratio, estimated on one set of assumptions about the cyclical adjustment, and table 5.2 shows the same categories, but estimated on an alternative set of assumptions about the cyclical adjustment. Table 5.3 compares the numbers used here with separate estimates of the cyclically adjusted PSFD/GDP ratio given by the Treasury. This essay's estimates of the adjusted PSFD/GDP ratio are close both to each other and to the Treasury's figures. Very similar conclusions emerge on both sets of assumptions, with the encouraging implication that they are genuine and not an artefact of the chosen method of cyclical adjustment. Using the first set of numbers (i.e., those in table 5.1), three years (1963, 1976, and 1986) saw hardly any change in fiscal stance, while the output gap itself was close to zero. They can therefore be eliminated from the sample as having no clear message for the matter in contention. Of the remaining forty-three years between 1949 and 1994 there were twenty-two years when the fiscal stance changed in a

Keynesian manner (that is, inversely to the output gap), but twenty-one years when it did not. Keynesian fiscal policy was more common in the period up to 1974 than afterwards, which is consistent with the view that the conduct of fiscal policy changed in the mid-1970s. Fiscal policy was countercyclical in fourteen of the relevant twenty-five years up to 1974 (that is, more than 55 percent of the years), but in only eight of the relevant twenty years from 1975 to 1994 (that is, in 40 percent of the years).

More rigorous econometric tests have also been performed, with the change in the cyclically adjusted PSFD regressed on the level of the output gap. It turns out that in virtually all of the equations – no matter which cyclical-adjustment assumptions or period is chosen – the coefficient on the output gap is not significantly different from zero. In other words, fiscal policy was not "Keynesian," in the usually received sense, in the period from 1949 to 1994 as a whole or in the two sub-periods, 1949 to 1974 and 1975 to 1994. On the face of it, there was no such thing as "the Keynesian revolution." (See the appendix for a fuller statement of these results.)

V.

The great majority of economists – particularly in Britain, but also in the United States and elsewhere – believe that something called "the Keynesian revolution" did happen. There is room for discussion about its precise meaning – for example, on the question of whether "fiscal policy" is best defined as the change or the level of the budget deficit. But the essence of the supposed "revolution" – that, in and after the 1940s, British fiscal policy (however defined) was used countercyclically in order to dampen fluctuations in output and employment, and to maintain a high average level of employment – is well known.

This essay has cast doubt, in the U.K. context, on the historical accuracy of this widely held view. First, it has demonstrated that Britain never had a Keynesian revolution in the usually understood sense. In the thirty years from the 1941 Budget, fiscal policy was not in fact conducted in a Keynesian manner, whatever leading politicians and economists claimed at the time. Much policy thinking in this era certainly was Keynesian, but theory and practice were a long way apart. Second, this essay has tried to describe the shift in policy thinking away from Keynesianism in the mid-1970s. There is little controversy that a shift of some sort occurred, although again its exact nature can be discussed. As has been shown, the government's rationale for action to restrict the PSBR varied over the years. Sometimes the argument relied on a presumed relationship between the budget deficit and monetary growth; at other times it reflected more traditional concerns about the accumulation of excessive debt, which would be expensive to service. But official references to fiscal policy as an instrument for cyclical stabilization were perfunctory or frankly dismissive.

The majority of British academic economists were unsympathetic to the shift in thinking about fiscal policy, with their discontents registered most famously in the letter of 364 economists to *The Times* after the 1981 Budget. The frankness of policy-makers' rejection of Keynesian precepts by the early 1980s ought perhaps to have encouraged these economists to examine the substance of "the Keynesian revolution" with care and skepticism. Whether the official ending of the Keynesian period (if it deserves the title) is dated as happening in 1975, 1976, or 1979, the statistical evidence is that the responsiveness of the budget deficit to the level of economic activity was weak, both before and after the change.

At any one period a great variety of personalities are involved in economic policy-making. As they usually come with different perspectives, it would be naïve to expect them to propound a single monolithic view of policy-making. Moreover, when the period of analysis is extended to a few decades, the cast of personalities changes, and no one canonical statement of theory and practice can bind them all. Keynes was a great man and a benign influence on British economic policy, and it is understandable that British economists should want to pay homage to his *General Theory*. But the substance of policy-makers' actions may have little connection with their advisers' descriptions of strategic intent. More bluntly, what people do may be quite different from what they believe they are doing. The U.K. is the homeland of Keynesian thought, but in the actual conduct of British fiscal policy "the Keynesian revolution" is and always has been an illusion.

STATISTICAL APPENDIX:
TESTING THE KEYNESIAN-REVOLUTION HYPOTHESIS

The author would like to acknowledge the help received from Professor Kent Matthews of Cardiff Business School and Mr. Stewart Robertson, senior economist at Aviva, in the preparation of this statistical appendix, which is, in effect, a joint product of three authors. (Mr. Robertson was working with the author at Lombard Street Research when the estimates were prepared.)

1. Collection and estimation of the data

Estimates of the "output gap" – the difference between the actual level and the trend level of national output expressed as a percentage of trend output – were the first requirement. The actual level of national output was measured by the Office for National Statistics' series for gross domestic product at factor cost in 1990 prices, starting in 1948. Trend output was estimated by assuming that it was determined by the quantity and productivity of inputs of labor and capital. (This is sometimes known as the "production function method," as production is represented as a function of inputs. The relative importance of the two inputs is calculated by assuming that their return is determined by their marginal products and that their share in national output is equal to their quantity multiplied by the return. The income share in national output is assumed also to be their contribution to output. For further discussion, see C. Adams and T. Coe, "A Systems Approach to Estimating the Natural Rate of Unemployment and Potential Output for the U.S.A.," published in the June 1990 *IMF Staff Papers*.)

Data for the labor force and the capital stock were supplied by the Organization for Economic Cooperation and Development from 1963 onwards. A trend rate of growth of "total factor productivity" (that is, the increase in the productivity of the two inputs) was obtained by smoothing the original figures by use of the Hodrick–Prescott filter. The use of the filter generates a potential output series with the characteristic that deviations of actual output from it sum to zero over the period as a whole. (Trend and actual output were equal in 1963. For years before 1963, when the OECD data for the capital stock and labor force were not available, trend output was estimated by taking a moving average.)

The Office for National Statistics publishes a series for the public sector's financial deficit back to 1948. In the text of essay 5 this deficit series was divided by gross domestic product at current market prices and multiplied by 100 to obtain the PSFD as a percentage of GDP. To calculate the change in the deficit/GDP ratio after cyclical adjustment, it was of course necessary to estimate a cyclically adjusted series for the level of the deficit/GDP ratio. As explained in the text, two distinct sets of assumptions were used to estimate this series. In both cases it was assumed that the difference between the actual and cyclically adjusted deficit depended on the output gap, for which a calculated series had already been prepared. (See the previous paragraph for this calculation. If output is beneath trend, tax revenues are also beneath trend, whereas various items of public expenditure, notably social-security expenditure, are above trend.)

The first assumption was that the PSFD was affected by the output gap only in the same year. For the years 1948 to 1979 the cyclically adjusted PSFD/GDP ratio, expressed as a percentage, was lower (higher) than the actual PSFD/GDP ratio by 0.4 percent of GDP for each 1 percent of GDP below (above) trend; for the years from 1980 to 1994 the coefficient was increased from 0.4 to 0.5, to reflect the increased size of the state sector. The second assumption was that the PSFD was affected by the output gap in the current and previous year, because, for example, of delays in tax payments. The coefficients 0.25 and 0.45 were assumed to hold for the first- and second-year effects from 1948 to 1979, while in the period from 1980 to 1994 the coefficients became 0.33 for the first year and 0.7 for the second year. The formula for the calculation was

$$\left(\frac{DEF}{Y}\right)_t = \left(\frac{DEF}{Y}\right)_t^* - aGAP_t - (b-a)GAP_{t-1}$$

where DEF is the deficit, Y is gross domestic product, GAP is the output gap, a and b are the coefficients for the first- and second-year effects, and the asterisk denotes the cyclically adjusted value of the deficit/GDP ratio.

The estimates of the cyclically adjusted deficit/GDP ratio using the first set of assumptions are set out in table 5.1; the estimates using the second set of assumptions are set out in table 5.2. The justification for the sets of assumption used in the cyclical adjustment was provided in two studies. First, Bredenkamp (1988) suggested that the first- and second-year effects on the PSFD (as a percentage of GDP) of a change in GDP relative to trend were 0.25 percent and 0.45 percent of GDP. (See H. Bredenkamp, "The Cyclically Adjusted Deficit as a Measure of Fiscal Policy," Government Economic Working Paper, no. 102, April 1988.) Second, the Treasury updated Bredenkamp's paper in the Winter 1990–91 issue of the *Treasury Bulletin*, in an article titled "Fiscal Developments and the Role of the Cycle," where it increased its estimates of the cyclical sensitivity of public finances and suggested the higher values of the coefficients, 0.33 and 0.7. (A further paper, "Public Finances and the Cycle," was published as Treasury Occasional Paper no. 4 in September 1995.)

The figures for the cyclically adjusted deficit/GDP ratio in the regression work (described below) related to calendar years and, as already noted, extend back to 1948. The Treasury has published its own estimates of the cyclically adjusted PSFD/GDP ratio on a fiscal-year basis from 1963–64 to 1986–87. These estimates are compared with those of the authors in table 5.3. The differences in the estimates are due to revisions to the data, different assumptions about the cyclical-adjustment factor, and different assumptions about the output gap.

2. Statistical relationships between the change in the cyclically adjusted PSFD/GDP ratio and the level of the output gap

As argued in the text, fiscal policy would have been Keynesian if the cyclically adjusted PSFD/GDP ratio had increased when output was beneath trend (that is, when there was a negative "output gap") and decreased when output was above trend. The test is therefore to regress the change in the cyclically adjusted PSFD/GDP ratio on the level of the output gap for both estimates of the PSFD/GDP ratio and for all three time periods, that is, 1948–94, 1948–74, and 1975–94.

i. Regression results using the first estimate of the cyclically adjusted PSFD/GDP *ratio (i.e., the* PSFD *is affected by the output gap in the current year only)*

1948–94

$$DUND_t = 0.03 \ OGAP_t + 0.293 \ DUND_{t-1}$$

$r^2 = 0.074$; only the coefficient on the lagged dependent variable is significant.

Note that here and in the other equations $DUND_t$ is the change in the underlying (that is, cyclically adjusted) public-sector financial deficit (expressed as a percentage of GDP at market prices) and $OGAP_t$ is the output gap as a percentage of potential output. (If the public-sector financial deficit falls from 2.3 percent to 1.6 percent of GDP, then $OGAP_t$ takes a value of 0.7).

1948–74

$$DUND_t = 0.048 \ OGAP_t + 0.358 \ DUND_{t-1}$$

$r^2 = 0.095$; only the coefficient on the lagged dependent variable is significant.

1975–94

$$DUND_t = 0.022 \ OGAP_t + 0.149 \ DUND_{t-1}$$

$r^2 = 0.031$; only the coefficient on the lagged dependent variable is significant.

In none of the three equations for the different periods was the coefficient on the output-gap term significant.

ii. Regression results using the second estimate of the cyclically adjusted PSFD/GDP *ratio (i.e., the* PSFD *is affected by the output gap in the current year and the previous year)*

1948–94

$$DUND_t = 0.112\ OGAP_t + 0.319\ DUND_{t-1}$$

$r^2 = 0.141$; only the coefficient on the lagged dependent variable is significant.

1948–74

$$DUND_t = 0.09\ OGAP_t + 0.448\ DUND_{t-1}$$

$r^2 = 0.163$; only the coefficient on the lagged dependent variable is significant.

1975–94

$$DUND_t = 0.148\ OGAP_t + 0.055\ DUND_{t-1}$$

$r^2 = 0.17$; neither coefficient is significant.

Again, in none of the three equations for the different periods was the coefficient on the output-gap term significant. (It is curious that the six coefficients on the output-gap terms are in fact all positive, whereas they ought to have been negative if policy had been on Keynesian lines. But – as the coefficients are all small and none of them is statistically significant – not too much should be made of this.)

TABLE 5.1
PSFD as a Percentage of GDP I
Both unadjusted and after adjustment according to first set of assumptions described in text

	Output gap as % of trend GDP	PSFD as % of GDP	Cyclically adjusted PSFD/GDP ratio	Cyclical adjustment as % of GDP
1948	−2.6	−2.3	−3.3	1.0
1949	−3.3	−2.5	−3.8	1.3
1950	−1.6	−2.7	−3.3	0.6
1951	−1.3	1.6	1.1	0.5
1952	−3.0	3.5	2.3	1.2
1953	−1.2	4.2	3.7	0.5
1954	0.6	2.4	2.6	−0.2
1955	1.9	2.0	2.8	−0.8
1956	0.5	2.6	2.8	−0.2
1957	−0.3	2.4	2.3	0.1
1958	−2.7	2.0	0.9	1.1
1959	−1.0	2.3	1.9	0.4
1960	1.5	2.7	3.3	−0.6
1961	1.0	2.7	3.1	−0.4
1962	−0.8	2.8	2.4	0.4
1963	0.0	2.7	2.7	0.0
1964	2.1	2.8	3.6	−0.8
1965	1.5	2.2	2.8	−0.6
1966	0.3	2.2	2.3	−0.1
1967	−0.7	3.6	3.3	0.3
1968	0.8	2.1	2.4	−0.3
1969	0.6	−1.0	−0.8	−0.2
1970	0.1	−1.3	−1.3	0.0
1971	−0.6	0.6	0.3	0.3
1972	0.0	2.4	2.4	0.0
1973	5.2	3.7	5.8	−2.1
1974	1.8	5.6	6.4	−0.8
1975	−0.7	7.2	6.9	0.3
1976	0.2	6.7	6.8	−0.1
1977	1.1	4.2	4.6	−0.4
1978	2.3	5.0	5.9	−0.9
1979	2.1	4.4	5.2	−0.8
1980	−1.7	4.5	3.8	0.7
1981	−4.8	3.1	0.7	2.4
1982	−5.2	2.7	0.2	2.5
1983	−3.7	3.4	1.6	1.8
1984	−3.9	4.0	2.0	2.0
1985	−2.0	2.9	1.8	1.1
1986	−0.1	2.1	2.0	0.1
1987	2.2	1.1	2.2	−1.1
1988	5.0	−1.4	1.1	−2.5
1989	5.3	−1.0	1.7	−2.7
1990	3.8	0.3	2.2	−1.9
1991	−0.3	2.5	2.3	0.2
1992	−3.3	6.3	4.6	1.7
1993	−3.9	7.6	5.7	1.9
1994	−3.0	6.6	5.1	1.5

Source: Office for National Statistics (ONS); and see text.

TABLE 5.2
PSFD AS A PERCENTAGE OF GDP II
Both unadjusted and after adjustment according to second set of assumptions described in text

	Output gap as % of trend GDP	PSFD as % of GDP	Cyclically adjusted PSFD/GDP ratio	Cyclical adjustment as % of GDP
1948	−2.6	−2.3	−2.9	0.6
1949	−3.3	−2.5	−3.8	1.3
1950	−1.6	−2.7	−3.7	1.0
1951	−1.3	1.6	1.0	0.6
1952	−3.0	3.5	2.5	1.0
1953	−1.2	4.2	3.3	0.9
1954	0.6	2.4	2.3	0.1
1955	1.9	2.0	2.6	−0.6
1956	0.5	2.6	3.1	−0.5
1957	−0.3	2.4	2.5	−0.1
1958	−2.7	2.0	1.2	0.8
1959	−1.0	2.3	1.5	0.8
1960	1.5	2.7	2.9	−0.2
1961	1.0	2.7	3.3	−0.6
1962	−0.8	2.8	2.8	0.0
1963	0.0	2.7	2.7	0.0
1964	2.1	2.8	3.3	−0.5
1965	1.5	2.2	3.0	−0.8
1966	0.3	2.2	2.6	−0.4
1967	−0.7	3.6	3.4	0.2
1968	0.8	2.1	2.2	−0.1
1969	0.6	−1.0	−0.7	−0.3
1970	0.1	−1.3	−1.2	−0.1
1971	−0.6	0.6	0.4	0.2
1972	0.0	2.4	2.3	0.1
1973	5.2	3.7	5.0	−1.3
1974	1.8	5.6	7.1	−1.5
1975	−0.7	7.2	7.4	−0.2
1976	0.2	6.7	6.7	0.0
1977	1.1	4.2	4.5	−0.3
1978	2.3	5.0	5.8	−0.8
1979	2.1	4.4	5.4	−1.0
1980	−1.7	4.5	4.7	−0.2
1981	−4.8	3.1	0.9	2.2
1982	−5.2	2.7	−0.7	3.4
1983	−3.7	3.4	0.3	3.1
1984	−3.9	4.0	1.3	2.7
1985	−2.0	2.9	0.7	2.2
1986	−0.1	2.1	1.3	0.8
1987	2.2	1.1	1.8	−0.7
1988	5.0	−1.4	1.1	−2.5
1989	5.3	−1.0	2.6	−3.6
1990	3.8	0.3	3.6	−3.3
1991	−0.3	2.5	3.8	−1.3
1992	−3.3	6.3	5.1	1.2
1993	−3.9	7.6	5.1	2.5
1994	−3.0	6.6	4.2	2.4

Source: Office for National Statistics (ONS); and see text.

TABLE 5.3
PSFD ESTIMATES USED IN ESSAY
COMPARED WITH THE TREASURY'S OWN ESTIMATES
All figures are % of GDP.

Year	Treasury unadjusted	Treasury cyclically adjusted	ONS unadjusted	Adjusted by first set of assumptions	Adjusted by second set of assumptions
1963–64	3.3	3.0	2.7	2.9	2.9
1964–65	2.3	2.8	2.7	3.4	3.2
1965–66	1.7	2.1	2.2	2.7	2.9
1966–67	2.6	2.6	2.6	2.6	2.8
1967–68	4.2	4.6	3.2	3.1	3.1
1968–69	0.8	0.9	1.3	1.6	1.5
1969–70	–1.7	–1.5	–1.2	–0.9	–0.8
1970–71	–0.4	–0.4	–0.8	–0.8	–0.8
1971–72	1.1	1.1	1.1	0.8	0.9
1972–73	3.0	2.8	2.8	3.3	3.0
1973–74	4.6	5.5	4.2	6.0	5.5
1974–75	6.7	7.4	6.0	6.5	7.2
1975–76	7.3	6.8	7.1	6.9	7.2
1976–77	5.7	5.1	6.1	6.3	6.2
1977–78	4.4	4.2	4.4	4.9	4.8
1978–79	4.8	5.1	4.9	5.7	5.7
1979–80	3.9	4.9	4.4	4.9	5.2
1980–81	5.0	5.2	4.2	3.0	3.8
1981–82	2.0	1.2	3.0	0.6	0.5
1982–83	2.9	2.3	3.0	0.6	–0.5
1983–84	3.7	3.5	3.6	1.7	0.6
1984–85	4.0	3.8	3.7	2.0	1.2
1985–86	2.3	2.1	2.7	1.9	0.9
1986–87	2.5	2.4	1.9	2.1	1.4

Source: *Office for National Statistics (ONS); and see text.*

ESSAY 6

KEYNESIANISM, MONETARISM, AND TWO CONCEPTS OF THE OUTPUT GAP

THE CONCEPT of the "output gap" is among the most prominent in modern macroeconomics. The relationship between inflation and the output gap is one of the three equations in the so-called "New Consensus Macroeconomics," while central banks, finance ministries, and private forecasting units devote considerable effort to the gap's measurement. (As discussed in the introduction, the three-equation system is sometimes also called "New Keynesianism," but the legitimacy of the label is questioned later in this essay.) It may therefore seem surprising to propose that the gap takes two distinct forms and that the two notions originate in rival systems of thought. However, that will be the contention of the present essay. To anticipate and simplify, one concept of the gap was first advanced by Okun in 1962 and may be termed "Keynesian," whereas the alternative concept stems from Friedman's presidential address to the American Economic Association in 1967 and may be regarded as "monetarist." The argument here will be that over time the monetarist concept of the gap has ousted the Keynesian and that the consequent refurbishment of economists' understanding of the "gap" made a vital contribution to the so-called "Great Moderation."

I.

In his 1936 *General Theory of Employment, Interest, and Money*, Keynes ventured a number of remarks on the relationship between the level of unemployment and the rate of wage inflation, and (as will emerge shortly) these are pertinent to the evolution of thinking about the output gap.[1] But the remarks were not central to Keynes's purpose, and the first extensive discussion of the topic, with supporting statistics, came in A.W. Phillips's 1958 paper in *Economica* on "The Relation between Unemployment and the Rate of Change of Money Wage Rates in the U.K., 1861–1957." As is well known, this paper's summary of almost a century of experience was that the rate of change of wages was inversely related to the level of unemployment. An essential attribute of the resulting "Phillips curve" was that, although the rate of change of wages varied with the unemployment rate, the rate of change of wages was stable at *any* particular unemployment rate.

A.W. ("Bill") Phillips was a professor at the London School of Economics when he collected the data from which his curve was derived. One of his colleagues at the LSE, Frank Paish, saw that the ideas could be generalized from the labor market to the whole economy. A 1961 paper titled "Output, Inflation, and Growth" appeared in Paish's 1962 collection *Studies in an Inflationary Economy* and included a theoretical section which referred in a footnote to Phillips's work. This section noted that

> The most important factor in determining the rate of rise in money wages is the proportion of productive capacity currently employed. If we accept this assumption, it follows that ... there must be a margin of unused capacity at which money incomes will rise at an annual rate equal to that of the growth of productive capacity. If the margin of unused capacity can be permanently stabilised at just this level ... we have ... the necessary conditions for long-term price stability.[2]

Paish went on to differentiate between short-term and long-term pressures on inflation, and noted one perhaps surprising possibility. This was that – because of lags in the inflationary process – demand expansion might reduce the margin of unused capacity beneath that associated with price stability in the long run and yet still be associated with stable prices in the short run. In his words, any equivalence "between a rise in incomes and a rise in output obtained by reducing the margin of unused capacity below the long-term equilibrium level is inevitably unstable and temporary."[3] This might sound like an anticipation of Friedman's 1967 presidential address, but that interpretation is not jus-tified by the rest of Paish's paper.

Although Paish's "margin of unused capacity" is indeed a concept of the output gap, he was writing within the confines of the Phillips-curve framework. He believed that in the long run, after all the lags had worked their way through the system, there was a stable relationship between the rate of inflation and the margin of unused capacity. Paish's work nevertheless deserves more attention than it has received. In par-ticular, Paish noticed in the U.K. context the phenomenon on which Okun was soon to place so much emphasis on the other side of the Atlantic. After drawing a graph with one axis showing the percentage of capacity utilized and the other axis the percentage of the labor force employed in the 1951–55 period, he said:

> It is at once clear that the fluctuations in the employment of labour are very much smaller than in the employment of total capacity, and in [the graph he had drawn] the labour employ-ment percentages are given on a scale five times as large as that used for the percentages of total capacity employed.[4]

However, he doubted that the five-to-one ratio would "hold good indef-initely as unemployment rises." In fact, one of his key conclusions was that price stability could be maintained only with a margin of unused capacity of 5 to 7 percent, "corresponding to between 2 and 2½ percent of unemployment," which he took to be in accordance with "Professor Phillips's estimate that just over 2 percent of unemployment is consis-tent with a rise in wage-rates of 2½ percent a year."[5] The lowness of the unemployment rate on which policy-makers might safely concen-trate their attention may seem extraordinary by later standards.

II.

American economists recognized the significance of Phillips's work soon after its publication. For example, Samuelson saw its relevance to what he, and others with Keynesian inclinations, regarded as the key policy problem facing the newly elected President Kennedy in January 1961. This problem was to assess how much fiscal stimulus might be administered in order "to get the economy moving" without raising inflation too much.[6] But – as in the U.K. – there was a case for analyzing the determination of inflation within the context of product markets and not merely that of the labor market.

In 1962, Arthur Okun published his analysis of "Potential GNP: Its Measurement and Significance" in the American Statistical Association's *Proceedings*. This analysis proposed a concept of "the GNP gap," which was obtained by distinguishing between potential and actual GNP. In Okun's words, "Potential GNP is a supply concept, a measure of productive capacity." Nevertheless, "it is not a measure of how much output could be generated by unlimited amounts of aggregate demand. . . . The full employment goal must be understood as a striving for maximum production without inflationary pressure." Potential output differs from actual output because aggregate demand may not be sufficient to deliver full employment. It follows that "If, in fact, aggregate demand is lower, part of potential GNP is not produced; there is unrealized potential or a 'gap' between actual and potential."[7] Without any particularly clear rationale in the paper itself, Okun selected an unemployment rate of 4 percent as that associated with full employment.[8] He said that potential output could be observed only at this unemployment rate and that it had otherwise to be estimated. Indeed, he used the word "leap" to describe three possible methods of using information on the size of the labor force to arrive at a series for potential output. At any rate, his own "subjectively weighted average of the relevant coefficients" from all three methods was 3.2, so that (with P denoting potential output, A actual output, and U actual unemployment)

$$P = A \left[1 + 0.032 \left(U - 4 \right) \right].$$

This equation was quickly baptized "Okun's law." Okun saw his work as helping to quantify the parameters for an expansionary fiscal policy. The "law" and the related notion of "the GNP gap" had immense influence over U.S. policy-making in the following decade.[9]

Plainly, Okun's definition of the gap allowed it to take only positive values (i.e., it was mono-directional), as the values of the gap increased with the rate of unemployment.[10] At full employment, inflation might be high, but – because of the properties of the Phillips curve – it would be stable. Implicitly, over-full employment was to be avoided as too inflationary. Nevertheless, the purpose of Okun's work was not the stabilization of inflation at a low rate. Instead its aim was to specify the appropriate fiscal policy for the maximization of employment, subject to the side constraint that inflation should not be excessive. With the short-run elasticity of output with respect to employment taking a value of 3, any shortfall in employment beneath full employment was deemed hugely costly in terms of lost output. In 1965 a book of papers titled *The Battle against Unemployment*, edited by Okun, was published in New York. As it included a prologue by President Kennedy, most of the papers must have been written two or more years earlier. In his own contribution, Okun deployed his law to justify a high pressure of demand. To quote,

> ... if we are to meet our targets of full utilization, we need expansionary measures that are large in relation to excess unemployment. ... [T]he demand for goods and services must rise relatively about three times as much as we can expect unemployment to fall.

In the same volume, James Tobin, looking forward to "The Tax-Cut Harvest" – as his paper was titled – noted that the difference between an unemployment rate of 5½ percent of the labor force and a rate of 4 percent "corresponds to a deficiency of ... 5 percent in total national spending for goods and services," a calculation that obviously appealed to Okun's law.[11]

The fact that, in Okun's own work, his gap took only positive values – or, in a phrase, the mono-directionality of the Okun "GNP gap" – recalled the structure of Keynes's argument in *The General Theory*. The analytical core of *The General Theory* was in books II to IV, in which the wage-unit (i.e., wages per worker) was assumed to be constant. With this assumption in place, an increase in aggregate demand led to the same proportionate increase in employment. This was a useful simplification for any theory intended to determine the level of employment. For example, it enabled Keynes to say that the effect of a rise in the quantity of money was to reduce the rate of interest and stimulate investment. He could postpone until book V the awkward possibility that a rise in the quantity of money might affect the wage-unit *and* the price level.

Okun, Tobin, and Samuelson did not see the GNP gap in exactly the same way as Keynes. The *General Theory* model applied to the Marshallian short run, with the capital stock given, and was expressed in terms of levels (i.e., the quantity of money affected the rate of interest and the price level), whereas Okun and his contemporaries were prescribing for a growing economy and thought in terms of rates of change. In particular, they viewed different rates of inflation, not different price levels, as being associated with differing degrees of demand intensity. But, because they viewed inflation as stable at any particular degree of demand intensity and any particular level of the GNP gap, the question of the determination of inflation was secondary in their thinking, in just the same way that the determination of the wage-unit was secondary in books II to IV of *The General Theory*.

In book V of *The General Theory* Keynes accepted that, once unemployment falls beneath a "critical level," an increase in the quantity of "effective demand produces no further increase in output and entirely spends itself on an increase in the cost-unit fully proportionate to the increase in effective demand."[12] A cut-off point is implied, between a zone of spare capacity in which the existence of unemployment allows extra demand to boost employment and output, and a zone of full employment in which extra demand affects only prices. An abrupt cut-off point on these lines is analytically consistent with the mono-directionality of the Okun gap. As in Keynes's book V, the gap applies to the zone of spare capacity and not to the zone of full employment. (Keynes acknowledged that the model of *The General Theory* contained an "asymmetry" between inflation and deflation, and even that there was, "perhaps, something a little perplexing" in it.[13])

In short, the Okun GNP gap was a construct that made sense when policy-makers believed in a stable trade-off between inflation and unemployment (i.e., a Phillips curve) and in a direct responsiveness of employment to demand (i.e., as described in books II to IV of *The General Theory*). The Okun GNP-gap concept can be fairly characterized as "Keynesian" in origin.

* * *

III.

In the 1960s and 1970s most of the criticism of Okun's work was directed at the value of the coefficient in his output/employment relationship. One such paper, "Economic Growth and Unemployment: A Reappraisal of the Conventional View" by John Tatom in the October 1978 *Federal Reserve Bank of St. Louis Review*, used the phrase "the output gap" in preference to Okun's "GNP gap."[14] But the main purpose of Tatom's paper was statistical, with the central conclusion being that the unemployment rate was more responsive to the growth of output and demand than Okun had allowed. Tatom did not question the conceptual validity of the Okun framework.

The fundamental theoretical challenge had in fact come earlier, from Friedman's 1967 presidential address to the American Economic Association and the related paper by Edmund Phelps. These two contributions together called into question the stability of the inflation/unemployment trade-off enshrined in the Phillips curve.[15] Their punch-line was that the rate of wage increases was stable at one, and only one, rate of unemployment, which Friedman termed "the natural rate." If unemployment were held beneath the natural rate, the entrenchment of expectations of rising prices in pay bargaining would cause inflation to accelerate without limit. The Friedman and Phelps critiques of the Phillips curve had clear significance for analysis of the labor market, and the threat to the viability of full employment as a policy target was soon understood. However, the extension of the ideas to the entire economy took surprisingly long. Whereas Paish and Okun had translated the Phillips-curve ideas into a whole-economy gap concept in little more than three years, the development of the whole-economy gap concept implied in the Friedman and Phelps contributions took over a decade.

At the Brookings Institution, economists continued to calculate a GNP gap, using much the same methods as Okun, through the 1970s. The main technical advance was to estimate the gap using a multi-factor production function instead of the single-factor output/employment relationship in Okun's 1962 paper. Perhaps because of the structure of the Okun approach, with the mono-directionality of its values, calculations of the gap in the 1970s invariably found that output was beneath its potential. At a conference organized by Brookings in April 1977, George Perry gave a paper on "Potential Output and Productivity," and accompanied it with a call for large-scale fiscal stimulus. Perry's paper was heavily criticized in separate comments by Robert Gordon and Michael Wachter as over-estimating the margin of spare capacity in the economy and, in Wachter's words, as having "major inflationary risks."[16] (In 1978 Okun and Perry were joint editors of a collection of papers, published by Brookings, with the title *Curing Chronic Inflation*. The change in emphasis from the title of Okun's 1965 book, *The Battle against Unemployment*, in itself speaks volumes.[17])

A year later, at the Carnegie-Rochester conference on public policy in April 1978, Wachter was joined by Jeffrey Perloff in the presentation of a paper on "A Production Function–Nonaccelerating Inflation Approach to Potential Output: Is Measured Potential Output Too High?" Perloff and Wachter went to some lengths to claim that they were working in the Okun tradition, saying in the main text that his 1962 paper "stated that potential output should be defined in terms of nonaccelerating inflation" and repeating the remark in a footnote. In fact, the Perloff and Wachter paper was a radical departure. They defined potential output as "that output which society could produce with the labor supply which is consistent with nonaccelerating rates of inflation. Thus, to provide estimates of potential output we need, besides the aggregate production function, an equation which determines the natural rate [of unemployment, denoted as U^*]."[18]

Perloff and Wachter proposed three ways of calculating U^*, which they also referred to as "equilibrium unemployment," and they tried out no fewer than six types of production function. The wide-ranging, rather diffuse character of the Perloff and Wachter paper may have been partly responsible for its later neglect. At any rate, it rejected – quite explicitly – the results of earlier work in the area. Previous estimates of potential output were, in their judgment, "almost certainly higher than the nonaccelerating inflation rate of potential output." After all it was "difficult to reconcile accelerating inflation between 1965 and 1977 with an estimated potential which shows deep and long periods of excess supply and shallow and brief periods of excess demand." In addition to the criticism of the inflationary dangers of the existing body of analysis, the Perloff and Wachter paper foreshadowed

later approaches by noting that their series "generates the kind of alter-
nating supply and demand gaps that could be consistent with periods
of rising and falling inflation."[19] Earlier studies had fitted trend lines
that tended "to hit only the peaks of the actual output series." The clear
suggestion was that calculations of the gap should not take only positive values and be mono-directional, but should take both positive and
negative values, and so be bi-directional. However, Perloff and Wachter
were loyal to Okun in one sense. They took positive values of the gap to
denote beneath-potential levels of output, just as he had done.

The Perloff and Wachter paper provoked two immediate sharp
responses. In his contribution to the 1978 Carnegie-Rochester conference, Gordon praised their contribution as "innovative," but disputed
that the association of potential output with non-accelerating inflation
had roots in Okun's work. In the early 1960s there was – in Gordon's
words – "no natural rate hypothesis." Instead, "the stable Phillips trade-
off curve reigned supreme." Indeed Gordon deprecated Okun's selection of 4 percent unemployment as "full employment," since this was
"entirely arbitrary." Gordon further remarked that the hypothesis of a
natural rate of unemployment, which he took to be 5½ percent in the
U.S., constituted a "macroeconomic revolution." He also found the use
of the phrase "potential output" misleading, since in the Perloff and
Wachter framework potential output was not a ceiling imposed by the
technical ability to produce. He suggested a different phraseology: that
the level of output associated with neither rising nor falling inflation
should be called the "natural rate of output."[20]

The second significant critique at the 1978 conference came from
Charles Plosser and G. W. Schwert. Neither Perloff and Wachter nor
Gordon used the phrase "output gap" in their published contributions.
But – in addition to commenting on some methodological weaknesses
in the Perloff and Wachter paper – Plosser and Schwert both used the
phrase and appreciated its ambiguity. To quote, the Okun approach
produces "an 'output gap' which is always positive, implying a contin-
ual need for stimulative government policies," whereas the new Perloff
and Wachter approach "implies that the 'output gap' can be both positive and negative." Plosser and Schwert also attacked Okun's law as
"infamous" and suggested that the short-run elasticity of output with

TABLE 6.1
TWO DIFFERENT CONCEPTS
OF THE OUTPUT GAP

This table shows values for the "output gap" implied by the two different approaches to its estimation. The short-run elasticity of output with respect to employment is assumed to be 3 in the Keynesian concept and 2 in the alternative, "monetarist" concept. High levels of employment are associated with negative values of the gap, as in Perloff and Wachter 1979, but the numbering scheme was inverted in later work.

Unemployment rate, as % of workforce	Keynesian concept of the output gap, originating in Okun 1962	Monetarist concept of the output gap, with roots in Friedman 1967, but first developed in Perloff and Wachter 1979
4	0.0	−3
4½	1.6	−2
5	3.2	−1
5½	4.8	0
6	6.4	1
6½	8.0	2
7	9.6	3

respect to unemployment was much lower than Okun claimed, perhaps having a value of only 2.[21]

One final comment needs to be made on the proceedings of the 1978 Carnegie-Rochester conference. There is little question that the Perloff and Wachter paper pointed towards a radical shift in thinking and terminology about the relationship between demand pressure and inflation. Gordon straightaway saw that this shift was a generalization of the natural-rate hypothesis, and Plosser and Schwert remarked that two distinct concepts of the output gap were implied. But not one of the conference participants referred to Friedman's 1967 presidential address.[22] Arguably, the obvious affinity between the natural-rate hypothesis and the new understanding of the gap justifies terming it a "monetarist" gap concept. Table 6.1 illustrates how – in the setting of the United States in the 1960s and 1970s – the two approaches would generate different values of the gap for the same unemployment rate.

IV.

In the 1960s and 1970s the Okun-originated (or Keynesian) concept of the output gap was estimated, in particular, by economists linked with the United States' Council of Economic Advisers and the Brookings Institution. By contrast, in the 1980s, work on the Friedman-originated (or monetarist) concept of the gap was centered in leading supranational institutions, particularly the International Monetary Fund and the Organization for Economic Cooperation and Development. A fair comment is that in both locales the task of estimation was carried out almost entirely by practitioner economists and not by economists affiliated with universities. Typically a policy prescription was implied by the estimates. The rise in inflation during the 1960s and 1970s had caused widespread disillusionment with "full employment" policies. Two important advantages of the monetarist concept of the output gap were that it helped to quantify both the degree of demand restraint needed to curb inflation, and the likely consequences for unemployment and lost output. Officials at the IMF and the OECD had regularly to prepare assessments of the future course of inflation, output, and unemployment in many countries. They found from experience that what has been termed here the monetarist concept of the gap was useful in their work. They dropped estimation procedures based on Okun's 1962 paper. The eventual result was that the monetarist concept of the output gap superseded the Keynesian and has now become dominant.

In 1987, three economists at the IMF published a paper on "Potential Output in Major Industrial Countries" in the IMF's *Staff Studies for the World Economic Outlook*. These authors, Charles Adams, P. R. Fenton, and Flemming Larsen, acknowledged that the Perloff and Wachter paper was the basis of their methodology.[23] One of these authors, Charles Adams, also contributed to an October 1989 paper in the IMF Working Paper series on "A Systems Approach to Estimating the Natural Rate of Unemployment and Potential Output for the United States."[24] The replacement of the full-employment rate of unemployment by the natural rate of unemployment as the fulcrum of the analysis is clear. The OECD – like the IMF with its *World Economic Outlook* – has to produce regular documents on the international economic prospect. In the words of the IMF's 1987 staff study, "the Fund's need for economy-wide estimates of potential output should be seen in the light of its surveillance function."[25] At some point in the late 1980s the teams at the IMF and the OECD started to exchange information and data. In May 1989 Raymond Torres and John Martin published "Measuring Potential Output in the Seven Major OECD Countries" in the OECD Working Paper series, and expressed thanks to Adams, Fenton, and Larsen "for supplying us with the IMF data on output gaps."[26]

Several more papers in this area of macroeconomics were published under IMF and OECD auspices in the early 1990s. Finally, the June 1995 issue of the OECD's *Economic Outlook* contained an annex table 11 on "Output Gaps," with data from 1980 to 1994 (and projections to 1995 and 1996) for twenty OECD countries. The numbers were drawn from a paper by four authors in the first 1995 issue of the OECD's *Economic Studies*. According to the notes on sources and methods in the June 1995 *Economic Outlook*,

> The output gap is measured as the percentage difference between actual GDP in constant prices, and estimated potential GDP. The latter is based on a production function approach . . . and underlying non-accelerating wage rates of unemployment or the NAWRU for each member country. It should be stressed that the estimated levels of potential are subject to significant margins of error.[27]

The only significant difference in presentation from the Perloff and Wachter paper of 1979 was in the system of numbering. Perloff and Wachter claimed – very debatably, according to the analysis in this essay – to be working in the Okun tradition. They therefore had positive values of the gap for unemployment levels higher than the natural rate of unemployment. The approach is counterintuitive, in that high levels of demand intensity and utilization have a negative output-gap value, and low levels a positive value. The OECD kept the bi-directional system of numbering, but inverted it. So in its paper above-potential output was associated with a positive value of the output gap and beneath-potential output with a negative value. The data now produced regularly in the OECD's *Economic Outlook* are probably used by several hundred economists around the world. As they have become the most quoted estimates of the output gap, the OECD has acted as a kind of Académie Française to the economics profession. Its definition of the gap is increasingly recognized as standard.[28]

Output-gap estimation in a policy-making environment can be very difficult. To estimate the gap at present it is necessary to have at least three reliable figures,

(1) the level of the gap in the recent past,

(2) the actual rate of growth of output in the latest period (or periods), and

(3) an understanding of the trend rate of growth also in the latest period (or periods).

In practice, analysts rarely agree on any of these three numbers. One way of overcoming the problems has been to harness business-survey information in an attempt to quantify the gap. A typical procedure is to compare historical series of the output gap with those for labor shortages and capacity utilization in business surveys, and so obtain benchmark values of survey answers associated with the potential level of output (or "the natural rate of output," in Gordon's terminology). As business surveys are published with hardly any lag at all, the latest values of the answers to labor-shortage and capacity-utilization questions provide a quick-and-dirty, but quite reliable, guide to the output gap.

The cross-checking of business-survey series against output-gap estimates based on the national accounts was not possible in most industrial countries in the 1950s, because most business surveys started after the Second World War and had had only a short life. Not much significance could be attached to the numbers. But by the 1980s the business surveys typically had been in existence for over twenty or even thirty years, and satisfactory levels of statistical significance were achieved when their data were compared with other macroeconomic information. In the United States the Federal Reserve started preparing a series on capacity utilization in 1967, and it gradually became recognized among analysts that a capacity-utilization level of about 81 to 83 percent was associated with stable inflation. Business economists and investment analysts also paid close attention to the monthly numbers in the National Association of Purchasing Managers' intentions survey, which was found from experience to be a good guide to the current state of the economy. Similar developments occurred in other countries. In the U.K., the Confederation of British Industry introduced a survey in 1958, but most of the series date from 1961 or later. Every quarter, questions about the intensity of labor shortages and plant capacity utilization are asked, and over time it has become possible to obtain benchmarks of the economy's "normal" degree of operation.[29] In Germany the IFO survey, conducted by the Institut für Wirtschaftsforschung in Munich, has served a similar purpose, also since the 1950s.

Nowadays a monthly survey of business intentions and experience, called the "PMI" (or "purchasing managers' index") is released by NTC Publications Ltd. for all the major economies. The PMI results often have an important effect on financial markets, because they often anticipate accurately the data in government-based statistical releases. At any rate, once a long series of business-survey results is available, it is a simple matter to work out which values of machine capacity and labor shortages are associated with an output gap of approximately zero. The calculation of the gap from official GDP and other statistics is still necessary for completeness, but business-survey results are timelier and easier to interpret than national-accounts data. The abundance of business-survey information today is in marked contrast to the situation in the 1950s and even the 1960s. The techniques of estimating the output gap from business-survey data are similar to those used in business-cycle identification, as pioneered by Arthur Burns and Wesley Mitchell in their work for the National Bureau of Economic Research.[30]

V.

This account so far demonstrates that by the early 1990s approaches for estimating the output gap were being increasingly standardized on the monetarist, natural-rate-based definition at the two international organizations that are leaders in the preparation of economic data, the

IMF and the OECD. Further, attempts were being made in many countries to relate output-gap estimates to business-survey information. Such attempts may have started in the survey organizations themselves, but they spread quickly to financial markets.[31] Because of the sensitivity of securities prices to movements in central-bank interest rates, and because central banks were known to react to actual and expected deviations of output from its trend level, financial institutions devoted large resources to the calculation of output gaps, the comparison of output-gap estimates with business-survey results, and the preparation of composite leading-indicator series for economic activity.[32]

The next two stages in the absorption of the natural-rate-based output-gap concept into the analytical bloodstream of economics were agreement on the concept's meaning at academic conferences, and frequent mentions in government and central-bank documents. On the first of these, the usual reference in academic literature to the endorsement of the output-gap idea is to John Taylor's 1993 paper on "Discretion versus Policy Rules in Practice," published in the Carnegie-Rochester Conference Series on Public Policy.[33] Taylor's paper proposed a central-bank reaction function with the key property that nominal interest rates were adjusted proportionately more than any change in inflation. The deviation of real GDP from "a target" was one term in his "quite straightforward" policy rule.[34] In the paragraphs surrounding the statement of his rule, Taylor clearly intended that "trend GDP" was to be the "target" notion of GDP. But he neither used the phrase "the output gap" nor made any general statement about the relationship between departures of output from trend and either the level or the change in inflation.

However, Taylor's paper did stimulate a large body of work in which the monetarist version of the gap was vital. A conference in the Florida Keys was held under the auspices of the National Bureau of Economic Research to bring together the various researchers, and its proceedings were edited by Taylor and published in 1999 in a book titled *Monetary Policy Rules*. In their paper on "Performance of Operational Policy Rules in an Estimated Semiclassical Structural Model," Bennett McCallum and Edward Nelson were concerned to ensure that their account of price-level adjustment, including the concept of the output gap embedded in it, was consistent with the natural-rate hypothesis. Two papers in the *Monetary Policy Rules* volume – one by Glenn D. Rudebusch and Lars E. O. Svensson, and the other by three economists at the Federal Reserve Board (Andrew Levin, Volker Wieland, and John C. Williams) – appealed to the natural-rate framework and used the associated concept of the output gap.[35]

The Levin, Wieland, and Williams paper also concluded that, "even in large models with hundreds of state variables, three variables (the current output gap, the current four-quarter average inflation rate, and the lagged funds rate) summarize nearly all the information relevant to setting the federal funds rate efficiently."[36] This was provocative, not least because it implied that the American central bank did not need to rely on money-supply data to make decisions on interest rates. The suggestion that policy-makers had the option to dispense with information on the money supply was in itself anti-monetarist, even though Levin, Wieland, and Williams endorsed an output-gap concept that pivoted on the natural rate of unemployment. Shortly afterwards, Richard Clarida, Jordi Gali, and Mark Gertler published their classic paper, "The Science of Monetary Policy: A New Keynesian Perspective," in the December 1999 issue of the *Journal of Economic Literature*. Its opening paragraph acknowledged that Taylor's rule for interest-rate setting was part of the motivation for their work, while the paper later said that its aim was to develop an avowedly "simple" macroeconomic framework. The framework set out the three equations of the New Consensus Macroeconomics, which were discussed in the first paragraph of this essay. The authors' justification for appending "New Keynesian" to the paper's title was that "we wish to make clear that we adopt the Keynesian approach of stressing nominal price rigidities, but at the same time base our analysis on frameworks that incorporate recent methodological advances in macroeconomic modeling (hence the term 'New')."[37] By this means the Keynesian label was attached to a set of ideas in which the natural-rate-based concept of the output gap was crucial.

The use of the phrase "New Keynesianism" to describe the now dominant approach to central-bank decision-making has become a commonplace.[38] Of course people are free to employ words in any way they wish, as long as they explain what they are doing. However, several economists have protested that the incorporation of the natural-rate-based concept of the output gap in a self-styled "Keynesian" policy

TABLE 6.2
THE TWO GAP CONCEPTS

	KEYNESIAN CONCEPT OF GAP	MONETARIST CONCEPT OF GAP
Concept of output relative to which the gap is measured	Full-employment level of output	Level of output associated with natural rate of unemployment
Scale of numbers by which gap is measured	Only positive values, taking value of zero at full employment and rising with unemployment	Positive and negative values, taking value of zero at natural rate of output and positive with output above natural rate
Seminal paper(s)	Okun in 1962 American Statistical Association *Proceedings* Paish in the 1950s, in association with Phillips, although both Paish and Phillips skeptical about "full employment" as goal	Friedman's 1967 AEA presidential address, published in 1968 Phelps 1967*, if from an otherwise Keynesian perspective Very debatably, Paish in the 1950s in association with Phillips
View on the inflation process	Level of inflation a function of level of gap, and change in inflation a function of change in gap	Change in inflation a function of level of gap **
Name of associated hypothesis on wage formation	Phillips curve	Accelerationist hypothesis
View on output as a policy objective	To be maximized (implicitly at lowest previously attained unemployment rate), as shortfall is expensive under Okun's law	Output to be kept at natural rate, even if this is less than the maximum "in an engineering sense"

View on inflation as a policy objective	Old "Keynesian" – i.e., to be controlled by incomes policy, and control of inflation is secondary to achieving full employment – although with many variations among "New Keynesians" and others	Meeting inflation target is paramount objective of policy and takes precedence over full employment
View on money and inflation	Monetary policy (e.g., behavior of bank deposits) not relevant to inflation; labor market critical instead	Output gap most reliable guide to direction of inflation in short run, but relationship between money and prices holds in the long run, and short-run fluctuations in real money affect asset prices, demand, and employment
Terminology	Initially "GNP gap," following Okun; now "output gap" in so-called "New Keynesian" policy framework, with Taylor rules etc.; but 1993 Taylor paper did not use phrase "output gap" or refer to link with inflation	First use of "output gap" in monetarist sense uncertain, but probably in Plosser and Schwert's comment on the Perloff and Wachter paper at the April 1978 Carnegie-Rochester conference Later the IMF and particularly the OECD developed the concept
Implied position of macro decision-making in the wider polity	Political; government to decide on right mix of inflation and unemployment	Technical; decisions on interest rates can be delegated to committee of experts

* Edmund S. Phelps, "Phillips Curves, Expectations of Inflation, and Optimal Unemployment over Time," *Economica*, vol. 34 (August 1967).
** In Friedman's 1967 address, the rate of change of real wages is a function of the divergence of unemployment from its natural rate, but in practice changes in real and nominal wages are closely correlated.

prescription is peculiar. These protests have come in particular from post-Keynesian writers who wish to maintain a degree of consistency between "what Keynes said" and the theories that have annexed his name as a branding exercise. According to Wendy Cornwall in *The Elgar Companion to Post-Keynesian Economics*, an "underlying assumption" of New Keynesianism is that "the economy is self-regulating in the . . . sense that it hovers around a macroeconomic equilibrium at the NAIRU (non-accelerating inflation rate of unemployment). Given this characteristic, New Keynesian models cannot be regarded as Keynesian: they are special cases of the neoclassical model."[39]

Also from a post-Keynesian perspective, Marc Lavoie has argued that the consensus three-equation model is "monetarism without money, since it is totally consistent with Milton Friedman's view of macroeconomics."[40] Given the rather questionable character of the "New Keynesian" label, it has been suggested that the three-equation policy-making model should instead be given a more neutral title, such as "the New Normative Economics" or (as in the opening paragraph of this essay) "the New Consensus Macroeconomics." The selection of an uncontroversial label of this kind allows an interpretation of events in which the achievement of the benign macroeconomic outcomes of the 1990s was largely due to the replacement of Keynesian ideas by their monetarist alternatives. The validity of that interpretation is of course a matter of debate. But it is surely wrong to try to close down the debate by giving a misleading name to a particular policy-making framework.

VI.

As the natural-rate-based concept of the output gap superseded the Okun-originated gap in thinking about economic policy, views on the structure of policy-making also changed. For the proponents of the New Economics in the United States in the 1960s, and indeed for many economists around the world for at least another twenty years, macroeconomics was a highly political subject. Since they believed in the Phillips curve and a long-run trade-off between unemployment and inflation, and since they accepted that economists had no right to prescribe a particular point in that trade-off, the choice between unemployment and inflation had to be given to politicians. In the Keynesian scheme, there was an obvious logic here. It made sense both to place the onus for deciding on the unemployment-inflation mix on the government, with its powers of taxing and spending, and to assert the superiority of fiscal to monetary policy. But the denial of a long-run unemployment/inflation trade-off, as implied by the accelerationist hypothesis, argued that the task of macroeconomic policy-making could be properly entrusted to technicians.

Technicians had of course ultimately to be accountable to democratic institutions. However, central banks could be granted operational independence and made subject to only occasional strategic oversight by the legislature. In practice most countries found that monetary policy was a more effective weapon in managing demand than fiscal policy, even though experience of money-supply targeting was mixed. By the mid-1990s the consensus was that macroeconomic policy could be reduced, more or less, to the setting of the short-term interest rate by the central bank, and that the central bank was likely to be most efficient in its task if its operations were cocooned from day-to-day political pressures. In short, macroeconomic policy became synonymous with monetary policy, and it was deemed to be a technical and not a political matter. Indeed, in those countries where politicians had for decades been actively involved in interest-rate setting (such as the U.K., Italy, and Spain), the shift in the 1990s to non-political, technical procedures under the auspices of an independent central bank was seen as a major step forward. But if the original Phillips curve and the Okun-originated gap concept had continued to dominate macroeconomic thinking, this shift could not have occurred. The expectations-augmented Phillips curve and the natural-rate-based concept of the output gap were, and remain, logical allies of central-bank independence.

This account of the development of the output-gap concept leaves unresolved such major issues as the place of monetary aggregates in the conduct of policy. However, no inconsistency arises in believing both that the change in inflation over the next few quarters is a function of the natural-rate-based output gap and that the underlying cause of inflation over periods of several years is excessive money-supply growth.[41] The use of output gaps in the specification of anti-inflation policy is not nowadays associated with the advocacy of an incomes policy, although Okun and a number of American Keynesian colleagues were articulate supporters of incomes policies in the 1960s. (Three British economists – Richard Layard, Stephen Nickell, and Richard Jackman – set out the case for a tax-based incomes policy in the 2005 issue of their book *Unemployment*. The book had extensive material on the calculation of the natural rate of unemployment, which they termed the "equilibrium rate."[42])

Table 6.2, on pp. 158–159, summarizes the differences between the two concepts of the output gap identified in this essay and tries to position the concepts within the wider debates.

VII.

In a widely cited paper, Athanasios Orphanides argues that the rapid inflation of the 1970s was to be explained by unsatisfactory contemporary calculations of the output gap.[43] According to Orphanides, policymakers in the 1970s behaved in accordance with the Taylor-rule prescription, but they had faulty numbers on the size of the gap. He sees difficulties in estimating the output gap as being inherent in the exercise and as undermining the concept's usefulness in real-world policy-making. In another analysis Nelson endorses Orphanides's assessment that policy-making suffered from incorrect output-gap measurement, but he also indicts the contemporary emphasis on cost-push factors rather than high money growth as the cause of inflation.[44] The Great Moderation of the 1990s therefore becomes attributable partly to economists' greater success in estimating the output gap, a concept taken to be unchanging over the last forty years. Neither Orphanides nor Nelson notices the ambiguity of the output-gap notion.

A quite different view of the Great Moderation is implied by the discussion in this essay. Economics has two concepts of the output gap, which – to repeat – are the Okun-originated, Keynesian concept and the Friedman-originated, monetarist concept. The Keynesian concept was formulated and refined in the 1960s, in association with active fiscal policies intended to deliver full employment. The critical step of reformulating the gap so that it pivoted on the natural rate of unemployment was taken in the paper given by Perloff and Wachter at the Rochester-Carnegie conference in April 1978. Gordon's comment on this paper at the 1978 conference was both pointed and correct. When

Okun prepared his gap estimates in the early 1960s, economics did not have the two key notions in Friedman's 1967 presidential address, namely the accelerationist hypothesis and the natural rate of unemployment. Despite Perloff and Wachter's insistence that they were working within the Okun tradition, their paper was a clear departure from previous approaches, including Okun's. The natural-rate-based concept of the gap has now replaced Okun's gap and provided a better guide to macro decision-making. An underlying premise of the natural-rate framework is that neither labor nor product markets are characterized by abrupt discontinuities in agents' price-setting behavior. In this respect the framework rejects the "asymmetry" between inflation and deflation postulated by Keynes in *The General Theory* and the mono-directional output-gap ideas associated with the Keynesian "New Economics" of the 1960s.

As the monetarist, natural-rate-based gap notion has superseded the Keynesian concept of the gap, major shifts have occurred in other aspects of policy-making over the last thirty years. Reliance on monetary policy has increased at the expense of fiscal policy, governments have shifted the focus of policy away from full employment towards low inflation, and, almost universally, central banks have been granted greater independence in the setting of interest rates. These changes were often discussed and prescribed in monetarist writings in the 1970s and 1980s. In other words, the Great Moderation should be interpreted as the result of changes in the focus of policy and the prioritization of instruments, as monetarist ideas supplanted Keynesian in policy-making praxis. Better outcomes were due not to economists' greater skill in estimating the output gap according to an unchanged concept, but to an improved conceptualization of "how economies work." ("Improved," but not "perfect." As discussed elsewhere in this volume, the Great Recession showed that economics still has great difficulty fitting banking and money into a larger general-equilibrium picture.)

Ironically, Friedman himself did not in his 1967 address see the potential for improved policy-making that it contained and never gave explicit blessing to the natural-rate-based concept of the gap that is now standard. A fair comment is that economists disagree not only about how the economy works, but also about the best labels for their favorite ideas. The evolution of the modern notion of the output gap owes much to demands from policy-makers and business clients, and to the attempts of practitioners (in supranational organizations, central banks, finance ministries, and commercial organizations) to answer these demands. Like most of the key advances in economics, it has come neither from pure theory nor from unreflecting practice. Instead it has resulted from a rather messy *tâtonnement* between the two.

ESSAY 7

WAS THE U.K.'S GREAT MODERATION DUE TO KEYNESIANISM, MONETARISM, OR WHAT?

ON WEDNESDAY, September 16, 1992 (known at the time as "Black Wednesday"), heavy selling of the pound on the foreign exchanges forced it out of the European Exchange Rate Mechanism. The U.K.'s exit from the ERM was regarded at the time as both a failure of economic policy and a national humiliation. As it is now, almost twenty years later, the event can begin to be analyzed from a wider historical perspective. The central point is surprising, but clear. The sterling crisis of September 1992 did not foreshadow increased instability, but instead was followed by fifteen years of greater macroeconomic stability than in any previous phase of the U.K.'s post-war history (and probably than ever before in British history). Black Wednesday became Golden Wednesday. (Of course, the U.K. was badly hit by the Great Recession in 2008–2010, but this essay focuses on the benign 1992–2007 period.)

The paradoxical outcome was highlighted by Sir Alan Budd, chief economic adviser to the Treasury between 1991 and 1997, in his lecture to the Julian Hodge Institute in April 2002. The lecture, entitled "The Quest for Stability," noted that new policy-making arrangements introduced in late 1992 had "exceeded all expectations."[1] Not only had the U.K. had "remarkably stable growth" in the 1990s, but it had "survived the recent world recession better than any other major economy."

165

Budd's lecture was a valuable starting point for discussion, but it prompted two further questions. The first related to quantification. If the decade after September 1992 was better than earlier decades, how much better was it, and what about the following five years running up to mid-2007, when the stability continued? Without an answer to this question, the impression of greater stability after 1992 remained only an impression. The second and perhaps more fundamental question was one of explanation. On the whole, the U.K.'s record in macroeconomic management between 1945 and 1992 had been mediocre. Indeed, this mediocrity had come to be seen not only as an aspect of a larger economic inadequacy, as the U.K.'s share in world output and exports declined year by year, but also as inevitable and never-ending. What happened in 1992 to interrupt the unsatisfactory record?

I.

Budd argued in his lecture that economic policy-making in the period starting in September 1992 had a considerable degree of continuity, with a focus on inflation targets and a de-politicization of decision-making. One way of assessing the stability of the fifteen years after September 1992 is to compare that period with previous periods in which U.K. economic policy and outcomes also had some sort of unity. For brevity the fifteen-year period can be labeled "the Great Moderation," in line with a common usage to describe a pattern that was in fact more or less universal. In this essay a comparison is made with two earlier periods – a stop-go period from the third quarter of 1945 to the second quarter of 1971, and a boom-bust period from Q3 1971 to Q3 1992. In the twenty-six-year period from the end of the Second World War to Q2 1971, the U.K. participated in the Bretton Woods system of fixed exchange rates. Although the pound suffered a heavy devaluation in 1949, it was then kept within the narrow limits ($2.78–$2.82) set by the Bretton Woods rules until November 1967. This fixity of the exchange rate conditioned all economic policy-making. The world economy was far more stable than it had been in the inter-war period, but the need to defend the pound's exchange rate led to frequent policy changes in the U.K., and economic activity fluctuated in mild stop-go cycles. (The stop-go period analyzed here roughly overlaps with the supposed "Keynesian era of demand management" reviewed – and debunked – in essay 5.)

The system of fixed exchange rates came to an end with the suspension of the dollar's convertibility into gold in August 1971. Apart from a brief flirtation with the European "snake" in the spring of 1972, the U.K. had a floating exchange rate against other major currencies until October 1990, when it joined the ERM. With no explicit external constraint on policy, monetary policy was extremely loose in the eighteen months starting in September 1971, and a wild boom developed. Although a degree of order was restored to policy-making by the introduction of money-supply targets in 1976, the operation of these targets was widely deemed to be unsatisfactory. With much uncertainty about the best policy regime for the U.K., the conduct of policy was often erratic. Big swings in interest rates and inflation were accompanied by two big boom-bust cycles (from 1971 to 1974, and from 1986 to 1992), and one smaller cycle (from 1977 to 1982). This period can be fairly described as "the boom-bust period." The analytical task becomes the comparison of macroeconomic stability in three periods – the stop-go period, the boom-bust period, and the Great Moderation.

The next step is to propose the macroeconomic magnitudes whose variability is to be measured. Macroeconomic instability has at least three dimensions: instability in demand and output, instability in inflation, and instability in interest rates. Of course, other policy goals are relevant. For example, a case could be made that fluctuations in employment have a more meaningful impact on people's welfare than fluctuations in demand and output. Much of the post-war period was indeed characterized by official concern to maintain so-called "full employment." However, the labor market saw such extensive structural and legislative changes over the decades that unemployment statistics have a quite different significance in 2002 or 2007 from what they had in 1945. By contrast, the concept of gross domestic output has remained much the same, despite great changes in its composition and level. Instability in the growth of GDP is therefore chosen as the first indicator. (The growth rate is the annual rate, and a quarterly series is analyzed.)[2]

A complication is that the phrase "instability in inflation and interest rates" begs the questions, Which inflation rate? and Which interest rate? As the policy target in the final post-ERM decade was expressed in terms of RPIX (i.e., the retail price index excluding mortgage interest rates), it might seem logical to use RPIX in the stop-go and boom-bust periods. But there is a difficulty, in that mortgage interest rates were included in the retail price index only from 1976, and the index is not wholly comparable before and after this date. A sensible answer is to regard both the "headline" RPI and the "underlying" RPIX as valid inflation measures. Hence the instability of both needs to be measured, and that is what is done here.

The post-war period saw a number of far-reaching changes in the structure of the British financial system. Associated with these changes were shifts in official emphasis on different interest-rate concepts, as well as a few re-designations of interest-rate concepts whose underlying economic meaning was quite stable. Fortunately, one instrument – the three-month Treasury bill – has changed little over the decades. Treasury-bill rate has therefore been chosen as the measure of interest rates for current purposes.

So the increase in GDP, the annual rates of RPI and RPIX change, and the Treasury-bill rate are taken to be representative of changes in output, inflation, and interest rates respectively. Statistical series are available for all three variables over the entire 1945–2007 period under consideration, with their instability measured here by the standard deviation. Their methods of compilation and estimation were consistent over the sixty-two-year period, and direct comparison of the numbers in the three sub-periods is a valid exercise.

The key results are given in the tables below. Table 7.1 shows the variations in output volatility in the three periods. The standard deviation of the output growth rate in the Great Moderation is less than half that in the two previous periods, plainly a major improvement. One surprise is that the boom-bust period does not appear to be more unstable than the stop-go period, with the two periods having roughly the same standard deviations of the output growth rate, 2.69 and 2.80, respectively. However, this is largely due to extreme output fluctuations in the immediate aftermath of the Second World War. Output fell heavily in 1946 because of demobilization, while the severe winter of 1946–47 also hit production badly. Conditions returned to normal only in 1948 and 1949, and so, arguably, a more valid alternative period for comparison runs from Q1 1949 to Q2 1971. The standard deviation of the output

TABLE 7.1
MEASURES OF OUTPUT VOLATILITY
IN THREE POST-WAR PERIODS

The figures below relate to the annual (i.e., four-quarter) change in gross domestic product (in market prices, using constant 1995 prices). The series analyzed is quarterly.

1. *The stop-go period, Q3 1945 – Q2 1971*
   Mean output growth rate   2.5%
   Standard deviation of output growth rate   2.80

2. *The boom-bust period, Q3 1971 – Q3 1992*
   Mean output growth rate   2.1%
   Standard deviation of output growth rate   2.69

3. *The Great Moderation, Q4 1992 – Q2 2007*
   Mean output growth rate   3.0%
   Standard deviation of output growth rate   0.79

Sources: National Statistics website, and calculations by the author and Richard Wild, then of Cardiff Business School

growth rate in this slightly shorter period is appreciably lower, at 1.94.

The effect of excluding the highly disrupted first three post-war years is therefore to make the stop-go period more stable than the boom-bust period, in accordance with the historical stereotypes. But it is worth noting that the difference between the standard deviations of the output growth rate in the Great Moderation and in the post-1949 stop-go period (1.94 minus 0.79, or 1.15) is greater than the difference between them in the post-1949 stop-go period and the boom-bust period (2.69 minus 1.94, or 0.75). As the stop-go era was commonly regarded by contemporaries as enjoying impressive economic stability compared with the inter-war period, and as it continued to be lionized for this reason during the boom-bust years, the scale of policy-makers' achievement from 1992 to 2007 emerges yet more emphatically.[3]

While the output-growth comparison demonstrates that the period from September 1992 was very good compared with both the stop-go and the boom-bust periods, the inflation comparison is even more favorable. Indeed, the stability of inflation in the Great Moderation has

TABLE 7.2
MEASURES OF INFLATION
IN THREE POST-WAR PERIODS

I. Inflation measured by the all-items retail price index

The figures below relate to the annual change in the all-items retail price index. The series analyzed is a quarterly average of the monthly values.

1. *The stop-go period, Q3 1945–Q2 1971*
   Mean annual inflation rate   3.84%
   Standard deviation of inflation rate   2.66

2. *The boom-bust period, Q3 1971–Q3 1992*
   Mean annual inflation rate   9.81%
   Standard deviation of inflation rate   5.70

3. *The Great Moderation, Q4 1992–Q2 2007*
   Mean annual inflation rate   2.66%
   Standard deviation of inflation rate   0.82

II. Inflation measured by RPIX, i.e., the retail price index excluding mortgage interest rates

The figures below relate to the all-items retail price index until the first quarter 1976, but to RPIX thereafter. As above, the series analyzed is a quarterly average of the monthly values.

1. *The boom-bust period, Q3 1971–Q3 1992*
   Mean annual inflation rate   9.61%
   Standard deviation of inflation rate   5.66

2. *The Great Moderation, Q4 1992–Q2 2007*
   Mean annual inflation rate   2.59%
   Standard deviation of inflation rate   0.44

Sources: National Statistics website, and calculations by the author and Richard Wild

to be described as astonishing after all the mishaps and wrong turnings in British macroeconomic policy in the preceding forty-five years. Inflation targets were introduced by the chancellor of the exchequer,

TABLE 7.3
MEASURES OF INTEREST-RATE VOLATILITY
IN THREE POST-WAR PERIODS

The figures below relate to the quarterly average of the Treasury-bill rate.

1. *The stop-go period, Q3 1945–Q2 1971*
   Mean interest rate   3.72%
   Standard deviation of interest rate   2.36

2. *The boom-bust period, Q3 1971–Q3 1992*
   Mean interest rate   10.55%
   Standard deviation of interest rate   2.65

3. *The Great Moderation, Q4 1992–Q2 2007*
   Mean interest rate   5.29%
   Standard deviation of interest rate   1.01

Sources: National Statistics website, and calculations by the author and Richard Wild

Mr. Norman (now Lord) Lamont, in October 1992. The annual increase in RPIX was to be kept within a 1 to 4 percent band for the rest of the parliament (which lasted to 1997), with a hope that it would be towards the lower end of the band by the parliament's end. In 1997 the newly elected Labour government reiterated the 2½ percent RPIX target as well as announcing the radical institutional change of making the Bank of England independent. The Bank's Monetary Policy Committee was given the job of keeping the annual RPIX increase to within 1 percentage point above or below the 2½ percent figure. In short, the U.K. had an inflation target – to be understood as a 2½ percent annual increase in RPIX – more or less without interruption for over a decade. In December 2003 the RPIX target was replaced by a target of a 2-percent-a-year increase in the consumer price index, but this was a change more of form than of substance.

What happened? The answer – given in table 7.2 – is that the mean increase in RPIX in the fifty-nine quarters to Q2 2007 was 2.6 percent, with a standard deviation of 0.44. So the target was met almost exactly. By contrast, in the boom-bust period the comparable measure of retail price inflation averaged 9.6 percent, with a standard deviation of 5.66.

Not only did the U.K. cut inflation during the Great Moderation to just a little over a quarter of the figure seen in the previous twenty years, but it also reduced the volatility of inflation to less than a tenth of the former level! Inflation was not much lower in the final decade of that period than in the 1950s and 1960s, but it was significantly more stable. Overall, the verdict on policy-makers' record in reducing and stabilizing inflation has to be highly complimentary.

The last variable to be considered is the rate of interest. Here, too, the post-ERM period stands out as by far the most stable phase in the sixty-two years of post-war experience under review, with markedly better macroeconomic management than in the preceding boom-bust period. Table 7.3 shows that the mean Treasury-bill rate in the period Q4 1992 to Q2 2007 was 5.29 percent, with a standard deviation of 1.01. In the boom-bust period the mean Treasury-bill rate was 10.55 percent, with a standard deviation of 2.65, and in the stop-go period it was 3.72 percent, with a standard deviation of 2.36. So – when measured in this way – the volatility of interest rates in the Great Moderation was less than half that in either the boom-bust or the stop-go period.

The contrast between the U.K.'s macroeconomic performance before and after September 1992 – that is, between the fifteen-year post-ERM period and the two previous periods of stop-go and boom-bust – is therefore obvious, easily quantified, and definite. The post-1992 period was far more stable than the boom-bust period, and it also had a far better record than the generally acclaimed stop-go period. It is time to move on to the more interesting and more difficult question of explanation. Why was the U.K. economy so much more stable after September 1992 than before?

Budd's answer in his lecture was institutional. In his view, the explanation for the greater stability was to be sought in the design of the system, with "the establishment of a clearly defined task," "the structure of the Committee," and "the requirement for transparency in the decision-taking process." The clarity of the task's definition stemmed from the technical nature of the objective. It was to meet the inflation target, with no awkward political distractions having to do with unemployment, growth, or the exchange rate. (Of course, unemployment, growth, and the exchange rate all mattered, but there were no explicit objectives for any of them.) Transparency was important, because there would be "no hiding place." In contrast to the Treasury-dominated and largely secret system of decision-making before 1992, policy-makers' views and voting records would move into the public domain. If they were wrong, it would be their fault and not that of anyone else. In short, the big changes in the system of decision-making after 1992 were that policy became focused on one and only one objective, and that the people involved were made fully accountable for mistakes.

Budd did not see the change in government in 1997 as a major break. The Treasury Panel of "wise men," which started business in early 1993, was not a decision-making body. But all its deliberations were on the record, and it therefore played a role in introducing transparency to policy advice. In 1993 the chancellor of the exchequer, Kenneth Clarke, announced that the minutes of the regular meetings between him and the governor of the Bank of England would be published, and Budd's lecture saw these meetings as foreshadowing the more complete transfer of power to the Bank in 1997. The Bank of England's *Inflation Reports* also pre-dated operational independence, and Budd evidently considers them to have had an influence on decision-making between 1993 and 1997. (The *Inflation Reports* informed the governor's position in his meetings with the chancellor.) So, when the Monetary Policy Committee was founded, it continued "an established system."[4]

II.

Institutions are vital, but an emphasis on a change in institutional structures is surely an incomplete way to explain the radical improvement in policy-making that seems to have occurred. It is also necessary to discuss policy-makers' beliefs and attitudes. The first forty-five years of the post-war period were marked by constant intellectual warfare between different tribes of British economists. Indeed, disagreement is popularly seen as a hallmark of modern economics and generates several standard jokes about the vocation. But one theme of Budd's lecture was that the excellence of the decisions made after 1992 reflected the domination of the decision-making process by economists. This would make sense only if economists shared a consensus view on the determination of inflation, a view that was well known and relatively uncontroversial to them but not familiar to people from other walks of life.

(Budd did not say so in as many words, but his lecture implied that politicians, bankers, civil servants, trade unionists, and so on should be kept out of monetary policy.)

The question becomes, What was the consensus about the determination of inflation that was so extensively shared by the Treasury Panel before 1997, the Monetary Policy Committee after 1997, and the large number of other economist advisers and commentators both within and outside the official machine in these years? It is important to be clear that the policy achievements of the 1990s were not due to the adoption of the most well-publicized prescriptions of the most well-known schools of thought. In particular, the simpler versions of neither "Keynesianism" nor "monetarism" were relevant.

A discussion of these two tribal belief systems is needed, if only to knock down some of the totem poles in macroeconomic debate. An influential view in Britain until the 1980s was that Keynesianism – in some shape or form – was responsible for the stability and prosperity of the immediate post-war decades. According to Mrs. Shirley (now Lady) Williams, writing in 1981, after the Second World War "government planning, public finance, and government intervention were used to bring about and sustain full employment and economic growth; deficit spending maintained demand during periods of recession . . . The lessons of Maynard Keynes, set out in *The General Theory of Employment, Interest, and Money*, had been devotedly learned."[5] Wynne Godley, a member of the Treasury Panel in the early 1990s, had written in 1983 that the twenty-five years after 1945 seemed at the time "a period of remarkable success with regard to all the main objectives of macroeconomic policy" and that this post-war prosperity was "the consequence of the adoption by governments of 'Keynesian' policies."[6]

This view of the beneficence of the so-called "Keynesian revolution" is heard less often nowadays, but it continues to lurk behind many debates about the state and the economy. It needs to be remembered that Keynesianism, in the version adopted by the British center-left in the post-war period, is a political doctrine about the optimal size of the state sector as well as a set of economic prescriptions about how to maintain full employment. In the final chapter of *The General Theory*, Keynes claimed that "a somewhat comprehensive socialisation of investment will prove the only means of securing an approximation to full employment."[7] This argument was part of the case for nationalization in the late 1940s, and it remained central to the defense of the mixed economy until the 1980s. As Anthony Crosland recognized in *The Future of Socialism* (first published in 1956), "Many liberal-minded people, who were instinctively 'socialist' in the 1930s . . . , have now concluded that 'Keynes-plus-modified-capitalism-plus-Welfare-State' works perfectly well."[8]

The current research exercise – like that in essay 5 – throws a different and much more skeptical light on the macroeconomic outcomes of the 1950s and 1960s. Crucially, the U.K. economy was far more stable in the 1990s and the opening years of the twenty-first century than at the apogee of the Keynesian revolution. It has been shown that in the Great Moderation the standard deviation of output growth was lower than in the years from 1945 to 1971, and it remained more stable when the troublesome 1945–49 period was excluded from the comparison. Further, inflation and interest rates were far less volatile in the 1990s than in the immediate post-war decades. Ironically, the inflation rate was the only variable that was not markedly worse during the period of the supposed Keynesian revolution. (Over the twenty-six years up to 1971 it was just under 4 percent. Many self-styled Keynesians profess themselves indifferent to inflation.[9])

But it is implausible to claim that the U.K.'s policies were still Keynesian in the 1990s. They certainly were not Keynesian in Shirley Williams's sense of government planning and intervention. On the contrary, the Conservative government from 1979 to 1997 was more committed to the free market than any of its post-war predecessors. In fact, public ownership was in retreat in the early 1990s, with the main energy utilities being privatized and their markets liberalized. But policies were not even Keynesian in the more humdrum sense that government spending and taxation were being varied to influence employment. Not one of the many policy statements from the Treasury in the 1990s envisaged an employment-promoting role for fiscal policy.[10]

So it was not Keynesianism that delivered the macroeconomic stability of the fifteen years from Black Wednesday. What about monetarism? Lamont's announcement of the inflation target in October 1992 was remarkably wide-ranging in its references to variables that policymakers would have to follow in future. It did mention monitoring ranges for money-supply growth, including the concept of "broad money," which Nigel Lawson had stopped targeting in 1985. But this was a charade. The Treasury itself pretended to be interested in narrow money (particularly as measured by the narrowest possible money measure, M0), but it had ignored an overshoot in M0 in the late 1980s, and its officials were not worried about broad money. Most members of the Treasury Panel did not want a discussion of monetary developments to figure in their meetings. It was only after a strong protest by one member of the Panel that a section on money was put on the agenda.[11] From the outset, the Bank of England's *Inflation Report* did include fairly extensive material on the monetary aggregates, but at least one of the Bank's published statements on the transmission mechanism of monetary policy paid scant attention to the quantity of money on any definition.[12] Indeed, when the Bank was given operational independence in 1997, it ended the monitoring range for broad money which had been in place from 1992. According to an article in the Bank's *Quarterly Bulletin*, the justification was that "Over policy-relevant time horizons, the monetary aggregates will be influenced by many factors, such as cyclical shifts in the demand for money and credit, and innovations in financial structure, products and regulation."[13]

III.

So monetarism – in the sense of money-target monetarism – had hardly any relevance to policy-making in the Great Moderation. Like Keynes - ianism, it cannot take any credit for the improved performance. However, monetarism encompasses a wide range of attitudes and beliefs. While most British economists have never been enthusiasts for money-supply targets, a clear professional consensus emerged in the 1980s and 1990s that one element in monetarist thinking was right. This was the view that there is no long-run trade-off between, on the one hand, output and employment and, on the other, inflation. Indeed, the emergence of this consensus was critical to the adoption of a policy-making framework focused on an inflation target. The rationale for the focus on inflation, and so for the demotion of full employment as a policy objective, had first been presented in the late 1960s, notably by Milton

Friedman, the leader of monetarist thought, in his presidential address to the American Economic Association in 1967.[14]

The heart of Friedman's argument was that government attempts to drive unemployment beneath the natural rate would lead not to high and stable inflation, but to hyper-inflation. Friedman was evasive about certain aspects of his argument. For example, he denied that central banks could measure the natural rate, even though one of his most famous early papers had emphasized the need to develop theories that were testable against data.[15] Other economists were not so cautious. It is, in fact, a simple matter to prepare series for unemployment, the rate of wage increases, and the change in the rate of wage increases, and to carry out some econometric tests. Despite many problems of interpretation, economists have been able to derive estimates of the natural rate and to see whether Friedman's "accelerationist hypothesis" is valid. In country after country the answer has been that, on the whole, it does fit the facts – or, when there is some lack of clarity in the data, that Friedman's hypothesis is more convincing than the alternatives.

But labor-market institutions – like financial regulation – are evolving all the time. To base monetary policy on an unemployment rate would be not only politically contentious, but also technically difficult. The key to applying Friedman's doctrine to policy-making was a generalization of the natural-rate idea. Instead of emphasizing that there is an unemployment rate at which inflation is stable, economists suggested that there is a level of output ("trend" or "sustainable output," or even "the natural rate of output") at which inflation is stable. When output is above the trend level, there is said to be a positive "output gap"; when it is beneath the trend level, the output gap is negative. Friedman's insight (i.e., the absence of a long-run unemployment/inflation trade-off) is captured, more or less, by the proposition that the *change* in inflation is a positive function of the *level* of the gap. (Essay 6 discussed the evolution of the modern output-gap concept from its origins in the 1960s.)

The implied approach to monetary policy was simple. In late 1992 the U.K. undoubtedly had a large negative output gap after the recession induced by the ERM. It could therefore enjoy several quarters, perhaps even a few years, of above-trend growth without any serious risk of rising inflation.[16] After a year of very strong growth in 1994, output had returned roughly to its trend level (i.e., the output gap was roughly zero) and the annual rate of RPIX inflation was about 2½ percent. Since then, monetary policy – to be understood almost wholly as changes in short-term interest rates – has been organized to keep the output gap at close to zero. According to the theory, if the output gap is kept at roughly nil, inflation should be stable. In the event, policy was successful in keeping the output gap at close to zero until the middle of the first decade of the twenty-first century, and inflation stayed remarkably steady at about 2½ percent. Here – in essence – is the explanation for the almost fifteen years of stability from 1992.[17]

In his "Quest for Stability" lecture, Budd acknowledged that this theory had motivated the official approach to monetary policy after the U.K.'s exit from the ERM. He noted that British governments had a long record of trying to maximize output and increase employment, and yet the result had been over-full employment, excessive inflation, and macroeconomic instability. But the new theory implied that the key to maintaining stability of inflation was to have "output stability"; and, in his words, "that is, in effect, what the [Monetary Policy Committee] does. It seeks to keep output as close as it reasonably can to its sustainable level, since that is usually a necessary condition for inflation stability." Budd did not elaborate the point, but, if the sentences here are to be dignified with a theoretical label, output-gap monetarism seems the most fitting.

IV.

Output-gap monetarism is hardly complicated. Although its adoption was particularly successful in the U.K., it now provides the dominant theoretical basis for central banking around the world. It has not eliminated the need for judgment and discretion in policy-making, as there are many difficulties in estimating the output gap and projecting its future course. Nevertheless, it helps to explain why the Nineties and early Noughties were a stable period not just in the U.K. but in many other economies too, including, crucially, the U.S. (See the appendix to this essay.) The puzzle is, surely, why it took economists in governments, central banks, financial institutions, and universities so long to find, develop, and accept the key ideas. In the U.K. the trouble may have stemmed partly from the prestige attached to Keynesian economics, with its very different concepts and emphases, and partly from many politicians' obstinate enthusiasm for basing monetary policy on the exchange rate.[18]

But the status of the natural rate of unemployment and the output gap in monetarist economics is also a little uncomfortable. There is no doubt that output-gap monetarism is derived from the accelerationist hypothesis, but Friedman himself failed to see the potential of his 1967 lecture for policy-making. Instead of advertising the positive agenda for stabilization implied by his ideas, he made a needlessly cautious remark about the difficulty of measuring the natural rate, and delivered a vital but entirely negative comment on full-employment policies. Further, the apparent triumph of output-gap monetarism does not mean the debates are over. There are still too many muddles about the role of money in the determination of demand and output, and continued disagreement about the tasks of the central bank and the status of different monetary aggregates in policy-making. The Great Recession demonstrated only too clearly that money and banking have not been properly integrated into macroeconomic analysis. (See, in particular, essays 17 and 18 for a critique of the Bernanke Fed's attitudes towards the money aggregates in the Great Recession.)

APPENDIX:
WHAT ABOUT THE UNITED STATES' GREAT MODERATION?

The United States' Great Moderation is usually deemed to have begun almost a decade before the U.K.'s, at some point in the mid-1980s. (The phrase "the Great Moderation" was introduced by the Harvard economist James Stock in a 2002 paper, "Has the Business Cycle Changed and Why?"[19]) In this exercise it is taken – somewhat arbitrarily – to have started in mid-1984. The three tables below compare output, inflation, and interest-rate volatility in three periods, the supposed "Age of Keynes" (1948 to 1960), the Great Inflation (1961 to mid-1984), and the Great Moderation (mid-1984 to mid-2007).

The message from table 7.4 is clear-cut: it is that, although growth was somewhat lower (by about ½ percent a year) in the Great Moderation than in the previous thirty-five years, the upward path of output

TABLE 7.4

MEASURES OF OUTPUT VOLATILITY IN THE U.S.
IN THREE POST-WAR PERIODS

*The figures below relate to the annual (i.e., four-quarter) change in real
gross domestic product, with the series analyzed being quarterly.*

1. *The 1950s ("the Age of Keynes"), Q1 1948–Q4 1960*
   Mean output growth rate   3.7%
   Standard deviation of output growth rate   3.71

2. *The Great Inflation, Q1 1961–Q2 1984*
   Mean output growth rate   3.6%
   Standard deviation of output growth rate   2.85

3. *The Great Moderation, Q3 1984–Q2 2007*
   Mean output growth rate   3.2%
   Standard deviation of output growth rate   1.39

*Sources: U.S. Department of Commerce, Bureau of Economic Analysis, and author's
calculations using website data as at October 2010*

was much smoother. The standard deviation of output growth in the Great Moderation was less than half that in the Great Inflation and, more surprisingly, even less than half that in the 1950s, taken to be part of the supposed "Keynesian era." The Great Moderation also saw a halving of inflation, which averaged 2.6 percent a year on the GDP deflator, compared with the Great Inflation, when it averaged 5.0 percent a year on the same measure. Further, the year-by-year variation in inflation was dramatically less in the Great Moderation than in either the 1950s or the Great Inflation, in line with the pattern also remarked in the U.K.

However, the greater stability in the inflation rate in the twenty-three years up to 2007 was not associated with particularly low and stable interest rates. Inflation was much the same in the Great Moderation as in the 1950s, but in the Great Moderation the Treasury-bill rate was on average more than twice as high as in the 1950s in terms of both levels and variability.

In short, the improvement in macroeconomic policy-making

TABLE 7.5
MEASURES OF INFLATION IN THE U.S.
IN THREE POST-WAR PERIODS

The figures below relate to the annual change in the GDP price deflator, with the series analyzed being quarterly.

1. *The 1950s ("the Age of Keynes"), Q1 1948–Q4 1960*
   Mean annual inflation rate   2.4%
   Standard deviation of inflation rate   2.25

2. *The Great Inflation, Q1 1961–Q2 1984*
   Mean annual inflation rate   5.0%
   Standard deviation of inflation rate   2.75

3. *The Great Moderation, Q3 1984–Q2 2007*
   Mean annual inflation rate   2.6%
   Standard deviation of inflation rate   0.79

Sources: U.S. Department of Commerce, Bureau of Economic Analysis, and author's calculations

TABLE 7.6
MEASURES OF INTEREST-RATE VOLATILITY
IN THE U.S. IN THREE POST-WAR PERIODS

The figures below relate to the monthly average of the Treasury-bill rate, with the series being analyzed also being monthly.

1. *The 1950s ("the Age of Keynes"), Q1 1948–Q4 1960*
   Mean interest rate   1.9%
   Standard deviation of interest rate   0.89

2. *The Great Inflation, Q1 1961–Q2 1984*
   Mean interest rate   6.40%
   Standard deviation of interest rate   3.09

3. *The Great Moderation, Q3 1984–Q2 2007*
   Mean interest rate   4.8%
   Standard deviation of interest rate   2.05

Source: Federal Reserve Bank of St. Louis's database ("FRED")

performance in the closing decades of the twentieth century was marked and well defined in the U.S. as in the U.K. But the U.S. had not seen such wrenching and destructive boom-bust cycles as the U.K., and so the improvement was less remarkable. A fair comment is that in the closing fifteen years of the twentieth century fiscal policy in the U.S. – under the Reagan, first Bush, and Clinton presidencies – was not conducted on Keynesian lines. So the Great Moderation delivered better macroeconomic outcomes than either the 1950s or the Great Inflation, and the good results were not due to Keynesian macro policies.

PART THREE

DOES FISCAL POLICY WORK?

Preface

THE KEYNESIANISM of the first post-war generation gave a warm embrace to fiscal policy and cold-shouldered monetary policy. But hovering in the background was the awkward topic of the relationship between money and national income. Suppose that a decrease in the budget deficit occurred at the same time as an increase in the quantity of money. Which of the two policy forces would win? Would fiscal policy overwhelm monetary policy or not? Would Keynesianism refute the monetarists' quantity theory of money, or *vice versa*?

Milton Friedman's answer was blunt. At the age of 83, in a 1996 interview with two British economists, Brian Snowdon and Howard Vane, he said,

> One of the things I have tried to do over the years is to find cases where fiscal policy is going in one direction and monetary policy is going in the opposite. In every case the actual course of events follows monetary policy. I have never found a case where fiscal policy dominated monetary policy and I suggest to you as a test to find a counter-example.[1]

The first essay here develops Friedman's views on fiscal policy in more detail, by comparing the 1996 interview with a 1948 paper in which the budget deficit and its pattern of financing were judged to be central to macroeconomic policy-making.

For any observer of the British economy in the mid-1970s the relative efficacy of fiscal and monetary policies was also fundamental. As a journalist on *The Times*, I was intrigued by the inconsistencies in official policy-making and the theoretical issues which they raised. The striking similarity of the rate of money-supply growth in 1972 and the rate of inflation in 1975, as well as my reading around the subject, convinced me that the monetarists' theories were largely correct. But what did that mean for fiscal policy and the income-expenditure model? I argued in an article in *The Times* on October 23, 1975 (reprinted as the second essay in this section), that, once a money-supply target had been announced, "reflating by fiscal means is like pumping air into a tire with a puncture – the puncture being massive sales of government bonds to the non-bank public." The conjunction in the mid-1970s of fiscal expansionism and persistent demand weakness was "the *reductio ad absurdum* of Keynesianism." (The article was very slight, but I think it is worth including here because of its relevance to the subsequent debates. It is a period piece, and the reader needs to be warned that I have left the contemporary references in the present tense. The macroeconomic conjunction – large budget deficits in association with demand weakness – was uncannily similar to that of today.)

The article in *The Times* also conjectured that cuts in public spending and increases in taxes would not necessarily deflate demand. The rather cryptic explanation I gave was that "Fewer bond sales would ensue, lowering interest rates, and promoting both investment and consumption." I had no notion when I wrote the sentence that – only a few years later – it would be relevant, indeed pivotal, to the justification of possibly the most controversial episode in British macroeconomic policy-making. The introduction of the Medium-Term Financial Strategy in the 1980 Budget, and the shoring up of the fiscal targets in that strategy by large tax increases in the 1981 Budget, provoked fury from academic economists. As mentioned elsewhere in this book, 364 of them wrote a letter to *The Times* protesting against "monetarist policies." The third essay in this section, "Did the 1981 Budget Refute Naïve Keynesianism?" criticizes the Keynesian income-expenditure model for its inability to incorporate monetary influences on asset prices and expenditure. It was written for a set of papers, edited by Philip Booth of the Institute of Economic Affairs, analyzing the 1981 Budget on its twenty-fifth anniversary.

ADDENDUM: The 1981 letter to *The Times* from the 364 is mentioned several times in these pages. The contents of the letter were as follows:

The following statement on economic policy has been signed by 364 university economists in Britain, whose names are given on the attached list:[2]

We, who are all present or retired members of the economics staffs of British universities, are convinced that:

(a) there is no basis in economic theory or supporting evidence for the Government's belief that by deflating demand they will bring inflation permanently under control and thereby induce an automatic recovery in output and employment;

(b) present policies will deepen the depression, erode the industrial base of our economy and threaten its social and political stability;

(c) there are alternative policies; and

(d) the time has come to reject monetarist policies and consider urgently which alternative offers the best hope of sustained recovery.

The letter was signed by seventy-six present or past professors, a majority of the Chief Economic Advisers to the Government in the post-war period, and the president, nine present or past vice-presidents, and the secretary-general of the Royal Economic Society.

Putting their names to the letter had no adverse effect on the signatories' subsequent careers. The letter was signed by Mervyn King, then a thirty-two-year-old professor at Birmingham University, who was to be appointed chief economist at the Bank of England only ten years later and became its governor in 2003. Another signatory, Martin Weale, was a research officer at Cambridge University's Department of Applied Economics at the time. He has recently (October 2010) been appointed to the Monetary Policy Committee of the Bank of England, to general acclaim.

ESSAY 8

FRIEDMAN (1948), FRIEDMAN (1996), AND THE EFFECTIVENESS OF FISCAL POLICY IN THE UNITED STATES

AS IS WELL KNOWN, views on the effectiveness of fiscal policy vary among economists. One position is widely held and, superficially, appears to be little more than organized common sense. Since government expenditure is part of aggregate demand, and since Keynes taught in *The General Theory* that demand generates output and that output requires employment, it follows (or seems to follow) that an increase in government expenditure is certain to boost demand, output, and employment. As Keynes's biographer, Robert Skidelsky, said in an interview in December 2009, if the aim is "to get aggregate spending up," "the surest way to do this is by the government spending the money itself."[1] The simplicity of this line of argument lends it plausibility, and, at first acquaintance, it goes a long way towards establishing a case for the effectiveness of fiscal policy. Nevertheless, many economists deny the effectiveness of fiscal policy as a means of influencing demand, while a high proportion of these fiscal skeptics believe monetary policy to be more important. Their problem is partly one of public relations, specifically that the argument for monetary policy is harder to formulate and project.

This essay has two purposes. The first is to show not only that different economists have sharply divergent views at any one time, but that the same economist can have contrasting views at different times. The economist chosen for the exercise, Milton Friedman, is accepted as having been one of the greatest of the twentieth century. The inconsistency between his standpoints in 1948 (when he said fiscal policy mattered enormously) and 1996 (when he said fiscal policy didn't matter at all) is so extreme that someone new to his work might ask questions about his intellectual integrity. The second purpose is to suggest that the Friedman of 1996 had learned from ideas and events. His position had evolved over years of thinking and research, and does need to be respected. Indeed, he knew that the views he held about fiscal policy later in his career put him in a small minority of economists, and he said so. Some data presented here will show that the United States' experience towards the end of the twentieth century did validate the mature Friedman's dismissal of the effectiveness of fiscal policy. The notion that extra government spending boosts demand and output may appeal to common sense, but it is not necessarily true.

I.

Friedman, born in 1912, was seventeen when the American stock market crashed in October 1929. He was then an undergraduate at Rutgers University, but he moved on to Chicago in 1932 and to Columbia in 1933 for postgraduate studies.[2] His student career thus coincided with the most traumatic cyclical upheaval ever inflicted on the United States, its Great Depression of 1929 to 1933. It is perhaps unsurprising that Friedman should have devoted much of his life to trying to understand what happened to the American economy in those years. According to his biographer, Lanny Ebenstein, in the early 1930s "Friedman was a hardworking student and took copious notes in class and of works that he read." At Chicago he "took, for example, eighty-seven pages of notes on Keynes's *Treatise on Money*."[3] In the *Treatise* Keynes was optimistic about the effectiveness of monetary policy as a means of combatting depression, with his favorite prescription for a slump being large-scale purchases of securities by the central bank, which he termed "monetary policy *à outrance*" (or "monetary policy to the uttermost").[4] More specifically, the operations Keynes had in mind in the *Treatise* were the combination of "a very low level of the short-term rate of interest" with central-bank purchases of "long-dated securities either against an expansion of central bank money or against the sale of short-dated securities until the short-term market is saturated." (Is it going too far to suggest that the "very low" short-term rates were to be maintained by "money-market operations," in the terminology of essay 4 in this collection, while the purchases of long-dated securities were to be by means of what are called there "debt-market operations"? Essay 2 in this collection considers the relative merits of Keynes's *Treatise* and his *General Theory*.)

Given the obvious keenness of Friedman's interest in monetary economics in his first postgraduate year, it might be expected that his earliest writings as a professional economist would highlight the advantages of monetary policy. Instead, his June 1948 paper on "A Monetary and Fiscal Framework for Economic Stability" had very different emphases. For a start it was less than flattering towards banks and the role of banking in a market economy.[5] In this respect it reflected the influence of Henry Simons, who had been professor of economics at Chicago until his early death at the age of forty-six in 1946. Simons claimed that the ability of banks to create money by extending loans to the private sector could result in large and untoward fluctuations in the quantity of money and, hence, to great and unnecessary macroeconomic instability.

Friedman latched onto this thinking, advocating that banks should not have the power to expand or contract money by altering credit to the private sector.[6] The aim should be rather that the state regulates directly the quantity of money. In Friedman's judgment, "the chief function of the monetary authorities" should be "the creation of money to meet government deficits or the retirement of money when the government has a surplus." An implication was that – in the middle, at a desired high-employment level of national income – the government's budget should be balanced and the quantity of money should not change. It followed that officialdom should estimate two budget concepts, "the stable budget," in which the figures were to be calculated as if the hypothetical desired level of national income prevailed, and the actual budget. Consequently, in Friedman's words, "The principle of balancing outlays and receipts at a hypothetical income level would be substituted for the principle of balancing actual outlays and receipts."[7]

Evidently Friedman (1948) did think that the equilibrium level of national income was a function of the quantity of money, in line with his later convictions. But – compared with his subsequent beliefs – the 1948 paper had two remarkable features. First, instead of favoring stable growth in the quantity of money to match increasing real output, he wanted the quantity of money to vary cyclically around a level that was to be kept constant across cycles. Second, fiscal policy was to be harnessed in order to deliver the desired countercyclical variations in the quantity of money. Booms would increase tax revenues and reduce unemployment costs, leading to budget surpluses. Such surpluses would allow "the retirement of money."[8] Conversely, recessions would undermine tax revenues and add to unemployment expenditure, resulting in budget deficits. The deficits could be financed by borrowing from the banks and by "the creation of money." In other words, monetary policy was to dance to the tune of fiscal policy. To quote, "Deficits or surpluses in the government budget would be reflected dollar for dollar in changes in the quantity of money." In this sense Friedman (1948) not only accepted the potency of fiscal policy, but also put fiscal policy before monetary policy.[9]

Now fast-forward almost forty-eight years. In January 1996 two British economists, Brian Snowdon and Howard Vane, were interviewing Friedman in the study of his apartment in San Francisco. (Coincidentally the American Economic Association was holding its annual conference in the same city.) Friedman had won the Nobel Prize for economics in 1976 and was by now a massively distinguished figure whose every utterance on economics was of wide interest. Snowdon and Vane asked Friedman, "in the light of your work on the consumption function and monetary economics in general, what role do you see for fiscal policy in a macroeconomic context?" Here is his answer:

> None. I believe that fiscal policy will contribute most if it doesn't try to offset short-term movements in the economy. I'm expressing a minority view here, but it's my belief that fiscal policy is not an effective instrument for controlling short-term movements in the economy.[10]

The contrast between this answer and the position stated in 1948 was sharp and obvious. In 1948 he saw the variations in the budget position that arose from the economy's cyclical fluctuations as worth exploiting by means of deliberate countercyclical policy adjustments to the quantity of money. So at that stage the budgetary position figured centrally in his favored approach to monetary management. But in 1996 Friedman favored a regime in which the budget balance did not have even a bit part in the larger drama of macroeconomic decision-making.

Why had Friedman changed his mind? And was he right to have rejected fiscal policy so emphatically?

II.

In the Snowdon and Vane interview, Friedman offered two informal theoretical arguments for the virtual irrelevance of fiscal policy, as he saw it. The second was that fiscal policy is "much harder" to adjust in "a sensitive short-term way" than monetary policy. But the first was the more telling and deserves detailed discussion. It was a direct challenge to hundreds of textbooks and the received wisdom of the majority of academic economists. In Friedman's words, "I believe it to be true . . . that the Keynesian view that a government deficit is stimulating is simply wrong." The explanation was the wider effects of the way the budget deficit is financed. To quote again, "A deficit is not stimulating because it has to be financed, and the negative effects of financing it counterbalance the positive effects, if there are any, on spending."[11]

Friedman's interviewers seem to have been startled by the forcefulness of his rebuttal of fiscal policy. Implicitly, Friedman was repudiating a view held almost universally among Keynesians, that the best policy response to the Great Depression of the 1930s would have been a large program of public works and an associated increase in the budget deficit. When Snowdon and Vane went on to ask whether Friedman would not have advocated "expansionary fiscal policy" in the 1930s, his reply was trenchant. "It wasn't fiscal policy, it was monetary policy that dominated. There was nothing you could do with fiscal policy that was going to offset a decline of one-third in the quantity of money." Bringing the discussion up-to-date, Friedman went on to condemn as futile the increases in the budget deficit on which Japan's government had embarked in the 1990s, in an attempt to break out of its macroeconomic doldrums. In his judgment, the Japanese were "wasting time and money in trying to have an expansive fiscal policy without an expansive monetary policy."[12]

Friedman's denigration of fiscal policy in the Snowdon and Vane interview relied, then, on his claim that monetary policy – by which he meant changes in the quantity of money – dominated fiscal policy, and the related implicit assumption that changes in the budget balance did not necessarily have any impact on the rate of money growth. It has to be said, in criticism, that this implicit assumption in Friedman (1996) is difficult to reconcile with Friedman (1948). In Friedman (1948) the creation of money by the private sector has been abolished by official fiat, and all money creation and destruction is the result, "dollar for dollar," of fiscal deficits and surpluses; in Friedman (1996) fiscal policy is irrelevant, because money dominates in the determination of macroeconomic outcomes, and the rate of money growth is not a function of the budget balance.[13] However, consistency could be restored to Friedman's position by appealing to an undoubted fact about the financing of budget deficits in most industrial nations in the two or three decades before 1996 (and in fact subsequently). In those two or three decades, governments almost invariably tried to finance budget deficits outside banking systems, partly to avoid difficulties in rolling over public debt as it came up for redemption, but more fundamentally in order to avoid the inflationary consequences of the monetization of budget deficits.

Friedman's position in the Snowdon and Vane interview then became intellectually coherent and rested on two points. First, if budget deficits are financed from non-banks and have no effect on the rate of money growth, then changes in the budget deficit (i.e., "fiscal policy," as usually understood) similarly have no effect on the rate of money growth. Second, if national income is a function of the quantity of money and not of the level of public debt, the unresponsiveness of money growth to fiscal policy means that fiscal policy is unimportant or even irrelevant to the macroeconomic situation. That was why – when asked, "What role do you see for fiscal policy?" – Friedman could say, "None."

The mature Friedman's scorn for fiscal policy therefore hinged on governments' deciding, in the late twentieth century, to finance budget deficits responsibly by medium- and long-term debt issuance – i.e., by the issuance of debt with an initial maturity of at least five years. (Friedman never denied that monetary financing of budget deficits would have all the macroeconomic consequences attributable to changes in the quantity of money.) The importance of the budget financing pattern was also central in the so-called "Treasury view" of Britain in the inter-war period. The Treasury resisted pleas by Keynes and others for extra public-works expenditure, on the grounds that long-term debt issued to finance public works would to some extent replace debt that might have been issued by the private sector. Public spending might be higher, but private spending would be lower, and the net impact on spending would not necessarily be positive.[14] The Treasury view remains one of the most effective critiques of naïve Keynesian confidence that increases in public spending and the budget deficit translate, almost automatically, into increases in national income. By the 1990s this sort of objection to Keynesian fiscal activism had become rather unfashionable within the economics profession, having lost ground to the so-called "Ricardian equivalence theorem" proposed by Robert Barro in a celebrated 1974 article.[15] Friedman seems to have appealed only infrequently to the neo-Ricardian ideas in the tendency to downplay fiscal play that marked the later stages of his career.[16]

III.

The Snowdon and Vane 1996 interview hinted that Friedman had been working for some time on research to compare the effectiveness of fiscal and monetary policy. That was confirmed in another interview at Stanford University four years later, with the questions now being asked by John Taylor. The 1948 paper was again a topic. Friedman admitted that this paper implicated the budget balance in the counter-cyclical variation of the money supply, but said that in the 1950s he came to the conclusion that the countercyclical money "policy rule was more complicated than necessary." Instead his verdict was that "you really didn't need to worry too much about what was happening on the fiscal end, that you should concentrate on just keeping the money supply rising at a constant rate." He was driven to this position by "the empirical evidence." Examination of the data persuaded him that "the link from fiscal policy to the economy was no use."[17]

But Friedman published nothing of any substance in his later career about fiscal policy.[18] (It needs to be remembered that he was in his late eighties when he gave the interview to Taylor. He did publish further heavily empirical work, but not on fiscal policy.)[19] So what was "the empirical evidence" he mentioned? Without access to his personal papers, it is impossible to say. At any rate, the rest of the present essay uses a database made available by the International Monetary Fund to see whether Friedman was talking sense or nonsense. The IMF website has data, covering the period since 1980, for the cyclically adjusted budget balance and the level of the output gap for a high proportion of its members, including the United States. From the data it is easy to calculate changes in the cyclically adjusted budget balance and the output gap, and to test whether the output gap responds to fiscal policy. As discussed in more detail in the appendix to essay 10, fiscal policy would "work," in the Keynesian manner, if increases in the cyclically adjusted budget deficit were accompanied by above-trend growth (i.e., by increases in the output gap, where "the output gap" is the monetarist concept whose evolution was discussed in essay 6). Was this the pattern observed in the United States from 1981 to 2008? Table 8.1 sets out the key numbers.

The table compares changes in the cyclically adjusted budget position (i.e., "fiscal policy," as measured by the IMF's concept of the general government structural balance) and changes in the output gap, using IMF data from its website as of December 2009. In several years, changes in both the output gap and the fiscal position were small (i.e., less than ½ percent of GDP), implying that no strong conclusions can be drawn about policy effectiveness. Such years are described as "?" when no conclusion whatever seems reasonable, and as "? Yes" or "? No" in borderline cases.

Some "naïve Keynesians" may be confident that increases in government spending and the budget deficit lead – with little or no further ado, and with next to no qualification – to similar or larger increases in aggregate demand. They may believe, in other words, the fable scripted in chapter 10 of Keynes's *General Theory*, and then rehearsed and replayed many thousands of times in textbooks and university lectures. For them table 8.1 may come as a profound shock. If naïve Keynesianism were correct, an inverse relationship would be expected to hold between changes in the budget balance and the rate of growth of output. That is, as the budget balance becomes more negative (i.e., the

TABLE 8.1
DOES NAÏVE KEYNESIANISM WORK IN THE U.S.?

	Levels of		Changes in		
	Output Gap, as % of Potential GDP	General Government Structural Balance as % of Potential GDP	Output Gap, as % of Potential GDP	General Government Structural Balance as % of Potential GDP	Years in Which Changes Have Opposite Signs and Behave in a Keynesian Manner
1980	−1.3	−6.2			
1981	−1.4	−1.7	−0.2	4.5	?
1982	−6.0	−2.6	−4.5	−0.9	No
1983	−4.6	−3.7	1.4	−1.1	Yes
1984	−0.0	−4.3	4.5	−0.6	Yes
1985	0.1	−5.0	0.1	−0.7	?
1986	0.4	−5.4	0.3	−0.4	? Yes
1987	0.7	−4.6	0.3	0.4	? No
1988	1.7	−4.2	1.1	0.4	? No
1989	2.3	−4.1	0.6	0.1	?
1990	1.4	−4.8	−1.0	−0.7	No
1991	−1.5	−4.4	−2.9	0.4	Yes
1992	−0.9	−5.3	0.6	−0.9	Yes
1993	−1.1	−4.5	−0.1	0.8	?
1994	−0.1	−3.5	1.0	1.0	No
1995	−0.8	−2.9	−0.7	0.6	Yes
1996	−0.5	−2.0	0.4	0.9	? No
1997	0.6	−1.0	1.1	1.0	No
1998	1.5	0.0	0.8	1.0	No
1999	2.6	0.9	1.2	0.9	No
2000	3.2	1.5	0.6	0.6	No
2001	1.3	0.5	−2.0	−1.0	No
2002	0.4	−1.9	−0.9	−1.4	No
2003	0.3	−2.9	−0.1	−1.0	?
2004	1.2	−2.5	0.9	0.4	? No
2005	1.4	−1.9	0.2	0.6	? No
2006	1.6	−1.6	0.2	0.3	?
2007	1.2	−1.6	−0.4	0.1	?
2008	0.2	−3.7	−1.0	−2.1	No

The period 1980–2008 contained 29 years, and 28 of those years saw changes in the variables under consideration. Of these 28 years there were:

5 years in which the output gap and the budget balance clearly changed in opposite directions, in the Keynesian manner,

1 year in which the output gap and the budget balance changed in opposite directions, but the changes were so small as probably to invalidate any conclusion about significance,

7 years in which changes in either or both the output gap and the budget balance were so small as probably to invalidate any conclusion about significance,

5 years in which the output gap and the budget balance changed in the same direction, but the changes in either or both were so small as probably to invalidate any conclusion about significance, and

10 years in which the output gap and the budget balance clearly changed in the same direction, contradicting naïve Keynesianism.

The 13 years in the middle were those in which changes in one of the two variables were under ½ percent of GDP, and their significance for the macroeconomic situation was therefore unclear. The benchmark of ½ percent of GDP is arbitrary, but reasonable.

With the 13 years of insignificant fiscal and/or output-gap changes excluded, the anti-Keynesian years (of which there were 10) outnumbered the Keynesian years (5) by two to one.

The anti-Keynesian or non-Keynesian years are clearly in a large majority. The U.S. economy behaved in an undoubtedly Keynesian fashion in less than 20 percent of these 28 years.

budget deficit increases), the rate of output growth should rise, and that ought to make above-trend growth more likely. The table shows that in fact – over a twenty-nine-year period in the world's largest and most well-studied economy – an inverse relationship of this kind held only a minority of the time. The American economy did not behave in the way expected and proselytized in one of the most influential chapters in *The General Theory*. On the contrary, as table 8.2 shows, in the twenty-nine-year period under review the years in which the economy responded in anti-Keynesian fashion to fiscal policy were twice as numerous as those in which it acted in accordance with the Keynesian script. To repeat, the economy behaves in anti-Keynesian fashion if an increase in the budget surplus or a decrease in the deficit is associated with above-trend growth, and if a decrease in a surplus or an increase in the deficit is associated with beneath-trend growth.

Various criticisms might be made of this survey of evidence on the effectiveness of fiscal policy. The approach is of course "casual empiricism," with a straightforward table of outcomes inviting quick appraisal, rather than sophisticated empiricism, with elaborate econometric techniques. But – bluntly – the exercise benefits from its simplicity and the clarity of the resulting answers. There is, of course, the objection that influences on demand were of two kinds, from fiscal policy and from all the other factors at work, and the most satisfactory analysis would be one in which the role of "all the other factors at work" could be isolated in a neat summary measure. So – a Keynesian might say – the conjunction of "restrictive fiscal policy" and above-trend growth in Clinton's second term proves nothing. The Keynesian might claim that, in that period, restrictive fiscal policy *by itself* was holding back demand growth, while "all the other factors at work" were motivating strongly above-trend growth. The Keynesian might then insist on the building of a full-scale "structural model" of the economy, so that the different sources of demand growth could be identified and measured.

Friedman was always suspicious of intellectual arguments of this kind. While a strong believer in confronting theories with evidence, he was skeptical about elaborate models and the incorporation of too many variables in a purportedly explanatory framework.[20] In building a structural model to test the relative effectiveness of fiscal and monetary policy, it is essential that the inherent properties of the model are not such as to bias the answer. But most models available at present are expansions of Keynesian income-expenditure analysis. Models of this kind, by their very method of construction, imply that an increase in the cyclically adjusted budget deficit boosts demand and output. Since the evidence on the effects of fiscal policy in the real world is murky and unimpressive, the income-expenditure models need to be handled with care. In any case the message of table 8.1 is that – even if fiscal policy could be shown to work in a properly specified structural model – in the real world the effects of fiscal policy must be largely overwhelmed by the effects of "all the other factors at work." If these factors include agents' adjustments of portfolios and expenditure to excess or deficient money holdings (see essays 15 and 16), there is at least a possibility that money is very important in "all the other factors at work." As Friedman showed in a large body of work, the power of monetary forces – in the sense of the power of changes in the quantity of money to affect changes in demand, output, and the price level – was an enduring feature of the American economy over many decades.

ESSAY 9

DOES FISCAL POLICY WORK?

THE PRESENT worldwide recession [i.e., the recession of the mid-1970s] is proving unusually stubborn. Large reflationary packages, involving cuts in taxation and higher public spending, have been announced in several leading Western economies, but the recovery so far has been fitful and uncertain. Accompanying the sluggishness of activity have been large public-sector financial deficits, particularly in the United Kingdom, the United States, and West Germany. These deficits were largely caused by the recession (as it has cut tax receipts), but at the same time they are seen as serving the benign function of combatting the weakness of spending (because the deficits represent a demand injection into the economy).

It may be thought unorthodox to argue that the deficits – or, more correctly, the deficits in conjunction with the strategies adopted to finance them – have done nothing to abate the recession. But the argument is not difficult to make. The key point is that extra spending by public authorities has been offset by reduced spending by companies and individuals. The more that governments have kept up their expenditures, the harder has it been for the private sector to carry out its investment and consumption plans. The mechanisms involved are not particularly complex and should be easy to understand, but their implications for economic policy are drastic and sometimes overlooked.

First, large public-sector deficits, when financed by debt sales to the general public, deter private investment. If the government sells bonds to non-bank private agents, it reduces their money balances and drives up interest rates. These higher interest rates lead industrialists to reconsider some of their projects and therefore crowd out investment that would otherwise have taken place. This "crowding out" effect has been much discussed in the United States recently, but it is not a new idea.

Indeed, it closely resembles the "Treasury view" which was influential in Britain in the late 1920s and early 1930s, before British officialdom had imbibed Keynes's analysis in his famous 1936 *General Theory of Employment, Interest, and Money.* The Treasury in those days resisted demands for deficit financing on the grounds that the money the government did not raise in tax revenue would have to be raised by borrowing, with no net effect on demand. Higher public spending would merely pre-empt resources that would otherwise have been utilized by the private sector. This apparently hard-faced attitude had been formed through experience of public-works programs in the 1920s. The Treasury found that, once these came to an end, there was a renewal of the initial problem, a lack of genuine jobs in private industry.

In the 1930s the Treasury view may have been misplaced because, with so many resources lying idle, the danger of less activity in one place because of more activity in another was minimal. Perhaps the Treasury could have safely financed deficits by printing money. The result of the expansion in the money supply would have been to bring idle resources back into employment, not to push up prices. But Keynes never denied that in other circumstances crowding out could be important.

More fundamentally, *with a given money-supply growth rate,* a higher level of public debt sales tends to lower the volume of bond issues by the private sector. The reduction in bond issues undermines private-sector capital spending and weakens the demand for labor. The comparative merit of public spending and private investment is a large subject. But the "consensus" is that private investment is "something we all need," "a national priority," and so on. Enthusiasm for public spending has, at any rate in the recent past, been less noisy.

Second, large sales of public-sector debt induce higher savings by individuals and result in less consumption. The abnormally high level of personal savings found in the advanced economies this year [i.e., 1975] can be largely explained in this way. It is interesting, for example, that the greatest departures from traditional savings behavior have occurred in West Germany and the United Kingdom, which also have the largest public-sector deficits (in relation to national income) of the major Western economies.

In the first quarter of 1975 individuals in the United Kingdom saved

14.2 percent of their disposable income, and in the second quarter they saved 13.4 percent. Throughout the 1960s the savings rate averaged well under 10 percent. Even in 1973, which at the time was thought to be an exceptional year, the savings rate was 11.3 percent. Much the same pattern is to be found in West Germany, although the level of savings has been consistently higher, with the savings rate around 17.5 percent this year. If people save more, they have less available to spend on consumption. The drop in demand for output is eventually reflected in the demand for labor and so counteracts the effect on employment of the public-sector deficit.

Why should a rise in public-sector deficits prompt higher savings? The basic reason is the high interest rates that are inevitable if the government denies itself the easy option of financing its deficit by increasing the money supply. Most obviously, high interest rates give a good income to savers. They affect the financial system profoundly in other ways as well. They make borrowing from banks and hire-purchase companies more expensive, and they encourage repayment of debt. (Note that there is another, less noticed way in which they make saving worthwhile, as emphasized by Keynes in *The General Theory*: If interest rates are above their long-run level, a holder of fixed-interest public debt should make good capital gains when they come down.)[1]

Although the level of interest rates is probably the best explanation of the recent financial behavior of individuals, something of a controversy has developed over other possible influences. A thought-provoking suggestion was made in Morgan Grenfell's latest *Economic Review*, edited by the firm's economics director, John Forsyth. The *Economic Review* argued that consumers try to keep their holdings of liquid assets in line with personal disposable income, because they need to have enough money or money-like assets to finance their transactions. If inflation is proceeding rapidly – at, say, 20 percent per annum – they need to add 20 percent each year to their existing holdings of liquid assets in order to keep their real value constant. Saving is sustained at a high enough level to ensure that this takes place.

The strands of the argument may now be brought together. If the government commits itself to a money-supply target, public-sector deficits and allegedly "reflationary" fiscal action have no positive effect on economic activity. As part of a strategy to ignite recovery, they are more or less futile. They do virtually nothing to pull economies out of recession, and their only true effect is to alter the balance between the public and private sectors. Higher public expenditure, paid for by long-dated bond issuance, crowds out private investment and causes higher personal savings. There is no addition to demand and no benefit in terms of employment.

The refusal of Western economies to pick up despite massive doses of supposed Keynesian "reflation" can be largely explained by the greater awareness of monetary aggregates in the mid-1970s. In the 1960s central banks sometimes seemed to have no rationally formulated policy at all, apart from day-to-day market maneuvering. But, to the extent that central banks had a policy, it was to maintain stable interest rates and allow the quantity of money to adjust to the economy. In that context extra government spending or lower taxation spilled over into the money supply and did stimulate economies. Now that the emphasis of monetary policy has changed, partly because of the lessons of the inflationary boom of 1971–73, fiscal policy is being neutralized by money-supply responsibility. In these new circumstances reflating by fiscal means is like pumping air into a tire with a puncture – the puncture being massive sales of government bonds to the non-bank public.

The argument can be taken a stage further. Governments reject calls for immediate massive cuts in public spending or sharp increases in tax rates on the grounds that they would deflate demand. The advice of a conventional "Keynesian" economist would be that such steps would substantially aggravate unemployment and cause a needlessly severe cut in output. But no such consequences follow. Fewer bond sales would ensue, lowering interest rates and promoting both investment and consumption. If accompanied by the appropriate monetary measures, fiscal restraint need have no unfavorable effects on demand and employment.

Of course, there would be adjustment difficulties. If public-sector employees are laid off as part of an economy campaign, they have to find jobs elsewhere. This takes time because of unavoidable labor-market frictions, even if the demand is there. The potential dislocations give a warning against making too abrupt changes in fiscal policy. But they do not weaken the essential argument. In any case, a different kind of unpleasantness arises if public expenditure is uncontrolled and the

TABLE 9.1
DIFFERENT ARGUMENTS TO EXPLAIN THE INEFFECTIVENESS OF FISCAL POLICY

1. The "crowding-out" argument

An increase in the budget deficit has to be financed. Unless the method of financing increases the quantity of money, the private sector has less finance than before the increase in the deficit and spends less, offsetting any boost to demand from the enlargement of the deficit.

2. The Treasury view

Much the same as the crowding-out argument, except that it is usually applied to public-works expenditures. This view was developed in the inter-war period, notably by Hawtrey in an article in *Economica* in 1925, to resist Keynes's demand for extra public-works expenditures.

3. Barro's "new Ricardianism"

An increase in public debt, due to the incurrence of a budget deficit, is not an increase in the nation's net wealth. Because net wealth is unchanged, changes in the size of the budget deficit or in its pattern of financing do not alter equilibrium national income.

4. Argument from sector flow of funds

An increase in the public sector's financial deficit implies an identical reduction in the private sector's financial deficit (or increase in its surplus), because for every new debt there must be an extra new financial claim. While the increased public-sector financial deficit may by itself imply extra spending, the reduction in the private sector's deficit implies an offsetting reduction in private spending.

5. Argument from confidence

Large budget deficits create concerns about long-run fiscal solvency, with the resulting uncertainty harming confidence and reducing private-sector expenditure. Strong action to restore fiscal solvency is good for confidence and hence for spending.

money supply is held back: private-sector employees are laid off and have to search for jobs in the public sector.

These qualifications need not be overdone. It is at last becoming clear that the coincidence of massive deficit financing with severe recession in most advanced economies, and the persistence of this state of affairs, signal the failure of fiscal policy. The present situation is the *reductio ad absurdum* of "Keynesianism," where Keynesianism is taken as the belief that an exclusive reliance can be placed on public spending and tax rates to control the economy. This belief, which never had any authority in Keynes's written work, is now being battered to death against a monetary brick wall.

ESSAY 10

DID THE 1981 BUDGET REFUTE

NAÏVE KEYNESIANISM?

THE 1981 BUDGET was undoubtedly a turning-point in British macro-economic policy-making. Its sequel put Keynesian fiscal activism into intellectual cold storage for over a generation. Only in the disastrous 2007–10 premiership of Gordon Brown were Keynesian considerations of short-term demand management briefly to dominate budgetary decisions once again. The key feature of the 1981 Budget was that taxes were raised by £4 billion (about 2 percent of gross domestic product) in a recession. In response, 364 economists wrote a letter of protest to *The Times*. As noted in the preface to this part of the book, they warned that "present policies will deepen the depression" and "threaten . . . social and political stability." It is fair to say, first, that the overwhelming majority of British academic economists disapproved of the 1981 Budget and, second, that they were quite wrong in their prognoses of its consequences. This essay discusses some of the issues in economic theory that it raised.

I.

Until the 1930s the dominant doctrine in British public finance was that the budget should be balanced. Keynes challenged this doctrine, and many authorities have subsequently cited his classic work, *The General Theory of Employment, Interest, and Money*, as the charter for discretionary fiscal policy. In fact, the remarks on fiscal policy in *The General Theory* were perfunctory. The case for discretionary fiscal policy was made more explicitly in two articles on "Paying for the War" that appeared in *The Times* on November 14 and 15, 1939.[1] These articles were a response to an unusual and very specific macroeconomic problem: the need to switch resources from peacetime uses to wartime production. Nevertheless, their influence was long-lasting. They contained an approach to macroeconomic analysis in which, given the present level of incomes, the sum of potential expenditures could be compared with the value of output at current prices. If potential expenditures exceeded the value of output, inflation was likely. In the 1939 articles, Keynes noted that equilibrium could be restored by "three genuine ways" and "two pseudo-remedies." After rejecting the pseudo-remedies (rationing and anti-profiteering), Keynes focused on the three "genuine" answers – taxation, deferred savings, and letting the inflation come through. He opposed inflation, and recommended taxation and deferred savings to eliminate excess demand.

Over time, Keynes's analysis had a powerful effect on official thinking. In a book published in 1982 R. J. Ball referred to "the almost total acceptance of Keynesian prescriptions by economists, public servants and politicians of both left and right in the United Kingdom."[2] The remarks in the two articles in *The Times* were elaborated in a theory of national-income determination which took hold in the textbooks of the 1950s and 1960s. Quoting from Christopher Dow (from his book *Major Recessions*, published in 1998),

> Interpretation of events cannot depend on unstructured observation, but has to be based on assumptions ... about the causal structure of the economy. ... Total demand is defined in terms of real final expenditure; its level (in the absence of shocks) is determined by previous income; its result is output, in the course of producing which income is generated; income in turn goes to determine demand in the subsequent period.[3]

In short, income determines expenditures, which determine income and output, which determine expenditures, which determine income and output, and so on, as if in a never-ending circle. The circular flow of income and expenditure is conceived here as being between passive private-sector agents with no way of adding to or subtracting from income from one period to the next, and without the inclination to vary the proportion of income that is spent. According to Dow's statement, the flow of private-sector expenditures would proceed indefinitely at the same level, were it not for "shocks." (Dow's view of the world also makes an appearance in essay 5, on p. 113 and pp. 115–118.)

However, the textbooks did allow for additions to or subtractions from the circular flow by an active, well-intentioned, and appropriately advised government. If the state itself spent above or beneath its tax revenue (if, in other words, it ran a budget deficit or surplus), it could add to or subtract from the circular flow.[4] The notion of a circular flow of income, and the related idea of the income-expenditure model of the economy (which was adopted in econometric forecasting in the late 1960s and 1970s), therefore made fiscal policy the favorite weapon in the macroeconomic armory. If all went well, the fiscal additions to and subtractions from the circular flow could be designed to keep the economy at full employment with price stability (or, at any rate, acceptably low inflation). The official judgment on the size of these additions and subtractions, announced with accompanying political theater every year in the Budget, was taken to be of great significance. For economists brought up to believe that the income-expenditure model was an accurate description of "how the economy worked" (and that included probably over 90 percent of the U.K.'s university economists at the time), the 1981 Budget was shockingly inept. They saw it as withdrawing demand in an economy where expenditure was weak and unemployment rising, and so as being totally misguided.

The circular flow of income is a useful, if rather elementary, teaching aid and is understandably popular in university macroeconomics courses. However, it is a primitive and incomplete account of national-income determination, and – as we shall see – it can be very misleading. If this is "Keynesianism," it is "naïve Keynesianism." Substantial amendments are needed to bring the story closer to the truth and, indeed, to the authentic Keynes of the major works.

At the level of the individual private-sector agent, it is incorrect that income and expenditure are the same in every period, for two reasons. The first is simple. As agents hold money balances, they can spend above income in any given period by running down these balances. (Of course, if they spend beneath income, they add to their money holdings.) The second is more troublesome. The motive of Keynesian analysis is to determine national expenditure and income, in order to fix the level of employment. So the relevant "expenditures" are those which lead to output in the current period and necessitate employment. It is evident that expenditure on existing assets – such as houses that were built decades ago, ships after they have been launched, antiques inherited from previous generations, and so on – does not result in more employment. (They are a legacy from past production and do not need to be made again.) But purchases and sales of assets, and of financial securities which establish claims to assets, are on an enormous scale. As with money, an individual agent can spend above income in any given period by selling an asset and spending the proceeds, or he can spend beneath income by purchasing an asset out of savings from current income. Goods can be bought with money arising from the sale of assets, and assets can be bought with money arising from the sale of goods.

At the aggregate level, the situation becomes even more complicated. Suppose, to ease the exposition, that an economy has no assets. If the amount of money is given for the economy as a whole, decisions by individual agents to run down or build up their money balances cannot alter the aggregate amount of money. However, even in this assetless economy, the amount of spending can vary between periods if the velocity of circulation of money changes. Of course, if the amount of money increases or declines from one period to the next, that also allows the level of expenditures to change even if the velocity of circulation remains constant.[5]

Now remove the assumption of an assetless economy. Money is used in three types of transaction. The first type relates to current expenditure (i.e., "aggregate demand"), output, and employment, and belongs to the circular flow. (I sell goods or services in order to purchase other goods or services.) The second type relates to expenditure on existing assets. (I sell assets in order to buy other assets.) This second type leads to asset re-dispositions and, typically, to changes in asset ownership. The third type is concerned with transactions that mix up current expenditure and expenditure on existing assets. (I sell assets in order to purchase goods or services, or I sell goods or services in order to purchase assets.) Total transactions consist of transactions in the circular flow, transactions in assets, and transactions that involve both the circular flow and assets.

These distinctions are not new, although economic theory has been rather shy about the third type of transactions, the transactions that bridge the current and capital sides of the economy. The distinction between the first and second types of transactions was in fact made by Keynes in his *Treatise on Money*, which was published in 1930, six years before *The General Theory*. To adopt his terms, "deposits" (money, in other words) are used partly in "industry" and partly in "finance." The "industrial circulation" was concerned with "maintaining the normal process of current output, distribution and exchange, and paying the factors of production their incomes"; the "financial circulation," on the other hand, was involved with "holding and exchanging existing titles to wealth, including stock exchange and money market transactions" and even "speculation."[6] Keynes's idea of two distinct circulations is thought-provoking, but he did not notice the constant interdependence of the two circulations. In the real world the same sum of money may be used in a transaction in goods one day and a transaction in assets the next. Money circulates endlessly. The distinction between the industrial and financial circulations – like any distinction relating to something as fluid as money – is to that degree artificial.

How are these ideas to be put to analytical use? It is immediately clear that, with the quantity of money given, the value of aggregate demand can change for two reasons. First, money's velocity of circulation in total transactions may alter, with the relative size of Keynes's industrial and financial circulations constant. Second, the velocity of circulation of money in total transactions may stay the same, but the relative size of the industrial and financial circulations changes. It should be unnecessary to add that, if the quantity of money increases or decreases between periods, that introduces yet another potential source of disturbance.

In short, once the economy is allowed to have both money and assets, the idea of a simple period-after-period equivalence of income and expenditure becomes implausible. The circular flow of income and expenditure would remain a valid description of the economy only if the following were constant:

(1) the quantity of money,

(2) the velocity of money in total transactions, and

(3) the proportion of transactions in the circular flow to total transactions (or, in Keynes's terminology in *A Treatise on Money*, the ratio between the industrial circulation and the industrial and financial circulations combined).

A brief glance at the real world shows that the quantity, the velocity, and the uses of money are changing all the time.

However, some economists brush these matters to one side and stick to a simple income-expenditure model when they interpret the real world. A common shortcut is to take expenditures as being determined in naïve Keynesian fashion and to claim that the quantity of money then adjusts to the level of expenditures. To quote from Dow again, "Change in nominal GDP determines change in broad money. Money is thus not the driving force in the economy, but rather the residuary determinant [*sic*]."[7]

But Dow is simply wrong. Banks are forever expanding and contracting their balance sheets for reasons that have nothing whatever to do with the recent or current levels of nominal GDP. For example, when banks lend to customers to finance the purchase of old houses, land, or long-established companies (that is, to finance the purchase of existing assets), they add to the quantity of money, but their activities do not in the first instance impinge on the industrial circulation. They have no immediate and direct effect on national income or expenditure. Nevertheless, agents have to reshuffle their money holdings and portfolios – in a second, third, or subsequent round of transactions – so that the extra money is again in balance with their wealth and current expenditure. The vital principle becomes that national income *and wealth* are in ongoing equilibrium, and so income and expenditure are likely to remain the same period after period *only* when the demand to hold money balances is equal to the supply of such balances (i.e., the quantity of money) at the end of each and every period, and when the quantity of money is constant. More briefly, national income is in equilibrium only when "monetary equilibrium" also prevails. After all, it was Keynes himself who said:

... incomes and price necessarily change until the aggregate of the amounts of money which individuals choose to hold at the

new level of incomes and prices . . . has come to equality with the
amount of money created by the banking system. That . . . is the
fundamental proposition of monetary theory.[8]

On this view, changes in the quantity of money – particularly big changes
in the quantity of money – shatter the cozy equivalence of income and
expenditure which is the kernel of naïve Keynesianism. Indeed, a sudden
sharp acceleration in the rate of money-supply growth might create a
severe "monetary disequilibrium" and initiate adjustment processes in
which first asset prices and later the prices of goods and services would
have to change.[9] A 25 percent jump in the quantity of money would –
with some technical caveats – increase the equilibrium values of both
national income and national wealth also by 25 percent. One interesting possibility cannot be excluded. It might be that – in the period of
transition from the old equilibrium to the new – some asset prices
would need to rise by more than 25 percent, in order to stimulate excess
demand in goods markets and motivate the required 25 percent rise in
national income. At any rate, for any comprehensive account of the
determination of national income, economists must have a theory of
money-holding behavior, and this theory has to recognize that money is
only one part of a larger portfolio of assets.

II.

All this may seem a long way from the 1981 Budget. It is therefore now
time to bring the discussion back to the contemporary context by discussing the values of income, money, assets, and related variables in
Britain at the time. The U.K.'s money GDPs in 1980 and 1981 were about
£215 billion and £233 billion respectively. The gross wealth of the personal sector at the end of 1980 was estimated at £658 billion, split
between £461 billion of physical assets (mostly houses) and £283 billion of financial assets, offset by £86 billion of debt, to leave net wealth
at £658 billon. Total national wealth – including public-sector and
corporate assets – was nearer £1,100 billion. At the end of 1980 the
quantity of money on the very broad M4 measure, which included
building-society deposits, was slightly above £130 billion, while sterling M3 (the subject of the official money targets then in force) was

£68.5 billion. The value of all transactions – including all check and other clearings among banks – in 1980 was over £4,000 billion.

A number of comments need to be made straightaway about these numbers. Two features are striking. First, the value of all transactions was a very high multiple of money GDP (or "national income"). Roughly speaking, total transactions were about twenty times as large as national income. Second, wealth was a high multiple of money GDP. To say that wealth was five times national income would be broadly correct, although the precise multiple depends on the valuation conventions adopted. Most wealth was owned by the personal sector, even though some of it was held indirectly via financial products of various kinds. Housing was the personal sector's principal asset.

It is obvious that national income and expenditure, the central actors in the naïve Keynesians' circular flow, took bit parts in the wider drama of total transactions. To repeat, national income was somewhat more than £200 billion, while total transactions exceeded £4,000 billion. Plainly, the majority of the transactions were not in goods and services, but in assets. In terms of size, the financial circulation dominated the industrial circulation. The preponderance of asset transactions was partly due to the second salient feature, that the value of national wealth was five times that of national income. The value of turnover on the London Stock Exchange in 1980 was £196.3 billion, not much less than GDP, while the value of turnover in gilt-edged securities was over £150 billion. In addition, there were transactions in foreign exchange, in unquoted companies and small businesses, in houses, commercial property, and land, and in such items as antiques, second-hand cars, and personal chattels.

How does this bear on the debate about the 1981 Budget? The 1980 Budget had proposed a Medium-Term Financial Strategy for both the budget deficit (defined in terms of the public-sector borrowing requirement, or PSBR) as a percentage of GDP and money-supply growth. Targets for both these variables had been set for the fiscal years up to 1983–84. The target for the 1981–82 PSBR in the 1980 Budget was 3 percent of GDP. In practice the PSBR in the closing months of 1980 proved much higher than expected, and the projections in early 1981 were that, on unchanged policies, the PSBR in 1981–82 would be over 5 percent of GDP. The government wanted to restore the credibil-

TABLE 10.1
VALUE OF THE MAIN ITEMS IN THE
U.K. PERSONAL SECTOR'S WEALTH, 1979–1982
All values in £m.

	1979	1980	1981	1982
Notes and coin	7,717	8,307	8,837	9,153
Bank deposits	36,210	43,188	47,662	51,685
Building-society deposits	42,442	49,617	56,699	66,993
▷ *All monetary assets*	86,369	101,112	113,198	127,831
Dwellings	276,600	313,200	323,700	345,900
Equity in life-insurance pension funds	37,000	49,000	57,000	75,000
U.K. ordinary shares	31,389	36,482	38,297	45,035
▷ *Three leading asset classes combined*	344,989	398,682	418,997	465,935
Net wealth	580,529	657,903	696,909	776,754

Source: *February 1984 issue of* Financial Statistics *(London: Her Majesty's Stationery Office),* table S12, p. 140

ity of the MTFS. It therefore, in the 1981 Budget, announced tax increases and other measures which would cut the PSBR/GDP ratio in 1981–82 by about 2 percent of GDP (i.e., about £4 billion). This "tightening" of fiscal policy at a time of recession was what provoked the letter to *The Times* from the 364. For economists who believed in naïve Keynesianism and the income-expenditure model, a demand withdrawal of 2 percent of GDP implied that over the year or so starting in March 1981 national expenditure and income would be at least 2 percent lower than would otherwise be the case. (Some economists of this stripe might appeal to the multiplier concept, also developed in Keynesian textbooks, to say that the adverse impact on demand would be 2 percent plus something extra because of supposed "multiplier effects.")

But hold on. As the last few paragraphs have shown, the total annual value of transactions in Britain at the time of the 1981 Budget was over £4,000 billion. The £4 billion tax increase might seem quite big relative to national income and expenditure, but it was a fleabite – a mere 0.1 percent – of total transactions. Given that national wealth is about five times national income, the impact of changes in national wealth on expenditure has to be brought into the discussion. As it happened, the 1981 Budget was accompanied by a reduction in interest rates, with the Bank of England's Minimum Lending Rate (then the name for the interest rate on which the Bank of England operated) falling from 14 to 12 percent. This cut followed an earlier one, from 16 to 14 percent, on November 25, 1980. The value of the U.K. housing stock and quoted equity market was rising throughout the period, partly because of rather high money growth and (starting in autumn 1980) the easing of monetary policy. Over the three years to the end of 1982, the value of the personal sector's money holdings advanced by over £40 billion. Meanwhile, the value of the three largest other items in its wealth (dwellings, equity in life-insurance and pension funds, and directly owned "U.K. ordinary shares") increased by more than £120 billion, and the value of its net wealth by almost £200 billion. (See table 10.1.) These numbers are an order of magnitude larger than the £4 billion tax increase in the 1981 Budget. Should anyone be surprised that the Budget was not followed by a deepening of "the depression" or by an erosion of "the industrial base of our economy," which would "threaten its social and political stability"? (Remember that third type of transaction outlined above, the transactions that bridge the current and capital sides of the economy. Expenditure on current items financed by the sale of increasingly valuable assets could and did swamp the fiscal "tightening.")

With "exquisite" timing (to use Lawson's word, from *A View from No. 11*), the recovery in the economy began almost immediately after the letter from the 364 appeared in *The Times*. Figure 10.1 shows the annualized growth of domestic demand, in real terms, in two-quarter periods from the start of the Conservative government in mid-1979 to the end of 1984. In every two-quarter period from mid-1979 to the first quarter of 1981, domestic demand fell in real terms; in every two-quarter period (with two minor exceptions) over the five years starting in Q1

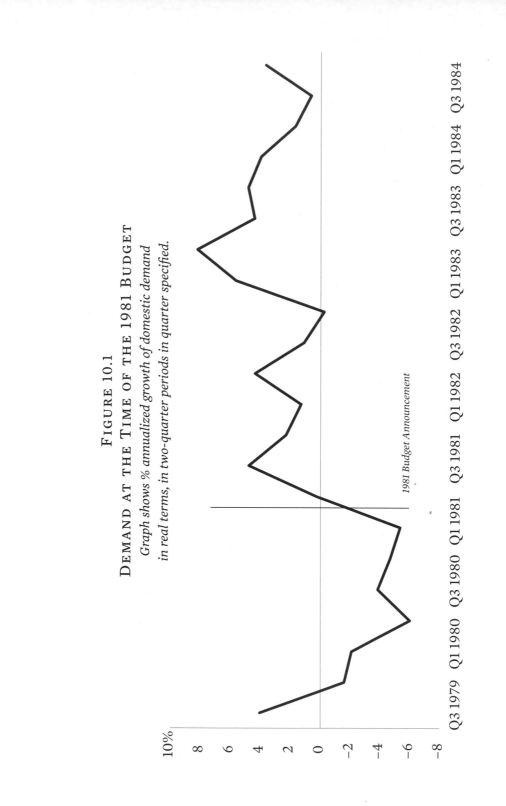

FIGURE 10.1
DEMAND AT THE TIME OF THE 1981 BUDGET
Graph shows % annualized growth of domestic demand
in real terms, in two-quarter periods in quarter specified.

1981 Budget Announcement

Q3 1979 Q1 1980 Q3 1980 Q1 1981 Q3 1981 Q1 1982 Q3 1982 Q1 1983 Q3 1983 Q1 1984 Q3 1984

10%
8
6
4
2
0
−2
−4
−6
−8

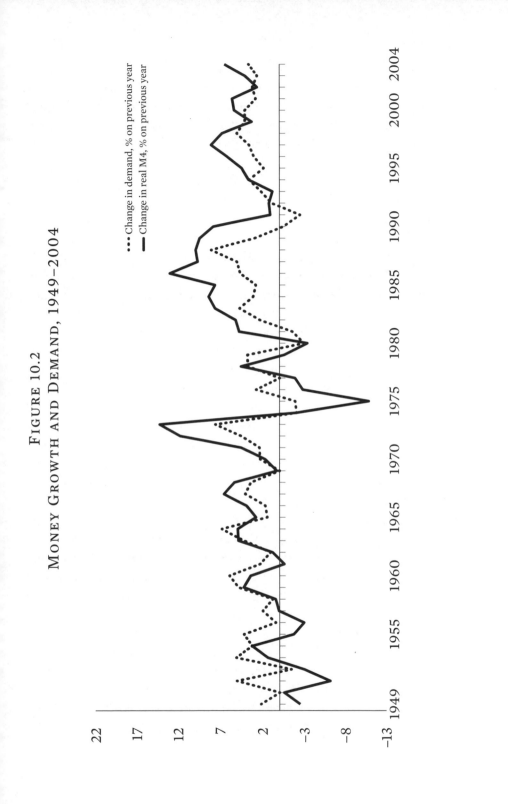

FIGURE 10.2
MONEY GROWTH AND DEMAND, 1949–2004

•••• Change in demand, % on previous year
—— Change in real M4, % on previous year

1981, domestic demand rose in real terms. From mid-1979 to Q1 1981, the compound annualized rate of fall in domestic demand was 3.8 percent; in the five years from Q1 1981, the compound annualized rate of increase in domestic demand was 3.3 percent. The warnings of a deepening of the depression were not just wrong, but hopelessly so.

III.

Of course there is much more to be said about the behavior of the economy in this period. A naïve Keynesian might ask why – if asset prices were gaining ground in 1980 and 1981 – a recession had occurred at all. While the causes of the 1980 recession are complex, the dominant consideration was plainly the very high level of interest rates. The Minimum Lending Rate had been raised to 17 percent on November 30, 1979, and the average level of clearing-bank base rate in 1980 was over 16 percent. While this had discouraged demand by familiar Keynesian mechanisms (such as the discouragement of investment), monetary forces had also been at work. Dear money had caused money-supply growth to be lower than would otherwise have been the case, and it had encouraged people and companies to hold a higher ratio of interest-bearing money balances to their expenditures. Although money-supply growth had been higher than targeted, real money balances had in fact been squeezed. The precise strength of these different "Keynesian" and "monetary" influences on demand is difficult to disentangle.

An appendix to this essay derives estimates of the change in the cyclically adjusted public-sector financial deficit as a percentage of GDP and the change in real broad-money balances on an annual basis from 1949 to 2004. The change in the PSFD/GDP ratio is usually regarded as a satisfactory summary measure of fiscal policy. The change in real domestic demand was then regressed on the two variables over four periods, the whole period (1949–2004) and three sub-periods (1949–1964, usually regarded as the era of "the Keynesian revolution"; 1965–1980, and 1981–2004). The resulting equation for fiscal policy over the whole 1949–2004 period was poor, although not totally disastrous, with an r^2 of 0.11 and a t statistic on the regression coefficient of 2.56, i.e., slightly less than the value of 3 usually thought necessary for a significant relationship. The equation for real broad money was better. It had an r^2 of 0.31 and a t statistic on the regression coefficient of 4.98. However, in the 1981–2004 period no relationship whatever obtained between the change in domestic demand and fiscal policy, whereas monetary policy – as measured by the change in real broad money – still seemed to be working. While this exercise is primitive, it suggests that the naïve Keynesian faith in fiscal policy was mistaken. By contrast, the role of the "real balance effect" – routinely dismissed by Keynesians as virtually irrelevant to the determination of demand – justifies much more investigation. (See the appendix for more details.)

The author of this essay wrote an article in *The Times* on July 14, 1983, under the title "How 364 Economists Can Be Wrong – with the Figures to Prove It." It argued that the thinking behind the MTFS was "that the economy had in-built mechanisms which would sooner or later lead to improved business conditions." It also pointed out that economies had grown, admittedly with cyclical fluctuations, for centuries before "the invention of fiscal fine-tuning, demand reflation, and the rest of the Keynesian tool kit." One key sentence read: "If we are to understand how the economy might recover without government stimulus today, we should look at wealth and credit." Particular attention was paid to the housing market and mortgage credit, since "borrowing for house purchase is the biggest financial transaction most people undertake." Data in an accompanying table showed that mortgage credit had more than doubled, from £6,590 million in 1979 to £13,795 million in 1982.

A reply appeared in the letters column of *The Times* on July 29 from Frank Hahn, one of the two economics professors at the University of Cambridge who had initiated the original letter criticizing the 1981 Budget. Hahn deserves two cheers because he did at least try to defend the 1981 letter, whereas most of the 364 have clammed up. (The author knows a few of them – who went on to later careers of great public prominence – who would prefer not to be reminded that they signed it.) The opening paragraph of Hahn's reply was lively and polemical, and may be recalled over twenty-five years later,

> Suppose 364 doctors stated that there is "no basis in medical theory or supporting evidence" that a man with an infection will

be cured by the administration of toad's liver. Suppose, none the less, that the man is given toad's liver and shows signs of recovery. Mr. Congdon (14 July) wants us to conclude that the doctors were wrong. This is slightly unfair since Mr. Congdon provides a "theory" of how toad's liver may do good to the patient.

The reply went on to claim that the recovery in the economy (which Hahn did not dispute) could be explained in "entirely Keynesian" terms, by the fall in interest rates and its impact on consumer spending.[10]

The trouble here is twofold. First, if Hahn had always believed that a fall in interest rates could rescue the economy, why did he help organize the letter from the 364? It is uncontroversial both that a decline in interest rates ought to stimulate demand and that the 1981 Budget was intended to facilitate a reduction in interest rates. Presumably Hahn's concern was about relative magnitudes. He thought that the £4 billion of supposed "demand withdrawal" announced in the Budget could not be offset by the positive effect on demand of the drop in interest rates and the rise in asset values. If so, he may have shared a characteristic of Cambridge macroeconomic thinking in the immediate post-war decades, namely, that demand is interest-inelastic and that policy-makers should instead rely on fiscal measures.[11] One purpose of the author's article of July 14, 1983, was to show that the housing market was highly responsive to interest rates and that pessimism about the economy's in-built recovery mechanisms was misplaced.[12]

Second, and much more fundamentally, Hahn's polemics concealed the deeply unsatisfactory state of Cambridge macroeconomics and indeed British macroeconomics more generally. To simplify greatly but not in a misleading way, part of Keynes's contribution to economic thinking had been to propose a new theory of national-income determination. In that theory national income was equal to national expenditure, and expenditure was a multiple of so-called "autonomous expenditure" (that is, investment and government spending). Dow's recapitulation of the circular flow of income and expenditure in *Major Recessions* was of course very much in this tradition. But Keynes fully recognized that the new theory was a supplement to an existing theory, "the monetary theory." As already explained, when money and assets are introduced into the economy, the equilibrium relationship between them and expenditure has inevitably to be part of the story. Keynes did not intend that the new theory should replace the old theory.

In a celebrated paper written in 1937, as a review article on Keynes's *General Theory*, John Hicks had tried to reconcile the two theories in a model (the so-called IS/LM model) where national income was a multiple of investment, and investment was equal to savings (i.e., the IS curve was defined), and where national income and the interest rate were at levels that equilibrated the demand for money with the supply (i.e., the LM curve was also defined). Full equilibrium, with the determination of both interest rates and national income, was achieved by the intersection of the two curves. But in practice most British economists had found the monetary side of the story complicated and confusing, and sidestepped the difficulties by the sorts of procedures adopted in Dow's *Major Recessions*. Like Dow, they fixed national income from their income-expenditure model and assumed that the quantity of money adjusted passively (or, in the jargon, "endogenously"). The quantity of money could then have no causal role in the economy. The LM part of the IS/LM model, and the possibility that asset prices and incomes might have to change to keep the demand to hold money (i.e., "liquidity preference," or L) in line with "the amount of money created by the banking system" (i.e., M), was suppressed. What Keynes deemed in *The General Theory* "the fundamental proposition of monetary theory" had disappeared from view.[13]

IV.

The message of the letter from the 364 was that British academic economists could not see national-income determination in monetary terms. They were angry because the Thatcher government had adopted monetary targets to defeat inflation and had subordinated fiscal policy to these targets, and because monetary targets made sense only if their pet theory were wrong and the monetary theory of national-income determination were correct. In retrospect, it is clear that the 364 had a poor understanding of the forces determining output, employment, and the price level. The LM part of the story mattered then (as it matters now), but the 364 could not see the connections between money growth and macroeconomic outcomes. Although policy-making improved dramatically in the 1990s, and a fifteen-year period of stability was enjoyed between 1992 and 2007, a fair comment is that British economists are still uncomfortable with monetary analysis. But it can be argued that the 1981 letter to *The Times* was part of a wider assault on money-supply targeting which led to the abandonment of broad-money targets in 1985 and 1986. The sequel was the disastrous Lawson boom and ERM bust of the 1985–92 period. That boom-bust cycle can therefore be blamed on British economists' weak knowledge of monetary economics; it reflected, in other words, "a great vacuum in intellectual understanding" and may be characterized as "the revenge of the 364" on the Thatcher government.[14]

At any rate, the 1981 Budget was an almost mortal blow to naïve Keynesianism. It was followed by a twenty-seven-year period in which fiscal policy was subordinate either to monetary policy or to rather vague requirements of "prudence." In decisions on the size of the budget deficit, governments respected the aim of keeping public debt under control over a medium-term timeframe. The central theme of macroeconomic policy-making was instead the discretionary adjustment of the short-term interest rate by an independent Bank of England to keep demand growing in such a way that actual output was, as far as possible, equal to trend output (i.e., the output gap was zero). The patient lapped up Professor Hahn's diet of toad's liver. The U.K.'s macroeconomic performance in the fifteen years from 1992 to 2007 was better than in any other period of comparable length. (See essay 7.) Nevertheless, it remains possible – depressingly – to come across textbooks that proclaim the virtues of fiscal policy and its ability to manage demand.[15]

As foreshadowed by the author's article in *The Times* in July 1983, the relationship between interest rates and the housing market became – and has remained – a more central part of macroeconomic analysis than the supposed impact of changes in the budget deficit in adding to or subtracting from the circular flow of income and expenditure. Nowadays the Bank of England is particularly active in research on the housing market.[16] Much attention is paid to the rate of house-price inflation (or deflation), because the change in the price of this asset is thought to have a major influence on consumer spending. But houses are only one asset class. In truth the level and rate of change of all asset prices matter. A key point has now to be reiterated: Any plausible theory of money-holding behavior has to recognize that money is only one part of a larger portfolio of assets. If a number of conditions are met (and over the long run they are met, more or less, in most economies), a 1 percent increase in the annual rate of money-supply growth is associated with a 1 percent increase in the equilibrium annual growth rates of both nominal national income *and the value of national wealth.* Moreover, national wealth is typically a high multiple of national income. It follows that a sudden acceleration in the rate of money-supply growth (of the kind seen in the early phases of the two great boom-bust cycles of the early 1970s and the late 1980s) leads to outbreaks of asset-price inflation. Big leaps in asset prices cause people and companies to sell assets, and to buy more goods and services, disrupting the smooth flows of incomes and expenditures hypothesized in the naïve Keynesian stories. Because the value of all assets combined is so much higher than the value of national income, the circular income-expenditure flow can become a thoroughly misleading way of thinking about the determination of economic activity.

The macroeconomic effects of the £4 billion tax increase in the 1981 Budget were smothered by the much larger and more powerful macroeconomic effects of changes in monetary policy. No doubt the naïve Keynesian would complain that this is to compare apples and pears, as hypothetical changes in asset values and their impact on expenditure are a long way from the readily quantified and easily forecast impact of budgetary measures. But that would be to duck the main question. As the sequel to the 1981 Budget showed, the naïve Keynesians are kidding themselves if they think either that the economy is adequately described by the income-expenditure model or that the impact of budgetary measures on the economy is easy to forecast.[17] (As the author argued in a series of articles in *The Times* in the mid-1970s on "crowding out," the effect of such measures depends heavily on how they are financed and, specifically, on whether they lead to extra money creation. One of these articles is republished here as essay 9.)[18] Macroeconomics must embrace monetary economics, and integrate the ideas of monetary and portfolio equilibria (and disequilibria) in the theory of national-income determination, if it is to come closer to reality.

It is ironic that the two instigators of the 1981 letter thought themselves to be protecting the "Keynesian" position in British policy-making and to be attacking "the monetarists."[19] As this volume demonstrates in several places, Keynes's writings – or at any rate his book-length writings – are replete with references to banks, deposits, portfolios, bond prices, and suchlike. No one can say whether he would have approved of the 1981 letter, but it is pretty definite that he would not have based a macroeconomic forecast purely on fiscal variables. The concepts of the industrial and financial circulations were proposed in the *Treatise* in 1930. They are building-blocks in a more complete and powerful theory of national-income determination than the simplistic income-expenditure notions advanced in the "Paying for the War" articles of November 1939. If the Keynesians had paid more attention to what Keynes said in his great works rather than in his journalism, and if they had been rather more sophisticated in their comments on money and wealth, they might not have been so embarrassingly wrong about the 1981 Budget.

STATISTICAL APPENDIX
DOES NAÏVE FISCALISM OR NAÏVE MONETARISM FIT
THE U.K. DATA BETTER?

Doubts have been raised about the validity of the monetary theory of national-income determination, with some of the skeptics adopting high-powered econometrics to make their point. In 1983 David Hendry and N. R. Ericsson published a well-known critique of the methodology used in Milton Friedman and Anna Schwartz's *Monetary Trends in the United States and the United Kingdom*.[1] Relatively little work has been directed at assessing the empirical validity of the proposition that changes in domestic demand are heavily, or perhaps even predominantly, influenced by changes in the budget deficit (which might be called the fiscalist [or naïve Keynesian] theory of national-income determination). The purpose of this appendix is to compare simple formulations of the fiscal and monetary theories of national-income determination. In view of British economists' inclination to downplay or even to dismiss the monetary theory (on the grounds that "it does not stand up to the facts"), and then to advocate changes in the budget deficit as an appropriate macroeconomic therapy, an exercise on these lines is needed. Series were obtained over the 1948–2004 period for:

1. The cyclically adjusted ratio of the public-sector financial deficit to GDP, and hence for the change in the ratio starting in 1949.

2. The change in real broad money, using the M4 measure of money adjusted by the increase in the deflator for GDP at market prices. (The M4 data after 1964 were taken from the official website of the Office for National Statistics. The M4 data before 1964 were based on a series prepared at Lombard Street Research, which drew on the data given in Forrest Capie and Alan Webber, *A Monetary History of the United Kingdom, 1870– 1982*, vol. 1 [London: Allen & Unwin, 1985].)

3. The change in real domestic demand, where the deflator for GDP at market prices was again used to obtain the real-terms numbers.

The cyclical adjustment to the PSFD data was conducted in the same way as in the author's paper "Did Britain Have a Keynesian Revolution? Fiscal Policy since 1941,"[2] which is reprinted in this collection as essay 5. (For fiscal years 1963–64 to 1986–87 the author's numbers for the cyclically adjusted PSFD/GDP ratio are virtually identical to those given in H.M. Treasury's Occasional Paper no. 4 on "Public Finances and the Cycle," published in September 1995.) The change in the cyclically adjusted public-sector financial deficit is usually accepted as a satisfactory summary measure of fiscal policy.

The change in real domestic demand was regressed against, first, the change in the cyclically adjusted PSFD/GDP ratio (to test a naïve fiscalist hypothesis) and, second, the change in real M4 (to test a naïve monetarist hypothesis) for four periods, 1949–2004 as a whole, 1949– 1964 (i.e., the "Keynesian revolution"), 1965–1980 (the period when the Keynesian dominance in policy thinking was being eroded), and 1981–2004 (the period when medium-term fiscal rules were adopted, initially because of "monetarism," but later because of Mr. Gordon Brown's "prudence"). The results are given in table 10.2.

TABLE 10.2
NAÏVE FISCALISM VS. NAÏVE MONETARISM

1. *The whole 1949–2004 period*

Naïve fiscalism
Change in real domestic demand (% p.a.) = 2.61 + 0.56
Change in PSFD/GDP ratio (% of GDP, in year in question)
r^2 = 0.11   *t* statistic on regression coefficient = 2.56

Naïve monetarism
Change in real domestic demand (% p.a.) = 1.74 + 0.28
Change in real M4 (% p.a.)
r^2 = 0.31   *t* statistic on regression coefficient = 4.98

2. *The 1949–1964 sub-period ("the Keynesian revolution")*

Change in real domestic demand (% p.a.) = 2.68 + 0.73
Change in PSFD/GDP ratio (% of GDP)
r^2 = 0.19   *t* statistic on regression coefficient = 1.82

Change in real domestic demand (% p.a.) = 2.87 + 0.34
Change in real M4 (% p.a.)
r^2 = 0.23   *t* statistic on regression coefficient = 2.03

3. *The 1965–1980 sub-period (the breakdown of the Keynesian consensus)*

Change in real domestic demand (% p.a.) = 1.96 + 0.98
Change in PSFD/GDP ratio (% of GDP)
r^2 = 0.35   *t* statistic on regression coefficient = 2.72

Change in real domestic demand (% p.a.) = 1.16 + 0.37
Change in real M4 (% p.a.)
r^2 = 0.66   *t* statistic on regression coefficient = 5.20

4. *The 1981–2004 sub-period (the period of medium-term fiscal rules)*

Change in real domestic demand (% p.a.) = 2.92 – 0.06
Change in PSFD/GDP ratio (% of GDP)
r^2 = 0.001   *t* statistic on regression coefficient = – 0.16

Change in real domestic demand (% p.a.) = 0.64 + 0.38
Change in real M4 (% p.a.)
r^2 = 0.28   *t* statistic on regression coefficient = 2.95

The econometrics here are primitive, but three comments seem in order. The first is that naïve monetarism works better than naïve fiscalism both over the whole period and in each of the three sub-periods. (See figure 10.2 above comparing the changes in real M4 and real domestic demand over the whole period.) However, naïve fiscalism was only slightly worse than naïve monetarism in the first sub-period (the period of "the Keynesian revolution"). The second is that in the final sub-period, when medium-term fiscal rules prevailed, the relationship between changes in the budget deficit and domestic demand disappeared. The results of the naïve fiscalist equation in the 1981–2004 sub-period are atrocious. (See figure 10.3, with its obvious absence of a relationship. As table 10.2 shows, the r^2 is virtually zero, and the regression coefficient has the wrong sign and is insignificant.)

It is not going too far to say that – in these years – naïve Keynesianism was invalid, and the standard prescription of its supporters ("fiscal reflation will boost employment") was bunk. The third is that the 364 were not entirely silly to believe in 1981 that a reduction in the budget deficit would be deflationary. Although the relationship between the changes in the cyclically adjusted budget deficit and domestic demand had been weaker than that between changes in real M4 and domestic demand in the preceding fifteen years, the naïve fiscalist hypothesis had not done all that badly in the second sub-period. Indeed, through the careful selection of years, one period of twenty-one years (1953 to 1973) could be found with an impressively strong relationship between fiscal policy and demand outcomes. (See figure 10.4.)

It was only in the final twenty-five years of the post-war period that – on the analysis here – a naïve Keynesian view of national-income determination became indefensible. The extremely poor quality of the fiscal equation in the final sub-period raises the question, Was its better performance in the 1949–1964 and 1965–1980 sub-periods, and particularly in the 1953–1973 sub-period, really because fiscal policy *by itself* was quite powerful, or was it rather because fiscal policy influenced money-supply growth, and monetary policy was the relevant, strong influence on demand? To answer these questions, the author regressed the rate of real M4 growth on both the level and the change in the PSFD/GDP ratio over the whole 1949–2004 period, and over the 1949–1964 and 1965–1980 sub-periods, and was unable to find a relationship

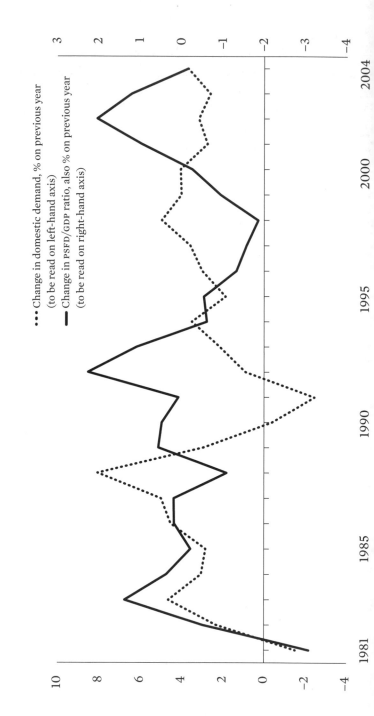

FIGURE 10.3
FISCAL POLICY AND DEMAND, 1981–2004
(The period of medium-term fiscal rules)

••• Change in domestic demand, % on previous year
(to be read on left-hand axis)

▬ Change in PSFD/GDP ratio, also % on previous year
(to be read on right-hand axis)

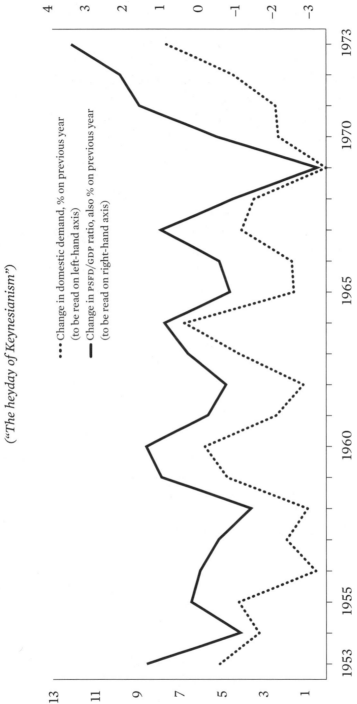

FIGURE 10.4
FISCAL POLICY AND DEMAND, 1953–1973
("The heyday of Keynesianism")

••• Change in domestic demand, % on previous year
(to be read on left-hand axis)

━━ Change in PSFD/GDP ratio, also % on previous year
(to be read on right-hand axis)

between the variables that met standard criteria of statistical significance. Much more work should be done, but it seems the apparent conclusion cannot be denied. To the extent that fiscal policy was effective between 1949 and 1980, it did not work largely though monetary policy, and it did have some independent effect on the economy. This may solace those (presumably most of the 364) who claim that fiscal policy mattered in these years, even though fiscal policy did not matter after 1980 and monetary policy has always mattered more.

However, a little more investigation raises more questions. The 1953–1973 sub-period – the best period for the Keynesian hypothesis – needs to be looked at more carefully. To repeat, fiscal policy ostensibly had a strong effect on domestic demand. (In the equation regressing the change in domestic demand on the change in the PSFD/GDP ratio, the r^2 was 0.62 and the t statistic on the regression coefficient was 5.57. The regression coefficient was remarkably close to unity, at 1.15. In other words, if the chancellor of the exchequer were to increase the budget deficit by £500 million over the next fiscal year, he could expect to increase domestic demand by slightly more than £600 million, just as the textbooks said.) Further, in this sub-period naïve Keynesianism worked better than naïve monetarism. (In the equation regressing the change in domestic demand on the rate of real M4 growth, the r^2 was 0.41 and the t statistic on the regression coefficient was 3.63.) Given that this was how macroeconomic policy operated over such an extended period, were not the Keynesians justified in the mid-1970s in believing in the effectiveness of fiscal policy and in the superiority of fiscal over monetary policy? The answer depends on how one views the relationship between fiscal and monetary policy in those years. When the author regressed the rate of real M4 growth on the level and the change in the PSFD/GDP ratio over the 1953–1973 period, the equation with the change in the PSFD/GDP ratio was much better than in other sub-periods and – exceptionally – it was quite good in its own terms. (The r^2 was 0.43 and the t statistic on the regression coefficient was 3.77.) This leaves open the possibility that fiscal policy "worked" between 1953 and 1973 because changes in fiscal policy were accompanied by changes in money-supply growth that operated in the same direction and had powerful impacts on demand in their own right. Fiscal policy "mattered" largely via a monetary channel, because the budget deficit affected the rate of the growth of the quantity of money.

In his celebrated attack on "the new monetarism" in the July 1970 issue of *Lloyds Bank Review*, Nicholas Kaldor scorned the role of monetary policy, claiming that changes in money-supply growth could be "explained" by fiscal policy. In his words, "I am convinced that the short-run variations in the 'money supply' – in other words, the variation relative to trend – are very largely explained by the variation in the public sector's borrowing requirement." He amplified the point in a footnote which read

> In fact, a simple regression equation of the annual change of the money supply on the public sector borrowing requirement for the years 1954–68 shows that the money supply increased almost exactly £ for £ with every £1 increase in the public sector deficit, with $t = 6.1$ and $r^2 = 0.740$, or, in fashionable language, 74 percent of the variation in the money supply is explained by the deficit of the public sector alone.[3]

The results of the regression reported in Kaldor's footnote are surprising, since the PSBR was not introduced as an official statistic until 1963, and thus (unless he had access to internal Treasury estimates, which is possible) no such regression could have been carried out for earlier years. The author has tried to replicate Kaldor's result by regressing the change in "the money supply" (i.e., the sum of notes and coin in circulation and clearing-bank deposits) on the public-sector financial deficit, for which (to repeat) data are available back to 1948. The equation was markedly weaker than the one reported by Kaldor (with a regression coefficient of 0.48, an r^2 of 0.38, and a t statistic of 2.81), but it was not rubbish. It is indeed plausible that – in the 1950s and 1960s, when bank lending to the private sector was officially restricted for much of the time – a major influence on the growth of banks' balance sheets was the increase in their holdings of public-sector debt. Fiscal and debt-management policies did affect money-supply growth, as most economists thought at the time (and despite the rather conflicting results mentioned in earlier paragraphs).

However, this does not mean – as Kaldor seems to have implied – that in all circumstances fiscal policy dominated monetary policy, and that monetary policy *by itself* was unimportant. In the 1980s and 1990s, after the removal of credit restrictions, bank lending to the private sector became by far the largest credit counterpart of M4 growth, and the change in money and the budget deficit were no longer correlated. But – as this appendix has shown – the influence of money on demand remained identifiable, whereas the influence of fiscal policy on demand vanished.

In retrospect it is clear that Kaldor went too far in his statement about the link between the budget deficit and money growth.[4] However, he did at least recognize that fiscal variables, and not monetary variables alone, needed to be cited as evidence in the debate. British Keynesians have later been much too ready to debunk monetary aggregates. The same standards of proof need to be applied to both monetary *and fiscal* variables.

ESSAY 11

DO CHANGES IN THE QUANTITY OF MONEY SMOTHER FISCAL POLICY?

A STANDARD PROPOSITION in macroeconomics is that national income and wealth take their equilibrium values only when agents' demand to hold money balances is equal to the quantity of money actually in existence.[1] The validity of this proposition is unaffected by whether it is stated in real or nominal terms. However, a specification in "real" terms – that real income and wealth are in equilibrium only when the demand to hold real money is equal to the quantity of real money balances – has an important merit. It reminds readers that this idea, so central to macroeconomics, is an outgrowth of the microeconomic theory of supply and demand, where "supply" and "demand" relate to real goods and services. A typical demand function for "real" things – socks, potatoes, foreign holidays – has a small number of explanatory variables, with three (price, income, and taste) being pre-eminent. Moreover, demand is usually a stable function of this small number of variables.

Milton Friedman, a champion of free-market economics, was a pioneer in the estimation of money-demand functions.[2] One of his central conclusions – that the demand to hold money is a stable function of a small number of variables – has acquired an ideological tinge, perhaps because of Friedman's well-known and sometimes controversial pro-capitalist political positions. However, no one would claim that there is anything ideological in the assertion that the demand for socks (or potatoes or foreign holidays) is a stable function of a small number of variables.

* * *

I.

In the modern world money is a liability of banks. Any worthwhile discussion of money necessarily spends time on banking institutions, including their idiosyncrasies, their frailties, and the often grubby motives of their managements. A common misapprehension is that in his *General Theory* Keynes demonstrated that the sordid (and highly capitalist) subjects of money and banking could be eliminated from macroeconomic analysis.[3] This is not so. As explained in essay 10 (pp. 220–221), *The General Theory* presented and reconciled two ways of thinking about national-income determination. In the first of these, which was given a new pre-eminence by Keynes, national income was seen as a multiple of investment, and as being in equilibrium when agents' desired levels of investment (I) and saving (S) were equal; in the second, which was rooted in traditional economic theory, national income was seen as a function of the quantity of money, and as being in equilibrium when agents' desired money holdings (or their "liquidity preferences," L) were equal to the quantity of money (M). John Hicks's demonstration that these two approaches could be reconciled in a single model – with both IS and LM equations, and a single diagram with the IS and LM curves intersecting – kept money in the analysis.[4] At no stage did Keynes deny the power of monetary influences on income and wealth, and hence the significance of banking developments for the macroeconomic prospect.[5]

Ultimately the usefulness of the monetary theory of the determination of national income and wealth is a matter of fact. Is there enough stability in the demand to hold money for economists to be able to make strong, interesting, and largely correct statements about movements in national income and wealth from what they know about the behavior of the quantity of money? A concession has to be made to the skeptics, namely that, in one respect, the monetary theory is ambiguous. What concept of "money" is at work in the standard LM proposition? For Keynes the answer was straightforward and explicit. In a footnote in *The General Theory* he said, "As a rule, I shall, as in my *Treatise on Money*, assume that money is co-extensive with bank deposits."[6]

For Friedman, too, the quantity of money was best understood as an aggregate including all bank deposits.[7] (See p. 376 and pp. 378–379 in essay 17.) If these remarks from the leaders of monetary thought are taken seriously, the LM equation is to be interpreted in terms of a broadly defined concept of money, a concept that is dominated nowadays by bank deposits and includes "time deposits" (that is, deposits which are not immediately available for transactions).[8]

In a fiat-money economy the creation of money requires virtually no resources. Certainly the nominal value of the bank notes issued by the state is an enormous multiple of the cost of printing them, while banks can add to both sides of their balance sheets by "a stroke of the pen." By contrast, the real values of output, employment, and the capital stock are determined – in the long run and preponderantly – by real variables, such as technology, demographics, skill acquisition, natural resources, and so on.[9] Two propositions follow from these remarks, which might be regarded as a *précis* of the realities – the realities of mainstream neoclassical economics – that confront every policy-maker in all nations. The first is relatively uncontroversial; it is that inflation is, in Friedman's words, always and everywhere a "monetary phenomenon." (Friedman's statement should really be expanded into "inflation and deflation are always and everywhere monetary phenomena." The virtual stagnation of money in Japan in the last fifteen years is the most obvious explanation for the falls in the price level that Japan has seen.)

The second proposition is less familiar and is indeed rejected by the majority of contemporary macroeconomists. This is that a major – and often pre-eminent – driving force in the business cycle is the variation in the rate of growth of real money balances. In the long run, in all economies, the rate of growth of real money balances is much the same as the rate of growth of real output. But in the short run, the growth rate of real money balances can diverge from the long-run or "equilibrium" level because of credit booms and busts, financial deregulation and re-regulation, inappropriate official interest rates, and so on.

II.

A few patterns seem to be recurrent. As the author's 2005 publication *Money and Asset Prices in Boom and Bust* showed, the nominal values of the key assets of a capitalist market economy (namely corporate equity, and both residential and commercial real estate) are far more volatile than the nominal values of individual incomes and the prices of most final goods and services.[10] (See also essays 15 to 17 in this volume.) Rapid growth of real money tends to be accompanied by bursts of asset-price inflation, which – by a variety of mechanisms – cause above-trend growth in spending and output. Conversely, stagnation or contraction of real money is associated with phases of asset-price deflation, and beneath-trend growth or, indeed, declines in spending and output.

It is here that the interactions between the banking system and macroeconomic outcomes become particularly evident. The condition of the banking system – as measured by its capital, cash, and liquidity relative to regulatory norms and management objectives – affects its ability (or sometimes its inability) to expand its deposit liabilities (i.e., the quantity of money). The rate of money growth is critical to current and future movements in asset prices, while a nation's wealth is typically five to seven times its current national income. Agents do not have to borrow in order to spend above income, as they can instead obtain extra money by selling an asset and running down their wealth. (Of course, they add to their wealth if they spend beneath income.) By implication, the deviation of asset prices from expected long-run values is basic to understanding the ups and downs in expenditure that characterize a typical business cycle.

The shenanigans in the British economy towards the end of the first decade of the twenty-first century were consistent with the monetary theory of national-income and asset-price determination. In 2005, 2006, and early 2007, U.K. money growth ran at an annual rate in the low double digits and was too high relative to the economy's trend increase in real output. Asset prices – notably house prices – took off and became unsustainably high.[11] After the Northern Rock affair broke in September 2007, banks reassessed capital adequacy and expansion plans, and money growth slowed markedly. The money balances of industrial and commercial companies, which were soaring at an annual rate of about 15 percent in 2006, fell in 2008. These falls in their nominal money holdings coincided with big increases in energy and raw-material costs at the tail end of a global boom. The implied squeeze on real money balances was associated with a slump of 40 percent in commercial-real-estate values, undermining the collateral for bank loans. Commentators feared that an implosion of the U.K.'s banking system could lead to large-scale loan repayments and an accelerating decline in bank deposits. The eventual outcome could even be an unstable "cumulative process" of credit and money contraction of the kind envisaged by Knut Wicksell in the 1890s, or the kind of self-reinforcing downward "debt deflation" spiral analyzed by the American economist Irving Fisher in the early 1930s.

In the traumatic environment of late 2008, a priority in macroeconomic policy became ensuring that the growth of bank deposits would resume. Here the government's own financial behavior was potentially important. If bank lending to the private sector was likely to contract over the next few quarters, bank deposits would also contract unless the banks were able to acquire other assets, such as claims on the public sector. Historically, British banks had held huge quantities of government debt. Indeed, in the late 1940s government securities and Treasury bills accounted for over three-quarters of their assets, whereas in late 2008 the corresponding figure was less than 2 percent.

But a debt-issuing government can do a deal with a debt-buying banking system only if the right kinds of government securities are created. Contrary to far too many newspaper reports in the 2007–09 crisis period, banks are inherently risk-averse institutions. They try to avoid buying any securities that may slump in value and become "toxic." In the ordinary course of business they will not buy long-dated, fixed-rate government securities.[12] Such securities fluctuate markedly in price as yields vary, causing large capital gains and losses, and unwelcome swings in the value of banks' capital. Banks instead favor Treasury bills (to be redeemed in three months) or short-dated government securities (with a life of less than five years). In late 2008 and early 2009, the contraction in bank credit to the private sector intensified, because of regulatory pressure on the banks to raise their capital/asset ratios. Loans to the private sector started to fall at a rate of ½ percent to 1 percent a month, not dissimilar to the pattern in the United States' Great Depression between 1929 and 1933. In such circumstances one way for the British government to restore a positive rate of money growth was for its debt agency, the Debt Management Office, to issue an abundance of Treasury bills and short-dated gilts, and to sell them to the banks.[13]

(The author advocated large-scale government borrowing, directly from the commercial banks, in his pamphlet *How to Stop the Recession*.[14] In the event, a collapse in the quantity of money was averted by the Bank of England's exercise in "quantitative easing," announced in early March 2009. The Bank borrowed from the commercial banks, by crediting them with cash-reserve balances, and used the proceeds to buy about £200 billion of government securities from non-banks. In the first instance the effect was to increase bank deposits [i.e., the quantity of money] by about £200 billion more than would otherwise have been the case. The QE exercise was an example of the "debt-market operations" discussed in essay 4. The British economy revived, quickly and impressively, as the QE operations took effect. Figure 11.1 shows a marked V pattern in the change in companies' real money balances and an accompanying rebound in companies' output plans in this period. The recoveries in real balances and output would have been inconceivable without the QE program. This program stopped the recession from becoming a depression. See also pp. 399–402 in essay 18 for more on the U.K.'s QE exercise.)

III.

What is the relevance of "fiscal policy" to the above analysis? The answer is that – contrary to a large number of textbooks – the size of the government's budget deficit is by itself not necessarily of any importance to aggregate demand.[15] Two theoretical arguments are commonly deployed to explain the ineffectiveness of fiscal policy. The first is the "Treasury view" elaborated most rigorously by Ralph Hawtrey in the journal *Economica* in 1925, according to which extra public spending "crowds out" an equivalent amount of private demand, with no net stimulus to the economy.[16] Alternatively, the neo-Ricardianism associated with Robert Barro in his classic 1974 paper in the *Journal of Political Economy* credits citizens with such forward-looking rationality that they "see through" the veil of paper claims and obligations that the public debt represents.[17] More precisely, they know they must pay taxes in order that public debt can be serviced, and therefore they see that budget deficits and the associated increases in public debt

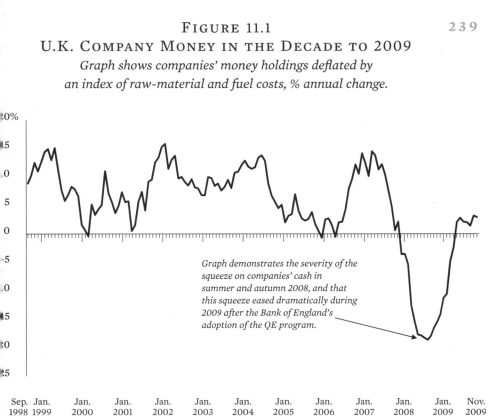

FIGURE 11.1

U.K. COMPANY MONEY IN THE DECADE TO 2009

*Graph shows companies' money holdings deflated by
an index of raw-material and fuel costs, % annual change.*

Graph demonstrates the severity of the
squeeze on companies' cash in
summer and autumn 2008, and that
this squeeze eased dramatically during
2009 after the Bank of England's
adoption of the QE program.

do not boost the private sector's net wealth. Because net wealth is
unchanged, so also is national expenditure.

But there is another line of reasoning, which is less widely noticed
and has much the same message. Any agent can spend above income in
a particular period by borrowing. But, if it borrows, that agent has to
divert spending power from other agents, and this diversion may reduce
the other agents' expenditure. Whether or not it does reduce other
agents' expenditure depends on a range of considerations, in particular,
the state of their balance sheets, wealth, and money holdings. There is
no guarantee – no guarantee at all – that an increased budget deficit
will expand total expenditure.

The vulnerability of the claim that "an increase in the budget deficit
is always expansionary" can be illustrated by an appeal to the identity
that the sum of the net acquisitions of financial assets by all sectors is

zero. The logic behind the identity is simple: that for new debts issued by one sector there must be matching new financial assets held by other sectors. It follows that, if the government's deficit contracts or moves into surplus, the deficits of all other sectors (household, corporate, and financial) must increase. Why is the increase in the combined deficit of these three sectors not expansionary in the same way that an increase in the budget deficit is supposed to be? Why should a reduction of the budget deficit – even a large reduction of the kind that occurred in the U.K. in the controversial 1981 Budget, and again between 1993 and 1996 – imply a net withdrawal of demand from the economy? It must – as a matter of logical necessity – be identically matched by an increase in the deficits of the other sectors.

As a matter of fact, the corporate-sector financial deficit has in some economies for many years been larger than the government's budget deficit, but no one has seen fit to identify this "corporate deficit financing" as an exogenous contribution to demand. If an increase in the government's budget deficit is "stimulatory," why isn't an exactly equal increase in the "budget deficits" of the economy's other sectors just as "stimulatory"? If an £x billion increase in the "budget deficits" of the economy's other sectors is "expansionary" in total demand, why isn't an £x billion reduction in the budget deficits of these other sectors "restrictive" in total demand? And – since an expansion of the public sector's net financial deficit must be accompanied by an identically equal contraction in the private sector's net financial surplus – what is the point of fiscal policy?

The trouble here is conceptual: too many economists have been bamboozled by the textbook account of the circular flow of income and expenditure. As noted in essay 10, in two articles in *The Times* in late 1939 Keynes elaborated the income-expenditure circular flow as the theoretical rationale for his recommendations to the British government about the financing of the Second World War. Crudely, income determines expenditures, which determine income and output, which determine expenditures, which determine income and output, and so on, as if in a constantly revolving circle. The circle goes on forever, unless an "injection" into or "withdrawal" from expenditures occurs from outside, say, from the government. By the manner of its exposition, the Keynesian income-expenditure model therefore accords government demand injections and withdrawals a starring role in the macroeconomic drama.

But the income-expenditure model simplifies to the point of carica-ture. In fact, economic agents use money to finance their expenditures, while it is not true that – in any particular period – any individual per-son's or company's expenditure is constrained by income in that or any previous period. An individual can sell some shares, obtain money from the sale proceeds, and – in any period – make consumption purchases way above the income of the period; a company can sell a subsidiary, again obtain money, and so finance an investment program that is many times greater in value than current profits. The income-expenditure circular flow is one of the earliest items in any university course on Keynesian macroeconomics, and it does indeed have some pedagogic value. But it must always be qualified by a recognition that expendi-tures can be paid for by asset sales as well as from current income. It must also not be used to support the Keynesians' claim that counter-cyclical adjustments of the budget deficit are the best means to regulate aggregate demand. That claim leads to a false and exclusive reliance on fiscal policy, when in fact the effects of fluctuations in the quantity of money and asset prices on demand may smother any impulse from changes in the budget balance.

IV.

The Keynesian enthusiasm for fiscal policy received a hard knock in the 1980s from the realization that perennial budget deficits lead not merely to rises in public debt, but in some conditions to self-reinforcing and unstable debt explosions.[18] An increase in the budget deficit in year 1 might or might not boost aggregate demand in year 1, but it certainly added to the debt in year 1, which implied higher debt-servicing costs and a yet larger budget deficit in year 2, which meant still higher debt-servicing costs and an even larger budget deficit in year 3, and so on. By year 4 or 5 a return to the same underlying budget deficit as in year 0 required measures to reduce the budget deficit by a sum much larger than the increase in year 1, and not for any good macroeconomic reasons, but because of the need to offset the extra debt interest charges. Most Western democracies abandoned Keynesian fiscal activism at some point in the two decades starting in the mid-1970s.[19]

Nevertheless, naïve Keynesian theories – with the income-expenditure circular flow as their center of gravity – continued to be taught in the universities. The Keynesian pabulum was fed to the latest generation of students, almost as if the experiences and priorities of decision-makers in the real world could be ignored. The Keynesians may have taken heart from the award of the Nobel Prize to the American economist Paul Krugman in 2008. He had spent much of the preceding fifteen years arguing that, because Japan was in a so-called "liquidity trap," demand in its economy ought to be promoted by a public-works program like that advocated by Keynes for Britain in the inter-war period. Krugman's claims about the liquidity trap were reviewed critically in essay 4, where it was shown that at least two quite distinct "liquidity traps" can be identified and that Krugman was confused about which trap really mattered in the Japanese context.

But another and equally fundamental issue was raised by Krugman's work. He took it for granted that fiscal policy "worked," in the sense that an increase in the structural (or cyclically adjusted) budget deficit would lead to stronger growth than would otherwise have been the case. Was this in fact a property of fiscal policy in Japan in the relevant period? In the last few years the International Monetary Fund has made available an impressive new database for all the leading economies, with numbers for both the structural budget deficit and the output gap. (For more on the development of the "output gap" notion now standard in macroeconomic research, see essay 6 above. The IMF database is mentioned elsewhere in this volume, notably on pp. 404–406 in essay 18.)

The database enables economists to compare changes in the structural budget deficit with changes in the output gap. If Keynesian fiscalism were correct, an increase in the structural budget deficit ought to be associated with an increase in the output gap. Figure 11.2 shows that this was just not true in Japan in the 1981–2008 period. Between 1991 and 1994 Japan's structural budget deficit increased in every year, and every year also experienced a reduction in the output gap, meaning that there was either beneath-trend growth or contracting output. In other words, the recession intensified while fiscal policy was, allegedly, "expansionary." Further, between 2004 and 2007 the structural budget deficit was reduced in every year, and every year enjoyed above-trend

FIGURE 11.2

DID FISCAL POLICY WORK IN JAPAN, 1981–2008?

*The increase in the structural, cyclically adjusted budget deficit
and the change in the output gap were in the opposite direction
on more occasions than they were in the same direction.*

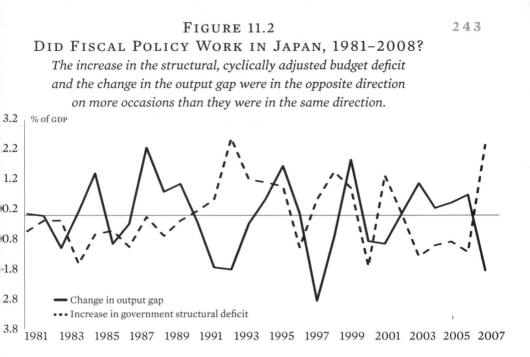

growth. While the economy was not exactly booming in this period, spare capacity and unemployment declined against a backdrop of supposedly "restrictive" fiscal policy. (See pp. 195–198 for a similar result in the U.S., pp. 224–232 for the U.K., and pp. 404–406 for the G7 as a whole. The finding that "fiscal policy doesn't work" is repetitive.)

Krugman was not the only economist to see the active use of fiscal policy as part of the answer to Japan's twenty years of macroeconomic doldrums from the early 1990s. In a much-praised book published in 2008, *The Holy Grail of Macroeconomics: Lessons from Japan's Great Recession*, Richard Koo, chief economist at the Nomura Research Institute, proposed that Japan suffered from what he called a "balance-sheet recession." According to this argument, the crux of the problem was that private-sector agents had excessive debt relative to the value of their assets, which had plunged in the early 1990s after the bursting of an extreme stock-market and real-estate bubble. With their debt too high, they did not want to borrow. This aversion to borrowing was – in Koo's view – the main cause of the sluggishness of expenditure. To quote, "a nationwide plunge in asset prices causes the value of business assets to fall sharply below the value of the corresponding liabilities . . .

Firms respond by minimizing debt, which reduces aggregate demand, and tips the economy into recession."[20] Koo went on to claim that, because the deadweight of past debts discouraged spending by the private sector, the public sector ought to run budget deficits and so fill a supposed "deflationary gap." While he accepted that strong public finances might be desirable "under ordinary circumstances," fiscal consolidation – meaning action to reduce the structural deficit – "can never be the right prescription during a balance sheet recession, which occurs only after the collapse of a nationwide asset-price bubble, a once-in-several-decades kind of event."[21]

V.

Implicit in Koo's discussion was a theory – or rather a quasi-theory – of the determination of aggregate expenditure. The Koo quasi-theory often appears in the financial press and broker reports, but it neither is recognized in economics as an academic discipline nor has the support of any leading thinker in the subject. According to the quasi-theory, the change in total expenditure depends on the amount of borrowing by agents. This notion seems to derive from the income-expenditure circular flow and the related idea that the flow continues endlessly unless spending injections or withdrawals occur "from outside," because of one sector of the economy incurring or repaying debt. If that were the real world, Koo's argument would be plausible. If extra demand depends on more borrowing, and if both private-sector agents and the government cannot or will not increase their borrowings, then total expenditure is stuck.

But the whole line of thought is wrong. The total value of payments in any economy is a vast multiple of the "expenditure" figure that appears in the national accounts, serves as the focus of elementary macroeconomic texts, and is the "effective demand" that Keynes explained in *The General Theory* was relevant to the determination of output and employment. The total value of payments exceeds the sum of consumption, investment, and changes in inventories (i.e., "private-sector aggregate demand," as understood in Keynesian macroeconomics) by the value of transactions in assets, intermediate transactions (i.e., purchases and sales between wholesalers, retailers, and so on), and assorted transfers between different agents, as well as by transfers between different accounts of the same agents. The critical constraint on the total value of agents' payments is imposed not by the amount of debt they owe, but by the quantity of money in their hands and the degree of inconvenience involved in making that money circulate faster (i.e., raising the so-called "turnover velocity of money"). In equilibrium, the total value of payments – which must be distinguished from national income and expenditure – can be viewed as the product of the quantity of money and the desired turnover velocity of money.[22] If the quantity of money rises, so also do the equilibrium values of all the payments in a society, and of such assets as real estate and corporate equity. Expenditure on goods and services – the total of consumption, investment, and the change in inventories – is a small fraction of the total value of payments, while the total value of payments is a vast multiple of new corporate credit. The total value of payments must have some sort of equilibrium relationship with the nominal values of national income, expenditure, and wealth, and both must maintain an equilibrium with the economy's money balances. But neither the value of total payments nor equilibrium national expenditure is limited by companies' inability or unwillingness to borrow, as Koo believes.

To repeat an argument developed particularly in essay 10, economic agents use money to finance their expenditures and can sell assets to pay for those expenditures. It is not true that – in any particular period – an individual person's or company's expenditure is constrained by the sum of income *and borrowing* in that or any previous period. (This is what Koo and far too many others appear to believe, with their thinking trapped in the box of the income-expenditure circular flow.) Agents can spend above current or recent income *without any borrowing*, either by running down their existing money balances or by selling assets to obtain additional money balances. In Japan as in all other economies, any sensible statement about the equilibrium values of total payments and aggregate expenditure must recognize the importance of money. As Keynes explained over eighty years ago, this recognition needs to allow for the use of money both for transactions purposes and as part of asset portfolios.[23]

If the quantity of money is rising by 10 percent a year, so also are the equilibrium values of corporate equity and real estate. If the equilibrium values of corporate equity and real estate are rising by 10 percent a year, it is almost certain that expenditures on goods and services will also be increasing – if not by exactly 10 percent a year, then at least by a figure similar to 10 percent a year. All that was required to end Japan's macroeconomic doldrums in the 1990s and the first decade of the twenty-first century was for public policy to organize an appropriately high rate of growth of the quantity of money. Contrary to Koo's contentions in *The Holy Grail*, the reluctance of companies to borrow was – by itself – neither here nor there.[24]

VI.

In terms of public relations, fiscal policy has a great advantage over monetary policy. There is common-sense plausibility in the idea that, when the government borrows more money and spends it on public works, the total amount of spending in the economy increases. The assumptions required to translate this increase in spending into "effective demand," and hence into output and employment, as in the Keynesian textbooks, are easy to grasp and appear to be quite realistic in the short run.[25] Moreover, by locating the responsibility for the extra spending in the government, fiscal activism appeals to the large number of intellectually alert people who see the state as an agent for social betterment.[26] By contrast, monetary policy works in seemingly mysterious ways, with many economists complaining about the elusiveness of "the transmission mechanism of monetary policy." The notion of "the demand to hold money balances" is difficult to pin down, given the multiplicity of money-holding agents and the variety of motives at work, while the proposition that macro equilibrium requires the equivalence of money demand and supply is far from intuitive. Even worse, any discussion of monetary policy almost necessarily leads to some analysis of banking systems. Bankers and their deal-making are both the epitome of capitalism and its worst advertisement. Whereas fiscal policy can be designed for social betterment, banking appears to be mostly for the enrichment of greedy individuals.

However, the truth is that fiscal policy is an unreliable, clumsy, and dangerous instrument for influencing macroeconomic outcomes. It is unreliable because of the overwhelming evidence that changes in the cyclically adjusted budget deficit are not accompanied by positive changes in aggregate demand, even if the textbooks assert that they ought to have this effect; it is clumsy because the implementation of fiscal policy involves changes in government spending and/or taxation, which disturb existing plans and may be wasteful; and it is dangerous because so-called "expansionary" fiscal policy can culminate in explosive increases in public debt. In the last twenty years Japan has seen larger budget deficits, relative to national income, than any other major industrial nation. Public-sector investment, in particular, has risen sharply relative to the twenty years before 1990. But the growth of total domestic demand has been pathetically weak, with many recent years experiencing a declining price level. The ratio of public debt to national income has soared. Although so far the debt-interest burden has been manageable, concern about the future sustainability of the debt has reduced Japan's international credit standing. Much of the public investment has been of the bridges-to-nowhere variety and has squandered resources.

Monetary policy also has many weaknesses, and it is not difficult to put together a diatribe in which it also is seen as unreliable, clumsy, and dangerous.[27] But monetary theory turns on a bedrock principle: that the demand to hold real money balances depends in the long run only (or at any rate almost entirely) on real variables.[28] The empirical validity of this bedrock principle is confirmed time and again in statistical exercises on official data. It is because of this principle that changes in the rate of growth of the quantity of money are invariably associated with roughly comparable changes in the rate of growth of nominal incomes. It then follows, first, that a reduction in the rate of growth of money is a necessary and sufficient condition for controlling inflation, and, second, that an increase in the rate of growth of the quantity of money is a necessary and sufficient condition to prevent deflation. As Friedman said on several occasions, stable growth of the quantity of money will not deliver Heaven on Earth, but it ought to avoid extreme fluctuations in output and employment, such as those seen in the United States' Great Depression between 1929 and 1933, and more generally across the globe in the Great Recession of 2008–2010.

Krugman and Koo have had considerable influence in their advocacy of fiscal activism in Japan. But fiscal policy has disappointed Japanese

TABLE 11.1
MONEY AND NATIONAL INCOME IN JAPAN

All figures are % annual changes

	Broad money	Nominal national output
1960–69	21.1	17.1
1970–79	21.3	13.0
1980–89	9.4	6.4
1990–99	4.4	1.6
2000–09	0.5	−0.1

In the 1960s and 1970s broad money grew much faster than nominal national output, largely because of the spread of "the banking habit" and the increasing sophistication of the financial system. A sharp rise in the ratio of broad money to income is common in the course of economic development.

Source: IMF

policy-makers, while the relevant evidence (on the relationship between changes in the structural budget balance and aggregate demand) is much the same in Japan as in other countries. This evidence supports the usual monetary relationships and, in particular, the medium-term similarity of the growth rates of the quantity of money and nominal income. (See table 11.1.) An implication of the evidence is that aggressive action to boost the *broadly defined* quantity of money, including all (or virtually all) bank deposits, could have checked Japan's deflation at any time in the last twenty years.[29] Changes in the quantity of money establish new equilibrium levels of total payments and national wealth in all nations. As a result, hugely powerful forces of equilibration are unleashed whenever the quantity of money alters by a significant amount (say, 5 percent, 10 percent, or more), and these forces smother and overwhelm fiscal policy in the determination of national income and expenditure.

PART FOUR

WAS THERE A "MONETARIST COUNTERREVOLUTION"?

Preface

THE UNITED STATES has a different intellectual outlook from the main European nations. It has never had a large and successful socialist political movement, while openly conservative principles (the rule of law, the sanctity of property rights, the civic value of patriotism) can still be expressed in the media and at public meetings without causing giggles. There is no doubt that, when the Keynesians first started to peddle their interpretation of *The General Theory* in textbooks and classrooms, they saw themselves as undermining the traditional American commitments to private enterprise and the free-market economy. In 1939 John Kenneth Galbraith contributed an article to the *Harvard Business Review* on his return to the United States after a year of pilgrimage to Keynes's Cambridge. To quote, "The government cannot logically place upon private enterprise the responsibility for solving unemployment if full employment is not the normal achievement of private enterprise." Ergo, ". . . it is a government responsibility to bring about this end." The academic Keynesian economists – at Harvard especially, but also at other universities – understood themselves to be the intellectual trendsetters, the forces of progress, in American public policy throughout the 1950s and 1960s. But – America being America – a powerful conservative backlash developed, slowly and rather quietly at first, but more emphatically and with greater articulacy in the 1970s. An early marker was set by William F. Buckley Jr. in the brilliant second chapter (given the sarcastic title "Individualism at Yale") of his 1951 *God and Man at Yale*. Its diatribe against the implicit socialist bias of macroeconomics instruction in an Ivy League university was both fresh in conception and difficult to answer. In 1981 the same John Kenneth Galbraith wrote a long essay for *The New York Review of Books* on "The Conservative Onslaught." He identified Arthur Laffer's supply-side ideas and Milton Friedman's monetarism as central strands in the "onslaught."[1]

The three essays in this section recognize the integral position of "the monetarist counterrevolution" in the conservative resurgence in the 1970s and 1980s. By implication, they also assert the continuing vitality and importance of monetarist ideas in the current American macroeconomic policy debate. The first essay – which is an updated and heavily rewritten chapter from my 1978 pamphlet *Monetarism: An Essay in Definition* – sets monetarism in the wider political context. It tries to explain why supporters of monetary control tend also to advocate the liberty of the individual, to support the free play of market forces, and to favor private ownership over state ownership.

The second essay is in one sense a period piece. The original version was written in 1987, to comment on the very different evolutionary paths of monetarist ideas in the U.S. and Britain, and much of it may now seem dated. However, monetary economics is a subject where the same ideas can be on display in one era, put into the deep freeze for a generation, then defrosted and displayed for a period, put back into the deep freeze for the next decade, then defrosted and displayed again, and so on. Keynes's writings from the 1920s helped to inform the debate between American and British monetarism in the 1980s, while that debate continues to echo in the policy disagreements stirred up by the recent Great Recession. American monetarists – unlike the proponents of "British monetarism," as it is described here – have tended to be interested in "the monetary base" (i.e., notes in circulation and banks' cash reserves) and to sidetrack or even ignore a broadly defined money measure. Friedman sometimes said that the debate about the relative merits of different money aggregates was unproductive, because ultimately all the aggregates moved together.[2] As the graph below shows, that observation is now untenable, even absurd.

In the first period of Bernanke's Fed chairmanship – the four years starting in February 2006 – the aggregates had widely divergent rates of change and, hence, totally different policy messages. In August 2010, Thomas Hoenig, the president of the Federal Reserve Bank of Kansas City, dissented from other members of the Federal Open Market Committee. For him the huge increase in the monetary base in late 2008 and 2009 contained significant risks of rising inflation in the future. Unlike all the other FOMC members he favored an early reduction in the Federal Reserve balance sheet. At the same time, the annual increase in the

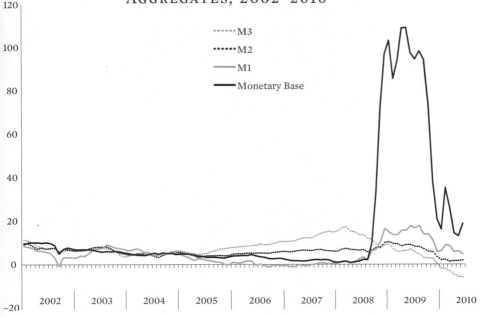

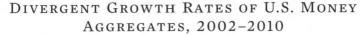

consumer price index, taking out the volatile food and energy items, was at 0.9 percent – the lowest it had been for over fifty years. Indeed, many observers were worried about deflation in 2011, not least because of the plunge in the broadest money aggregate, M3, in the year up to summer 2010. The difference between the rates of change of the monetary base and M3 in the eighteen months up to summer 2010 was not a minor gap, but an immense chasm.

Which money concept matters to the determination of national income and wealth? The battle of the aggregates will not go away. The third essay here rebuts the many criticisms of monetarism and argues – like essays 6 and 7 earlier – that it was a key intellectual input to the achievement of the Great Moderation. But Friedman, who was undoubtedly the leader of the monetarist counterrevolution, gave some poor forecasts in the early and mid-1980s, and damaged the reputation of the ideas he had done so much to promote. I suggest that his mistakes came from switching his attention towards the M1 aggregate and away from his long-term favorite, M2 broad money. In the next and final section the case for broad money is developed more rigorously and at greater length.

ESSAY 12

THE POLITICAL ECONOMY OF
MONETARISM

IT IS ALWAYS a double-edged compliment to characterize an idea as fashionable. The description tends to suggest impermanence and fragility, as if the idea in question could be shrugged off as a topical irrelevance. In the case of monetarism in the 1970s and 1980s, this danger was particularly acute. Many of its detractors found that the sharpest critical approach was to admit that it had gained widespread support, but to imply that such support fluctuated with the ebb and flow of opinion, and made no real difference to economic knowledge.[1] This sort of attack was unfair. Certain propositions branded as "monetarist" were not, in fact, distinctive of any school of thought, but formed part of the core of received economic theory. Moreover, many distinctively monetarist themes, far from being an evanescent response to the inflationary excess of the 1970s, had been recognized in one form or another for decades or even centuries.

The Keynesians in Britain were hostile – or at least apathetic – towards the teaching of monetary economics in British universities and the application of monetary theory in policy-making. But the allegation that monetarism was a fashion and nothing else was strange, since the monetary tradition in British economics was at one time full of vitality. Indeed, in the first half of the twentieth century Cambridge was the acknowledged center of monetary theory, not just in Britain but in the world, with original contributions from Marshall, Pigou, Robertson, and, above all, Keynes. In the 1950s and 1960s this legacy was neglected. The leading economists at Cambridge, who called themselves "Keynesians" and enjoyed the esteem conferred by Keynes's name, scoffed at small and diminishing bands of die-hards in provincial universities who obstinately insisted on the importance of money.[2] They also isolated Dennis Robertson, who had worked closely with Keynes in the 1920s (although quarrelling with him in the mid-1930s) and had become Cambridge's foremost monetary theorist. (According to the author of Robertson's intellectual biography, Keynes's influence at Cambridge "lived on through his disciples, and the battles Robertson fought with them in the Faculty over teaching arrangements and new appointments continued to shadow his declining years.")[3] Arguably, the strength of opposition to monetarism, and the lack of intellectual preparedness in the policy-making establishment when it was confronted by the double-digit inflation that followed the Barber boom of 1972–73 and the Lawson boom of the late 1980s, was due to the Cambridge Keynesians' pooh-poohing of the quantity theory of money in the 1950s and 1960s. Would it then be right to blame Keynes himself for Britain's economic difficulties in the 1970s and 1980s?

I.

The reply to this question reveals much about the development of economic thought in Britain. One point must be made straightaway. The titles of Keynes's four main books on economics – *Indian Currency and Finance* (published in 1913), *A Tract on Monetary Reform* (1923), *A Treatise on Money* (1930), and *The General Theory of Employment, Interest, and Money* (1936) – suggest that Keynes was obsessed by money and finance.[4] Further, there is no doubt that he always considered the influence of money on fluctuations in output and employment to be fundamental. He thought that the weakness of economics in his day was its inability to reconcile the determination of individual prices by supply and demand with the determination of the aggregate price level by the quantity of money. His aim in *The General Theory* was

to escape from this double life and to bring the theory of prices as a whole back to close contact with the theory of value. The division of economics between the theory of value and distribution on the one hand and the theory of money on the other hand is, I think, a false division. The right dichotomy is, I suggest, between the theory of the individual industry or firm and the distribution between different uses of a *given* quantity of resources on the one hand, and the theory of output and employment *as a whole* on the other hand. So long as we limit ourselves to the study of the individual industry or firm on the assumption that the aggregate quantity of employed resources is constant . . . it is true that we are not concerned with the significant characteristics of money. But as soon as we pass to the problem of what determines output and employment as a whole, we require the complete theory of a monetary economy.[5]

Keynes devoted over thirty years of study to analyzing the interaction of the real and financial sides of a capitalist economy. It is true that at the outset he considered money to be a benign or at worst harmless contrivance for facilitating transactions, whereas at the end he had convinced himself that it could be the jinx of the free-enterprise system. But, whether money was beneficial or pernicious, he had no doubt that money mattered. That an influential set of academics was able so easily and successfully to promote their own "Keynesianism," in which decisions to spend were severed from the quantity of money and the banking system, was an extraordinary intellectual fabrication. How did moneyless "Keynesianism" emerge? What were its main elements, and can they be related, even distantly, to *The General Theory*?

It has to be conceded that the Keynesian approach of the 1960s and 1970s – as adopted, for example, by the Brookings Institution and President Kennedy's Council of Economic Advisers in the U.S., and by the Treasury and the National Institute of Economic and Social Research in the U.K. – was not altogether divorced from Keynes's thinking. The principal Keynesian theoretical construct is the income-expenditure model of aggregate demand determination. Reduced to its essentials, this model says that demand depends on how much economic agents decide to spend and that certain categories of spending (such as exports and government expenditure) are "exogenous." That is, they do not depend on the current level of national income, but instead regulate its future value by the multiplier process. The U.K. Treasury's econometric model, which by the mid-1970s already had scores of equations, was nothing more than an elaboration of this simple insight.

The income-expenditure model is advanced in *The General Theory*, constituting the subject matter of books II to IV. These take up 160 of *The General Theory*'s 385 pages and are the work's analytical heart. The model is expressed in wage-units, which may be equated with the wage payment to the average worker. This device could be represented as purely technical. It has the great convenience that, if demand is measured in so many wage-units, an increase in demand leads to an identical increase in the number of wage-units and, as long as wages are constant, to an identical increase in the number of men in work. The wage-unit assumption therefore facilitates the determination of demand, output, and employment. (In the 1930s it enabled Keynes to proceed quickly from the level of aggregate demand to the level of employment, an undoubted merit when mass unemployment was the major economic problem.) But expository convenience is obtained at significant cost in theoretical completeness, because the result is that – within books II to IV – *The General Theory* has no method of determining the wage-unit. (The importance of the wage-unit assumption is also discussed in essay 1, on pp. 12–13.)

For this reason book V of *The General Theory* is concerned with "Money-Wages and Prices." Now a key issue becomes the determination of the wage-unit itself. Not surprisingly, the hypothesized effects of changes in the quantity of money are very different in this book from what they are in books II to IV. In books II to IV an increase in the money supply lowers the rate of interest, stimulates activity, and does not change the price level; in book V, by contrast, a rise in the money supply boosts effective demand, and "the increase in effective demand will, generally speaking, spend itself partly in increasing the quantity of employment and partly in raising the level of prices."[6] In the extreme case of full employment, monetary expansion leads only to inflation. Clearly, the income-expenditure model is outlined in books II to IV *before* the discussion of wages and prices because it is valid only if the wage-unit is constant. Keynes was fully aware of the ramifications, and the peculiarities, of the wage-unit assumption when he organized the argument of *The General Theory*.

But the Keynesians of the immediate post-war decades overlooked these qualifications. Their income-expenditure models – both in the textbooks and in large-scale forecasting models – were (and still are, in the early twenty-first century) constructed in real terms, as if a change in wages could not occur while income and expenditure were being determined. Within the context of the model, the absence of a clear economic mechanism for determining changes in price and wage levels was defensible. It is a common property of Keynesian forecasting models that an x percent rise in wages is sooner or later accompanied by an x percent rise in prices, implying that the real purchasing power of earnings and, hence, consumption and national income are unaffected. But the habit of forecasting the macroeconomic aggregates in real terms had very serious consequences. It persuaded the economists concerned to believe that real variables and the level of inflation were determined by two separate processes, and it allowed them to banish money from their models. As Keynes recognized, his theory was not able to disentangle the effects of a money-supply increase on real output and the price level (except, of course, in long-run equilibrium, when quantity-theory conclusions hold). The Keynesians came to believe not only that national income depended on decisions to spend, but also that decisions to spend had no systematic connection with the main items in the economy's balance sheet (the level of the nominal and real money supply, the market value of stocks and shares, and house prices and other real-estate values). If money and asset prices had major effects on expenditure, the empirical validity of the income-expenditure model would be undermined and the whole conceptual edifice of Keynesianism – as the term was understood in the policy-formation establishments of the English-speaking world – would dissolve.[7]

As this account demonstrates, the story of the degeneration of Keynes's pure theory to the Keynesian "orthodoxy" of the 1970s was quite complicated. But it could be argued that one theme of this story was the reinstatement of an invalid dichotomy. The dichotomy was invalid because it separated two aspects of the economy which, in the real world, are intertwined. One aspect was the determination of national income in real terms by the level of demand; and the other was the determination of the rate of inflation by supposing that collective bargaining drives up wage costs (i.e., Keynes's wage-unit) and, in the same proportion, the price level. Here lay the intellectual origin of the Keynesian assertion that effective demand had no bearing on the increase in prices and the theoretical background to the advocacy of incomes policies. If spending changes output and not prices, demand management is a useless instrument for controlling inflation. Reliance ought instead to be placed on direct political and administrative action. That such action might distort the structure of relative prices was a minor drawback to the typical Keynesian economist because his income-expenditure model was aggregative and did not bother itself with the supply-and-demand problems of individual businessmen.

The dichotomy under discussion here was an associate of "a technique of thinking" in which the signaling function of relative price movements was regarded as unimportant. Of course the signaling function of relative price movements is basic to microeconomics. The "apparatus of mind" of some British Keynesians in the 1970s was therefore a kind of anti-economics. The advocacy of "planning," the suppression of microeconomics, and the neglect of monetary economics were interrelated. It was consistent that the Department of Applied Economics at Cambridge – where this type of anti-economics was developed most fully – should in the late 1970s propose an "alternative economic programme" including import controls. Perhaps more than any other single factor, it was this anti-economics which was responsible for the succession of misguided policies, both micro- and macroeconomic, pursued by the British government in the 1960s and 1970s.[8] (Fortunately, import controls were never implemented, but they were the subject of extensive, unnecessary, and largely misguided discussion during the various crises of the 1970s. Some participants in the public debate seemed to yearn for an almost Stalinist "socialism in one country." Economists disagree about many things, but there is a strong professional consensus that import controls reduce welfare and are a mistake.)

Moreover, the dichotomy that was central to the Keynesian anti-economics resembled the classical dichotomy rebutted by Keynes. The classical dichotomy said that the output of the individual industry depended on supply and demand, *and* that the aggregate price level depended on the quantity of money. Keynes insisted that, via the rate of interest, money affected relative prices, output, and the aggregate price level, and that money, banking, and asset markets had profound effects on demand and employment. The Keynesian dichotomy of the 1960s and 1970s was, in some respects, even more unrealistic than the classical dichotomy because – in its extreme forms – it dispensed with money altogether. Keynes, who thought that "as soon as we pass to the problem of what determines output and employment as a whole we require the complete theory of a monetary economy," would surely have repudiated it. The income-expenditure models of the Treasury and the National Institute were sometimes characterized as a "vulgar," "hydraulic," or "bastardised" version of what "Keynes really said."[9] But that was too flattering. They simplified to the point of misrepresentation and would be better described as fakes.

The resistance to monetarism in Britain cannot be attributed to the fact that Keynes was an Englishman, rather than an American or a European, and that he therefore had a disproportionate intellectual influence in Britain. It was not his fault that, from the time of his death and particularly from the early 1960s, the prestige of monetary economics at Cambridge collapsed. Indeed, monetarism could be interpreted not as an assault on Keynes's work, but as an attempt to rescue it from his successors. Friedman compared Keynes's disillusionment with the stability of capitalist financial markets in the 1930s with similar views held by Henry Simons, a professor of economics at the University of Chicago. He also described Keynes's monetary theory as "sophisticated and modern."[10] By contrast, one would not have guessed from the sort of statements that emanated from the National Institute or the Department of Applied Economics at Cambridge in the 1970s that Keynes had a monetary theory or, indeed, that such an entity as monetary theory, whether derived from Marshall, Keynes, or Friedman, was worth discussing at all. The lack of sturdy intellectual defenses in the U.K. against monetary abuse on the scale of the 1972–74 period, when the annual rate of money-supply growth exceeded 20 percent, and the 1985–88 period, when it approached 20 percent, is not to be explained by Keynes and the special position he holds in the pantheon of British economists.

II.

Part of the explanation for the shrillness of the debates between Keynesians and monetarists was that much more than textbook economics was at stake. As its critics understood, monetarism was not – and is not – politically neutral. It was and is an ally of a certain disposition towards political problems. This disposition was basically liberal, in the best nineteenth-century sense of valuing the freedom of the individual. But, since the need to respect existing institutions was also emphasized, it had conservative implications. It was not tendentious to associate it with such thinkers as F. A. Hayek and Michael Oakeshott, although Hayek in his later years disowned technical monetarism. The purpose of this and the next section is to identify some of the links between monetarism, liberalism, and conservatism.

Money is usually termed "the medium of exchange," but this does not go far enough. The phrase "the instrument of choice" brings into stronger relief its significance for a liberal philosophy. Of course, choice exists in a barter economy, but the possibilities for transacting are more circumscribed. Because money is universally accepted, its introduction into an economy reduces the size of the stock of goods that merchants need to engage in trade. It thereby lowers marketing costs and extends the area in which consumers are able to select the combination of products most suited to their preferences. This extension of choice is an essential preliminary to widespread specialization. If it is expensive to trade, the market may be too small to allow an individual to concentrate on one form of production. But, with exchange facilitated by a universally accepted instrument of choice, the division of labor can begin.

The ensuing gains from economies of scale and experience were first described by Adam Smith in *The Wealth of Nations* in 1776, and they have formed part of the folklore of the free-market economy ever since. The division of labor can, of course, be taken a long way in a socialist, centrally planned economy, but traditionally it has been a process associated with market freedom and decentralized decision-making. The advances in productivity associated with the division of labor are an effective illustration of how self-interested individuals, not working at the behest of a single co-ordinating unit under government control, can achieve a harmonious and socially optimal result. It is one component, and perhaps the most persuasive component, of the argument for permitting the "invisible hand" to allocate resources without interference from the state.

Hayek reinforced this argument by pointing out the dependence of a complicated economy on the fragmentation of knowledge, on the fact that each member of society can have only a small fraction of the knowledge possessed by all and that each is therefore ignorant of most of the facts on which the working of society rests.[11] Here, too, the role of money is crucial. It is a common standard of value, a *numéraire* in which the value of all goods may be expressed. Its presence excuses traders from having to inform themselves of the price of a good in terms of other goods (such as the exchange ratio of wheat into coffee, of cars into furniture, and so on), since it is instead adequate to know the price of a good in terms only of the money *numéraire* (how many pounds, dollars, euros, or whatever have to be paid for a given weight of wheat, for a particular type of car, and so on). Since the amount of information required for successful marketing and trading is reduced by this device, energies are released for other tasks, and economic efficiency is improved. The advantage conferred by money in this respect is weaker if its quantity and, consequently, its exchange relationship to goods in general (that is, the overall price level) change too much in a short space of time. The monetarist distrust of sharp fluctuations in the money supply finds here its most basic rationale.

The connection between money and freedom therefore pivots on Adam Smith's theory of the division of labor and Hayek's concept of the division of knowledge. One of the characteristics of economists who believe in these ideas is that they respect the relative price structure which arises from free production and exchange. They consider that – except in certain special circumstances, which need to be carefully (and skeptically) specified – unfettered market forces set prices which achieve the right equilibrium between consumer wants and scarce resources. Not surprisingly, monetarists recommend a high degree of wage and price flexibility, since restrictions on price movements impede the attainment of this equilibrium. Such restrictions sometimes stem from monopoly power, but governments and regulatory bodies are often to blame.

In the U.K. in the 1960s and 1970s pay and price controls designed to curb inflation were the most prominent form of government interference. Although they were commonly formulated as if they were to be impartial in effect (for example, the same percentage pay increase was allowed to the whole labor force), they always discriminated in practice. It is almost part of the definition of a dynamic economy that the relative price structure should come under pressure from different rates of productivity growth in different industries, varying income elasticities of demand, and so on. To proclaim the same proportional pay increase for every worker or the same proportional price increase for every good was to freeze the relative price structure and weaken its allocative power. That might have been an acceptable price to pay if prices and incomes policies did in the end deliver lower inflation, but experience showed that they did not.

The monetarists' condemnation of incomes policies stemmed partly from their philosophical attitude towards market freedom and partly from the failure of such policies when attempted in practice. Of course, if it could be shown that monetary mismanagement was the cause of inflation, that lent weight to the proposition that monetary responsibility was a sufficient policy response. In that case, direct controls, with the infringement of freedom they entailed, were unnecessary. This conclusion could not be reached by the more extreme Keynesians since money formed no part of their system. Their world-view was such that only changes in wages could account for changes in the aggregate price level, and only political measures to check the collective greed of the unions could prevent prices from rising.[12]

The divide between monetary and non-monetary approaches to British inflation in the 1960s and 1970s was related to another fundamental split in economic theory, between those theories which say the distribution of income is determined by productivity and those which say it is determined by comparative bargaining power. The productivity theories belong to the neo-classical strand in economics and the power theories to the Marxian.[13] In the post-war decades the thought habits associated with the wage-unit assumption placed the Keynesians on the Marxian side. (Indeed, Schumpeter once referred to the more left-wing representatives of the cause as "Marxo-Keynesians."[14])

Nevertheless, much of the reasoning in *The General Theory* itself is conducted in terms of standard price theory, and book V makes explicit references to a marginal-productivity basis for wages. Because the wage-unit assumption implied that wages were not governed by the workings of the income-expenditure model, but were given by forces outside the model, it was open to the Keynesians to attribute pay movements, and the balance between wages and profits, to political factors. The frequent references to union militancy in Keynesian writings were a logical consequence. In the more embroidered versions, phrases such as "class conflict" and "revolutionary struggle" even made an appearance. On this reckoning, inflation was a manifestation of "social crisis," a sign that the system was under threat from tension between selfish workers and profiteering capitalists.

Since the problem was seen as political, so was the supposed solution. Hence, there was a need for the government to involve itself in peace-making between the different groups, by laying down pay and profit limits to be binding on all of them. Keynes's wage-unit assumption therefore culminated in centralized pay negotiations between, on the one hand, the "peak organizations" of labor and capital, and, on the other, the government and the leading politicians of the day. Moreover, in the opinion of some Keynesians, these negotiations ought not only to help in overcoming inflation, but also to contribute to the attainment of "social justice." According to Opie, writing in 1974, "certainly all Keynesians in the early days and most Keynesians later on were radical in some sense or other, and few would have shrunk from the egalitarian implications" of increased government activism in the economy.[15] By permitting larger pay increases to the low-paid than to the well-off, an incomes policy could reduce inequality. The Keynesians considered this a desirable end, partly because equality was good in itself, but also partly because they felt that the prevailing distribution of income, being determined by power, had no worthwhile economic function.

Monetarist-inclined economists took the opposite view. Their sympathies were with the neoclassical school of pricing and distribution. Because they believed that the relative price structure reflected market forces, they saw wages – which were also prices, the prices of labor – as being determined by supply and demand. A worker is paid for what he produces; if he is paid less than the value of his product, employers are induced to compete for his labor services until his wage rises and their surplus is removed; if he is paid more, he is either made redundant or obliged to suffer a wage cut. There is a definite, if rough-and-ready, justice in this equating of pay with marginal productivity because it matches reward to effort and skill. Centralized pay controls disturb this equivalence and, aside from the potentially harmful side-effects in the misallocation of labor, they tend to lead to industrial unrest. The monetarist suspicion of incomes policies was validated, therefore, not merely by the tenet that inflation was caused by excessive monetary expansion, but also by acceptance of the structure of relative wages, salaries, and other rewards determined by market forces. (The typical monetarist view was that, if the market-determined pattern of income distribution offended against some distributive principle or other, it should be remedied by the tax system, not by interference in relative prices and wages. In qualification, this preference for tax-based redistribution is widespread among professional economists and should not be associated too closely with monetarism.)

To summarize, the monetarists' criticism of incomes policies was part of a broader defense of economic freedom. Economic freedom was seen as beneficial because of the gains arising from Smith's division of labor and Hayek's division of knowledge. A trustworthy instrument of choice, in the form of a monetary unit that maintained a constant value (or, at any rate, a degree of stability) through time, was thought necessary for the smooth operation of the free-market economy which the monetarists favored.

III.

By its intrinsic nature, money is private, not public, property. Since the state is able to manufacture money at zero (or minimal) cost, it has no need to hold large money balances. For most of the twentieth century central governments in the industrial world financed their expenditure partly by a continuous overdraft from the banking system. The government's money holdings are negligible in most countries, but the banks lend it large sums for ongoing commitments by taking up issues of Treasury bills and other short-dated paper. (Again, in many countries – although not the United States or the Eurozone – states, provinces, local authorities, and public corporations can never face bankruptcy, because the government will bail them out however extreme their financial incompetence. One consequence of their immunity from risk is that they do not need to have sizeable balances in the banks.) British money-supply statistics confirm these observations. At the end of 1976 – when the debates between Keynesianism and monetarism were livening up – the M3 measure of money totaled £45.1 billion, while deposits held by the public sector were about £0.9 billion. Public expenditure was over 45 percent of national output, but money held by public-sector bodies was a mere fiftieth of money held by the private sector. (The situation was much the same at the end of 2005, to take a more recent illustration. Sterling deposits held by the public sector at U.K. "monetary financial institutions" – that is, banks and building societies – were £28.7 billion, whereas such deposits held by the private sector amounted to £1,324.7 billion.[16]) Evidently, no private-sector agent can operate with the same financial freedom as the government. Every individual and company outside the public sector must own some cash or bank deposits, or risk the possibility of going bankrupt because of an inability to service debt. There are far-reaching – although often overlooked – implications for stabilization policy. Monetary control is not a complete macroeconomic agenda. Guidelines for fiscal policy, and government spending in particular, also need to be spelled out.[17]

The political message of the macroeconomic theory in Keynes's *General Theory* was that, because of the instability of the speculative demand for money, monetary policy was an unsound tool for regulating demand and that greater reliance should be placed on fiscal policy. So it might on occasions be necessary to combat recession by raising public expenditure. Keynes had not noticed that money was relevant only as a determinant of private-sector fluctuations. By contrast, as explained above, the public sector can borrow from the rest of the economy almost at will and cannot be constrained by a lack of liquidity. One of the major flaws latent in his advocacy of fiscal activism was therefore hidden from Keynes.

This flaw came gradually to be exposed in the 1960s and 1970s. The Keynesian predilection for using public expenditure as a demand regulator aided those politicians and bureaucrats who wanted, for ideological reasons, to see remorseless expansion of the public sector.[18] It would not have mattered if, after recessions were accompanied by spending increases, booms saw equivalent spending cuts. But that was not the way the cycles worked out. Instead, recessions induced increases in public spending and booms prompted restrictive monetary policy. The private sector was disadvantaged in either situation. When demand was weak, the government's inclination to stimulate public expenditure was not associated with comparable pressures to raise private expenditure; and, when demand was strong, the resort to higher interest rates was detrimental to the private sector alone.

The tendency of this asymmetry to expand the size of the state, which was implicit in Keynesianism, was reinforced by the characteristics of government employment. Because such employment is only rarely justified by marketed output, the government cannot dismiss employees on the grounds that demand has dropped and sales revenue is insufficient. The state is quite unlike a private-sector company subject to commercial disciplines, which can offer a practically convincing (and morally reasonable) defense for declaring workers redundant if it does not have enough money to pay their wages. Private-sector redundancies, the ultimate cause of which is often a cyclical downturn due to monetary restraint, can be attributed to the lack of demand for a particular product. They have a clear – if disagreeable – rationale, even to those who go without jobs. Since public-sector output is financed by general taxation, the same argument cannot be made. It is more difficult to make redundancies in the public sector than in the private sector.[19]

There is a further, related point. Keynes's attack on the effectiveness of monetary policy did not stop with his call for the activation of fiscal policy. A further implication was that fiscal policy could have the necessary impact only if the public sector were sufficiently large. The logical corollary was, to use Keynes's own phrase, "a somewhat comprehensive socialisation of investment." An apparently technical and non-ideological judgment about the efficacy of monetary policy became the background to an openly socialist proposal. There was much to be said against Keynes's argument even on its own premises. For example, difficulties in predicting the consequences of monetary policy might be thought a reason for paying more attention to it, not less. Further, precisely because government employment was (and remains) more inflexible than private-sector employment, variations in public expenditure were not (and still are not) an adaptable and easily deployed macroeconomic policy instrument.

But there was a more sweeping objection to the Keynesians' proposed harnessing of the state's fiscal powers for the short-term management of demand and output. The monetarists were critical of fiscal activism largely because they doubted that the relevant authorities – the government, the finance ministry, and the central bank – had the wisdom, foresight, and political detachment required for the role. According to one characteristic monetarist argument, the supposed unpredictability and waywardness of the lag between changes in the money supply and money national income did not validate the greater use of fiscal policy. Instead it justified abandoning the discretionary approach to economic policy altogether and adopting an automatic money-supply rule. The crowding-out argument buttressed the monetarist position, because it implied that – once a money-supply target was in place – an activist fiscal policy was futile and pointless. (See essay 9 for a statement of the crowding-out argument in an article in *The Times* of London in October 1975.)

Aside from the crowding-out thesis, mainstream Keynesians had produced conflicting estimates of the size of the so-called "multiplier" by which national income rises in response to an increase in government spending. Economists' uncertainties about the demand implications of public spending – about whether a £1 billion increase in public expenditure added £2 billion, £1 billion, or nothing to effective demand in the economy – were symptomatic of wider difficulties with fiscal activism. These difficulties established a case for skepticism about Keynes's call for an overhaul of property relationships as radical as that implied by the phrase "comprehensive socialisation of investment." Donald Moggridge, the editor of Keynes's writings for the Royal Economic Society, once mentioned "Keynes's tendency towards rather wild asides."[20] Surely the recommendation of a socialization of investment, on the spurious grounds that it was needed to make fiscal activism effective, was one such "wild aside."

The strength of the correlation between monetarist sympathies and a liberal or conservative approach to political problems in the debates of the 1970s and 1980s was not an accident. It remains logical and important today. Money is one of the principal kinds of private property, and variations in its quantity have the greatest effect on the private sector. The "Friedman money-supply rule" was intended first and foremost as the answer to inflation, but – if adopted – it would also have gone some way towards protecting the private sector from the politicians. It is sometimes said that there is no intellectual connection between, on the one hand, monetarist macroeconomics and, on the other, an aversion to excessive public expenditure and interventionist industrial policy. But support for sound money and free markets forms part of a coherent and integrated political outlook.

A socialist government could have a program of constant money-supply growth and a balanced budget, while maintaining a high ratio of public expenditure to national income and embarking on schemes for subsidizing or penalizing private industrial ventures. But a high ratio of public expenditure to national income reduces the scope for individually motivated choices and thus makes the management of the money supply less important. In addition, the more obvious is the state's determination to plan the economy, "to pick winners" and "to accelerate industrial change," and the more politicians and government officials arbitrate on the allocation of scarce inputs, the less important is the financial system's role of enforcing market-related priorities according to profitability. The monetarist advocacy of stable money sits easily with the defense of private property. Meanwhile, in Oakeshott's words, private property is the institution that "allows the widest distribution and discourages most effectively great and dangerous concentrations of power" and, hence, is "most friendly to freedom."[21]

In an article in the November 1976 issue of *Encounter* Friedman tried to make more precise the warnings about how over-expansion of state spending might undermine political freedom. He advanced the notion of a "tipping point," a particular ratio of public expenditure to national income at which political liberty is in peril and totalitarianism is imminent. For a fairly unsophisticated country, such as Chile, the tipping point might be 40 percent; for a richer country, like Britain, it might be higher, perhaps 60 percent.[22] These remarks received heavy criticism, notably from such leading economic commentators as Samuel Brittan of the *Financial Times*, as being glib and unscientific. (At the time Brittan was usually sympathetic to monetarist ideas.) But Friedman's *Encounter* article, even if it could not substantiate the specific figure in contention, was based on some clear and indisputable features of democratic societies. The vital contrast, in his view, was between political and economic markets. The political mechanism had "the fundamental defect" that

> ... it is a system of highly weighted voting under which the special interests have great incentive to promote their own interests at the expense of the general public. The benefits are concentrated; the costs are diffused; and you have therefore a bias in the political

marketplace which leads to ever greater expansion in the scope
of government and ultimately to control over the individual.

The economic market was "very different."

> In the economic market – the market in which individuals buy
> and sell from one another – each person gets what he pays for.
> There is a dollar-for-dollar relationship. Therefore, you have an
> incentive proportionate to the cost to examine what you are get-
> ting. If you are paying out of your own pocket for something and
> not out of somebody else's pocket, then you have a very strong
> incentive to see whether you are getting your money's worth.[23]

Although in his *Encounter* article Friedman did not join this essentially
political argument to his well-known economic prescriptions, it would
not have been difficult to do so. Today, as in the 1970s, the machinery of
the political market is oiled by votes. More generally, competing interest groups are able to extract resources from the state (which has a
monopoly of coercion, and the powers to tax and to print money) if they
can assemble voting coalitions. Whether the distribution of resources to
particular groups then has any relation to economic merit or social justice can be arbitrary. By contrast, in the economic market people receive
income according to the value of what they produce, and they can
express their preferences for different products when they purchase
goods and services. Production and consumption therefore respect individual choice and personal freedom; and the outcomes have an obvious
logic, even if market forces are sometimes harsh and capricious. The
lubricant of the economic market is money, and the advantages of the
economic market are most obvious when the monetary system is in good
working order. It is the hallmark of societies undergoing a hyperinflationary experience that pressures on the government to act as the
guardian of particular sectional interests are particularly strong. In such
circumstances some citizens may prefer the political market because
the lack of a stable monetary unit reduces the efficiency of the economic
market. Only when the value of money is steady and reliable over a
period of years can the economic market develop to its full extent.[24]

* * *

IV.

The last two sections showed that sound money furthers the widening of choice found in a free economy and lends support to the institution of private property. Both these themes connected monetarism with liberalism and conservatism in the 1970s and 1980s, and helped to account for the typical political attitudes of monetarist economists. The argument remains central to the positioning of participants in the public debates of the early twenty-first century, particularly now that a sharp ideological left-right split has returned under the Obama presidency. This final section will suggest that an important theme in monetarist economics was skepticism about the rationalist and managerial style of politics which was dominant in the late twentieth century. Misgivings about this type of politics were expressed by Popper and Hayek and, more particularly, by Oakeshott in his *Rationalism in Politics*.

Keynesianism of the kind practiced by the American and British policy-making establishments had several rationalist characteristics. It was highly ambitious in that it asked the state to pursue four goals – full employment, price stability, economic growth, and balance-of-payments equilibrium – and to have a precise conception of what these goals were or should be. Once defined and (probably) quantified, these goals were to be sought by means of "demand management." Notice how the word "management" had crept in, rather as if the state were a business and politicians were its board of directors. The concept of demand management presumed not only that policy-makers had a good grasp of the applicable economic theory, but also that the empirical relationships highlighted by theory were stable and reliable. Implicit throughout was the notion that the more scientific was the approach, the deeper would be policy-makers' understanding and the better would be their decisions. The electronic gadgetry of the major econometric forecasting models (Wharton in the U.S., the Treasury model in the U.K.), with their pretense of giving exact answers to difficult questions, indicated the cast of mind involved. Also fundamental was the Keynesian assumption that all the requisite knowledge and wisdom could be concentrated, in the U.S., in a few minds in Washington (or in Washington and the East Coast, saltwater "elite" universities) or, in the U.K., in Whitehall (or in Whitehall and a handful of colleges at Cambridge

University).[25] Ultimately the economy's fate – and that of dozens of industries and businesses across the land – was to be determined at a sort of central committee meeting where the crucial decisions were to be made. (Hence, all the attention paid in the Britain of the 1970s to meetings of the National Economic Development Council or "confrontations" between the chancellor of the exchequer and the Trades Union Congress or the Confederation of British Industry.) The committee's decisions would have, if some Keynesian accounts were taken to their logical conclusion, a purely technical character, rather as though the problem of steering the economy were like that of steering a ship on an agreed course. Ideally, debate and uncertainty were to be banished, rather as if – in Keynes's own words – economics could be reduced to a kind of dentistry.

Monetarism was in conflict with the rationalist tendency in two main ways. First, it denied that enough was known for policies to be framed with the exactitude needed. Friedman's original case for the monetary rule was negative and skeptical. It was not based on an extravagant boast that he knew more about the economy than the Keynesians, but instead rested on the perhaps less vulnerable foundations of partial ignorance. Friedman argued that – precisely because so little was understood – it was sensible not to expect too much from monetary policy. A similar admission of incomplete knowledge came with his theory of the natural rate of unemployment. In the 1967 presidential address to the American Economic Association, he said quite candidly that, although he thought the natural rate was an empirically valid concept, he could not measure it. This may be branded as obscurantist or applauded as prudent intellectual modesty, but either way it was not rationalist or managerial in its implications.

Secondly, monetarists distrusted the political authorities to whom Keynes felt the task of demand management should be granted. To Keynes, and arguably to most of the British upper and middle classes of his time, it was safe to believe that governments acted as servants of the community as a whole and that their members were basically honest and conscientious. This was plausible in the early twentieth century because Britain had been ruled by a political elite of unusually high quality for at least 150 years. The Benthamite and melioristic mood of Keynes and his establishment colleagues reflected this long tradition of honesty, fairness, and decency in public life: it duped them into thinking that altruism among politicians was the rule rather than the exception. Henry Simons, and other social and economic observers in the inter-war United States, did not have the same respect for the political process. The American Constitution has many strengths, but the rough-and-tumble of democratic vote-catching in large American cities from the late nineteenth century on was not edifying. Chicago School economists have tended to take a cynical view of politicians' motives, as Friedman's antithesis between the economic and political markets demonstrates. The monetarists of the 1970s were influenced by the new theory of public choice which was then emerging.[26] They were alert to the possibility that politicians, far from watching over the interests of the community as a whole, often put their own interest first. Taken to the logical extremes, public-choice theorists argued that politics was to be analyzed, not as the maximization of social utility, but as the maximization of politicians' utility. It followed that the government's powers in the economic sphere should be restricted. The monetary rule was seen as an effective barrier to political discretion. When consistently applied, it excluded "management" of the exchange rate, "management" of fiscal policy, and "management" of individual prices and incomes. The implied critique of Keynesianism was far-reaching. Monetarism and Keynesianism were motivated by quite different interpretations of democratic politics.

In the first three post-war decades Britain's experience of democracy became much more like the United States', with the two main parties – the Conservatives and Labour – competing for votes with electoral promises in such areas as full employment and inflation control. The boom of the early 1970s was a particularly blatant attempt to court political popularity by over-stimulating the economy. Precedents were to be found in 1955, when the Conservatives held a general election shortly after a Budget that cut income taxes, and again in 1959, when Prime Minister Macmillan's slogan of "You never had it so good" was declared in the midst of an unusually vigorous cyclical upswing. Keynesianism – with its hope that governments would publicly commit themselves to full employment – encouraged a version of democracy in which political parties competed with each other to have the best management team. But managerialism refuted itself. By becoming embroiled in party politics, demand management lost its innocence and ceased to be a purely technical item on a committee's agenda. Moreover, as economic policy became increasingly contentious and political in nature in the 1960s and 1970s, macroeconomic outcomes got worse rather than better.

The progress of monetarism in public debate in the 1970s may be seen, therefore, as partly a reflection of the disillusionment with politicians that marked the decade. This disillusionment may in turn be attributed to a realization that rationalism in economic policy had not solved problems, but increased them, and had not made disagreement about policy less heated, but intensified it. Keynesianism, a managerial style of economic policy-making, and pork-barrel politics were, and are, confederates. Managerialism and Keynesianism give politicians plenty to say at elections and plenty to do between them. An alternative set of ideas (such as monetarism) which envisages a smaller state and a less adventurous economic policy may always be difficult to reconcile with the competitive, adversary style of present-day democratic politics. Since 2007 the Great Recession has again given intellectual ammunition to the opponents of free-market capitalism. In these dangerous times the interrelated arguments for sound money and a small state need to be restated and re-emphasized.

HOW DO BRITISH AND AMERICAN MONETARISM COMPARE?

THE SPREAD OF monetarism in the 1970s did not occur by a simple process of intellectual conquest. In most countries monetarist ideas could not be incorporated into policy formation until they had adapted to local economic conditions and recognized existing traditions of monetary management. The U.K. posed a particular problem. With its long history of monetary debate and practice, and with its unusually long-established institutional structures, it did not readily assimilate Chicago School doctrines. Nevertheless, in the late 1970s and early 1980s the media, leading politicians, and the public at large believed that British macroeconomic policy was becoming progressively more monetarist. Perhaps the apex of monetarist influence on policy came in the Budget of 1980 with the announcement of the Medium-Term Financial Strategy, in which targets for both monetary growth and the budget deficit were stated for four years into the future. In a statement to regional city editors on June 9, 1980, Mr. Nigel (later Lord) Lawson, financial secretary to the Treasury (later to be chancellor of the exchequer), said that the "Medium-Term Financial Strategy is essentially a monetary – or, if you like, monetarist – strategy."[1]

The purpose of this essay is to compare the "monetarism" referred to by Nigel Lawson with the "monetarism" that is conventionally associated with the Chicago School. The monetarism that once dominated policy formation in the U.K. is called British monetarism, and the monetarism of the Chicago School, American monetarism. Of course, these simple labels are to a degree misleading. So many ideas have been in play, and they have undergone such constant evolution, that there is an inevitable arbitrariness in talking of this monetarism, that monetarism, or the other monetarism. Despite the difficulties, a short description of British monetarism is ventured in the next section. No precise definition is given of American monetarism, but Friedman's work and Thomas Mayer's book on the structure of monetarism are taken as broadly representative.[2] In the following four sections contrasts are drawn between British monetarism and American monetarism. The tensions between them were reflected in a number of perplexities which are critical to understanding the decline and fall of monetarism in U.K. policy formation in the mid-1980s. The final section therefore discusses, among other things, the corrosive impact of certain distinctively Chicagoan beliefs on the staying power of British monetarism in the policy debate.

It would be wrong to give the impression that there was a bitter transatlantic intellectual duel. The divergence between British and American monetarism certainly did not reflect a controversy as intense or long-standing as that between monetarism and Keynesianism. However, there were points of contact between the two debates. Perhaps it is not surprising, in view of the range of his work, that Keynes himself touched on several of the topics that have subsequently been disputed between American and British monetarists. As we shall see, the relationship between his views and the Anglo-American monetary disagreements of the 1980s turns out to be many-sided and ambivalent.

I.

The opening months of 1980, coinciding with the introduction of the Medium-Term Financial Strategy, have already been mentioned as a period of particular confidence in the virtues of monetary policy. Two official documents prepared at the time may be regarded as defining statements of British monetarism. The first is the March 1980 Green Paper *Monetary Control*, which was the joint work of the Treasury and the Bank of England; the second is the "Memorandum on Monetary Policy" prepared by the Treasury for the Treasury and Civil Service Committee of the House of Commons in June 1980.[3]

The focus of both documents was a target for the growth of broad money, measured by sterling M3. Sterling M3 consisted of notes and coin and nearly all deposit liabilities of the banking system. Sterling M3 was monitored not for its own sake, but as an intermediate target thought to have a definite – if rather elusive – relationship with the ultimate target of inflation. The government's faith in this relationship was expressed strongly in the Treasury's "Memorandum on Monetary Policy." While conceding that the mechanisms linking money and prices change over time and space, the "Memorandum" insisted that "the proposition that prices must ultimately respond to monetary control holds whatever the adjustment process in the shorter term may be."[4] An accompanying note on "The stability of the income velocity of circulation of money supply" stated that, although velocity had fluctuated in the previous seventeen years, "at times quite sharply," there appeared to be "a clear tendency for the series to return to the underlying trend."[5]

If the monetary targets were to be achieved, it was essential to understand what caused monetary expansion. The favored account of the money-supply process gave pride of place to bank credit. With the deposit liabilities of the banking system representing the greater part of broad money, it was logical to attempt to limit the growth of bank assets. Since the growth of bank assets depended on the extension of new credit to the public, private, and overseas sectors, monetary control was guided by an analysis of the so-called "credit counterparts." More specifically, the authorities used a credit-counterparts identity which set out the relationship between, on the one hand, the public-sector borrowing requirement, sales of public-sector debt to non-banks, bank lending to the private sector, and a variety of external and other influences, and, on the other hand, the growth of broad money.[6]

The chosen approach to managing monetary growth was therefore to operate on the credit counterparts. Bank credit to the public sector could be influenced by varying the public-sector borrowing requirement (PSBR) and the amount of public debt sold to non-banks; bank credit to the private sector was thought to be responsive to changes in interest rates; and bank credit to the overseas sector was related to intervention tactics on the foreign exchanges.[7] In this spirit, the Green Paper *Monetary Control* began with the observation that "There are a number of policy instruments available to the authorities in influencing monetary conditions. Of these the main ones are fiscal policy, debt management, administered changes in short-term interest rates, direct controls on the financial system and operations in the foreign exchange markets."[8]

Officials at the Treasury and the Bank of England had few illusions about the precision of monetary management by these means. Indeed, there was an uneasy slide from the use of the ambitious word "control" in the title of the Green Paper to the more modest notion of "influence" in the key opening paragraph. Nevertheless, the authorities were confident that, with their "basic weapons," they could "achieve the first requisite of control of the money supply – control, say, over a year or more."[9]

Restraint on the budget deficit was seen as integral to monetary control over such annual periods. At Budget time a careful assessment was made of the consistency of the PSBR estimate with the broad-money target, and the tendency of policy was to subordinate fiscal decisions to the monetary targets. In the early 1980s the humbling of fiscal policy was regarded as almost revolutionary, since it appeared to end the Keynesian demand-management role traditionally assigned to the government in post-war British political economy. The intention was not to vary the PSBR to counter cyclical ups and downs in the economy, but rather to ensure – in the words of the Treasury "Memorandum" – that "the trend path" of the PSBR be "downwards."[10]

If the authorities were skeptical about their ability to target broad money over short-run periods of a few months, the government was reluctant to make exact predictions about how long it would take for inflation to respond to monetary restraint. The emphasis was very much on the medium-term nature of the commitment to monetary targets. It was readily conceded that a check on broad money this year would be followed by slower inflation not in the immediate future, but in two, three, or perhaps even four years' time. One consideration thought particularly likely to confuse the money/inflation link in the U.K. was the influence of a powerful trade-union movement on wages and prices. This influence was sometimes regarded as having autonomy from strictly economic variables, such as the state of demand and the level of unemployment. The size of the public sector, and its insensitivity to monetary conditions, was a special problem.[11]

To ask what Keynes would have thought about British monetarism in its 1980 version may seem an ahistorical impertinence. However, it is not far-fetched to see similarities between the system of monetary management envisaged by the Thatcher government in its early years and the idea of a managed currency advocated by Keynes throughout his life. Indeed, in one particularly interesting respect they coincided. The proposal for a managed currency was first made in *A Tract on Monetary Reform* (published in 1923), which was intended as a reasoned polemic against the gold standard. It contrasted the gold standard ("a barbarous relic"), focusing on the stability of foreign exchange, and a managed currency ("a more scientific standard"), with its goal of "stability in an index number of prices."[12] A preference for domestic price stability over a fixed exchange rate was also embodied in the Medium-Term Financial Strategy, as originally formulated. In the 1981 Mais Lecture, Sir Geoffrey Howe, the chancellor of the exchequer, remarked that, if monetary targets had been adopted, "you cannot have it both ways and also hold the exchange rate at a particular level. If any inconsistency emerges, the monetary targets have to come first."[13] In accordance with this prescription, exchange intervention was minimal for several years in the early 1980s.

In summary, British monetarism could be said to have four distinctive features: (1) the selection of broad money as the appropriate intermediate target, and a consequent emphasis on the control of bank credit as the central task of monetary management; (2) as part of the overall control of credit, a belief that fiscal policy should be made consistent with monetary policy and lose the demand-management functions attributed to it in the 1960s and early 1970s; (3) an admission that the link between money and inflation was medium-term in nature and difficult to predict, partly because of the strength of British trade unionism; and (4) the avoidance of any specific exchange-rate objective, for reasons that Keynes would probably have understood and approved.

II.

The first area of disagreement between British and American monetarism lay in the relative emphasis placed on broad and narrow money, and in related questions about the implementation of monetary control. As we have seen, in Britain in the early 1980s broad money was the focus of policy-makers' attention. Although Friedman himself believed that all measures of money conveyed a valuable message (and he had blessed broad money in the classic *A Monetary History of the United States*, which he wrote jointly with Anna Schwartz), there is no doubt that the majority of American monetarists favored the monetary base or a narrow money aggregate as the best policy indicator. According to Mayer, the monetary base was chosen for two reasons. One was that the American monetarist's "analysis of the money supply process" told him that this was "the variable which best reflect[ed] monetary policy actions"; the other was that he believed "the monetary base to be the best indicator of future changes in the money stock."[14] Both aspects of Mayer's statement are important and need to be discussed, but to understand them a sketch of the American monetarists' view of the money-supply process is required.

American monetarists, like their British counterparts, normally included bank deposits in their definition of the money supply.[15] Since banks (in the 1980s and now) have to be able to repay deposits with cash, they are obliged to hold a fraction of their assets in the form of cash or balances with the central bank. In American monetarism, empirical investigation was said to demonstrate a reasonably stable ratio between cash and deposits over the long run, while the quantity of cash – a liability of the central bank – was fully under the monetary authorities' control. It was therefore claimed that changes in the quantity of cash, reflecting central-bank operations, determined the level of bank deposits and, hence, of the money supply. Cash (that is, notes, coin, and balances with the central bank) is also known as "high-powered money," the "monetary base," or the "reserve base." Economists who believed in this account of the money-supply process tended also to favor deliberate variations in the quantity of cash as the main instrument of monetary policy. This system, known as monetary-base control, was widely advocated by American monetarists. (A version of monetary-base control was indeed implemented, briefly and rather reluctantly, by the Federal Reserve in a three-year experiment from 1979 to 1982. In the recent Great Recession the Federal Reserve massively expanded its balance sheet and hence the monetary base. This led in early 2009 to warnings of rising inflation from some American economists, including most notably Alan Greenspan, even though unemployment and spare capacity were unusually high.)

The first part of Mayer's statement is therefore readily explained. Changes in the monetary base were taken, by American monetarists, as the clearest guide to what the central bank had been doing, and so to the intended thrust of monetary policy. It is clear from the previous section that the approach of British monetarists was quite different. With bank deposits viewed as the counterpart to bank credit, British monetarists concentrated their attention on variables believed to be relevant to the behavior of bank credit. By far the most important of these was the short-term rate of interest, set by Bank of England operations in the money market. The contrast with the American monetarist position, with its concern over the quantity of reserves rather than the price at which they were made available to the banking system, was radical. Moreover, whereas in British monetarism the level of bank lending to the private sector was seen as critical to the monetary outlook, American monetarists were largely indifferent to it. (Bank credit mattered to British monetarism because it determined the quantity of money, not for any wider role in the determination of macroeconomic outcomes. The notion that bank lending did have such a role began at Harvard University in the late 1980s, where it was proposed by – most prominently – Ben Bernanke. For the later significance of "creditism" in the Great Recession, see particularly essays 17 and 18.)

Some doctrinal purists might protest at this stage that a preference for the interest rate over the monetary base cannot plausibly be attributed to monetarists of any kind, not even to "British monetarists." They might say that, if that is the implication of the definition of British monetarism given here, then the definition is too idiosyncratic and peculiar to be taken seriously. The answer to this objection is to recall the pattern of public debate in the early 1980s. The official policy framework prevailing at that time, and the attitudes informing it, were labeled as "monetarist" in the media, in Parliament, and in many other contexts. Furthermore, its emphasis on broad money and the credit-counterparts arithmetic did logically entail that close attention be paid to interest rates. Of course, to say that interest rates mattered was not to make them a target of policy. On the contrary, the intention was that interest rates (the instrument) were to be varied to influence credit and money (the intermediate targets) in order to exert leverage over the inflation rate (the ultimate target).

American reaction to monetary-control procedures in Britain varied from technical puzzlement to frank outrage. A consequence of the British arrangements was that official sales of gilt-edged securities to non-banks often had to be stepped up in order to reduce the excessive quantity of deposits created by bank credit to the private sector. In other words, long-term "funding" was a basic instrument of monetary policy. An official at the Federal Reserve Bank of New York remarked at a conference in May 1982 that this "emphasis on selling intermediate and long-term securities to mop up money balances always sounds a bit strange to us."[16] Friedman's comments to the Treasury and Civil Service Committee in 1980 were much sharper. He expressed incredulity at the opening paragraph of the Green Paper *Monetary Control*. In his view, "Only a Rip Van Winkle, who had not read any of the flood of literature during the past decade and more on the money supply process, could possibly have written" the key sentence with its list of instruments for influencing monetary conditions. He judged that "This remarkable sentence reflects the myopia engendered by long-established practices, the difficulty we all have of adjusting our outlook to changed circumstances." He declared strong support for direct control of the monetary base instead of the British system.[17] (The subject of money-supply control remains awkward to this day. Essay 4 explained how – in the extreme – the government itself can transact with the commercial banks and create money, entirely bypassing the central bank. The "debt-market operations" discussed there are just another name for the "funding" which so baffled Federal Reserve officials in the early 1980s.)

The dismay that many American monetarists felt in the early 1980s – and continued to feel for many years thereafter – about the Bank of England's monetary-control procedures did not go unnoticed in the U.K. Several economists advocated that Britain adopt some form of monetary-base control. The most notable were Professor Brian Griffiths of the City University (later to be head of the prime minister's Policy Unit at 10 Downing Street), Professor Patrick Minford of Liverpool University, and Professor (later Sir) Alan Walters, who was appointed the prime minister's economic adviser in 1981. As all three were British and were called monetarists, it may seem odd that in this paper "British monetarism" is associated with broad money, credit control, and funding. It perhaps needs to be repeated that British monetarism is defined here as the system of macroeconomic management established in the late 1970s and early 1980s, not a set of beliefs held by self-professed "monetarist" economists.

What about the second part of Mayer's statement, that American monetarists followed the monetary base because it was "the best indicator of future changes in the money stock"? It may or may not be true that the monetary base had this property in the United States. (Much depends on the economists and technical econometric papers one decides to trust.) But in the U.K., where the institutional apparatus is different, the monetary base is not – and for several decades has not been – a reliable guide to future changes in the money stock on any definition. Under the British arrangements the Bank of England traditionally supplied cash in the required amounts to keep banks' balances at the daily clearing just adequate for them to fulfill their obligations.[18] In consequence, the quantity of cash held by the banks adjusted to the size of their balance sheets rather than the other way round. The monetary base is – and long has been – determined by what is happening in the economy today; it does not determine what banks, the money stock, or the economy will do in future.[19] (The traditional arrangements were severely challenged in late summer 2007. The closure of the international inter-bank market implied cash shortages for several British banks, causing them to offer AAA-rated asset-backed paper to the Bank of England as collateral for loans. To their surprise the Bank made difficulties and declined to lend cash against the paper. The run on Northern Rock – one of the most embarrassing episodes in the Bank's history – followed a few weeks later.)

Indeed, one of the remarkable features of the British system in the 1980s was that – because of the flexibility of official money-market operations – the banks could keep very low ratios of cash reserves to deposit liabilities. Since cash reserves did not at that time pay interest, the lowness of cash-reserve holdings was an attractive feature to profit-seeking overseas bankers. (This was one reason for the intensity of foreign competition in the British financial system at the time. Other countries have subsequently also reduced banks' cash-reserve requirements. As just explained at the end of the last paragraph, in the Great

Recession, starting in late 2007, the Bank of England was sometimes unhelpful to banks in their cash-management decisions. Large numbers of foreign banks left London in 2008 and 2009.)

American economists did not appear fully to understand either the method of operation or the purpose of the British practices. The same Federal Reserve official who was puzzled by the significance of funding in the U.K. was also "struck by the minimal role that reserve requirements play in the monetary control process." He wondered whether "the amount of leverage available" was "sufficiently large for the central bank to pursue monetary and other policy targets effectively in all seasons."[20] But the point of the British system was that – in contrast to the situation in the United States – the quantity of cash reserves was not supposed to exert any leverage on the monetary targets. In his evidence to the Treasury and Civil Service Committee, Friedman proposed some reforms which he thought would tighten the link between the base and the money supply. He noted that banks could hold a variety of assets to meet reserve requirements in the U.K. and suggested that

> It would be highly desirable to replace this multiple reserve system by one in which only a single asset – liabilities of the Bank of England in the form of notes and coin (that is, base money) – satisfies reserve requirements. This is probably the most important single change in current institutional arrangements that is required to permit more effective control of the money supply.[21]

But Friedman was confused. He was talking about a 12½ percent reserve-asset ratio, the assets in which could be sold to the Bank of England for cash if an individual bank or indeed the banking system as a whole had a shortfall at the daily inter-bank settlement. Money-market operations were not intended to alter the level of reserve assets in the 12½ percent ratio; rather, they were intended to alter the amount of cash in a much smaller 1½ percent cash ratio. This cash ratio was the operational fulcrum of monetary policy. Since the confusion was shared to some degree by British economists and officials, Friedman's misinterpretation was perhaps excusable. But his imperceptiveness on the question reflected a wide gap between American and British approaches to monetary management and undoubtedly symptomized a certain amount of mutual incomprehension.

The differences between central-bank techniques in the U.K. and the U.S. are not new, but can be dated back to the early years of the Federal Reserve System. Unlike some recent participants in the debate, Keynes was well aware of their nature and origins, and devoted many pages of his *Treatise on Money* (published in 1930) to their analysis. He drew a contrast between "the bank-rate policy" applied in Britain and the "open-market policy" adopted in the United States. Essentially, the bank-rate policy involved a varying bank rate in order to control "the aggregate of the central bank's assets," whereas open-market operations of the American kind produced "a direct effect on the reserves of the member banks, and hence on the volume of deposits and of credit generally."[22] Although Keynes saw some merits in a bank-rate policy, it is quite clear that he preferred an open-market policy. He expressed great admiration for Governor Strong of the Federal Reserve, whom he regarded as the pioneer of scientific open-market operations, remarking that

> open-market operations can be so handled as to be quite extraordinarily effective in managing the currency. The successful management of the dollar by the Federal Reserve i.e. from 1923 to 1928 was a triumph ... for the view that currency management is feasible, in conditions which are virtually independent of the movements of gold.[23]

The sympathy here for the American approach connects with some of Keynes's later themes, since he also considered that, "whilst the bank rate may be the most suitable weapon for use when the object of the central bank is to preserve international equilibrium, open-market sales and purchase of securities may be more effective when the object is to influence the rate of investment."[24] This fitted in neatly with Keynes's emphasis in *The General Theory* on the need to influence investment in order to mitigate fluctuations in output and employment.

However, it should be noted that in *The General Theory* Keynes says rather little about central-bank techniques and almost nothing about the Federal Reserve. There is a short comment, in "Notes on the Trade Cycle" in chapter 22, about how "the most enlightened monetary control might find itself in difficulties, faced with a boom of the 1929 type in America, and armed with no other weapons than those possessed at the time by the Federal Reserve System."[25] But that is all. Is it reasonable to conclude that – in this area of the technicalities of monetary control – Keynes inclined more towards American monetarism than towards British? In qualification, in virtually all his discussions about monetary practice Keynes was concerned about the behavior of bank deposits and so of broad money. The focus on broad money was particularly obvious in his distinctions between income deposits, business deposits, and savings deposits, and between industrial and financial "circulations," in the first volume of *A Treatise on Money*.[26]

III.

Basic to the Medium-Term Financial Strategy, and indeed to the monetarist enterprise in Britain more generally, was control over the fiscal position. Recognition of the importance of restricting public-sector borrowing can be dated back to the mid-1970s. At that time extremely large budget deficits had been accompanied by difficulties in controlling the money supply and by fears that the substantial demands made by the public sector on the savings pool were crowding out private-sector investment. Targets for the PSBR were included in the International Monetary Fund's Letter of Intent in December 1976, which set out conditions for its loan to the U.K. In his speech to the lord mayor's dinner on October 19, 1978, Denis Healey – as chancellor of the exchequer in the Labour government – said that the government was "determined to control the growth of public expenditure so that its fiscal policy is consistent with its monetary stance."[27] The stipulation of precise numbers for the PSBR in the Medium-Term Financial Strategy from 1980 onwards should be seen not as a surprise innovation, but as the logical culmination to events over several years.

The thinking behind this approach was implicit in the credit-counterparts arithmetic. If bank lending to the private sector, external influences on money growth, and public-sector debt sales to non-banks were all given, there was – and, of course, still is – a direct accounting link between the PSBR/PSNCR (public-sector net cash requirement) and the growth of the money supply. For every £100 million of extra PSBR, there was an extra £100 million of M3. If an excessive PSBR threatened the monetary target, high interest rates would be needed to discourage lending to the private sector or encourage more buying of public-sector debt. According to Peter Middleton (later to become Sir Peter and also permanent secretary to the Treasury), in a seminar paper given in the 1977–78 academic year, "as a general proposition, a big fiscal deficit will tend to lead to a rapid growth of money supply and/or to higher interest rates . . . It follows that it is essential to examine fiscal and monetary policy simultaneously and coordinate them as far as practicable."[28]

This relationship between flows of public-sector borrowing and the growth of the money supply can be easily reformulated in terms of the stocks of public-sector debt, bank lending to the private sector, and money.[29] The main conclusion is that, if the ratios of public debt and bank lending to gross domestic product are constant, a higher ratio of the PSBR to GDP is associated with a higher growth rate of broad money and so with more inflation. In practice, ratios of public-sector debt and bank lending to GDP fluctuate substantially over time. But it is plausible that a government committed to extensive privatization of productive assets would favor, over the medium term, a rising ratio of private-sector bank borrowing to GDP, rather than a high ratio of public debt to GDP. In the early 1980s that implied a need for the PSBR/GDP ratio to be maintained at a low level for several years.

What about the American monetarists' attitude towards fiscal policy? In the late 1960s there was a fierce debate in the United States – known as the "Battle of the Radio Stations" after the initials of the main researchers involved (AM, FM, for Ando–Modigliani, Friedman–Meiselman) – about the relative effectiveness of fiscal and monetary policy.[30] Arguably, it was the starting point of monetarism. Not only did it prompt Professor Karl Brunner to coin the term "monetarist," but also it revolved around the idea – later to become a commonplace in the British policy debate – that discretionary changes in fiscal policy were misguided as a means of influencing the economy.

In view of this background, American monetarists might reasonably have been expected to welcome the demotion of fiscal policy in the

Medium-Term Financial Strategy. Curiously, that was not the reaction. Friedman, in his evidence to the Treasury and Civil Service Committee, said that the attention paid to the PSBR targets was "unwise," partly "because there is no necessary relation between the size of the PSBR and monetary growth."[31] Friedman's remarks were picked up by British critics of monetarism, notably by the Oxford economist Christopher Allsopp, who was emboldened to claim that "The standard monetarist line is that it is only the money supply that matters for inflation control, and that fiscal policy has little direct effect on the economy, or on the ease or difficulty of controlling money."[32] Although Friedman may have been particularly forthright in denigrating the place of PSBR control in British monetarism, there is no doubt that most American monetarists did not integrate fiscal policy into their thinking and policy advice. Thus a prescription for fiscal policy does not figure in Mayer's list of key monetarist propositions. Is the explanation perhaps to be sought in the separation of powers between the Federal Reserve (responsible for monetary policy) and the Treasury (which, along with other agencies, controls the federal budget) in the American system? For institutional reasons it perhaps made less sense to attempt to co-ordinate fiscal and monetary policy in the American context than in the British.

IV.

There was never any pretense in British monetarism that x percent growth of broad money over the next year would be followed by an exactly predictable y percent growth of money GDP at an exactly known date in the future or, indeed, that x and y would be virtually identical. It was readily admitted that the link between money and inflation was imprecise, while there were no illusions that the impact of monetary restraint on inflation would assert itself – or even be identifiable – over periods of time as short as three to six months. Instead, the connection between broad money and the price level was regarded as rather difficult to forecast and essentially medium-term in nature. When British monetarism was at its most influential, policy-makers probably thought in terms of an x percent rate of broad-money growth leading to an inflation rate of x plus or minus 2 or 3 percent at some date two to four years away. That may sound too flimsy as a basis for decision-making, but it is vital to remember the context in which British monetarism first made headway in the public debate. In the mid-1970s, when the inflation rate was frequently at about 20 percent or more, politicians were less fussy about an annual error in forecasting inflation equivalent to 2 or 3 percent of the index than they are in the early twenty-first century. Moreover, in the early 1980s there was little respect for computer-based macroeconomic forecasting methods which aspired to great exactitude. Such methods had totally failed to predict the scale of the inflationary retribution for the monetary policy mistakes of the Heath-Barber period.

American monetarists also refused to make bold claims about the precision of monetary impacts on the economy. Friedman coined an often-repeated phrase when he said that the relationship between money and inflation was marked by "long and variable lags." In his evidence to the Treasury and Civil Service Committee, he cautioned that "failure to allow for lags in reaction is a major source of misunderstanding." After suggesting that "for the U.S., the U.K., and Japan, the lag between a change in monetary growth and output is roughly six to nine months, between the change in monetary growth and inflation, roughly two years," he immediately inserted the qualification that, "of course, the effects are spread out, not concentrated at the indicated point of time."[33] Arguably, this reluctance to be specific reflected an aspect of monetarism highlighted by Mayer, namely, a preference for small reduced-form models over large-scale structural models of the economy.[34]

The differences between American and British monetarists in this area may not, therefore, seem to be all that wide. Keynes also recognized, although with reservations, the medium- and long-term validity of the money/inflation link. In chapter 21 of *The General Theory*, he said that the question of the relationship between money and prices outside the short period is "for historical generalizations rather than for pure theory." He continued by observing that, if liquidity preference (that is, the demand for money) tends to be uniform over the long run, "there may well be some sort of rough relationship between the national income and the quantity of money required to satisfy liquidity preference, taken as a mean over periods of pessimism and optimism together."[35] This is an interesting quotation because it shows that Keynes never dismissed the relevance of money to the long-run behavior of prices, not even after the refinement of his theoretical ideas on the short-run determination of output in *The General Theory*. However, the section that contains the quotation also makes several references to wages and productivity as fundamental influences on prices. Keynes may have been reluctant to give a wholehearted endorsement to either a monetary or a wage-bargaining theory of the price level. Perhaps he thought that both had something to say.

Keynes's equivocation on the subject may have reflected the central position of the trade unions in British society. A strong and influential trade-union movement continued for most of the first fifty or so years after the publication of *The General Theory* and obliged economists in the U.K. to pay trade unionism more attention than did their counterparts in the U.S. Not surprisingly, therefore, greater anxiety in the U.K. about the trade unions' impact on the labor market and the economy differentiated American and British monetarism, although the differences were more matters of emphasis than of substance. British monetarists were more inclined to claim that trade unions, by disrupting the setting of market-clearing wages, aggravated the problem of unemployment. This argument was integrated into a specifically monetarist framework by saying that trade-union activity increased the natural rate of unemployment. The point was that, in a situation such as the U.K.'s, where there had traditionally been strong political pressures to reduce unemployment below the natural rate, inflation expectations were contaminated by occasional phases of excess demand. As long periods of unemployment above the natural rate were then needed to remove the inflationary virus, and as these always involved restrictive and unpopular monetary policies, trade-union activism indirectly stigmatized the deliberate use of monetary policy. British monetarists therefore accorded trade unions a more prominent and active role in the inflationary process than American monetarists.[36]

Friedman's position on the trade unions was that they could alter relative wages (that is, the ratio between union and non-union wages), but could not influence the absolute level of wages (that is, union and non-union wages combined), which was determined by, among other things, the money supply. Moreover, a given amount of trade-union power could not explain continuing inflation. When asked at an Institute of Economic Affairs lecture in 1974 whether trade unions could increase the natural rate of unemployment, Friedman acknowledged that this was "a very difficult question to answer," but reiterated that "what produced ... inflation is not trade unions, nor monopolistic employers, but what happens to the quantity of money."[37]

The problem posed by trade unionism for British monetarism was exacerbated by the dominance of trade unionism in the public sector. While there are reasonably obvious transmission mechanisms between monetary policy and private-sector inflation, it is far from evident how monetary policy affects the public sector. One exercise on the demand for money in the U.K. recognized this by regressing the money supply on private-sector GDP, not GDP as a whole.[38] It did not occur to American monetarists – with the United States's smaller government sector and weaker trade unions – to be so fastidious.

V.

The British economy also differed (and still differs) from the American in being smaller and more susceptible to international influences. Since this difference made British monetarists more concerned about external pressures on domestic monetary policy than their American counterparts, it stimulated a lively debate about the appropriateness of alternative exchange-rate regimes. This debate has continued over many decades, with Keynes's argument for a managed currency in *A Tract on Monetary Reform* being one of the seminal contributions. Indeed, it could be claimed that when Sir Geoffrey Howe expressed such a decided preference for monetary targets over a fixed exchange rate in 1981 he was echoing a famous passage in the *Tract*. In Keynes's words, "If the external price level is unstable, we cannot keep both our own price level and our exchanges stable. And we are compelled to choose."[39]

In the mid-1970s, however, the British government – with Denis Healey the chancellor of the exchequer – failed to choose. Some interest-rate changes were motivated by external factors, some by domestic considerations, and some by both. The result was rather unhappy not just intellectually, but also practically, with 1976 seeing the most prolonged and embarrassing sterling crisis in the post-war period.[40] The monetarist commitment to floating exchange rates in the early 1980s can be interpreted largely as a reaction to the muddles of the first three years of the Healey chancellorship. But a number of key theoretical inputs also molded the climate of opinion and need to be mentioned. They can be dated back to the late 1960s, when lending economic journalists – egged on by Professor Harry Johnson of the University of Chicago and the London School of Economics – thought that the abandonment of a fixed exchange rate would remove an artificial barrier to British economic growth. More immediately relevant in the late 1970s was work done by David Laidler and Michael Parkin at the Manchester Inflation Workshop.[41]

An episode in late 1977 is basic to understanding the clarity of the monetarist support for a floating exchange rate in 1980 and 1981. After the excessive depreciation of 1976, the pound revived in 1977, and for much of the year its rise was restrained by heavy official intervention on the foreign exchanges. (The Bank of England sold pounds and bought dollars, to prevent the value of the pound from rising.) This intervention had the effect of boosting the money supply, which in consequence grew much faster than envisaged by the official target. The target was for an increase of 9 to 13 percent in sterling M3 in the 1977–78 fiscal year, whereas the actual result was an increase of 15.1 percent. Monetarist economists argued that the high monetary growth jeopardized the financial progress achieved under the IMF programs and that, after the usual lag, it would be punished by higher inflation. More conventional economists at the Treasury and elsewhere thought that a "low" exchange rate was needed for reasons of export competitiveness. The debate was conducted at several levels and proceeded with particular intensity inside the official machine.

When the government stopped intervening and allowed the pound to float upwards in October 1977, the monetarists seemed to have won. But their victory was not final. Although they were vindicated by a sharp upturn in inflation in late 1979 and early 1980 (after a fairly standard Friedmanite two-year lag), there were constant complaints that the government's permissive attitude towards the exchange rate allowed undue exchange-rate appreciation. Among the most active participants to the 1977 debate were economists at the London Business School. On the whole they favored adhering to the money-supply targets and allowing the exchange rate to float. A particularly notable contribution was made by Mr. Terry (later Lord) Burns, who was to become the government's chief economic adviser in January 1980.[42]

The views of British monetarists in the late 1970s and early 1980s on the choice of exchange-rate regime were not radically different from those of their American counterparts. One of the classic statements on the merits of floating was given by Friedman in his 1950 paper "The Case for Flexible Exchange Rates."[43] This paper was perfunctory in its treatment of the impact of foreign-exchange intervention on money growth, which was basic to the U.K. debate in the late 1970s. But its mood, with its aspersions on the forecasting ability of central-bank officials and its praise for market forces, was close to that of the Thatcher government in its early years. In his evidence to the Treasury and Civil Service Committee in 1980, Friedman said that "of course" an attempt to manipulate the exchange rate would limit the authorities' ability to control the money supply. He also criticized the government's announced policy of preventing excessive fluctuations in the exchange rate. In his opinion, "this exception is a mistake; better to leave the market entirely free . . . certainly for such a broad and efficient market as exists in British sterling."[44]

As it happened, the government in 1980 and early 1981 did not make an exception, even for a patently excessive fluctuation in the exchange rate. The pound became seriously overvalued, reaching $2.42 in October 1980 (compared to $1.63 in October 1976), and in February 1981 reaching almost 5 deutschemarks (compared with 4 one year earlier). These exchange-rate oscillations were subsequently singled out as the principal policy disappointment of the monetarist experiment. Inevitably, there has been much soul-searching about the suitability of monetary targets in an intermediate-size economy subject to all the volatilities of contemporary international finance. It is interesting that Keynes, when describing the alternatives of price stability and exchange stability in the *Tract*, conceded that the right choice must "partly depend on the relative importance of foreign trade in the economic life of the country."[45] Indeed, the book's final paragraph suggested that "there are probably no countries, other than Great Britain and the United States, which would be justified in attempting to set up an independent standard." Other countries could decide to peg their currencies to either sterling or the dollar until, "with the progress of

knowledge and understanding, so perfect a harmony had been established between the two that the choice was a matter of indifference."[46]

VI.

The period of strong monetarist influence over policy-making was
short-lived, although its precise length is a matter for discussion and
depends on whose version of events one selects. At one extreme it has
been argued that broad-money targets were discredited in July 1980
when the abolition of the "corset" was followed by a jump of over 5 percent in sterling M3 in only one month. (The corset was an artificial
device for restricting credit, which imposed penalties on banks when
their balance sheets increased faster than given percentage figures.)[47]
However, a more plausible account would treat the erosion of the system set up in early 1980 as a gradual process. There are various possibilities, but mid-1985 is probably best regarded as the terminal phase. It
was then that broad-money targets, and hence the defining feature of
British monetarism, were scrapped. Just as monetarism did not gain
ground by a simple process of intellectual conquest, so it did not retreat
through a straightforward failure to meet key practical tests. Instead
there were a number of distinct and intermittent challenges to monetarist arrangements. Although none of them individually might have
been decisive, their cumulative impact was difficult to resist.

The first major problem was the pound's clear overvaluation in late
1980 and early 1981. The reasons for sterling's appreciation have been
much debated, but one thesis – that above-target broad-money growth
obliged the government to maintain high interest rates, and high interest rates drove up the sterling exchange rate – made obvious sense. As
we have seen, both Sir Geoffrey Howe and Keynes had argued, in their
different ways, that "You cannot have it both ways" – you cannot simultaneously control the domestic price level and the exchange rate. But
the experience of 1980 and 1981 suggested that Britain should try to have
it both ways. It was better to have an intellectually muddled monetary
policy than a politically unacceptable industrial recession. In 1982 and
1983 official thinking was that the exchange rate should have some role
in assessing monetary conditions, while the monetary targets should be
retained. After severe exchange-rate overvaluation had caused a dras-

tic fall in industrial production between mid-1980 and mid-1981, the government was less concerned about the logical niceties of the matter than about avoiding further damage to the manufacturing base.

The second difficulty was that sterling M3 proved awkward to manage. The 1980 Green Paper *Monetary Control* may not have been particularly optimistic about month-by-month control, but at least it thought that sterling M3 could be brought within target "over a year or more." A large overshoot in 1980–81 undermined the credibility of even that rather unambitious statement. When there was another overshoot in the 1981–82 fiscal year, with sterling M3 up by 13 percent compared to a target range of 6 to 10 percent, many economists agreed with the then chief opposition spokesman on Treasury and economic affairs, Peter Shore, that sterling M3 had become "a wayward mistress." There was a widely held view that sterling M3 was no longer a reliable intermediate target and that policy should be stated more flexibly. For those who still favored monetary targets in one form or another, the disappointments with M3 targeting implied that monetary-base control deserved more sympathetic consideration. The disillusionment with broad money was accompanied by increased interest in narrow money, either in the monetary base itself (also known as M0) or in M1 (cash in circulation with the public, plus demand deposits). (The subsequent travails of M0 – for which the Bank of England ceased to publish data in 2006 – are discussed below on pp. 298–299, pp. 346–349, and pp. 361–362.)

These changes in official allegiances and informed opinion, away from money targets to the exchange rate and from broad money to narrow money, were largely determined by the pattern of events. But intellectual rationalization was not far behind. A key figure in the dethronement of sterling M3 was Sir Alan Walters. Although his credentials when appointed as the prime minister's economic adviser in 1981 were avowedly "monetarist," his monetarism was different in character from the "British monetarism" described here. He had been much influenced by the American enthusiasm for monetary-base control and was doubtful about the merits of operating on the credit counterparts to achieve broad-money targets. His preference was for a measure of money used in transactions, which he thought was best approximated in the U.K.'s case by M1. Despite problems because of institutional change, he believed that "It is money in this transactions sense that plays the central role in the theoretical structure and the propositions of monetarism." He judged that credit had "but a minor role," and he was correspondingly skeptical about "such credit magnitudes as M3." (However, the Alan Walters of the mid-1980s was different from the Alan Walters of the early 1970s. He had been critical of the explosion of *broad* money during the boom of the early 1970s, emphasizing the connection between it and rapid asset-price inflation.[48])

A consequence of the demotion of broad money was that less concern was felt about the rapid growth of credit in the private sector. Indeed, there was a school of thought – best represented by the Liverpool Research Group under Professor Patrick Minford – that bank lending to the private sector was always good for the economy, since it made possible more private-sector spending and investment. In some of its publications this group also suggested that large increases in broad money contained no inflationary threat. According to one issue of its *Quarterly Economic Bulletin*, credit – even credit in the form of bank lending – cannot be inflationary, regardless of the effect of its rapid growth on the quantity of money. The *Bulletin*'s argument was that, since borrowing by some individuals must be accompanied by lending by others, there is no net addition to or subtraction from wealth, and there should be no effect on behavior. Thus, when both sides of a balance sheet increase, "This is a straightforward portfolio adjustment and is not inflationary."[49] Minford, like Walters, had been much influenced by the American literature. As a reflection of this background, he regarded narrow money (particularly M0) as the most trustworthy money-supply indicator and favored monetary-base control.

By 1983 and 1984 the views of Walters and Minford had been important in undermining the original monetarist arrangements. These arrangements suffered most from policy surprises and disappointments, and from criticisms from non-monetarist or frankly anti-monetarist economists. But the willingness of these two economists carrying the "monetarist" label to repudiate certain aspects of the existing policy framework reinforced the suspicion and distrust with which British monetarism had always been viewed by the press, Whitehall, and the majority of academic economists. Since Walters and Minford had undoubtedly been keen students of monetarist thought coming from the other side of the Atlantic, their susceptibility to its teachings meant that American monetarism contributed – if somewhat indirectly – to the decline of British monetarism.[50]

In another respect, however, Walters and Minford were loyal to the policy structure envisaged in 1979 and 1980. Although Walters promoted a 1981 report by Jürg Niehans, which identified sterling's sharp appreciation as a symptom of monetary tightness, he was adamantly opposed to attempts to manage the exchange rate by foreign-exchange intervention. He wanted policy to be geared towards domestic monetary objectives and not towards the preservation of a fixed exchange rate or a target exchange-rate band. Indeed, he thought that these conditions still "broadly" applied to the U.K. in 1985, when he wrote, in *Britain's Economic Renaissance*, that "The authorities announce that the level of short-term interest rates will depend primarily on the assessment of the movement in the monetary aggregates. The exchange rate is to be the object of benign neglect."[51] Minford was equally hostile to systematic foreign-exchange intervention. In a paper first presented in 1980, he took it for granted that an "independent monetary policy is possible" and noted that this "presupposition is only valid under floating exchange rates."[52]

Unlike the tendency to play down the significance of credit and broad money, the increasing official preoccupation with the exchange rate in the early and mid-1980s therefore cannot be ascribed to pressure from Walters and Minford, or to the influence of American monetarist ideas. In the end it was the completeness of the shift in official priorities from domestic monetary control to exchange-rate stability that was primarily responsible for monetarism's downfall. Although several official statements had already hinted at the precedence of exchange-rate stability as a policy goal, the Plaza Accord of September 1985 may have been the key turning-point. At the Plaza meeting the finance ministers of the five leading industrial nations decided that in future they should co-operate more actively to achieve an appropriate pattern of exchange rates. Thereafter the chancellor of the exchequer, Nigel Lawson, was constantly mindful of this international responsibility and gave less attention to domestic monetary issues.

Other considerations, more local and humdrum, pointed policy in the same direction. The standard British practice of long-term funding, which had so bewildered Federal Reserve officials in 1982, was beginning to cause technical problems in the U.K.'s short-term money markets by mid-1985. The authorities decided that they could no longer "overfund" the PSBR in order to keep broad money on target. Without this technique, which had proved immensely useful as a means of curbing the growth of the monetary aggregates, there were likely to be great difficulties meeting broad-money targets.[53] In addition to all the other supposed weaknesses of broad money, sterling M3 was now condemned for complicating the management of the money markets. In his Mansion House speech on October 17, 1985, Lawson suspended the broad-money target for the 1985–86 fiscal year.

This was effectively the end of British monetarism as a policy-making framework. Although ostensibly only "suspended," broad-money targets had in fact been abandoned. A broad-money target was announced in the 1986 Budget, but the envisaged growth rate was so high that it was not a worthwhile constraint on inflation. Despite that, the target was soon exceeded, and Lawson suspended it again. By late 1986 the U.K. was in the early stages of a vigorous boom driven by extraordinarily rapid growth in the quantity of money, broadly defined. Although the government refrained from fiscal reflation, the credit and money excesses of 1987 and early 1988 were curiously similar to those seen in the Barber boom of the early 1970s. This was richly ironic, since the inflation that followed the Barber boom had been largely responsible for policy-makers' initial receptiveness to American monetarist ideas in the late 1970s.

The government did announce and observe narrow-money targets, expressed in terms of M0, throughout 1986 and 1987. But M0 completely failed to warn the government about the widening payments gap and rising inflation trend that emerged in late 1988. If Lawson had a meaningful anti-inflation policy in these years, the key instrument was the exchange rate for the pound, and the central idea was that exchange-rate stability would ensure rough equivalence between inflation in the U.K. and in other industrial countries. As the dollar was falling heavily starting in early 1985 because of the United States' enormous trade and current-account deficits, it seemed sensible to watch the pound/deutschemark exchange rate more closely than the pound/dollar exchange rate or, indeed, the effective exchange rate against a weighted basket of other major currencies. Throughout 1987, sterling was held fairly stable in a band of 2.85 to 3 deutschemark.

This shadowing of the deutschemark meant that the U.K. was virtually an associate member of the Exchange Rate Mechanism of the European Monetary System. Lawson had opted for an external financial discipline in preference to the domestic focus associated with money-supply targets. Since this was obviously a major change in strategy from the early years of the Thatcher government, an active public debate developed about the advantages and disadvantages of full EMS membership. Most academic economists approved of Lawson's new approach and thought it a welcome change from the doctrinaire monetarism he had espoused as financial secretary to the Treasury in 1980. But old-style monetarists (as they now were being called) were mostly hostile to EMS membership, while Walters and Minford were particularly outspoken in their attacks on it. In *Britain's Economic Renaissance*, Walters described the EMS as "rather messy" and remarked that the periodic exchange-rate realignments, far from being determined in an economically rational way, were "grand political events which present many opportunities for horse-trading, threats, counterthreats, bluff, etc."[54] In his view, it would be best if the U.K. had nothing to do with it. In adopting this position, Walters was following the mainstream monetarist tradition, in favor of freely floating exchange rates, associated with Milton Friedman and Harry Johnson.

After Walters had persuaded the prime minister, Mrs. Margaret (later Lady) Thatcher, that the EMS was a bad idea, she was increasingly worried about how Lawson was organizing monetary policy. Their private disagreements became steadily more acrimonious and eventually could not be hidden from the press or their Cabinet colleagues. On March 7, 1988, Margaret Thatcher indicated to the Bank of England her wish that foreign-exchange intervention be more limited in scale. The pound soon appreciated sharply against the deutschemark. However, this did not foreshadow a return to money-supply targets. In the Budget on March 15, Lawson did not reinstate a broad-money target, and even narrow money received a sharp snub. The M0 target was rendered ineffective by the admission, in the Treasury's *Financial Statement and Budget Report*, that no specific action would be taken to correct an overshoot which was expected to emerge early in the coming fiscal year.

By mid-1988 economic policy was in a fairly standard British muddle.

The monetarist framework, as understood in 1979 and 1980, had been coherent and relatively simple in conception. It had been replaced by a confused and eclectic pragmatism reminiscent of the Healey chancellorship in the mid-1970s. Government policy involved "looking at everything" (the exchange rate, bank lending, house prices, and the trade figures), and decisions were often the result of a lucky dip between options suggested by events in the financial markets. The U.K. had dropped broad-money targets of a kind favored by British monetarists; it had not adopted monetary-base control as recommended by American monetarists; it had had an unsatisfactory experience with narrow-money targets supported by American-influenced monetarists such as Walters and Minford; and it had procrastinated before rejecting, at least in appearance, full membership of the EMS.

The many fluctuations in policy fashion in the 1980s should not be allowed to disguise a number of successes which were clearly attributable to the original monetarist program. Most obviously, the inflation rate was reduced from an average of almost 15 percent in the late 1970s to about 5 percent in the five years starting in 1982. In view of the substantial monetary overshoots in 1980–81 and 1981–82, this achievement may have seemed due more to serendipity than to scientific management. But in all of the next three fiscal years the broad-money target was met, and in early 1985 the annual growth of sterling M3 was down to under 10 percent. Meanwhile the government broadly adhered to the fiscal side of the Medium-Term Financial Strategy. The result was that in the years of moderate growth from 1982 to 1986 the ratio of public-sector debt to national output was falling, while in the Lawson boom of 1987 and 1988 tax revenues were so buoyant that the government actually ran a large budget surplus. The U.K. was therefore saved from the worries about long-run fiscal solvency that troubled some other European nations.[55] The soundness of the U.K.'s public finances was also, of course, in sharp contrast to the United States' problems with budget deficits throughout the 1980s. With the benefit of hindsight, fiscal issues seem to have been handled more prudently by British monetarists than by their American counterparts.[56]

Indeed, there is something of a puzzle about the government's – or, at any rate, Nigel Lawson's – decision in 1985 to scrap the monetarist machinery with which it (and he) had been so closely associated five years earlier. As we have seen, there were many pressures tending to undermine the monetarist approach throughout the early 1980s, but one central point could not be overlooked. Monetarism had accomplished most of the original objectives held by its supporters as set out in the key policy documents of 1979 and 1980. Why, then, had the monetarist approach to macroeconomic policy disintegrated so quickly?

Perhaps the main solvents were the hostility of the traditional policy-making establishment, particularly academic economists in the universities, and the incomprehension of many influential commentators in the media. The aversion of the policy-making establishment may have had political roots. It is a safe sociological generalization that the majority of university teachers in Britain did not like Mrs. Thatcher and did not in the 1980s (and do not now) vote Conservative. They are more sympathetic to socialism or the mixed economy than to competitive capitalism. It would be consistent if they disliked monetarism as much for the free-market evangelism of its high priests as for its technical content. Also important in explaining their attitudes was British economists' habit of basing macroeconomic policy on external criteria, notably the exchange rate, instead of analyzing domestic monetary conditions. Officials at the Bank of England, which for most of its history had been charged with keeping the pound stable in value against gold or the dollar, undoubtedly found it more natural to adjust interest rates in response to exchange-rate movements than to deviations of the money supply from its target level. (The historical roots for U.K. policy-makers' preference for external, exchange-rate-based signals are discussed above in essay 3, "Keynes, the Keynesians, and the Exchange Rate.")

In this context the debates between British and American monetarists were important. In the circumstances of the early 1980s, when monetarism was very much on trial, the new system needed to be defended with simple and convincing arguments by a cohesive group of advocates. Instead the arguments were typically of extreme complexity, while often they were more heated between rival members of the monetarist camp than between monetarists and non-monetarists. The differences between the British and American methods provided material and personnel for these disputes, and therefore weakened the monetarist position in public debate. Samuel Brittan of the *Financial Times*, the U.K.'s most influential economic commentator at the time, referred dismissively on several occasions to "monetarist mumbo-jumbo," well aware that most of his readers were bored by technicalities. To him, and to many other people, membership of the EMS – with its uncomplicated exchange-rate discipline – had great appeal.

There is a paradox here. Many critics of monetarism assumed the label of "Keynesian" and clearly believed that their views were in a direct line of descent from Keynes himself. But, as we have seen, this is questionable. One theme throughout almost all of Keynes's career was that monetary policy should be directed to the attainment of domestic policy objectives (price stability and full employment), not to fixing the international value of the pound (in terms of either gold or another currency). In 1923 he mentioned in *A Tract on Monetary Reform*, with evident approval and sympathy, "the pioneer of price stability as against exchange stability, Irving Fisher."[57] It is intriguing that Irving Fisher is usually seen as an intellectual ancestor of Milton Friedman. But the determination of monetary policy by reference to domestic economic goals, and not to a numerically arbitrary exchange rate, was the central policy implication of Keynes's idea of a managed currency.

When Keynes wrote the *Tract* in 1923, Britain had extensive commercial influence throughout the world, and its empire had an economic weight not much less than that of the United States. Its size relative to other countries' justified it "in attempting to set up an independent standard" as a complement to the dollar area. By contrast, in the late 1980s the U.K. was in a transitional and historically ambiguous position. It was no longer large enough to dominate a supranational currency area, but it was not so small that membership of a European currency arrangement was self-evidently optimal. This dilemma, posed by the decline in British economic and financial power in the sixty-five years after the publication of the *Tract*, was basic to understanding policy-makers' resistance to a managed currency over the whole period. Perhaps the detailed blueprint for a managed currency would still have been unattractive if it had come not in the form of monetarism, but in a less ideologically unpalatable and far-reaching package. The trouble was that the Treasury and the Bank of England, knowing that the U.K. was in long-term financial retreat, lacked the self-confidence to make a managed currency work. American monetarists, resident in a large, self-contained economy, could more confidently recommend an ambitious and independent style of monetary policy than their British equivalents. It may always have been rather naïve to expect that ideas nurtured at the University of Chicago could be easily transplanted to Whitehall and Threadneedle Street.

At any rate, when the U.K. did eventually join the ERM (notionally as a stepping-stone to the EMS) in October 1990, it was in the worst possible circumstances for the success of the enterprise. Intolerably high interest rates were needed to preserve the fixed rate with the deutschemark. Home-owners and small businesses were delighted by the drop in interest rates that followed the pound's expulsion from the ERM on September 16, 1992. The U.K.'s association with the European fixed-exchange-rate system had lasted less than two years, a shorter period than that of money-supply-target monetarism (from 1976 to 1985), and it was a fiasco. Since 1992 monetary policy has been guided neither by the exchange rate nor by the money supply, but by a variety of indicators, of which one – the output gap, whose origins were discussed in essay 6 – has probably been the most important. The U.K. has had a form of "managed currency," although it is not the same as that proposed in *A Tract on Monetary Reform*, and no one can know whether Keynes would have approved of how policy-making has evolved in the last fifteen to twenty years. The Britain of the early twenty-first century is very different from the Britain in which he lived.

ESSAY 14

CRITICIZING THE CRITICS OF MONETARISM

BY THE START of the twenty-first century, monetarism – unlike a surprisingly mutable Keynesianism – was being referred to in the past tense. For some people "monetarism" was a convenient swearword, used to express their loathing for everything that had gone wrong (as they saw it) since conservative governments in the U.S. and the U.K. embraced free-market economics in the 1980s. A more sympathetic author, Michael Oliver, interpreted the rise and fall of monetarism in Britain as a problem in "social learning." As Oliver put it, writing in the mid-1990s,

> The social learning process since 1979 has been a mixed affair. The 1980s were a time of policy experiments ... While it would be wrong to see policy as an unqualified success in the 1980s, it would be equally incorrect to conclude that nothing positive has come from the past 16 years.[1]

A particularly interesting discussion by Thomas Mayer and Patrick Minford appeared in the spring 2004 issue of *World Economics*. Their paper, "Monetarism: A Retrospective," concluded that "Monetarism as a distinct school is in decline, but monetarist ideas are flourishing and form a major part of the modern synthesis."[2]

The various assessments generally saw monetarism as an outgrowth of theoretical ideas revived by (mostly) American economists in the 1950s and 1960s, and translated into policy across the industrial world to combat the high inflation of the 1970s; and they correctly recognized the strong influence that monetarism had on policy-making in the early years of the Thatcher government in the U.K., starting in 1979, and, to a lesser extent, in the Reagan administration in the U.S., starting in 1981. But a common tendency – shared by Mayer and Minford – was to underestimate the success of the monetarist challenge to the styles of policy-making (corporatism and fiscalist Keynesianism) that had prevailed, particularly in the U.K., before the 1970s.

One line of attack on monetarism was technical. In the 1980s a conventional wisdom emerged from a large body of econometric work that demand-for-money functions had become unstable. In some circles the breakdown of money-demand stability was thought not only to invalidate the case for money-supply targets, but also to argue against the practice of tracking the money-supply aggregates for their macroeconomic information. The following discussion is intended as a critique of the criticisms of monetarism. It will concentrate on the U.K., although the argument has wider relevance.

I.

In their opening remarks and in a section on "Basic Ideas and History," Mayer and Minford compared monetarism with other schools of macroeconomic thought, particularly Keynesianism. In their view the differences were hardly fundamental. Whereas the monetarists believed in the importance of money to national-income determination in the short and long runs, the Keynesians accepted the role of money in national-income determination in the long run, but questioned it in the short and medium terms; monetarists such as Milton Friedman regarded the proposition that money and national income have similar rates of changes as a reasonable working hypothesis (but acknowledged that the theory of money is an aspect of the theory of portfolio selection), while Keynesians emphasized that desired money holdings may change relative to other types of wealth and income, put questions of portfolio selection first, and repudiated a mechanical one-to-one relationship between money and national income; and so on. In this ball of economic theory the dancers changed their partners from time to time, but they all knew the sequence of steps in the Cambridge cash-balances equation, the routines of the IS/LM model, and other familiar

tunes and rhythms. Everyone enjoyed everyone else's company, and the
gap between monetarism and other schools of thought arose from differences of nuance and emphasis. There was no clash of worldview and
ideology, and no need for polemics.

But that was not how matters stood in Britain in the mid-1970s or
for many years afterwards. The study of monetary economics in British
universities had declined in the 1950s and 1960s, and most university
teachers rejected both a monetary theory of inflation and a role for
money in the determination of national income.[3] Inflation was widely
attributed to trade-union greed or "pushfulness," with one commentator remarking that "pulp forests have been consumed" in discussing the
role of the trade unions in the inflationary process.[4] The standard view
about national-income determination was that both output and income
were equal to expenditure, and that current expenditure was dependent on past income plus or minus demand withdrawals by the state (i.e.,
by the use of fiscal policy) and on events overseas (as the world economy
waxed and waned, or because the exchange rate changed).[5] As a consequence of these beliefs, mainstream professional opinion favored two
policy approaches. First, incomes policy (or "wage and price controls")
should be used to control inflation, with high-level bargaining between
the government, the trade unions, and industry on dividend freezes,
pay norms, and suchlike. Second, fiscal policy should be used to manage
demand, with the annual "Budget judgment" (i.e., the net injection or
withdrawal of demand by the state, approximated by the change in the
cyclically adjusted budget deficit) being critical. The purpose of demand
management was to achieve full employment, in line with an agenda
widely attributed to the 1944 White Paper on Employment Policy.

Monetary policy – often defined only in terms of interest rates rather
than in terms of the quantity of money – was widely considered to be
peripheral to the economy. Interest rates were recognized as having
some effect on the exchange rate, but that was all. According to Charles
Goodhart,

> Throughout most of the 1960s . . . interest rates varied mainly in
> response to external conditions, being raised whenever there
> was a need to support the fixed exchange rate, which was often
> under pressure, and lowered – in a spirit of general benevolence

towards investment – as each balance-of-payments crisis tem-
porarily receded. With interest rate policy mainly determined by
external considerations, the money supply was allowed to vary
passively.[6]

Support for incomes policy and active fiscal management, and disdain
for monetary policy, had huge political significance. They did not
reflect merely technical differences of opinion about the effectiveness
of the various economic instruments, but were instead motivated by
deeper ideological commitments in British society. The high-level bargaining associated with incomes policy gave the trade unions considerable political power. Comparisons were made between the style of
British economic government in the two decades starting in 1960 – as
politicians sought economy-wide deals with senior figures in the trade
unions and large companies – and the state capitalism or "corporatism"
of several European nations earlier in the twentieth century.[7] Clearly,
the greater the reliance on incomes policy to curb inflation, the
stronger was the position of the trade unions in key policy debates.

The pre-eminence of fiscal policy also had implications for the
U.K.'s social and political structure. In his *General Theory*, published in
1936, Keynes had said that fiscal policy would work best in a nation
with "a somewhat comprehensive socialisation of investment." He
thereby established a persuasive argument for a mixed economy with
an extensive state-owned sector. To quote Keynes's words, "The central controls necessary to ensure full employment will, of course,
involve a large extension of the traditional functions of government."[8]
In short, both corporatism and Keynesianism accorded with the interventionist bias of most British writers and thinkers, including most
British economists, in the early post-war decades.[9]

A fair comment is that by the early 1970s the macroeconomic thinking of many British economists, and the often rather pugilistic espousal
of such thinking as "Keynesianism," had become idiosyncratic by international standards. James Tobin, an American economist of undoubted
Keynesian leanings, later commented sharply on these trends in
an article in *The Economist*. In his words, "Particularly in Britain, the
view that money and financial markets are a self-contained sideshow to
the main macroeconomic performance held sway for much too long.

Mainstream American Keynesians did not dispute Friedman's contention that 'money matters.'"[10]

At any rate, a blend of Keynesian and corporatist doctrines conditioned economic policy-making. Taken to extremes, it prescribed a policy mix in which incomes policy set a politically determined and administratively enforced limit on inflation, and fiscal expansionism – justified by rhetoric about full employment – drove output to its employment-maximizing level. A policy mix of this kind was indeed favored by the National Institute of Economic and Social Research in the 1960s and 1970s. However, it could not be freely pursued in the 1960s because the Bretton Woods system of fixed exchange rates constrained U.K. policy-making.[11] But in August 1971 President Nixon – for reasons of American public policy quite separate from the U.K.'s troubles – decided to end the dollar's convertibility into gold. (The U.S. also had a dose of the Keynesian-corporatist remedies at that time, with many economists both indifferent to rapid money growth and supportive of incomes policies. Nixon imposed wage and price controls in conjunction with the ending of gold convertibility. When Nixon told Friedman at a private meeting in September 1971 that he should not blame George Shultz, a member of the administration and an old friend of Friedman's, for "this monstrosity" of wage and price controls, Friedman hit back: "I don't blame George, I blame you." They never met again.[12])

The breakdown of the Bretton Woods arrangements enabled the British government for the first time in the post-war period to combine incomes policy with aggressive fiscal reflation. The external barrier to high money-supply growth was removed, while an increased budget deficit could be financed to a large extent from the banking system. In the two years up to the end of 1973 the sterling M3 money-supply measure – which consisted mostly of sterling bank deposits – increased by over 25 percent a year. A wild boom in 1972 and 1973 was followed by rising inflation in 1974 and a peak inflation rate (as measured by the annual change in the retail price index) of 26.9 percent in August 1975.[13] Well-respected commentators warned of the possible collapse of British democracy.[14]

Monetarism in the U.K. developed partly under the influence of academic ideas from the U.S. (such as the quantity theory of money associated with Milton Friedman and the Chicago School), but mostly it was a response to the U.K.'s own economic and political crisis of the mid-1970s. Its central tenet was that inflation had monetary roots, in the sense that inflation was caused by the quantity of money rising too rapidly relative to the quantity of goods and services. To monetarist participants in the British public debates at that time, the facts supporting this proposition were compelling. Particularly eloquent was the similarity of the peak rate of retail price inflation in 1975 to the peak rate of money growth two to three years earlier. But Friedman's thinking supplemented the education by events in one very important way. In his presidential address to the American Economic Association in 1967 he had argued that there is no long-run trade-off between unemployment and inflation. His core thesis was that the pursuit of "full employment" (meaning a low level of unemployment with an excess demand for labor) would be accompanied not by a stable high rate of inflation, but by ever-accelerating inflation. As economists examined the data, evidence for this "accelerationist hypothesis" could be found in the U.K. and many other countries.[15]

Three vital implications followed. The first was that incomes policy was an ineffective answer to inflation and should be dropped; the second was that fiscal policy should be subordinated to monetary control; and the third was that policy-making should not try to achieve full employment, but should instead be focused on the reduction of inflation (and the eventual achievement of price stability) by lowering the rate of money-supply growth. Heavy emphasis must be placed on one point. While the agenda could be presented as largely technical, its wider social and political consequences were far-reaching. Keynesianism and corporatism were ideas that fitted the post-war so-called "Butskellite" consensus, with a large public sector, extensive state ownership of the nation's capital assets, and close relations (or, at any rate, attempted close relations) between the trade unions and the government.[16] Even into the 1960s many leading figures in British public life saw the mixed economy as a half-way house between the *laissez-faire* capitalism of the nineteenth century and a Communist end-state that was certain to arrive at some future date.[17] Despite bitter controversy, the first post-war generation of Labour politicians kept Clause Four (in favor of government ownership of all the means of production) in their party's constitution. In 1979 Tony Benn published a book of *Arguments for Socialism*, which included the proposition that Clause Four had "growing relevance today as capitalism moves into decline." In his view, it "must remain at the core of our work."[18]

Monetarism represented not just an alternative to Keynesianism and corporatism in technical macroeconomics. More fundamentally, it was an expression of an utterly different worldview. Without an incomes policy, Cabinet ministers did not need to negotiate with the trade-union movement; without an activist fiscal policy, the Keynesian case for a large state sector collapsed; without a full-employment commitment, the government could concentrate on the provision of a sound currency to promote the efficiency of a market economy. Monetarism welcomed the liberation of market forces to collect the nation's savings, and their management by private-sector companies and financial institutions ("the City," in the U.K. context), according to profitability. By rejecting the traditional arguments for the state ownership of the so-called "commanding heights of the economy" (steel mills, nuclear reactors, state-subsidized aluminum smelters, and suchlike), it laid the intellectual foundations for the privatizations of the 1980s.

Hundreds of thousands, indeed millions, of British people – in the trade unions, in the media, in the universities, and indeed in positions of trust as civil servants – had believed from the 1930s that the inevitable long-run drift in U.K. policy-making was towards increased state ownership, more planning and intervention, and an ever-growing public-sector supply of services. After all, non-defense public expenditure rose relative to national income even under the Conservative government from 1951 to 1964. It came as a shock to such people to find that in the mid- and late 1970s there were advocates of a diametrically opposite point of view. This clash of worldviews – about which Mayer and Minford said almost nothing in their 2004 appraisal of monetarism – must be mentioned if it is to be understood in a British setting.[19]

II.

In May 1979 the intellectual jolt to Britain's left-leaning chattering classes became a real-world political trauma. The Conservative Party, led by Mrs. Margaret (later Lady) Thatcher, was elected with a comfortable majority in the House of Commons. It quickly set about implementing an agenda quite different from its Labour predecessor's. Within a few weeks, prices and incomes policies, and the accompanying institutional machinery, were scrapped. In October, exchange controls – which had been in force for forty years – were also abolished. The task of inflation control was to fall exclusively on monetary policy. Thatcher and her ministers were prepared to test the theory that inflation has only monetary causes, and they pledged themselves not to commit a U-turn ("The lady's not for turning") and restore incomes policy. They received intellectual reinforcement from a television series, *Free to Choose*, which appeared in the spring of 1980 and was in effect a dramatization of Friedman's 1962 book *Capitalism and Freedom*. Each program ended with a discussion between Friedman and a number of British academics, businessmen, and politicians. According to Peter Jay (who hosted the discussions), "Friedmanism" had become the "central issue in British domestic political debate."[20]

Ideas were again translated into action in the March 1980 Budget, when Sir Geoffrey (later Lord) Howe announced the Medium-Term Financial Strategy. The strategy envisaged year-by-year targets for reductions in the rate of money-supply growth and in the ratio of the budget deficit (as measured by the "public-sector borrowing requirement" – PSBR) to gross domestic product. It was intended as an exercise in monetary "gradualism," not as shock therapy to move the economy rapidly onto a lower inflation path. In the 1981 Budget, Howe raised taxes sharply in order to keep the budgetary position under control. This was a direct challenge to Keynesianism, as the cyclically adjusted budget deficit was being cut despite high unemployment and weak demand. (Essay 10 discusses the context and sequel to the 1981 Budget in more detail.)

This is not the place to provide a narrative account, even in a potted version, of the main policy decisions and outcomes over the subsequent thirty years. However, in any meaningful assessment of British monetarism, the main features of policy-making after the 1981 Budget must be discussed. Mayer and Minford's paper was quite friendly towards monetarism, but it failed to provide such a discussion. Instead, their section on "Monetarism in the United Kingdom" contained an outline of events between the mid-1970s and 1982, implying that – although monetary policy was rather disorganized – "shock tactics" did get inflation down and eventually "restored the fortunes of Mrs. Thatcher and her supporters." Almost nothing was said about events after 1982, as if the second Thatcher election victory marked the end of "the monetarist experiment." Mayer and Minford's implicit view – that, in some sense, British monetarism ended in 1982 or 1983 – may be partly responsible for their judgment that "as a distinct school" it had fallen into "decline." The next few paragraphs will argue that, at the level of real-world policy-making, this conclusion is almost wholly wrong. Far from slipping into decline, monetarism demolished Keynesianism and corporatism.

What happened in the three crucial areas of incomes policy, fiscal policy, and the conduct of monetary policy? Incomes policy may be taken first. If monetarism had really fallen into "decline," a fair expectation might be that British economists would in the early twenty-first century be lauding the virtues of incomes policy as a way of curbing inflation. But that is not so. In sharp contrast to "the pulp forests" consumed in comment about and advocacy of incomes policy in the 1960s and 1970s, it is difficult to think of a single recent book on the topic. Academic articles and historical monographs may still be written about Jack Jones, Vic Feather, Arthur Scargill, the Counter-Inflation Program, "the son of £6 a week," and that sort of thing, but incomes policy is no longer a live and relevant option for policy-makers. Trade-union membership has fallen heavily, while newspapers no longer feel obliged to report the proceedings of the Trades Union Congress as if the "union barons" were a major power in the land. In this respect the contrast between Britain today and Britain in the early 1970s could hardly be more total. For all practical purposes, incomes policy is dead.

Incomes policy did not become a permanent fixture in standard macroeconomics texts and has been easy to forget. Fiscal policy is another matter. Its validity as a stabilization tool has been asserted in most textbooks since 1945, and its supposed effectiveness in this role is still widely seen as the explanation for the increased stability of the American and British economies compared with the 1930s. But in fact the textbooks have lost touch with reality. The announcement of the MTFS in 1980 marked the beginning of a period of over twenty-five years in which fiscal-policy decisions were set within a medium-term framework, with one key objective being to ensure that the ratio of debt to GDP was kept under control. Mayer and Minford implied that a veil was drawn over the MTFS by embarrassed policy-makers in the early 1980s. In their words, "the MTFS was widely written off as a failure at this time . . . and it came to be seen as a temporary interlude before traditional politics resumed."[21] On the contrary, a version of the MTFS was retained in all the Budgets until 1997. Although its contents evolved over the years and the monetary element was downplayed, the MTFS continued to set the context for fiscal-policy decisions throughout the long period of Conservative rule. The MTFS undoubtedly had a major effect on public-finance outcomes. Whereas in the 1970s the U.K. was bracketed with Italy as an incorrigible fiscal spendthrift, by the late 1990s the ratio of public debt to GDP was below the average for the industrial world and down to about a third of that in Italy. The British banking system – whose assets had been dominated by claims on the public sector in the 1950s and which therefore was subject to official restraints on its lending to the private sector – held virtually no public-sector debt at the start of the twenty-first century.

Sure enough, a big debate about the wisdom of orienting fiscal policy on medium-term debt sustainability rather than short-run demand management did return during the Great Recession of 2008–2010. But from the early 1980s to the Great Recession, discussion of fiscal-policy issues in the U.K. was muted. When a Labour government replaced the Conservatives in 1997, the MTFS was dropped, but Gordon Brown, the new chancellor of the exchequer, did not revert to old-style Keynesianism. Instead a commitment to medium-term fiscal stability was a hallmark of Mr. Brown's supposedly innovative policy regime. He announced a "golden rule" (in which current expenditure was to be covered by taxation) and a "sustainable investment rule" (which set a limit on the ratio of public debt to GDP). Both these rules had nothing whatever to do with the type of fiscal demand management recommended by British Keynesians in the 1950s and 1960s, and could more plausibly be interpreted as a modern refurbishment of Gladstonian principles of public finance.[22] Again, for all practical purposes Keynesianism – in the sense of short-run changes in the fiscal position to manage demand – had been rendered obsolete in the U.K. (Whether a refurbished version of Keynesian fiscalism will come back at a later date is uncertain, but the present Conservative–Liberal Democratic coalition appears at the time of writing [December 2010] to have repudiated the brief and disastrous indulgence in so-called "fiscal expansionism" during the Gordon Brown premiership.)

Finally, as far as the conduct of monetary policy is concerned, many years have now passed since it was directed to the maximization of employment. The first half of the Thatcher premiership showed that monetary policy could be used to reduce inflation, without relying on the crutch of incomes policy. (The second half – which saw a marked acceleration in money-supply growth in the unfortunate "Lawson boom" and a subsequent rise in inflation – also demonstrated the validity of the monetary theory of inflation, and is discussed below.) In the 1990s decision-making on interest rates was transferred from politicians to monetary specialists in two steps: first, the publication of the minutes of the monthly meetings between the chancellor of the exchequer and the governor of the Bank of England starting in early 1993; and second, the granting of operational independence to the Bank of England in 1997. This transfer of power was possible only because informed opinion was quite different from what it had been in the 1960s. The U.K.'s sorry experience of boom and bust had persuaded almost everyone who mattered in policy formation (politicians in all three main parties, their advisers, leading civil servants, and the most influential newspaper commentators) of the validity of Friedman's 1967 proposition that no long-run trade-off exists between inflation and unemployment. The phrase "full employment" had lost its totemic status in public debate. It was therefore sensible for the setting of interest rates to be taken out of the political domain and given to technicians.

Paradoxically, the decade starting in 1994 saw almost uninterrupted increases in employment and falls in unemployment, so that by the mid-Noughties the U.K. had high labor-force participation and low unemployment by European standards. These gains can be interpreted as partly due to policy and, in particular, to supply-side reforms to improve labor-market flexibility, which dated back to the early 1980s. But no one in officialdom had planned them, in the sense of having a quantified target for either employment or unemployment, and no one in the Treasury or the Bank of England would have dreamt at any stage in the 1990s of adjusting interest rates to raise or lower employment. Indeed, the fifteen years starting in 1992 were characterized by extraordinary macroeconomic stability compared to any period of comparable length since the Second World War, including the years from 1948 to the early 1970s, the heyday of the supposed "Keynesian revolution."

A case can be made that the vital theoretical basis for this policy achievement was a generalization of Friedman's ideas on the link between changes in inflation and departures from the so-called "natural rate of unemployment."[23] If so, it is monetarism – and certainly not corporatism or Keynesianism – that deserves the accolades for Britain's much improved macroeconomic performance. Mayer and Minford's 2004 statement that monetarism was "in decline" was a travesty. It may have been in decline in the sense that the number of references to it in newspapers and parliamentary debates had fallen heavily, but the lack of attention was due to the general acceptance of its core recommendations on the structure of policy-making.[24] On a wider canvas, the Labour Party had dropped Clause Four from its constitution, while Tony Blair, the Labour prime minister from 1997 to 2007, embraced the market economy and was attracted to private-sector supply as a means of delivering public services. (His successor, Gordon Brown, is another story. The binge in public spending and the attack on the U.K. banking system during his three-year premiership are increasingly being regarded as calamitous. It is of course too early to have a historical perspective.)

III.

The technical critique of monetarism is directed not against its broad political and philosophical message, but against the practical value of the style of monetary management with which it was associated in the late 1970s and early 1980s. The centerpiece of this style of monetary management was an annual target for the growth rate of the quantity of money. Superficially, the rationale for such targets was simple. If the quantity of money and the level of nominal national income grew at similar rates in the long run (as evidence from many nations suggested they did), then control over monetary growth would deliver control over the growth of nominal national income and, at a further remove, the rise in prices. In the U.K. context in the early 1980s gradual reductions in money-supply growth – of the kind announced in the MTFS from 1980 onwards – ought in due course to achieve lower inflation.

In informal presentations of the argument, the velocity of circulation of money (that is, the ratio of national income and expenditure to the quantity of money) was said to be stable and predictable, like some of the constants in nature (such as the freezing and boiling points of water, or the speed of light). Even Friedman was tempted to invoke analogies between "laws" in physics and economics. In his 1992 book *Money Mischief: Episodes in Monetary History*, he claimed, "Fisher's equation [$MV = PT$] plays the same foundation-stone role in monetary theory that Einstein's $E = mc^2$ does in physics."[25] The trouble with this sort of assertion was that it overlooked that money and banking are human institutions, and the way in which people use their media of exchange is always changing. The U.K. experience with money-supply targeting was important to the reputation of monetarism, partly because of the ideological passions aroused by the larger debates over Thatcherism and its challenge to middle-way Butskellism.

Unfortunately for the monetarists, both the radicalism of the supply-side reforms introduced after 1979 and the rigor of the anti-inflationary policy disturbed the relationship between money and money national income. A host of changes – discussed at more length in footnote 26 – upset the thinking behind official policy.[26] Whereas from 1945 to the late 1970s money had been growing more slowly than national income, after 1979 its long-run tendency was to increase at an annual rate of 2 or 3 percentage points faster than national income. The targets in the first version of the MTFS made insufficient allowance for this change in behavior. As a result, the money-supply targets were pitched much too low and were routinely exceeded. The overshoots caused the whole machinery of money-supply targets, and not just the particular set of target numbers chosen, to be derided by critics as inappropriate and harmful. Far from being a natural constant, the velocity of circulation was shown to vary in the long run, as institutions, technology, and regulations evolved. Although its behavior could still be explained in economic terms, expectations of a stable velocity were shown to be naïve.

This experience helps to explain why, according to Mayer and Minford, a stable demand function for money "disappeared," so that "monetarism was providing no reliable way of predicting GDP." Other authors reached a similar conclusion. In the words of a 2003 textbook, *Monetary Economics: Policy and Its Theoretical Basis*, by the mid-1980s "it was clear both that the authorities' ability to target the broad money stock with any degree of accuracy . . . had been severely undermined, and that the rationale for monetary targets had itself broken down in the face of a sharply falling velocity."[27] The instability of money-demand functions and the inadequacy of money as a forecasting tool became part of the conventional wisdom.[28]

Particularly embarrassing for the monetarist cause was that Friedman made serious forecasting mistakes in the 1980s. As will be explained in essays 15 and 16 on the transmission mechanism from money to the economy, an all-inclusive, broadly defined money measure is the most relevant for analytical purposes and the most effective in policy-making. Friedman's long-term preference was indeed for a broadly defined measure, M2. Unfortunately for his reputation, in the early 1980s he was seduced into supporting the M1 aggregate, which at that time was being targeted by the Federal Reserve.

When interest rates dropped sharply from 1981 to 1984, interest-bearing deposits became less attractive to hold, and people and companies switched into non-interest-bearing demand deposits in M1. The result was that M1 jumped by 8 percent in 1982 and 10 percent in 1983, convincing Friedman that inflation would accelerate sharply. In July 1983 he averred in a *Newsweek* column that the United States would be "fortunate . . . if we escape either a return to double-digit inflation or renewed recession in 1984"; in April 1984 he warned, "I believe [the consumer price index] will be rising in the neighborhood of 8 to 10 percent in 1985"; even in November 1985 he conjectured that inflation "will emerge again and be higher next year than it is this year." Nothing of the sort happened. As noted by Edward Nelson in a fascinating paper on Friedman's magazine commentaries in his mid- and late career, inflation was in fact "below 5 percent in every month from 1983 to 1986 . . . and was lower in 1986 than it was in 1985."[29]

IV.

Nevertheless, the critics of monetarism went much too far. As an analytical matter, a change in the velocity of circulation of money does not imply that the demand for money has become unstable. The velocity of circulation of money may alter because of large shifts in the value of the arguments in the money-demand function other than national income itself. (For example, the desired ratio of money to income may depend on real interest rates and financial technology. If rises in real interest rates and improvements in financial technology cause agents to want a higher ratio of money to income, their underlying preferences for the quality of "money-ness" in their portfolios may be stable.) Moreover, the finding of instability in money-demand functions was not new in the 1980s. In the U.K., research at the Bank of England and elsewhere had usually found stable demand functions for broad money in the 1960s, but two well-regarded papers published by Michael Artis and Mervyn Lewis in 1974 and 1976 argued that these functions had broken down.[30] What had changed by the mid-1980s? Indeed, well before the challenge from Artis and Lewis, Walters had carried out empirical work on money and incomes spanning the 1880–1962 period, and found sub-periods when the link between money and incomes was weak. But this did not prevent Walters from becoming one of the leading advocates of control over the growth of the money supply as a means of curbing inflation. He was appointed personal economic adviser to the British prime minister, Margaret Thatcher, in 1981 principally because he was a committed believer in the potency of monetary policy.

The critics of monetarism also became sloppy in their use of words and careless in their judgments. It was one thing to show that the quality of an econometric relationship between money and incomes was lower in the 1980s than it had been in the 1960s. That meant that – even if the regression coefficient in a simple two-variable money/income equation were 1 in both the 1960s and the 1980s – any forecast in the 1980s would be made with less confidence than in the 1960s.[31] But it was something else to leap from there to the conclusion that the economy would not be affected at all by a shift from a lower to a higher rate of money-supply growth. If the regression coefficient were indeed 1 in both the 1960s and the 1980s, the correct forecast in both decades was that the most likely outcome of an acceleration in annual money-supply growth from 5 percent to 15 percent was an acceleration in the annual rate of increase in nominal national income also from 5 percent to 15 percent.

There seems little doubt that – when the technicians produced their statistical results for senior officials and their political masters – the message was garbled. In a speech at Loughborough University on October 22, 1986 – given when the annual growth rate of the money supply on the M3 measure had climbed well into the teens – the governor of the Bank of England, Mr. Robin Leigh-Pemberton (later Lord Kingsdown), said that it was "fair to ask whether a broad money target continues to serve any useful purpose" and that perhaps "we would do better to dispense with monetary targetry altogether." (One is reminded of Mr. Polly, in the H. G. Wells novel, who thought that he could not go bankrupt if he dispensed with an accountant.)[32]

The lower quality of the statistical relationships between money and income in the U.K. in the 1980s did *not* mean that the behavior of the quantity of money had no macroeconomic impact whatsoever. (A remarkably large number of people seemed to think that this is what it did mean.) Mayer and Minford – following the conventional wisdom – asserted, in their 2004 paper, that "monetarism was providing no reliable way of predicting GDP." But this was to ignore entirely the unhappy sequence of events between 1985 and 1992 in the U.K., and the success of monetarist analysts in their prognostications during the period.

In 1986 and 1987 the growth rate of bank deposits increased markedly, and the consequent excess supply of money led to large asset-price increases and a wider economic boom. At the beginning of 1988 the overwhelming majority of forecasting groups were nevertheless afflicted by "forecasters' droop" and expected 1988 to see a slowdown in the economy. (For an explanation of the phrase "forecasters' droop," see p. 54 in essay 3.) They were hopelessly wrong – and their indifference to money-supply developments was the fundamental reason for their misjudgments. In fact, 1988 saw the highest increase in private-sector domestic demand (in real terms) in the post-war period. Severe overheating resulted in a widening payments deficit and rising inflation. Policy-makers had to more than double interest rates between the spring of 1988 and the autumn of 1989 to compensate for earlier mistakes. In 1990 the annual rate of inflation reached double digits, while money-supply growth collapsed. The squeeze on real money balances hit asset prices, with real estate (including, for the first time in the post-war period, residential housing) suffering significant price falls. Recovery was delayed until 1993. The Conservative Party was stigmatized for economic mismanagement, with its traditional support among the home-owning middle classes being sharply lower in the general elections of 1997, 2001, and 2005 than in those of the 1980s.

The boom-bust episode was every bit as much the result of incompetence as the one between 1971 and 1975, which had developed from the 1971–73 explosion in money growth under Heath (as prime minister) and Barber (as chancellor). Ironically, it was the Heath-Barber boom which had caused Keith Joseph to protest against "inflationeering," and so had provided the initial stimulus to the adoption of monetarist ideas by leading figures in the Conservative Party. At any rate, the Lawson boom and the subsequent bust demonstrated yet again the validity of the monetary approach to national-income determination. Economists who monitored the behavior of the money supply (on the broadly defined measures) were the most successful in anticipating the large fluctuations in asset prices, demand, and inflation that occurred in the decade starting in 1985. When Mayer and Minford claimed that monetarism "was providing no reliable way of predicting GDP," they were being very misleading. It would be closer to the truth to say that, in the more extreme phases of the last major U.K. boom-bust episode, only the monetarists provided reliable forecasts of GDP.[33] In this respect the British monetarists – unlike Friedman in the United States – gained extra credibility in the public debate from their forecasting records.

V.

Whatever one's doctrinal affiliations, there is not much dispute that in the 1970s U.K. macroeconomic policy-making was in crisis. The U.K.'s problems were far more severe than those of other industrial nations, including the United States. The monetarists set out an agenda for change which was adopted rather haphazardly by the Labour government after the 1976 crisis and, with more commitment, by the Conservatives from 1979 on. It cannot be emphasized too strongly that in these years the monetarists were heavily outnumbered in the academic debate. Remarkably, the monetarist agenda was implemented in the early 1980s in defiance of beliefs held by the great majority of British university economists.[34] The 364 economists who wrote the March

1981 letter to *The Times* in protest against monetarism were quite wrong in their forecasts of the economy. Over the following few years their jeremiads about the U.K.'s "industrial base," and its "social and political stability," came to look ridiculous.

Nevertheless, they and their students continue to dominate the academic profession in the U.K., and like-minded economists are in the majority in the academic profession in other English-speaking nations. As far as monetary economics is concerned, the two Cambridges – the one in Cambridgeshire, England, and the other in Massachusetts, U.S.A. – are very much together. Leading economists in the colleges of Cambridge, England, share with their counterparts at Harvard University and the Massachusetts Institute of Technology an aversion to monetary analysis, and contempt for the notion that "money and banking" are vital in macroeconomic discussion.[35] There should be no surprise that a conventional wisdom has emerged which is carping and mean towards monetarism, and fails to recognize its contribution to the improvement in American and British macroeconomic performance during the Great Moderation. The technical element in the conventional wisdom – with its aspersions on the instability of velocity, the unreliability of forecasts, and so on – is largely wrong and needs a critical re-appraisal. The opponents of monetarism have had it too easy for too long.

PART FIVE

HOW DOES THE ECONOMY WORK?

PREFACE

THE EVIDENCE of a long-run relationship between the quantity of money and national income is overwhelming in the United States, as in other countries. (See the table on p. 97 in essay 4, and the table on p. 326.) But critics can readily put together contrary evidence for periods of, say, one to three years. They often then go on to claim that – because of the wobbles and bumps in these "short runs" – supporters of monetary analysis lack a plausible account of the so-called "transmission mechanism." As noted in essay 15, Keynes made roughly this point as long ago as 1911 in a review of Fisher's *The Purchasing Power of Money*. The critique was sharpened in 1970, by Paul Samuelson in remarks on Friedman and Schwartz's *A Monetary History of the United States*. According to Samuelson, the book was light on theory, and the mechanisms at work in the monetary interpretation of the economy were "a black box." The "black box" allegation was repeated in the title of an influential 1995 paper "Inside the Black Box: The Credit Channel of Monetary Policy Transmission." The paper's two authors were Mark Gertler and Ben Bernanke, who – little more than a decade later – became chairman of the Federal Reserve. As I say in both essays 17 and 18, Bernanke's statement must be taken at face value. When someone of Bernanke's intellectual depth, breadth, and fluency says that he believes something is a black box, he does believe that it is a black box. He wouldn't make it up.

The argument in the first two essays in this section is that the black-box allegation is false. Loose and impressionistic accounts of a link between money and expenditure, and so between the quantity of money and the price level, go back to the sixteenth century. But the key advance – in terms of economic thought – was made early in the twentieth century by the Swedish economist Knut Wicksell. He realized and spelled out the consequences of a rather obvious insight. This was that, when one agent tried to reduce or to increase his money balances (by

Money and Nominal GDP in the U.S., 1959–2009
% compound annual increase

	Nominal GDP	M2	M3
1960s*	6.9	7.0	7.5
1970s	10.2	9.6	11.4
1980s	7.8	7.9	8.5
1990s	5.5	3.9	4.9
2000s**	4.0	6.2	8.1
Whole period***	6.9	6.9	8.0

* I.e., Q4 1959–Q1 1969, and so on for the other decades

** I.e., Q4 1999–Q4 2009

*** I.e., Q4 1959–Q4 2009

Sources: St. Louis Federal Reserve Economic Data; for nominal GDP, quarterly data originally from Department of Commerce; for M2, data originally from Federal Reserve, with last month in quarter taken to define quarter's value; for M3, data since 2006 from Shadow Government Statistics

spending above or beneath income, or by purchasing or selling assets), that did not alter the aggregate quantity of money in a society. Alternatively put, millions of attempts by individuals to change their money balances (or "individual experiments," as they have become known, following Patinkin in his 1956 *Money, Interest, and Prices*) may alter the distribution of money balances between individuals, but they do not affect the total quantity of money held by them all. Transactions of all kinds – transactions in goods, transactions in financial securities, transactions in tangible assets – are conducted endlessly in order, first, that the distribution of money balances between agents approaches a desired pattern, and, second, that all prices and quantities move towards an equilibrium with the total quantity of money. It follows that changes in the total quantity of money (or "market experiments") – because of the creation and destruction of money by the banking system and its customers – alter the equilibrium levels of national income *and wealth*, and of the price levels of goods and services *and assets* (i.e., corporate equity and real estate, most importantly, although also corporate and government bonds). The value of the transactions conducted in this search for the equilibrium values of goods, services, and assets, and also for the desired distribution of money between individuals, is a very high multiple of national income and expenditure.

The discussion in the last paragraph may seem banal. Nevertheless, its implications are profound and provoke strong intellectual resistance. Many people are subject to the illusion – the understandable illusion – that, when one agent spends money, that money disappears from the economy. No, it doesn't. The money re-appears in another bank account and keeps on circulating, possibly forever. The equilibrium value of total transactions depends on the quantity of money and the desired ratio of money to transactions; and the equilibrium level of national income depends on the quantity of money and the desired ratio of money to incomes. Keynes did not dissent from these basic ideas. In two admittedly rather clumsy sentences at the end of chapter 7 of *The General Theory*, he said that after a rise or fall in the quantity of money,

Incomes and [the] prices [of securities] necessarily change until the aggregate of the amounts of money which individuals choose to hold at the new level of incomes and prices thus brought about has come to equality with the amount of money created by the banking system. This, indeed, is the fundamental proposition of monetary theory.

Further, with the quantity of goods given by real forces (technology, demographics), the equilibrium price level of goods and services can be seen as reflecting the quantity of money, the desired ratio of money to nominal incomes, and the quantity of goods and services.

What about the price level of assets? In *The General Theory* Keynes integrated one asset – and only one asset – into the analysis, namely a fixed-interest bond. If – starting from equilibrium – the quantity of money is disturbed, the price of bonds has to change. It follows that the equilibrium bond yield – "the rate of interest," as Keynes called it – also changes. If the quantity of money rises, the excess demand for bonds raises their price; if the quantity of money falls, the excess supply of bonds (relative to the reduced amount of money) lowers their price. Given the inverse relation between the price of fixed-interest bonds and their yield, an increase in the quantity of money lowers Keynes's "rate of interest." This was the nub of Keynes's "liquidity preference theory of the rate of interest," usually deemed to be one of his most revolutionary theoretical innovations. (Contrary to a widespread misconception, the "rate of interest" in Keynes's *General Theory* was *not* the short-term money-market rate set by operations in the money market. I explained the difference between two types of official operation – those which affect the quantity of the monetary base and the money-market rate, and those which affect the quantity of money and the bond yield – in my rebuttal of Krugman in essay 4.)

But why limit the discussion to bonds? An economy with money, goods, *and equities* (not bonds) could be imagined, or an economy with money, goods, *and real estate* (again no bonds), or even a fairly realistic economy with money, goods, *equities, and real estate*. Those economies would be closer to everyday business life than the rather restricted, unusual, and special economy in Keynes's *General Theory* (i.e., an economy with money, goods, and only bonds). And would not the effect of a sudden, sharp increase in the quantity of money in these real-world economies be to boost the prices of equities and real estate, in just the same way that in Keynes's special economy an increase in the quantity of money boosts the price of bonds? And what does that then tell us about "the transmission mechanism" from money to the economy? Is there anything "black box"–ish about people spending more because the value of their mutual funds and houses has increased, or about companies purchasing more plant and equipment because they can readily sell new shares to finance such investment?

Essays 15 and 16 are about the relationship between money and the economy, where the economy explicitly has assets other than bonds. Essay 15 is mostly about the U.K., and essay 16 mostly about the U.S., but they have a common message. If residential real estate is put to one side, the dominant asset types of the modern world – corporate equity and commercial real estate – are typically owned by specialist long-term savings institutions (pension funds, mutual funds, life-insurance companies, and so on). The evidence is that – in the long run – they keep their ratios of money to total assets fairly stable. By implication, if the total quantity of money rises by x percent (for whatever reason), the money held by the specialist long-term savings institutions *and the value of all the assets in these institutions' hands* are likely to rise by a number not dissimilar to x percent. The behavior of asset prices is therefore central to the transmission mechanisms from changes in the quantity of money to changes in all macroeconomic variables.

The last two essays are critical of Bernanke and the conduct of American monetary policy during his Fed chairmanship. The role of money in asset-price determination, and hence in the determination of macro outcomes more generally, makes sense only if the quantity of money is defined to include all potentially relevant deposit balances. Balances that can be used to settle transactions only after a notice period must be included. After all, much of the money held by large companies and financial institutions nowadays is not – strictly speaking – in readily available demand-deposit form, but those companies and financial institutions certainly operate in the expectation that they can use the money if they have to. The right money concept is therefore "broadly defined," such as M2 or M3 (or, in the U.K. context, M4), not M1 and certainly not the monetary base by itself.

Bernanke prefers to think in terms of "credit," "credit spreads," "credit conditions," and "credit availability" rather than in terms of the quantity of money. In essay 17 I argue that, by allowing the quantity of money to stagnate in 2009 and early 2010, Bernanke did not keep to the spirit of a promise he had made to Milton Friedman in 2002. In essay 18 I propose that Bernanke's "creditism" was the most important "intellectual mistake" responsible for the policy blunders of the last few years. The Great Recession of 2008–2010 would have been avoided if Bernanke had organized monetary policy on the lines recommended repeatedly by Milton Friedman over a period of more than fifty years, namely to maintain stable growth of the quantity of money.

ESSAY 15

MONEY, ASSET PRICES, AND
ECONOMIC ACTIVITY IN THE U.K.

HOW DOES money influence the economy? More exactly, how do changes in the level (or the rate of growth) of the quantity of money affect the values of key macroeconomic variables such as aggregate demand and the price level? As these are straightforward questions that have been asked for over four hundred years, economic theory ought by now to have given some reasonably definitive answers. But that is far from the case.

Most economists endorse the proposition that in the long run inflation has monetary causes. They agree – if rather loosely – that inflation is associated with faster increases in "the quantity of money" (defined according to taste) than in the quantity of goods and services. But they disagree and squabble about almost everything else in monetary economics. Particular uncertainty attaches to the so-called "transmission mechanism." The purpose of this essay is to outline a theoretical sketch of the transmission mechanism from money to the economy. Heavy emphasis will be placed on the importance of the quantity of money – broadly defined to include most bank deposits – in asset-price determination. However, in order better to locate the analysis in the wider debates, a discussion of the origins of certain key motivating ideas is necessary. Although the focus here is on the U.K. experience, the conceptual framework and analytical approach are vital preliminaries for the next essay, which concentrates on the United States.

* * *

I.

Irving Fisher of Yale University was the first economist to set out, with rigorous statistical techniques, the facts of the relationship between money and the price level in his 1911 study, *The Purchasing Power of Money*. Fisher's aim was to revive and defend the quantity theory of money. In his review of Fisher's book for *The Economic Journal*, John Maynard Keynes was mostly friendly, but expressed some reservations. In his words, "The most serious defect in Professor Fisher's doctrine is to be found in his account of the mode by which through transitional stages an influx of new money affects prices."[1] In the preface to the second edition Fisher summarized Keynes's criticism as being the claim that, although the "book shows *that* changes in the quantity of money do affect the price level," it "does not show *how* they do so."[2] In other words, Keynes felt that Fisher had not provided a satisfactory version of the transmission mechanism.

Fisher quickly responded to Keynes. In fact, he used the opportunity of the preface to the second edition of *The Purchasing Power of Money* to direct Keynes to pp. 242–247 of another of his works, *Elementary Principles of Economics*, which had been published in 1912, between the first and second editions of *Purchasing Power*. In those pages, entitled "An Increase in Money Does Not Decrease Its Velocity," Fisher noted that economic agents have a desired ratio of money to expenditure determined by "habit" and "convenience." If "some mysterious Santa Claus suddenly doubles the amount [of money] in the possession of each individual," economic agents have excess money balances. They try to get rid of their excess money by increasing their purchases in the shops, which leads to "a sudden briskness in trade," rising prices, and depleting stocks. It might appear that only a few days of high spending should enable people to reduce their money balances to the desired level, but "we must not forget that the only way in which the individual can get rid of his money is by handing it over to somebody else. Society is not rid of it." To put it another way, the payments are being made within a closed circuit. It follows that, under Fisher's "Santa Claus hypothesis," the shopkeepers who receive the surplus cash "will, in their turn, endeavor to get rid of it by purchasing goods for their business."

Therefore, "the effort to get rid of it and the consequent effect on prices will continue until prices have reached a sufficiently high level." The "sufficiently high level" is attained when prices and expenditure have risen so much that the original desired ratio of money to expenditure has been restored. Prices, as well as the quantity of money, will have doubled.[3]

Three features of Fisher's statement of the transmission mechanism in his *Elementary Principles of Economics* are

> ▷ the emphasis on the stability of the desired ratio of money to expenditure,

> ▷ the distinction between "the individual experiment" (in which every money holder tries to restore his own desired money/expenditure ratio, given the price level, by changing his money balances) and "the market experiment" (in which, with the quantity of money held by all individuals being given and hence invariant to the efforts of the individuals to change it, the price level must adjust to take them back to their desired money/expenditure ratios), and

> ▷ the lack of references to "the interest rate" in agents' adjustments of their expenditure to their money holdings.[4]

These are also the hallmarks of several subsequent descriptions of the transmission mechanism. In 1959 Milton Friedman – who became the leading exponent of the quantity theory in the 1960s and 1970s – made a statement to the U.S. Congress about the relationship between money and the economy. He recalled Fisher's themes. After emphasizing the stability of agents' preferences for money, he noted that, "if individuals as a whole were to try to reduce the number of dollars they held, they could not all do so; they would simply be playing a game of musical chairs." In response to a sudden increase in the quantity of money, expenditure decisions would keep on being revised until the right balance between money and incomes had returned. While individuals may be "frustrated in their attempt to reduce the number of dollars they hold, they succeed in achieving an equivalent change in their position, for the rise in money income and in prices reduces the ratio of these balances to their income and also the real value of these balances."[5] Friedman also emphasized throughout his career the superiority of monetary aggregates over interest rates as measures of monetary policy.

The claim that, in a long-run equilibrium, the real value of agents' money balances would not be altered by changes in the nominal quantity of money was also a central contention of Patinkin's *Money, Interest, and Prices*, the first edition of which was published in 1956. *Money, Interest, and Prices* exploited the distinction between the individual and market experiments in a detailed theoretical elaboration of what Patinkin termed "the real-balance effect." In his view "a real-balance effect in the commodity markets is the *sine qua non* of monetary theory."[6] The real-balance effect can be viewed as the heart of the transmission mechanism from money to the economy.[7] (The distinction between the individual and market experiments is also noted in the next essay, on pp. 356, where the original thought is attributed to the Swedish economist Knut Wicksell.)

II.

Despite the lucidity of their descriptions of the transmission mechanism, the impact of Fisher, Friedman, and Patinkin on the discussion of macroeconomic policy in the final forty years of the twentieth century was mixed, and in the opening years of the twenty-first century their work was increasingly ignored. In the 1970s Friedman had great success in persuading governments and central banks that curbing the growth of the money supply was vital if they wanted to reduce inflation. However, his theoretical work on money was contested by other leading economists and did not command universal acceptance. By the 1990s the preponderance of academic work on monetary policy focused on interest rates, with the relationship between interest rates and the components of demand in a Keynesian income-expenditure model attracting the most attention.[8] When asked by the Treasury Committee of the House of Commons for its views on the transmission mechanism, the Bank of England prepared a paper in which "official rates" (i.e., the short-term interest rates under the Bank's control) influenced "market rates," asset prices, expectations and confidence, and the exchange rate, and these four variables then affected domestic demand and net external demand. In a twelve-page note, it reached page 10 before acknowledging that "we have discussed how monetary policy changes affect output and inflation, with barely a mention of the quantity of money."[9] The links between money, in the sense of "the quantity of money," and the economy were widely neglected or even forgotten.

The relatively simple accounts of the transmission mechanism in Fisher's *Purchasing Power of Money* and some of Friedman's popular work were particularly vulnerable on one score. They concentrated on the relationship between money and expenditure on the goods and services that constitute national income, but neglected the role of financial assets and capital goods in the economy; they analyzed the work that money performs in the *flow* of income and expenditure, but did not say how it fits into the numerous individual portfolios that represent a society's *stock* of capital assets. As Keynes had highlighted in his *Treatise on Money* (published in 1930), money is used in two classes of transaction – those in goods, services, and tangible capital assets (or "the industrial circulation," as he called it), and those in financial assets ("the financial circulation").[10] (Keynes's distinction between the two circulations formed part of the argument of essay 10, on the weakness of the textbook income-expenditure model.) The need was therefore to refurbish monetary theory, so that money was located in an economy with capital assets and could affect asset prices as well as the price level of goods and services. Much of Friedman's theoretical work for a professional audience was a response to this requirement. For example, in a 1964 paper written with David Meiselman he contrasted a "credit" view, in which monetary policy "impinges on a narrow and well-defined range of capital assets and a correspondingly narrow range of associated expenditures," with a "monetary" view, in which it "impinges on a much broader range of capital assets and correspondingly broader range of associated expenditures."[11]

But most macroeconomists have remained more comfortable with the notion that interest rates affect investment (and, at a further remove, the level of national income) than with the claim that the quantity of money has an empirically significant and verifiable role in asset-price determination (and that asset-price movements are fundamental to cyclical fluctuations in national income). This essay and the next will challenge the dominant view; they will show that in the four closing decades of the twentieth century and in the decade running up to the Great Recession of 2008–2010, money was crucial to asset-price fluctuations in the U.S. and the U.K. They will appeal, in particular, to the first two of the three distinctive features of the naïve transmission mechanism discussed by Fisher in 1912 and Friedman in his 1959 congressional testimony, namely the stability of the relevant agents' demand for money, and the need to differentiate between the individual and market experiments. It will argue that these ideas are useful in the context of the financial markets where asset prices are set, just as they are in the markets for the goods and services which enter consumer price indices.

III.

Before we relate money to asset prices, some remarks on ownership patterns are necessary. Ample official data on the U.K.'s wealth are available for the five decades under review here. The main constituents of the capital stock throughout the period were residential houses, land and infrastructure, commercial property, and plant and equipment, including ships, planes, and cars. Ultimately all these assets were owned by people. But often they were in the names of companies, and people owned claims on the companies in the form of equities or bonds. Partly to achieve diversity in their asset portfolios and partly to enjoy the advantages of specialized investment management, many households build up their assets through long-term savings products marketed by financial institutions.

The twentieth century saw a rise in the proportion of corporate equity quoted on the stock exchange in tandem with the institutionalization of saving. As a result, financial institutions became the principal holders of U.K. quoted equities in the closing decades of the century. (See table 15.1.)[12] They also held – and of course continue to hold – substantial portfolios of commercial property and other assets, such as government and corporate bonds. Indeed, over most of the last fifty years the institutions have been so large that their activities have been crucial in the determination of asset prices and particularly of share prices.

A key question arises from the institutions' heavyweight role in

TABLE 15.1
OWNERSHIP OF U.K. SHARES, 1963–1989
Table shows % of total equity owned

	1963	1975	1989
Insurance companies	10.0	15.9	18.6
Pension funds	6.4	16.8	30.6
Unit trusts	1.3	4.1	5.9
Investment trusts and other OFIs	11.3	10.5	2.7
Total institutional	29.0	47.3	57.8

Source: Economic Trends, *January 1991 article on "The 1989 Share Registry Survey"*

asset markets. What was the significance of money in their portfolio decisions? Is it sensible to view their attitudes towards their holdings of equities, and other assets, as being powerfully influenced by their money balances or not? Fortunately, abundant information has been published on the money-supply holdings of the different sectors of the U.K. economy. Following the Radcliffe Committee's recommendation that more money-supply statistics be compiled, the Bank of England and the Office for National Statistics (formerly the Central Statistical Office) have since 1963 collected information on the bank deposits held by various categories of U.K. agent. The three types of private-sector agent tracked in the data are the personal (or "household") sector, the corporate sector (known more technically as "industrial and commercial companies" or "non-financial companies"), and the financial sector (also called "non-bank [or other] financial institutions"). Separately the Office for National Statistics has collected and published data on the asset holdings of the main types of financial institutions in the U.K., including their short-term assets such as bank deposits, also since 1963. Together the sector-by-sector money-supply numbers and the information on institutions' portfolios represent a rich body of statistical material relevant to the process of asset-price determination in the U.K.

Some noteworthy facts about the monetary behavior of the three components of the private sector are presented in table 15.2. It demonstrates, in a particularly striking way, some important differences

TABLE 15.2
KEY FACTS ABOUT DIFFERENT SECTORS' MONEY
HOLDINGS IN THE U.K. ECONOMY, 1964–2003

Table relates to annual changes, based on quarterly data, with the first rate of change calculated in Q2 1964. (Note that the differences in the "level" series are often very different from those in the "changes" series published by National Statistics, because of changes in population and definition.)

	Mean increase, %	Standard deviation of growth rates
Personal sector	10.9	4.1
Corporate sector	11.0	10.6
Financial sector	18.3	15.7

Source: National Statistics database, as at February 2004

between the sectors in the forty years starting in the mid-1960s. The growth rate of money held by the financial sector was almost double that of money held by the personal and corporate sectors. In addition to the long-run institutionalization of saving already mentioned, the period saw radical financial liberalization. The effect of liberalization was to enhance the competitiveness of non-bank financial institutions relative to banks and other types of business organizations, and to allow them profitably to expand both sides of their balance sheets, and hence their monetary assets, much faster than the quantity of money as a whole. The growth rate of financial-sector money was also characterized by more pronounced volatility than that of other sectors' money. The standard deviation of the growth rate (as defined in table 15.2) of financial-sector money was four times that of personal-sector money and markedly higher than that of corporate-sector money.

The contrast between the different sectors' monetary behavior is vital in understanding the transmission mechanism from money to the economy. Econometric work on the personal sector's demand-for-money functions in the U.K. during this period routinely found them to be stable, in the sense that standard tests on the significance of the relationship between personal-sector money and a small number of other

variables (including nominal incomes) were successful.[13] Similar work
on the demand to hold money balances by companies and financial
institutions was less convincing.[14] However, it would be a serious mistake to believe that companies' and financial institutions' monetary
behavior was entirely erratic and unpredictable.

Figure 15.1 contains a striking message: the ratio of money assets to
total assets of life-insurance companies and pension funds combined
was much the same ten years into the twenty-first century as it had
been in the mid-1970s, even though their assets had climbed more than
seventy times.[15] As shown in table 15.1, life-insurance companies and
pension funds were the two principal types of long-term savings institutions in the U.K. in this period, and it is therefore legitimate to focus
on their behavior in an analysis of asset-price determination. (A small
complication is that investment institutions often manage their holdings of all liquid assets, rather than money as such, relative to all assets.
Assets are "liquid" if they can be quickly and cheaply converted into
other assets. Bank deposits are an example of a liquid asset, but the
institutions might from time to time also hold liquidity in assets such as
short-dated Treasury or commercial bills, which are not money.) The
long-run uniformity of the ratios of money and liquidity to the total
assets held by the U.K. institutions is surely remarkable. The final three
decades of the twentieth century and the opening years of the twenty-
first saw considerable financial turmoil and much institutional upheaval,
yet these institutions' demand for liquidity (i.e., their "demand to hold
money," roughly speaking, or their "liquidity preferences," as Keynes
would say) was quite stable. The stability of the institutions' desired
ratio of money to assets may serve the same purpose in a discussion of
asset markets as Fisher's stability of persons' desired ratio of money to
expenditure in a discussion of goods markets.

IV.

Given the approximate long-run constancy of the desired money/asset
ratios in the leading financial institutions, it is easy to sketch – in a simplified way – a link between financial-sector money and asset prices.
As already noted, a crucial feature of Fisher's and Friedman's descriptions of the transmission mechanism was that payments were being

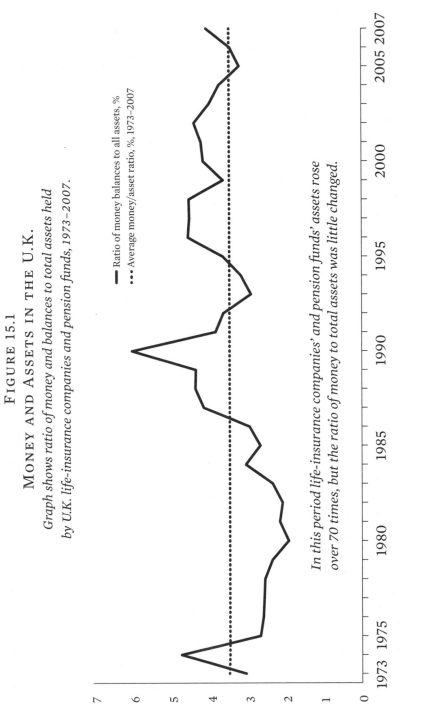

FIGURE 15.1

MONEY AND ASSETS IN THE U.K.

Graph shows ratio of money and balances to total assets held
by U.K. life-insurance companies and pension funds, 1973–2007.

— Ratio of money balances to all assets, %
••• Average money/asset ratio, %, 1973–2007

In this period life-insurance companies' and pension funds' assets rose
over 70 times, but the ratio of money to total assets was little changed.

made within a closed circuit. As a result, if agents had excess money, individuals' attempts to unload their excess balances by increased expenditure would not change the quantity of money. The direction of causation was from the quantity of money to spending and national income, not from spending and national income to the quantity of money. An analogous argument is readily presented in the case of financial institutions in asset markets.

To help in understanding the processes at work, a highly stylized "asset market" may be assumed. It could be regarded as a naïve characterization of Keynes's "financial circulation." Suppose that the U.K.'s financial institutions are the only holders of and traders in U.K. equities (i.e., they operate within a closed circuit), that equities constitute all of their assets, and that the stock of equities (i.e., the number of shares in issue) never changes. Suppose that – for whatever reason – the financial institutions' money balances jump sharply and that they have excess money. Whereas in the long run they try to keep their ratio of money to total assets at, say, 4 percent, their money/assets ratio (or "cash ratio") now stands at 6 percent. In terms of figures, they might have £60 billion of money and £1,000 billion of equities, whereas recently they had £40 billion of money and £1,000 billion of equities. Each individual institution tries to get rid of its excess money by buying equities. *But the purchase of equities by one institution is the sale by another. For all the institutions taken together, the assumptions ensure that the flow of purchases and sales cannot change the £60 billion of money in the system.* No matter how frenetic the trading activity and no matter the keenness of particular fund managers to run down their cash, the aggregate £60 billion cannot rise or fall. The value of trading in equities in a year may be an enormous multiple of this £60 billion, but still the £60 billion cannot change.

How, then, is the 4 percent cash ratio restored? In one round of transactions the excess supply of money causes buyers to be more eager than sellers, and the price of equities edges up, perhaps by 10 percent, so that the value of the stock of equities is £1,100 billion. The cash ratio falls to £60 billion divided by £1,100 billion multiplied by 100, or just under 5½ percent. This is a movement towards the equilibrium 4 percent ratio, but it is not enough. The institutions still hold "too much money." In the next round of transactions the excess supply of money again causes buyers to be more eager than sellers, and the price of equities moves forward again, perhaps by 15 percent. The value of equities rises to £1,265 billion, and the cash ratio drops to £60 billion divided by £1,265 billion multiplied by 100, or to about 4¾ percent. And so on. In every round the value of the money balances stays at £60 billion. *It does not change because – within the closed circuit assumed in the exercise – it cannot change.* The return of the institutions' cash ratio to the equilibrium 4 percent is achieved, after however many rounds of transactions, by a rise in the value of equities to £1,500 billion. The institutions' asset values have adjusted to the amount of money they hold. It is a striking, but entirely realistic, feature of the example discussed that a rise in their money balances from £40 billion to £60 billion (i.e., a rise of only £20 billion) is associated with ("causes") a rise in equity prices of £500 billion. The argument can be generalized freely. In the advanced economies of today, specialized financial institutions are the characteristic holders of assets. It follows that, when they hold excess money, there is likely to be upward pressure on asset prices; conversely, when they have deficient money balances, asset prices tend to fall.

The realism of the analytical sketch above is open to question and needs more exposition, some of which is provided in the next essay. By contrast, the claim that asset prices are relevant to spending behavior should not need extensive discussion. It should be sufficient to emphasize the ubiquity of arbitrage in asset markets, and to note two kinds of linkage between asset markets and the rest of the economy. These linkages ensure that asset prices affect spending. Arbitrage is important, because it links the price of equities with the price of the tangible assets and goodwill to which they relate and, at a further remove, to the price of all financial securities and all tangible assets.

An excess supply of money may in the first instance boost the price of existing equities traded on the stock exchange, including – for example – the equities issued by real-estate companies in the past. But that induces new equities issuance by quoted companies and the formation of new unquoted companies with a view to seeking a quotation. So owners of real estate package their buildings in a corporate vehicle and try to sell these vehicles to financial institutions. The market price of all real estate is boosted by the ambitious stock-market valuations. In a modern economy, similar processes are at work for all assets. Further,

TABLE 15.3
AN EXAMPLE OF AN ASSET MARKET IN THE U.K. IN 1994 BUYERS AND SELLERS OF QUOTED ORDINARY SHARES (I.E., EQUITIES)

Net sellers of equities	Amount sold (£m.)	Net buyers of equities	Amount bought (£m.)
Banks	393	Life-insurance companies and pension funds	8,531
Personal sector	679		
Industrial and commercial companies	9,261	Remaining financial institutions	1,097
Public sector	3,646	Overseas sector	4,351
Sum of sales by net sellers	13,979	Sum of purchases by net buyers	13,979

The sum of net sales and purchases was zero.

Note: Each of the identified types of equity-market participant had substantial purchases and sales. The gross value of their transactions was a very high multiple of their net purchases or sales. Stock-exchange turnover in U.K. and Irish listed equities was £577,526 million in 1994. (In 1994 the U.K.'s gross domestic product at market prices was about £670,000 million.)

Source: Financial Statistics, *June 1998, tables 8.2A and 6.3A*

arbitrage operates between different assets as well as between different forms of the same asset. If equities rise sharply in price, they may appear overvalued relative to commercial or residential real estate. The wide variety of wealth holders found in a modern economy – including rich individuals and companies, as well as the large financial institutions – may then sell equities and use the proceeds to buy real estate. The excess supply of money – the condition of "too much money chasing too few assets" – has pervasive effects.

Of course the power of arbitrage to remove asset-price anomalies relies on the ability to switch payments between different types of asset markets. A key assumption in the analysis – that of a specialized asset market, which constitutes a closed circuit where certain asset prices are set – has to be relaxed. Instead, agents compare prices in all asset markets, and sell overvalued assets in one market and buy undervalued assets in another. (Not only do they sell overvalued stocks to buy under-valued stocks and sell small-capitalization stocks to buy big-capitaliza-tion stocks and so on, but they also sell houses to buy shares and sell shares to buy houses.) Does that destroy the concept of a closed circuit of payments in which the ability of excess or deficient money to alter asset prices depends on the quantity of money being a given? The short answer, in an economy without international transactions, is, Not at all. It is true, for example, that, if quoted equities become expensive rela-tive to unquoted companies of the same type, the owners of unquoted companies will float them, which withdraws money from the pool of institutional funds. Conversely, when quoted companies become cheap relative to "asset value," entrepreneurs organize take-overs, which inject money back into the institutional pool. To the extent that one type of participant has been a net buyer and has satisfied its purchases by drawing on its bank balances, its bank deposits (i.e., its money hold-ings) must fall. But the money balances of another type of agent must rise. In fact, it is possible to identify particular types of participant in asset markets, and to collect data on their purchases and sales. Table 15.3 gives data on the market in U.K. quoted ordinary shares in 1994 as an illustration. It needs to be understood that – because purchases are matched by sales – the net value of purchases (+) and sales (–) in a par-ticular market, and indeed of all asset purchases and sales in the econ-omy as a whole, must be zero. But the logically necessary *ex post* equivalence of the value of purchases and sales does not mean that the prices of the assets bought and sold cannot change. In particular, prices change when all the agents participating in the numerous asset mar-kets have *ex ante* excess or deficient money holdings. The arena of pay-ments – the closed circuit within which the rounds of transactions take place – becomes the entire economy.[16]

What about the two kinds of influence of asset prices on spending on goods and services? First, investment in new capital items occurs when the market value of assets is above their replacement cost. If the value of a new office building would be $10 million and it would cost only $5 million to purchase the land and build it, it is obviously prof-itable for an entrepreneur to organize the construction of the new office building. On the other hand, if the value of a building is lower than the replacement cost, no investment takes place. Assets will continue to be bought and sold, and investments will be undertaken or suspended, until the market value of assets is brought into equivalence with their replacement value.[17] Second, consumption is affected by changing levels of wealth. When asset-price gains increase people's wealth, they are inclined to spend more out of income.[18]

Another way of stating the wider theme is to emphasize that, in the real world, markets in goods and services and markets in assets interact constantly. Keynes's two circulations – the "industrial circulation" and the "financial circulation" – are not separate.[19] If excess money in the financial sector causes asset-price gains, agents of all kinds will be inclined to sell a portion of their assets and buy more goods and services (i.e., to spend a higher proportion of their incomes). On the other hand, if deficient money in the financial sector causes asset-price falls, agents will spend a lower proportion of their incomes on goods and services. The adequacy of money balances relative to a desired level, the direction of pressures on asset prices, and wealth-influenced changes in the propensity to spend out of income should be seen as an indissoluble whole.

A polemical note can now be injected into the discussion. In none of the above has a reference been made to "interest rates." Agents have been adjusting their spending on goods and services, and their asset portfolios, in response to excess or deficient money, and the prices of goods, services, and assets have been changing in order to bring agents back into "monetary equilibrium" (i.e., a condition where the demand to hold money balances equals the supply of such balances). The Bank of England's version of the transmission mechanism in its 1999 note to the Treasury Committee – like the innumerable other accounts in which interest rates do all the work – is far from being the only way of approaching the subject or a definitive statement of the matter. Further, we saw in the introduction to this volume that some economists – like the New Keynesians – believe that the central bank's money-market rate is the *factotum* of macroeconomics. These economists are wrong. The models revered by the New Keynesians – the three-equation encapsulations of the entire economy and suchlike – omit variables so basic to the understanding of reality that their relevance to macroeconomic analysis and policy-making is highly debatable.

A central motif of the argument has been that spending and asset prices change in response to the quantity of money. Money motivates asset dispositions and spending; it is a dominant causal factor in the adjustment processes that alter quantities and prices as companies and individuals seek new equilibriums. These adjustment processes constitute the ceaseless hurly-burly of a free-market economy. The current essay has therefore provided a monetary theory of the determination of both income *and wealth*. The next essay applies that theory to the United States in recent decades.

ESSAY 16

MONEY AND ASSET PRICES

IN THE U.S.

In the 1970s and 1980s most central bankers said that they accepted Friedman's dictum that inflation "is a monetary phenomenon." More precisely, they followed Friedman and the monetarist school is believing that persistent and significant increases in the price level could not happen unless they were accompanied by increases in the quantity of money at rates above the trend rate of growth in real output. However, non-monetarist and anti-monetarist economists had an awkward question: Which definition of "the quantity of money" was relevant to the key monetarist propositions?

I.

Two classes of definition, "narrow" and "broad," were available. (See table 16.1. It relates to February 2006, because – as soon to be discussed – this was the last year for which official data for M3 were prepared in the U.S.) The main narrow definition in the U.S. context was M1, which included banks' demand deposits (or "checkable accounts"), but some economists were even more selective and equated "money" with "the monetary base." In the 1970s – when the debates aroused by Friedman's work were most intense – the narrow and broad aggregates were already hugely different in size and composition. Since then the differences have increased.

The heyday of the monetarists' influence on American policy-making was in the late 1970s and early 1980s. It is fair to say not only that the monetarists failed to reach a consensus on the relative appropriate-

TABLE 16.1

COMPOSITION OF U.S. M3 AS OF FEBRUARY 2006

Figures are not seasonally adjusted and relate to a make-up day late in February 2006. They are all in $b.

Currency and travellers' cheques	741.7*	741.7	741.7	741.7
Demand deposits		319.8	319.8	319.8
Other checkable deposits		309.1	309.1	309.1
M1		= 1,370.6		

The base and M1 are "narrow" aggregates.

Savings deposits			3,610.4	3,610.4
Small time deposits			1,028.5	1,028.5
Retail money funds			713.0	713.0
M2			= 6,722.5	

M2 and M3 are "broad" aggregates.

Large time deposits				1,394.8
Repos				574.3
Eurodollars held by U.S. residents				430.2
Institutional money funds				1,161.4
M3				= 10,283.2

Components do not add up exactly to the Federal Reserve's non–seasonally adjusted published total as of February 2006, which was $10,276.1b.

* *"Currency held by the non-bank public" is usually regarded as the retail component of the monetary base and sometimes as "the monetary base" itself.*

ness of the different aggregates, but also that the squabbles between competing points of view undermined the credibility of their case. Anthony Harris of the *Financial Times* compared the debate to that between Big Enders and Little Enders (about the best way to open a boiled egg) in Swift's *Gulliver's Travels*. The ritual repetition of the statement "Inflation is a monetary phenomenon" became hollow. By the late 1990s most key personnel in the central banks of the English-speaking world understood it to mean that inflation could be explained by monetary policy (by interest-rate setting) within a New Keynesian framework; they did not in fact believe that inflation was caused by excessive growth of the quantity of money, however defined. In the Great Recession very few American academic economists paid attention to "money" on any of the available definitions. The practice in central banks ran parallel with theory in the universities, particularly the leading East Coast universities in the United States, where the skepticism about money was particularly marked. (The point is developed in more detail in essay 18, which identifies Harvard as the source of the "creditist" thinking so prominent during the Great Recession.)

But participants in financial markets – including commentators, and economists in banks, brokerages, and consulting firms – continued to watch the money data for clues on the economy. Interest in the "Which money?" debate was revived by the Federal Reserve's decision to stop publication of the M3 monetary aggregate, which took effect on March 23, 2006. The decision was attributed in the media to the then newly appointed Fed chairman, Professor Ben Bernanke, and was criticized by several market participants. One newsletter feared that "all sorts of speculations and conspiracy theories" would run rampant.[1] Another information service – John Williams' Shadow Government Statistics – opined that the decision, relating to "probably the most important statistic published by the U.S. central bank," had been taken "unilaterally and without reasonable explanation."[2] Shadow Government Statistics has since March 2006 prepared and published its own unofficial estimates of M3. It has been able to do so from publicly available information on M3's various components.

The discontinuance of M3 data followed a long period of estrangement from the monetary aggregates at the Federal Reserve and recalled its earlier abandonment of a "liquidity" aggregate in 1998.[3] However, Bernanke himself may not be wholly unsympathetic to monetary interpretations of major macroeconomic events. In the first chapter of his collection of essays on the Great Depression (drawn from an article in the 1995 *Journal of Money, Credit, and Banking*), he remarked, "the new gold-standard research allows us to assert with considerable confidence that *monetary factors played an important causal role*."[4] Most of the discussion in Bernanke's collection related to the M1 measure of money, which he saw as being determined – in accordance with the conventional textbook accounts – as a multiple of the monetary base. By implication, he views narrow money measures – not broad money – as being of most value in central-bank decision-making.[5] (Bernanke's intellectual position was of great significance for the conduct of American monetary policy in the late Noughties, as explained in essay 17.)

Other influential central bankers pay – and have long paid – considerable attention to broadly defined money aggregates. In the 1970s the Bundesbank was well known as a bastion of monetary orthodoxy, with its research department committed to the Friedmanite message that moderate growth of money was essential to the control of inflation. Dr. Otmar Issing, who was chief economist at the Bundesbank in the 1990s and took up the same position at the newly founded European Central Bank in 1998, was very much in this tradition. In an article in the *Financial Times* of December 15, 2005, he reiterated the European Central Bank's commitment to a "two pillar" approach to monetary policy-making, with adherence to a money-supply target as one of the two pillars. In his view, the monetary data served as a cross-check on inflation forecasts prepared by other methods. Although the ECB – like the Bundesbank before it – normally focused on the M3 aggregate, Issing said that the work had become more wide-ranging. In his words, "Monetary analysis goes beyond focusing exclusively on developments in one particular aggregate – M3 in our case – to encompass a rich assessment of other measures of liquidity, as well as credit and financial flows and asset prices."[6]

The Bank of England also staked out a position in the debate. On September 26, 2006, it announced that it would cease publishing data for M0, an aggregate that had started life in 1984 and resembled the concept of "the monetary base" so prominent in American-style monetarism. (See pp. 51–53 in essay 3 for more on the trials and tribulations of M0.) As the Bank had for many years not given any publicity to the M1 or M2 money measures, and as it had earlier scrapped a long-standing M3 series, in 1989, it might seem to have been as indifferent to monetary quantities as the Federal Reserve. But occasionally its officials did claim that money trends could affect decisions. For example, in a surprise statement on June 14, 2005, the Bank's governor, Mervyn King, observed that the high growth rate of the M4 aggregate was a constraint on interest-rate cuts in the U.K.

With the publication of the Monetary Policy Committee's subsequent *Minutes*, it seemed that the reporting of Mr. King's remarks may have exaggerated the Bank of England's worries about high money growth. According to the *Minutes*, the Bank regarded financial-sector money as of little relevance to the behavior of demand or inflation, and it monitored a measure of M4 without financial-sector balances. Non-financial M4 had been growing at a much more moderate pace than M4 as a whole. The Bank's distrust of financial-sector money ran parallel to Fed thinking, since a high proportion of the money balances in the United States' M3 but not in its M2 were – and continue to be – held in the financial sector.

II.

The argument here will be that an all-inclusive, broadly defined measure of money is and always has been the most useful for policy-makers. It will suggest that the Federal Reserve's and the Bank of England's doubts about the usefulness of tracking financial-sector money were unjustified in the mid-Noughties and remain so today. Of course views about the usefulness and appropriateness of an aggregate depend largely on the purpose of the exercise being undertaken. In the following pages it is taken for granted that the main task of monetary analysis is to understand the forces which, in the real world, determine the nominal levels of national income *and wealth*.[7]

Notice that the last paragraph closed with a reference to the "levels of national income *and wealth*." Wealth must be part of the story. A standard university macroeconomics course teaches that income depends on past expenditure, which depends on previous income (plus or minus injections or withdrawals of demand), which depends on earlier levels of expenditure, and so on. If the ratio of one type of expenditure (consumption) to income is constant and if various other apparently plausible assumptions are made, a classroom exercise shows that national income is a multiple of investment. With a bit of algebraic embroidery, the proposition is expanded so that national income is a multiple of investment plus other types of so-called "autonomous" expenditure, including government expenditure. Variations in government expenditure can then perform the salutary role of offsetting the fluctuations in the private sector's expenditure and so steering the economy. The income-expenditure approach and the associated multiplier theory are often called "Keynesian," as they have their intellectual roots in chapter 10 of *The General Theory*. According to some accounts, Keynesianism on these lines can and should rescue capitalism from the deep-seated instability that arises – or at any rate allegedly arises – from the private sector's actions.[8]

Unhappily, textbook multiplier analysis ignores asset values and national wealth, and their potential impact on spending decisions. This version of Keynesianism is therefore baffled when it has to handle the interaction between wealth and spending. In their 2009 book, *Animal Spirits*, George Akerlof and Robert Shiller professed their enthusiasm for Keynesian economics, and their opening chapter recalled the multiplier analysis pioneered in the 1930s. They devoted many words to the impact of changes in consumer confidence and business sentiment – "animal spirits," in a phrase – on spending decisions. Indeed, they claimed that their book, "which draws on an emerging field called behavioral economics," recognized that people are possessed of "all-too-human animal spirits" and so described "how the economy really works."[9] In a chapter titled "Why Are Financial Prices and Corporate Investments So Volatile?" their verdict was unsettling: "No one has ever made rational sense of the wild gyrations in financial prices, such as stock prices." They said that economists had tried to give a convincing explanation for aggregate stock-price movements, but – even in retrospective analysis with all the data available – "no one has ever succeeded." The stock market – in their view – did not appear "to be explicable by changes in interest rates, by subsequent dividends or earnings, or by anything else."[10] They appealed to Keynes to add weight to this negativism. In chapter 12 of his *General Theory* Keynes had indeed offered scathing remarks about the superficiality and copycat behavior of investors in the stock market.[11]

One aim of the current essay is to refute Akerlof and Shiller's negativism. To repeat, the discussion in the next few sections will argue that the forces determining the nominal value of income need to be analyzed alongside those determining the nominal value of wealth, while the key variable at work is the quantity of money. Again, to repeat, the specific "quantity of money" relevant to macroeconomic adjustment is

– and has to be – broadly defined to include all bank deposits. A central finding will be that certain types of money balance play a crucial role in asset-price determination. They are the balances held by financial institutions and large companies, and typically classified in official data as "wholesale money." Ironically, these are exactly the types of money that the Federal Reserve dismissed as uninteresting – and hence as not justifying the cost of data collection – in its rationale for ending the publication of M3 in early 2006. The Fed's indifference towards the role of money, and particularly wholesale money balances, in asset-price determination continues today.

It is important to understand that the Fed's position is in no way unusual or iconoclastic. Most American academic economists reject or ignore the proposition that money is relevant to the determination of asset prices and, hence, national wealth. For example, in *Animal Spirits* Akerlof and Shiller include just one reference to "the money supply" and then only to the M1 measure. In their words,

> ... the money supply is in fact very small: in 2008 in the United States the M1 measure of the money supply, consisting of cash and demand deposits (that is, checking accounts), amounted to only $1.4 trillion, of which $800 billion was currency. And most of the currency is stashed away by a relatively small number of hoarders, often in foreign countries; most of us have only a few bills in our purses or wallets at any given time. The other component of the money supply, the demand deposits and other checkable deposits, amounted to only about $600 billion in 2008, about 1% of national wealth. How can it be that by managing the quantity of demand deposits the Fed can fix all of the problems that we have so far detailed in this book? It can't.[12]

Much has gone wrong here. The key error is to regard "the quantity of money" and the M1 aggregate as synonymous. In order to understand why Akerlof and Shiller have so badly misjudged the role of money in the economy, the merits and demerits of different money aggregates therefore need to be reviewed at some length. Three arguments are presented here for believing in the primacy of a broadly defined money aggregate in macroeconomic analysis:

1. the role of "money transfers" in nullifying a causal role for narrow money in the transmission mechanism from money to asset prices and demand (or, for short, *the money-transfers argument*),

2. the insignificance of narrow money in asset portfolios and the implausibility of claims that narrow money has a major role in portfolio decisions (or *the money-in-portfolios argument*), and

3. the undoubted importance of the demand for certain types of narrow money (particularly high-denomination notes) in the black and/or criminal economies, which are not included in official measures of national expenditure and income (or *the black-economy argument*).

The arguments will be given a section each in coming pages. The first two arguments – the money-transfers argument and the money-in-portfolios argument – are particularly effective in demonstrating the macroeconomic significance of an all-inclusive, broad measure of money. The third argument is the only one where Akerlof and Shiller's comments draw blood. They are correct that the currency issue and M1 are too small to figure meaningfully in the spending and portfolio decisions of mainstream economic agents (companies, financial institutions, and most households in the formal, non-criminal, and non-black economy). The currency issue and M1 are indeed therefore irrelevant to macroeconomic appraisal nowadays. However, the effectiveness of the black-economy argument against M1 arises from the facts about money holding in modern industrial economies. In that sense it is contingent on the nature of these economies. It is less compelling in some backward economies of today, with only limited banking systems, and it did not apply to industrial economies of a hundred or two hundred years ago. Monetary theory began when economies were more primitive than they are today, and notes and coin were a high proportion of the quantity of money. To some extent, theorizing has remained stuck at a rudimentary stage of monetary development, and so failed to keep abreast of modern institutions.[13]

* * *

III.

The cogency of the money-transfers argument depends on a particular view about the transmission mechanism from money to national income. A flood of articles has been written about the transmission mechanism *of monetary policy* in recent years, but this is a somewhat different subject from the transmission mechanism *from money to the economy*. Indeed, several descriptions of the transmission mechanism of monetary policy have been given in which the quantity of money plays no role at all in the determination of national income. These typically focus on the relationship between the central-bank discount rate and the main components of national expenditure, and they either do not mention money or mention it only as a variable which is determined *after* national income has been derived by adding up the demand components.[14]

However, economics does have a line of argument in which money plays a central role in national-income determination. It starts from the relatively uncontroversial notion that national income and wealth cannot be in equilibrium unless the demand to hold money balances is equal to the actual quantity of money in existence. (Alternatively, "national income and wealth are determined only when the demand for money equals the money supply.") It then posits an injection of extra money balances, which comes adventitiously from outside the economy.[15] (In the jargon, the new money is "exogenous.") If the role of assets is put to one side for the moment, the question becomes, Given that the additional money has disturbed the pre-existing equilibrium, what happens to national income?

The answer is simple enough in principle. Agents have an excess supply of money and try to eliminate the excess balances by transactions among themselves (that is, within a closed circuit of payments). Agent A, having too much money (relative to income and wealth), purchases goods and services from agent B, and so gets rid of the excess. But agent B, the seller of the goods and services to A, in turn has excess money, and purchases goods and services either from A or from another agent, C. As all agents have excess money, the value of the transactions in the economy rises and in due course prices increase. The successive rounds of transactions between A, B, C, and so on raise the money value of transactions (i.e., and hence, national expenditure and income) until the demand to hold money is again equal to the money supply.[16] Assuming that the demand to hold money balances *in real terms* is a function only of *real* variables (as is true, more or less, in all economies) and assuming also that nothing real is affected by the rounds of transactions, the equilibrium value of national income rises in proportion to the money supply. (Notice that – in the successive rounds of transactions – no credit is granted. Although extra money may have entered the economy because of the growth of bank credit, the adjustment of expenditure and the price level to money need have nothing whatever to do with credit.)

Numerous accounts of a transmission mechanism on these lines are available in the literature of monetary economics, from David Hume in the eighteenth century onwards. A terse but particularly clear state-ment was given by Milton Friedman in testimony to the U.S. Congress in 1959.[17] Any one person may think that he can control the amount of money in his bank account, but, in Friedman's words,

> For all individuals combined, the appearance that they can con-trol their money balances is an optical illusion. One individual can reduce or increase his money balance only because another or several others are induced to increase or reduce theirs; that is, they do the opposite to what he does. If individuals as a whole were to try to reduce the number of dollars they held, they could not all do so ... they would simply be playing a game of musical chairs.

Nevertheless, the game of musical chairs is not futile. While individuals in the aggregate may be

> [f]rustrated in their attempt to reduce the number of dollars they hold [if they all have an excess supply of money], they suc-ceed in achieving an equivalent change in their position, for the rise in money incomes and in prices reduces the ratio of these bal-ances to their income and also the real value of these balances. This process will continue until this ratio and this real value are in accord with their desires.

In his 2004 book, *Monetary Theory*, Alan Rabin suggested that the adjustment of expenditure and incomes to money be called "the Wicksell process," as it was given an early and lucid description in Wicksell's 1898 *Interest and Prices*.[18] Wicksell may have been the first economist to see the importance of distinguishing between the adjustment problem at the level of a single individual ("the individual experiment") and at the level of all individuals interacting in a market ("the market experiment"). The distinction between the two types of experiment was elaborated most rigorously in Patinkin's account of the "real-balance effect" in his classic *Money, Interest, and Prices*, of which the first edition was published in 1956. In a 1963 paper, Tobin poked fun at the approach by remarking that "it is the beginning of wisdom in monetary economics to observe that money is like the 'hot potato' of a children's game: one individual may pass it to another, but the group as a whole cannot get rid of it. If the economy and the supply of money are out of adjustment, it is the economy that must do the adjusting."[19]

Suppose that this version of events – whatever it may be called – is accepted as the preferred description of the transmission mechanism *from money to national income*. What are the implications for the choice of money aggregate? Notice that the key to the power of money over the economy is that, when individuals try to reduce their own money holdings, they do not reduce money holdings in the aggregate. Because of this feature of the process, disequilibrium between money demand and supply can be eliminated only by changes in aggregate spending and so in national income.[20]

Does a narrow-money aggregate work here? The economy under consideration has three types of "thing" (or category) in it:

▷ narrow money,

▷ money balances in an all-inclusive money measure, but not in narrow money, and

▷ the goods and services that constitute national expenditure and output.

(Assets are ignored, for the time being, in order to ease exposition.) It follows from the assumption of a three-category economy that individual A, with excess narrow money, can pursue only two courses of action. First, he can use the excess to purchase goods and services from B. If B then also has excess money, he can try to get rid of it by purchases of goods and services from C. And so on. A game of musical chairs is played, in the manner proposed by Friedman in his 1959 congressional testimony, and expenditure and income adjust until equilibrium between money demand and supply is restored.

Alternatively, individual A can make a transfer from a balance in narrow money to a balance not in narrow money. For example, money can be transferred from a demand deposit (included in the M1 money measure) to a time deposit (not in M1, but part of a broader measure such as M2 or M3). When an individual does this, his excess holding of M1 is reduced, *and so also is the aggregate quantity of M1*. Again, an individual may have too large a note holding relative to his expenditure requirements. The excess notes can be deposited with a bank, eliminating the disequilibrium in the individual's money position and, on usual definitions, *in the aggregate quantity of narrow money*.[21] In short, when an excess supply of or demand for narrow money is removed by a transfer between money balances (that is, by money-into-money transactions, or "money transfers," for short), the process has no effect on the demand for goods and services, and is without any wider macroeconomic interest. If disequilibrium in narrow money is ended by money transfers, such transfers nullify the causal role that narrow money might have played in the transmission mechanism from money to the economy.[22]

The relative importance of the two ways of eliminating disequilibrium in narrow money is an empirical matter. If it were true that people often eliminate an excess supply of narrow money by, for example, important retail purchases, it would have some macroeconomic significance. But the reality of the modern world is that most people adjust their narrow-money holdings by money transfers that are a routine, dull, and uninteresting part of their financial planning. They make frequent switches between notes and bank deposits, and between different types of bank deposit, and these switches are the main influence both on each individual's M1 holding and on the aggregate amount of M1.[23] (My weekend spending is not determined by my withdrawal of $100 in notes from the bank late on Friday, and by my possession of an average balance during the weekend of $50. On the contrary, my with-drawal of $100 in notes from the bank late on Friday is determined by my prior decision to spend $100 over the weekend, a decision that reflects numerous other considerations – including, to some extent, the size of my total bank balance.) Indeed, it is not going too far to say that money transfers make narrow money "endogenous." When Kaldor derided claims for the exogeneity of money by asking whether the money supply (in the sense of the note issue) determined Christmas, he was making a good analytical point which the monetarists have never properly answered.[24]

But money transfers cannot nullify the macroeconomic role of an all-inclusive, broadly defined measure of money. As I wrote a few years ago,

> A distinguishing feature of broad money is that it includes the widest possible range of monetary assets. The nearest alterna-tive is therefore not a constituent of the money supply. This is crucial. If an individual economic agent . . . is in monetary dis-equilibrium, adjustment has to occur through [transactions in goods and services, or in assets]. It cannot take place through money transfers.
>
> Consider a person who has an excess supply of broad money balances. He cannot remove this by switching into another money balance because, by definition, no such balance exists. He has to purchase an asset, a commodity or a service from another economic agent. Similarly, if someone has an excess demand for broad money balances, he cannot eliminate it by a money trans-fer from another bank account, because his holdings of broad money constitute his entire money balances. He has to sell some-thing if he is to return to equilibrium.[25]

In other words, with an all-inclusive money measure, the traditional account of the transmission mechanism from money to the economy can work without a hitch. Whereas narrow money is uninteresting (because it is nowadays largely determined by prior decisions to spend), broad money is of great macroeconomic importance. If an economy is in approximate monetary equilibrium and the quantity of broad money changes abruptly in a short period, the standard account of the transmission mechanism applies. The equilibrium level of national income has been altered, and a sequence of transactions takes place to change national income, and so to restore the equivalence of the demand for money with its supply.[26]

The money-transfers argument may or may not be immediately convincing. The analyst needs to accept that the transmission mechanism set out above ("the real-balance effect" view, or the view based on the musical-chairs or the hot-potato story) is a persuasive description of everyday business and finance. If one believes that the real-balance effect is the heart of the transmission mechanism from money to the economy, then the money-transfers argument is a decisive critique of the claim that it is narrow money which matters to macroeconomic outcomes. By extension, the rationale for the Fed's decision to stop calculating the M3 aggregate but not the M2 aggregate is far from clear. Since M2 can be changed at little cost by a money-into-money transaction between a balance in M3 but not in M2, the M3 aggregate must logically be at least as important to money holders' decisions as M2.[27]

The argument of this section can now be put more concisely, with non-money assets restored to the discussion. An economy consists of assets with a given nominal value, and goods and assets with nominal values (i.e., prices) that vary in the course of transactions. Assets with a given nominal value are conventionally called "money."[28] If the analytical interest lies in understanding how the rates of changes of the prices of goods and non-money assets are determined, it must surely be the entire amount of money – a money measure of assets which embraces all assets with a given nominal value – that is relevant. To exclude a particular type of money balance (such as the wholesale money – large time deposits and money-market institutional funds – which forms part of U.S. M3 but not M2) leaves the analysis incomplete and begs certain questions. Specifically, what are the economic relationships between the excluded and included types of money, and between the excluded types of money on the one hand and goods and non-money assets on the other? The Federal Reserve might argue that it has been unable to find interesting relationships between wholesale money and other macroeconomic variables. The view that U.S. wholesale money is unimportant to macroeconomic outcomes will be disputed shortly, in an account of the attitude towards their money holdings taken by large

U.S. financial institutions. But, first, the role of money in portfolios needs to be discussed in general terms.

IV.

The above account of the transmission mechanism was largely concerned with how agents balance their money holdings against their expenditure on goods and services. However, in the real world every economy also has assets (financial securities, houses, land, antiques, and so on). Agents' asset portfolios, as well as their income and expenditure, are relevant to their demand to hold money balances.[29]

The economy contains four categories:

▷ narrow money,

▷ other money balances (i.e., balances in a broad money measure, but not in narrow money),

▷ goods and services, and

▷ non-money assets.

All money balances – both narrow and non-narrow – have two properties: that their nominal value is certain (or as near to certain as makes no difference) and that their nominal value does not change in the course of transactions. By contrast, the future nominal value of goods and services, and assets, is uncertain, and their nominal value can change in the course of transactions. Obviously, in a full general equilibrium, equilibrium relationships between all the categories have to be satisfied. There is an equilibrium relationship between narrow money and non-narrow money, between non-narrow money and expenditure on goods and services, between expenditure on goods and services (or "national income," which is the aggregate value of all goods and services) and asset values (or "national wealth"), and so on. It may seem reasonable to claim, when starting from equilibrium, that a change in narrow money alters the equilibrium value of everything else, including asset values. But does this proposition ring true in a modern economy with a sophisticated banking system and large asset portfolios? Two points need to be made.

The first is that the money-transfers argument applies here again. The nearest alternative to a money balance in narrow money (to repeat, notes and coin in the M0 aggregate, and notes, coin, and demand deposits in the M1 aggregate) is another money balance, not a non-monetary asset. When agents think about the place of narrow money in their portfolios, they are concerned with the choice between holding wealth in the form of notes rather than demand deposits, or in the form of demand deposits rather than time deposits. In a modern economy with deep capital markets, very few agents balance their narrow-money holdings against non-monetary assets.

Second, an important purpose of holding money is to minimize transactions costs. It is true that certain components of broad money – such as large-denomination certificates of deposit – cannot be used in small-scale retail transactions. According to Sir Alan Walters, "one would clearly not count £50,000 negotiable CDs as money; so far as I am aware no one would ever accept such an instrument to pay an outstanding expense."[30] But it is also true that notes are an extremely inconvenient way of settling debts arising from major capital transactions, such as the purchase of houses, large blocks of commercial property, or financial securities. The costs of counting and bundling up notes for such capital transactions would be inordinate compared to the cost of making entries in a check register. This is one reason why the most important participants in capital markets typically have small, negligible, or even zero holdings of notes. It follows that these notes play no role in their portfolio decisions. The notion of a "portfolio" demand for monetary-base assets by non-banks is merely silly.

In the U.K. – where the Office for National Statistics collects data on the currency and money holdings of different sectors – the relevance of these points to the financial sector's demand for money is easily demonstrated. At the end of 2009 the currency holdings of all non-bank financial intermediaries in the U.K. were under £0.1 billion. By contrast, the value of all their currency and deposits (including foreign-currency deposits, and both sterling and foreign-currency deposits outside the U.K.) was over £1,300 billion, and the value of all their assets was above £3,000 billion. In other words, these organizations' total money holdings were more than 13,000 times as large, and their total assets were more than 30,000 times as large, as their currency holdings! The United States' flow-of-funds data have less detail on the subject, but the same message comes out. At the end of the first quarter of 2010 the United States' private pension funds had total assets of almost $5,800 billion, while their holdings of money assets were just over $225 billion. Within this $225 billion, only $18.8 billion were "checkable deposits and currency," and holdings of currency as such were undoubtedly negligible. At any rate, pension funds' total assets were 300 times the size of their narrow-money balances and – almost certainly – a few thousand times a multiple of their currency.

The management of checkable deposits is not an entirely mechanical exercise in large financial institutions, and sporadically the level of checkable deposits may affect the timing and other execution details in equity and bond transactions. But checkable deposits have no bearing on the substance (i.e., prices and quantities) of such transactions. The relative size of different types of deposit within the overall total of monetary assets is a much less significant influence on returns than either decisions on the relative size of monetary and non-monetary assets or decisions on asset allocation more broadly understood (i.e., the relative size of holdings of equities, bonds, and so on). In his influential 1956 paper "The Quantity Theory of Money: A Restatement," Friedman – following the lead of Hicks and Keynes – argued that money needed to be analyzed as part of wealth portfolios. In his words, "the theory of the demand for money is a special topic in the theory of capital." But it is clear that – as a practical and empirical matter – the theory of the demand for *narrow* money is *not* a special topic in the theory of capital. (See also footnote 7 to essay 15, which emphasizes the same point.)

On the other hand, the theory of the demand to hold an all-inclusive, broadly defined money aggregate is undoubtedly a topic in the theory of capital. The U.K. evidence suggests a rough-and-ready but persistent relationship – arguably of considerable importance in understanding the course of the U.K.'s disastrous boom-bust cycles in the 1970s and 1980s, and the Great Recession of 2008–2010 – first, between the rates of growth of broad money and of money in the hands of financial institutions, and then between the rates of growth of financial-sector money and asset-price movements.[31] The relatively stable ratio of financial institutions' liquid assets to their total assets – illustrated in figure 15.1 in the previous essay – helps in understanding the causal relationships at work. On this basis, the Bank of England has always needed to pay attention to financial-sector M4 as well as non-financial M4 in its macroeconomic assessments, despite the greater closeness of the link between non-financial M4 and nominal GDP. But what about the United States? What about the money-holding patterns of American financial institutions?

V.

More exactly, is it the case that the long-run growth rates of American financial institutions' money holdings and assets are similar? And, if such similarity is found, what are the implications for the Fed's decision to discontinue M3? A large body of information on the asset holdings of the United States' financial institutions is contained in the Federal Reserve's flow-of-funds data. Data on these institutions' holdings of money and near-monies are part of the material, and invite analysis of their attitudes towards the holding of money and liquid assets. With most of the series starting in 1952, they offer insights into behavior over an unusually long period by the standards of most macroeconomic analysis. Moreover, there is no doubt that the financial sector was and still is the principal holder of the wholesale-money balances in the M3 measure, which the Federal Reserve stopped compiling.[32]

In the current exercise several types of non-bank financial institution are covered. The discussion here concentrates on those which have substantial long-term assets (such as quoted equities), more specifically,

▷ private pension funds,

▷ state and local governments' employee retirement funds,

▷ life-insurance companies,

▷ property and casualty insurance companies, and

▷ mutual funds.

At the start of 2010 these institutions held in aggregate total assets of over $21,100 billion, a sum almost 50 percent higher than the United

States' GDP. They undoubtedly played a critical – perhaps even a dominant – role in American asset-price determination. At the end of the first quarter of 1952 the total assets of these five categories of institution were $99.7 billion. Between that date and the first quarter of 2010 their total assets increased by 222 times, with a compound annual rate of increase of 9.8 percent. In the same period, their money assets (or, at any rate, assets identifiable as monetary from the flow-of-funds data) increased from $3.3 billion to $561.6 billion, which is by 172 times, with a compound annual rate of increase of 9.3 percent. So while total assets increased by somewhat more than 200 times and money holdings increased by somewhat less than 200 times, the ratio between money and assets changed from 3.3 percent to 2.5 percent, or by just under 25 percent (i.e., at a compound annual rate of about 0.5 percent).

While suggestive, do these facts establish a case for believing that U.S. financial institutions' money holdings have a powerful influence on the nominal value of their assets? A great deal of further analysis would no doubt be needed to persuade skeptics of money's significance. Figure 16.1 shows the ratio of the five types of financial institutions' money holdings (again, insofar as these could be identified from the flow-of-funds data) to their total assets over the 1952–2010 period, using quarterly data. It is clear that the ratio varied considerably at times, despite changing little in the whole period. Critics of the monetary approach to asset-price determination might say that the graph is far from persuasive.

It cannot be denied that both institutional money holdings and asset prices are extremely volatile series. Akerlof and Shiller may be right in asserting that in the short term the desired ratio between money and assets is a plaything of investors' confidence, more a matter of "animal spirits" than of scientific calculation. But the possibility remains that the relationship between changes in institutional money and asset prices is fairly reliable over the medium term. More detailed statistical analysis of the 1952–2010 data finds that, in periods of only one year, changes in the ratio of money to assets were roughly as important as changes in money as an influence on the value of institutions' total assets. But, when the length of the period under scrutiny increases, the influence of changes in the ratio of money to assets diminishes and eventually disappears. Money becomes the dominant factor in changes in the nomi-

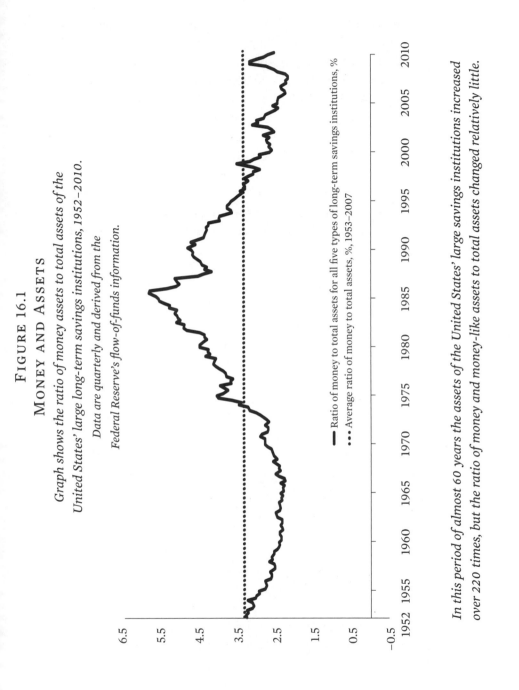

FIGURE 16.1

MONEY AND ASSETS

Graph shows the ratio of money assets to total assets of the
United States' large long-term savings institutions, 1952–2010.

Data are quarterly and derived from the
Federal Reserve's flow-of-funds information.

—— Ratio of money to total assets for all five types of long-term savings institutions, %
····· Average ratio of money to total assets, %, 1953–2007

In this period of almost 60 years the assets of the United States' large savings institutions increased
over 220 times, but the ratio of money and money-like assets to total assets changed relatively little.

nal value of total assets. Figure 16.2 shows five-year moving averages of the annual rates of change of money and total assets. The relationship is clear and definite, and withstands rigorous statistical testing.[33]

Skeptics may still question the relevance of financial institutions' money balances to asset-price determination. The subject is certainly difficult. Even if financial institutions' demand-for-money function is characterized by long-run stability, the institutional money/assets ratio is likely to alter in response to large shifts in the arguments in that function. Particularly important are changes in the attractiveness of money relative to other assets, as, for example, banks pay interest on an increasing proportion of their liabilities and real interest rates fluctuate. Moreover, frequent changes in the institutional framework disturb the clarity of the underlying relationships. The impact of such institutional change would be evident in a thorough review of the money-holding behavior of each of the five types of institution taken individually, but space constraints prohibit detailed discussion.[34]

Three final points conclude this section. First, a high proportion of the money balances held by the five types of long-run savings institutions analyzed here belong in M3, but not in M2. The thesis here is that the wholesale-money balances held by these institutions have in recent decades played an important role in asset-price determination. They therefore need to be monitored for their significance in the transmission mechanism from money to the economy. By discontinuing the publication of the M3 series, the Federal Reserve sent a message that it did not regard wholesale-money balances as relevant to macroeconomic analysis. Given the apparent fact of the long-run similarity of the rates of growth of long-run savings institutions' money and their asset totals, that verdict seems debatable.

Second, the allegation made by Akerlof and Shiller in *Animal Spirits* needs to be recalled. According to them, modern macroeconomics does not have a well-organized and widely accepted theory of the determination of the nominal value of the general level of asset prices (that is, the prices of common stocks and real estate). The analysis here and in essay 15 challenges their skepticism. It has proposed, first, that asset prices are determined by the interaction between investors' money holdings and their desired ratio of money to assets, and, second, that in

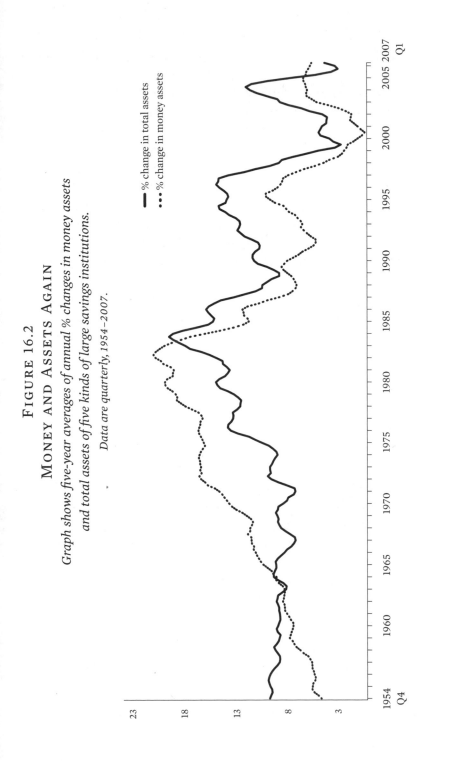

FIGURE 16.2
MONEY AND ASSETS AGAIN

*Graph shows five-year averages of annual % changes in money assets
and total assets of five kinds of large savings institutions.
Data are quarterly, 1954–2007.*

—— % change in total assets
••••• % change in money assets

the medium and long runs investors' desired ratio of money to assets is stable. This statement begs certain questions, notably about how money relevant for investment decisions is to be segregated from the rest of the economy's money holdings. Nevertheless, the policy message is obvious. Periods of rapid growth in the quantity of money are likely to be associated with high asset-price inflation, while periods in which the quantity of money contracts tend to see weak stock markets and falling real-estate values.

Third, an alternative to the money-based argument is that asset-price bubbles are largely to be attributed to excessive growth of "credit." In work carried out under the auspices of the International Monetary Fund and the World Bank, and discussed at academic conferences, the relationship between asset prices and bank lending (or "domestic credit expansion" – DCE) was tested in a number of countries and was found to meet standard tests of statistical significance in several instances.[35] However, a very high correlation often prevails between, on the one hand, bank lending and DCE (which is invariably a measure of credit *extended by the banking system*) and, on the other, money-supply growth. Tests of the relationship between bank credit and asset prices therefore do not discriminate between credit-based and monetary views of asset-price determination. One way of meeting this difficulty is to examine the relationship between *non-bank* credit (such as credit in the form of new bond issuance) and asset prices, since no correlation is to be expected between non-bank credit and money growth. No economist has identified a robust relationship between the rates of change of non-bank credit and asset prices or proposed a theory in which non-bank credit could have an effect on the overall level of asset prices.

An even more decisive objection to a credit-based theory of asset prices rests on brute fact: in most leading industrial nations the long-term savings institutions do not borrow at all. This is certainly true of the five categories of financial institution in the United States discussed in this essay. Yet these institutions usually hold the majority of the outstanding stocks of quoted equities and bonds, and their transactions largely determine the prices of these assets. Bank lending to the real-estate sector is significant in most nations, and it may sometimes be possible to find correlations between either aggregate bank lending or lending specifically to real-estate investors, on the one hand, and real-estate prices, on the other. However, it is easy to cite historical examples in which the growth of bank credit to the private sector has been negligible or even negative, but rapid increases in the quantity of money – due to purchases of government securities by the banks – have been accompanied by rapid increases in asset prices.[36] In short, the view that the quantity of money is pivotal in determining the general level of asset prices is easier to reconcile with certain well-established features of modern economies than the credit-based argument.

At any rate, it is clear that narrow money cannot be relevant to asset-price determination. In the U.S. – as in the U.K. and other industrial nations – many of the organizations most active in financial markets do not hold meaningful amounts of narrow money, in the form of notes, at all. The Federal Reserve's flow-of-funds data simply do not refer to the note holdings of non-bank financial institutions. In a modern economy, notes are not used in large capital transactions and play virtually no role in the balance-sheet decisions of substantial financial institutions. These institutions may hold narrow money in the form of demand deposits, but it is striking that demand deposits are usually very small compared with both time deposits and such assets as security repurchase agreements and open-market paper. The money aggregate critical to their portfolio decisions must be an all-inclusive, broadly defined one.

VI.

Defenders of the macroeconomic role of narrow money might protest that, for the majority of economic agents, their cash and demand deposits are the types of money most immediately available for spending. Since money matters because it can be used in transactions, this appears to establish a case for concentrating attention on cash and demand deposits, the components of M1. The logic may sound reasonable, but inspection of the data shows that so-called "transactions balances" – the types of money found in the United States' M1 – are held to a remarkable extent in other countries and in the "black economy." Since the black economy, however defined, is only a fraction of the formal economy tracked in official figures for GDP, neither the monetary base (currency) nor M1 can be plausibly viewed as particularly important in determining total spending.

This black-economy argument against narrow money appeals to salient features of the United States' currency issue. At various times in recent decades almost half of it has been held by non-U.S. citizens, predominantly outside the United States itself. The U.S. flow-of-funds data contain a line 22 (in table L.204, on "Checkable Deposits and Currency," in the latest data set), which gives a number for the currency holdings of the "rest of the world." In the first quarter of 2010 it was $316.0 billion, while the total U.S. currency outside banks was $882.7 billion. In other words, over a third of the United States' non-bank currency holdings (and almost 20 percent of M1) had not remained in the United States at all. Non-U.S.-held dollar notes are of course put to a wide variety of uses around the world, notably in assisting legitimate retail transactions in societies suffering from rampant inflation. However, the incidence of hyperinflation (or even of the milder "galloping inflation" of over 50 percent a year) is much less common today than ten or twenty years ago, and still the rest of the world's dollar holdings continue to climb. There can be little doubt that a high proportion is held in the black economies of numerous societies. In particular, U.S. dollar notes are the principal media of exchange in the international narcotics trade, although of course hard evidence is elusive.[37]

What about note holding in the United States itself? The flow-of-funds data have a figure for vault cash held by the commercial banks ($52.9 billion in the first quarter of 2010), but the holdings of the various kinds of non-bank agent are not published. If the foreign holdings are deducted from the $882.7 billion figure for total currency held outside banks, the total held by non-banks came to $566.7 billion in the first quarter of 2010. With the United States' adult population at about 240 million, the implied average holding per non-bank individual was just under $2,500. With some of the non-bank holdings in corporate hands (such as in the retail sector), a reasonable guesstimate is that the average holding of U.S. adults in their own hands may have approached $2,000.

The proportion of U.S. families without a transaction account (which would normally be at a bank) fell to 10.6 percent in 2004.[38] These were, overwhelmingly, families with low incomes whose assets were too small to justify the retention of a bank account. Given their modest overall wealth, it seems unlikely that a large average note holding – say, a note holding of much above $1,000 per person (or of $2,000 per household) – could have been common in this tenth of the United States' population. The average level of cash withdrawals from automated-teller machines was $100 in 2006, pointing to an average note holding of well beneath $2,000 for those people using ATMs.[39] A fair deduction is that in the United States a large part of the dollar-note issue is held by outright criminals or by groups on the borderline between the legitimate and criminal economies. It is therefore difficult to see how the United States' monetary base *by itself* can have much relevance to macroeconomic conditions.[40]

What about M1, data for which continue to be published by the Federal Reserve? Many economists still believe that M1 is the most useful measure of money in the United States, and, as noted at the outset, Bernanke referred to it in his work on the Great Depression.[41] However, M1 now suffers from a serious drawback – namely, that it is very small compared with both M2 and M3. Historically, balances inside M1 were larger than non-M1 balances in wider measures of money. When the quantitative significance of demand deposits was combined with the view that time deposits outside M1 were "not available to spend immediately," a focus on M1 seemed valid. But M1 now represents only slightly above 20 percent of M2, while M3 is about seven times as large as M1. Banks' increasing tendency to pay interest on deposits (particularly on time deposits) has led to agents' holding most of their monetary wealth in balances outside M1. (See table 16.1.) It is difficult to believe that M1 should still receive the preponderance of macroeconomic attention and comment.

VII.

The points made in this essay together constitute a powerful argument for believing that broad money – not narrow money – is the important aggregate for macroeconomic analysis. To summarize:

1. Because of the ease of transferring money between different types of money (i.e., of making money-into-money transactions), it is unlikely that narrow money plays a significant causal role in motivating expenditure decisions (i.e., money-into-goods-and-services transactions) or portfolio adjustments (i.e.,

money-into-assets transactions), whereas excess or deficient holdings of broad money are eliminated by macroeconomically interesting portfolio adjustments and/or decisions to spend on goods and services.

2. Narrow money does not have a significant position in asset portfolios, and it is difficult to believe that, for example, the note issue has any bearing on the portfolio adjustments that determine asset prices in a modern economy, whereas a large body of evidence can be assembled (for the U.S., the U.K., and no doubt elsewhere) that the levels and changes in broad money influence the levels and changes in asset prices.

3. Narrow money – and especially the very narrow concept of the monetary base (i.e., "currency" in the U.S.) – is held disproportionately in the black economy and in that sense is of limited relevance to economic developments in the formal economy.

If an all-inclusive, broadly defined money aggregate plays a vital role in the determination of national income and wealth in nominal terms, should the Federal Reserve have discontinued the publication of the M3 series in 2006? The money balances inside M3 but not M2 are characteristically held by financial institutions. The argument of this essay has been that financial institutions' non-M2 M3 holdings are particularly relevant to the determination of asset prices. A case can be made that, since asset prices are important to cyclical fluctuations in the U.S. economy, so also must be the non-M2 M3 balances involved in asset-price determination. As the determination of the general level of asset prices is a highly contentious area of macroeconomics, further research is clearly needed. The Federal Reserve should consider preparing data on the money-supply holdings of the U.S. economy's different sectors (i.e., the household, corporate, and financial sectors), in order better to understand these sectors' monetary behavior. The Bank of England has been preparing such data for nearly fifty years. Arguably, the data have shown several interesting patterns which throw vital insights into the transmission mechanism from money to the economy. (See essay 15 for an illustration of the shuffling of money between sectors and agents, as they buy and sell goods and assets.)

Interestingly, the ECB has also started to assemble such information for the Eurozone.[42]

Broad money is superior to narrow money in macroeconomic analysis. It is striking that virtually all the leading theorists of traditional monetary economics – Wicksell, Fisher, Keynes, Robertson, Hawtrey, Friedman, and Johnson – either expressed a clear preference for broad money or discussed the relationship of money to the economy in the context of a commercial-banking sector which they viewed as important to macroeconomic outcomes.[43] The shift since the late 1950s to favoring the base – largely due to the influence of New Classical Economics and particularly of Eugene Fama – is a radical intellectual change which seems to have had more impact on American macroeconomists (and perhaps on American central bankers) than on European central bankers.[44] The next essay argues that the Federal Reserve's neglect of broad money contributed to the monetary-policy mistakes of the late Noughties which led to both the housing-price bubble of 2005–07 and the Great Recession of 2008–10.

ESSAY 17

DID BERNANKE BREAK HIS
PROMISE TO FRIEDMAN?

ON NOVEMBER 8, 2002, the University of Chicago organized a ninetieth-birthday reception in honor of Milton Friedman. Ben Bernanke, who had then been a governor of the Federal Reserve for three months, was a guest speaker. He concluded his remarks by addressing Friedman: "Regarding the Great Depression. You're right, we [meaning the Fed] did it. We're very sorry. But, thanks to you, we won't do it again." This was a reference to the classic study *A Monetary History of the United States, 1867–1960*, co-authored by Friedman and Anna Schwartz, and published in 1963, which argued that the Fed should take much of the blame for the 1929–33 slump.[1] Friedman believed that a more activist Fed policy could have prevented the Great Depression.

By early 2010 Bernanke had been chairman of the Fed for a four-year term which included the period widely regarded as the most difficult for the American economy since the 1930s and hence as a veritable "Great Recession." Although many of his decisions had been controversial, he was reappointed for a second four-year term by President Obama. Indeed, Bernanke was widely applauded for his handling of the banking crisis in 2008 and 2009. The December 2009 issue of the journal *Foreign Policy* identified him as number one of the "top 100 global thinkers" in 2009 "for staving off the Great Depression."[2]

But, in his handling of the Great Recession, had Bernanke in fact kept his promise to Friedman? For the purpose of discussion, the promise is taken here to have committed the Fed in three ways:

> ▷ to prevent the recurrence of the Great Depression,

▷ to apply Friedman's understanding of monetary economics in the Fed's policy-making approach, and

▷ to respect at least the spirit of Friedman's main policy prescription, that the growth of the quantity of money should be stable over time.[3]

Each aspect of the commitment merits discussion.

I.

In his November 2002 remarks Bernanke paid tribute to Friedman and Schwartz's *Monetary History*, remarking that what he took "from their work is the idea that monetary forces, particularly if unleashed in a destabilizing direction, can be extremely powerful."[4] Bernanke appeared not only to offer an enthusiastic endorsement of Friedman and Schwartz's work, but also to agree with the main themes of their monetary theorizing. As will become clear as the discussion proceeds, his true position was (and probably remains) more ambivalent.

A central finding of Friedman and Schwartz's study was that an extraordinary collapse in the quantity of money, not an inherent failing of the capitalist system, was the main cause of the United States' "Great Contraction" (as they termed it) between 1929 and 1933. Their favored measure of money fell on a peak-to-trough basis by almost 40 percent in less than four years (that is, typically at an annual rate of about 10 percent), from $48.2 billion in October 1929 to $29.7 billion in April 1933.[5] According to Friedman and Schwartz, the critical failure in operational terms was that the Fed did not initiate sufficiently expansionary open-market purchases of securities (meaning: purchases to expand the quantity of money) until too late. So Bernanke's promise to Friedman had one clear interpretation: If he were at the helm in the Federal Reserve, a similar plunge in the quantity of money would not be allowed to happen. What, then, has been the behavior of the quantity of money since Bernanke became Fed chairman in February 2006 and, more critically, since the escalation of the crisis after the Lehman bankruptcy in September 2008?

Unfortunately, a thorny technical issue is basic to any analysis.

Which money aggregate is most relevant to assessing the macroeconomic situation? In their *Monetary History*, Friedman and Schwartz recognized that this topic could be awkward and contentious, and were explicit about their own preferences. To quote, "we have found in our work that a concept of money which includes both categories of deposits [i.e., demand and time deposits] often displays a more consistent relationship to other economic magnitudes than a concept which excludes time deposits." In other words, their predilection was for M2 (which includes time deposits) over M1 (which does not). In his subsequent career Friedman was indeed a fairly – but not wholly – consistent supporter of M2.[6]

What, then, happened to M2 in Bernanke's first term as Fed chairman? The accompanying figure – with both the three-month annualized growth rate and the annual growth rate – sets out the key numbers. The annual rate of M2 growth was fairly stable at about 5 percent a year in the two years starting in early 2006, if with some tendency to rise. It then slowed markedly in 2008, a development better illustrated by the three-month annualized rate of change than by the annual figure. In fact, by August 2008 the three-month annualized rate of change had dropped to almost zero. With the escalation of the financial crisis in September 2008, and in particular with the bankruptcy of Lehman Brothers and public intervention in the AIG insurance company, the trajectory of M2 changed abruptly. Heavy purchases by the Fed of commercial paper and, to a lesser extent, of other assets caused a leap in M2. (These purchases were largely from non-banks, leading to a direct addition to bank deposits. In 2009 the commercial paper was sold and replaced by other securities, especially mortgage-backed paper. The Fed financed the purchases by issuing cash reserves to banks, so that the monetary base soared.) For a few weeks in late 2008 the annualized three-month rate of M2 increase was in the area of 15 to 25 percent. Given the widespread fears at that time of another Great Depression, Friedman would surely have approved of these highly expansionary open-market operations.

But what would he make of the subsequent record? As figure 17.1 shows, money growth may have flipped up in the immediate aftermath of the Lehman crisis, but then it flopped. From February 2009 to April 2010, when Bernanke had been reappointed, the growth of M2 was

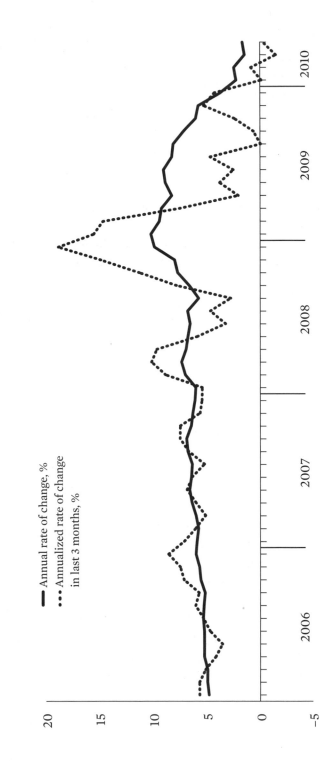

FIGURE 17.1
M2 GROWTH IN BERNANKE'S FIRST TERM
*Note surge in late 2008, followed by
stagnation from early 2009.*

— Annual rate of change, %
••• Annualized rate of change
  in last 3 months, %

negligible. The annualized rate of increase in the fourteen-month period was a mere 1.4 percent. The Fed's programs of asset purchases did by themselves sustain money growth, with the most obvious evidence being the dramatic climb in banks' cash assets. But the effect of the programs was barely powerful enough to outweigh the contractive effects on M2 of the shrinkage of banks' risk assets. This shrinkage was largely driven by newly imposed regulatory requirements to raise capital/asset ratios, which were supposed to make banks safe. The Fed was one of the ringleaders in the regulatory push. It ought to have understood that the removal of risk from bank balance sheets would inevitably lead to a slowing of asset acquisition and hence of monetary expansion. Given that an imperative in American public policy in 2009 was to lift the economy out of the worst downturn for over seventy years, the feeble growth of M2 was a big disappointment. Even in autumn 2010 it remained a source of worry. (Unemployment, which had peaked at just above 10 percent of the labor force in late 2009, was still at 9.8 percent in November 2010. The post-1947 average is 5.7 percent.)

What is the verdict on the first of the three elements in the Bernanke promise? A second Great Depression was avoided, at least in part because of Bernanke's support for expansionary asset purchases in late 2008. But surely more could have been done to raise the rate of money growth in 2009. Particularly if the Fed had worked with the U.S. Treasury to organize a large scheme of buybacks of government securities, it could have taken a far more active approach to boosting money growth.

II.

What about the second part of the promise? Did Bernanke and the Fed make decisions that showed sympathy and respect for Friedman's contributions to economics? The discussion so far has centered on the M2 data, as M2 was Friedman's pet aggregate for most of his life. However, monetary statistics – like the banking institutions to which they relate – are in constant flux. A case can be made that the closest present-day equivalent of the money measure favored in *A Monetary History* is in fact M3. M3 was introduced as an official money aggregate in 1971, with a back run of data starting in 1959.[7] The late 1960s and 1970s were the heyday of academic controversy about the interpretation of the events and data set out in *A Monetary History*, and the introduction of more aggregates should be seen in that context. At the start of the M3 series, the differences between it and M2 were minor. M3 included, but M2 excluded, large time deposits and Eurodollar deposits held by U.S. residents. But – as has been noted at several points in this volume – time deposits are the type of money that is being balanced against non-money assets in wealth portfolios. They should not be cut out of monetary analysis. (See, particularly, pp. 83–86 in essay 4 for Keynes's emphasis on broad money in his discussion of portfolio selection.) Indeed, there are grounds for claiming that M3 was in the late 1960s and 1970s – and remains today – a much better approximation to the notion of a money aggregate encompassing *all* demand and time deposits than M2.

In particular, the exclusion of "large" time deposits from M2 seems arbitrary and odd. The Fed's procedure is to exclude all deposits with an opening value in excess of $100,000 from M2 money. So a deposit of $90,000 is "money," but one of $110,000 is not. Does one need to point out that this is absurd? An obvious comment is that, as nominal incomes and wealth grow, a rising proportion of deposits will have an opening value above $100,000 and so will be excluded from M2, with the result that M3 will expand relative to M2. In December 1959, M2 was $297.8 billion, only fractionally less than M3 at $299.7 billion; in December 2009 M2 was $8,543.9 billion, 40 percent less than M3 at $14,370.0 billion.[8] Undoubtedly, an ever-increasing proportion of deposits in the hands of companies and financial institutions are no longer eligible for inclusion in M2. For those economists who believe – not unreasonably – that corporate and financial-sector money balances have an important bearing on macroeconomic conditions, the M2 money measure has become less interesting and useful than it was when Friedman and Schwartz used it in their work on the Great Depression.

Several participants in financial markets have said that there is a genuine need for M3 data. But in November 2005, when Greenspan was still chairman, the Fed announced that it would stop publishing M3 numbers. According to Johan van Overtveldt in his book *Bernanke's Test*, the decision to end M3 was a mistake that was "as much attributable to Bernanke as Greenspan."[9] Bernanke's apparent aversion to M3 suggests that he looks at money data in a very different spirit from Friedman. As his book of essays on the Great Depression focused on the

M1 measure when it referred to money at all, Bernanke's approach clearly diverged from that of Friedman and Schwartz in their *Monetary History*. There is no sign in Bernanke's statements as Fed chairman that he has rethought his position on this subject.

How important was the suppression of M3 data starting in early 2006 to American monetary policy over the next four years? Figures 17.2 and 17.3 suggest that it was hugely important. The Fed may have stopped publishing M3 numbers, but its staff continues to prepare and release data on nearly all its main components. A private research company, Shadow Government Statistics, has therefore been able to compile an estimate – or anyhow a good guesstimate – of monthly M3 data. On this showing the M3 money aggregate has seen a dramatic boom and bust in the last few years. It started the Bernanke chairmanship with a single-digit annualized six-month growth rate, but this growth rate moved up to low double digits in early 2007, and to the teens in late 2007 and early 2008. (Admittedly, interpretation is complicated by the disintegration of the so-called "shadow banking system.")[10]

Monetary economists who favor broad money would surely have blown the whistle about excessive money growth as early as mid-2007, if they had known what was going on. (The argument here has been that Friedman did worry about broad money, although his views on the 2007–09 crisis are conjecture. He died on November 16, 2006, at the age of 94.) At any rate, the Fed did become concerned in late 2007 and early 2008 about the need to dampen inflation pressures, which were becoming more evident. Money growth started to decelerate. The subsequent plunge in M3 was startling. With the *level* (not the *growth rate*) of M3 falling by 4 percent in the six months up to March 2010 (i.e., at an annualized rate of over 8 percent), the rate of contraction of U.S. broad money was unprecedented since the 1930s. Questions must be raised about the management of the money supply – or rather, the lack of management of the money supply – during the Bernanke chairmanship. Figure 17.2 shows the annual growth rates of M3 since 1959; figure 17.3 concentrates more specifically on the Bernanke chairmanship, demonstrating an extreme boom-bust in M3 growth. Recall – when looking at these figures – that Friedman's injunction in 1960 was that "The stock of money [should be] increased at a fixed rate year in and year out without any variation in the rate of increase to meet cyclical needs."

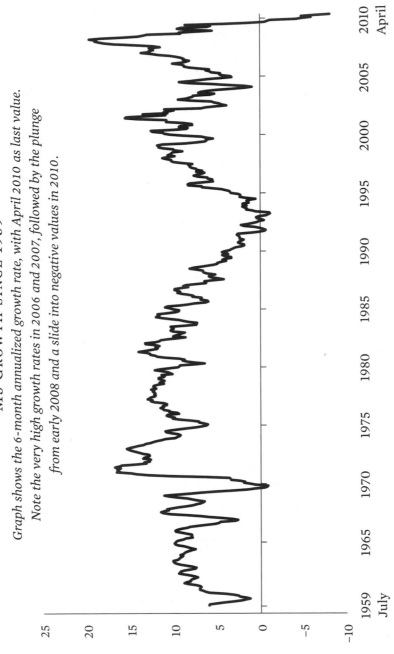

In a celebrated paper on the so-called "credit channel of monetary policy transmission," co-authored with Mark Gertler and published in the 1995 *Journal of Economic Perspectives*, Bernanke said that the relationship between money and the economy was "a black box." In a number of other places, Bernanke has proposed that credit, as measured by changes in bank lending to the private sector, is just as important in understanding the economy as changes in the quantity of money. (For a more extended critique of Bernanke's "creditism," see essay 18.)

Friedman's position here was almost the exact opposite of Bernanke's. He spent most of his career condemning economists who – in his view – placed too much emphasis on credit, and so failed to understand how money affected asset prices and economic activity. For example, he had a decades-long tussle with the Nobel Prize–winning American Keynesian James Tobin on precisely this subject. In another joint work, their 1982 volume, *Monetary Trends in the United States and the United Kingdom*, Friedman and Schwartz pooh-poohed Tobin's focus on the monetization of commercial lending, which Tobin saw as a vital first-round impact of bank credit on spending. Their rebuttal was that money was turned over many times a year. To quote, ". . . remember that the transactions velocity of money may well be 25 to 30 or more times a year, to judge from the turnover of bank deposits. So the first-round effect covers at most a two-week period, whereas the money continues circulating indefinitely."[11]

In short, Bernanke has different views from Friedman on both the merits of alternative money aggregates and the relative significance of credit and money. Further, these differences were of great practical importance in Bernanke's first term as Fed chairman. When orchestrating the large purchases of commercial paper in late 2008, Bernanke let it be known that he regarded the operations as "credit easing," not "*quantitative* easing" (that is, it was not designed to boost the *quantity* of money). He wanted the expansionary asset purchases to lower credit spreads and did not see their key impact as being on the quantity of money.[12] By contrast, Friedman's argument for stimulatory open-market operations always pivoted on the boost to the money supply.

* * *

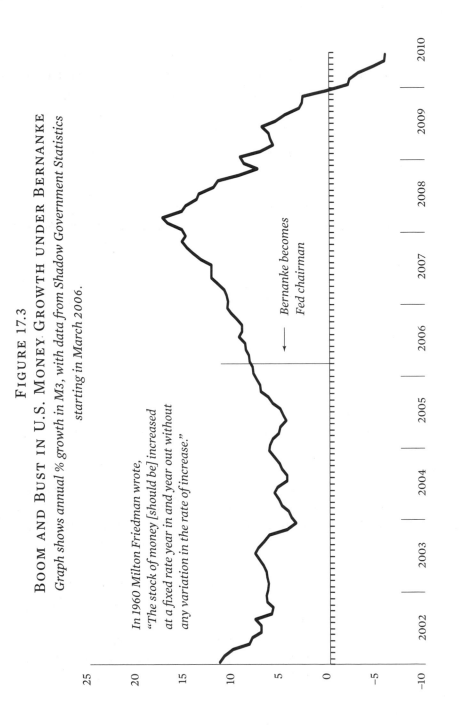

FIGURE 17.3

BOOM AND BUST IN U.S. MONEY GROWTH UNDER BERNANKE

Graph shows annual % growth in M3, with data from Shadow Government Statistics starting in March 2006.

In 1960 Milton Friedman wrote, "The stock of money [should be] increased at a fixed rate year in and year out without any variation in the rate of increase."

Bernanke becomes
Fed chairman

III.

Despite the length and intellectual turmoil of his academic career, Friedman held to one theme from the mid-1950s onwards. This was that stable growth of the quantity of money – stable growth of a broadly defined quantity of money, let it be repeated – would contribute to better macroeconomic outcomes. Famously, Friedman advocated that the Fed should pursue a "constant money-growth rule," with its decisions motivated by the objective of keeping the growth rate of the quantity of money more or less the same year after year.

In his final paper – a note given in 2006 for the *festschrift* of his former pupil David Laidler – he referred to the variability of M2 growth as an influence on variability in output. (See figure 17.4.) He wanted to provide a general explanation for the improvement in macroeconomic performance in the preceding twenty years, the so-called Great Moderation. (The United States' Great Moderation is discussed in more detail above on pp. 179–182 in the appendix to essay 7.) The final paragraph of the 2006 note, the very last words that Friedman wrote for public consumption, were:

> The collapse of the variability of output is clearly an effect of the collapse of monetary variability. In my opinion, the same results could have been obtained at any earlier time and can continue to be achieved in the future. What is involved is not a trade-off but direct cause-effect.

It follows that, if Bernanke were loyal to Friedman's ideas about monetary policy, he would try to prevent undue fluctuations in M2 and M3 growth. What in fact has happened to the variability of M2 and M3 growth since 2006? The answer is that money growth has been highly volatile. This is particularly obvious from figure 17.3 on M3 growth, but it also emerges clearly if more formal estimates of the standard deviation of quarterly money growth rates are calculated. In fact, the volatility of M2 and M3 growth may have been greater in the late Noughties than at any time since the Great Depression. As figure 17.5 brings out, the swings in money growth in recent years have been similar to those in the early 1970s, also a period of macroeconomic instability and uncertainty.

* * *

FIGURE 17.4

FRIEDMAN'S INTERPRETATION OF THE GREAT MODERATION

*Graph shows standard deviation of annualized 6-month growth rate
of M2 over previous two years; final date is December 2006.*

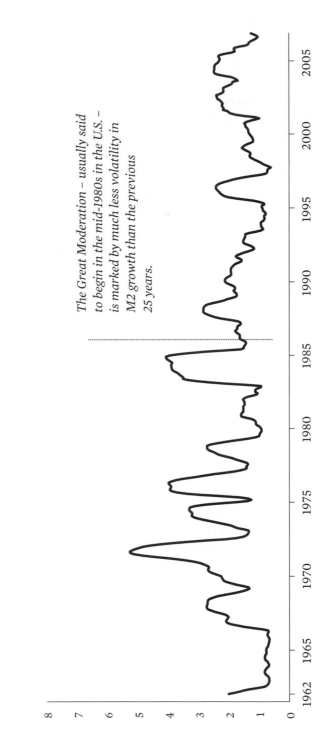

*The Great Moderation – usually said
to begin in the mid-1980s in the U.S. –
is marked by much less volatility in
M2 growth than the previous
25 years.*

IV.

What is the conclusion? To give Bernanke his due, the large-scale purchases of commercial paper in late 2008 were an astute and appropriate operation to stop severe deflation. In that sense the Fed did not repeat the "it," the gross mismanagement of money in the Great Depression, which he discussed at Friedman's ninetieth-birthday celebration. However, in the last few years American monetary policy has otherwise been conducted with almost blatant disregard of Friedman's research messages. Friedman emphasized the benefits of stable broad-money growth, but M3 money growth under Bernanke has been more erratic than at any time since the 1930s. Whereas Friedman disliked references to credit variables, Bernanke downplays money aggregates and instead concentrates on credit. Most damning of all, the Fed allowed the growth of both measures of broad money, M2 and M3, to stall in 2009, despite the most difficult and sluggish macroeconomic conditions since the Great Depression.

To say that Bernanke has broken the promise he made to Milton Friedman in November 2002 may be too harsh; to suggest that he has not kept to the underlying spirit of that promise is surely fair. What should he and his colleagues on the Federal Open Market Committee have done? They might at least in early 2009 have considered adopting the Bank of England's approach, with massive purchases of medium- and long-dated government securities *from non-banks* in order – consciously and frankly – to increase the quantity of money on the broad definitions. This may have too monetarist a flavor for some, but it is worth recalling Keynes's advice to the Fed via his letter to President Roosevelt in *The New York Times* on December 31, 1933. He wanted the Fed to imitate the Bank of England's successful conversion of the War Loan issue of government debt in 1932, which, in his view, had marked "the turn of the tide" in the U.K.'s battle with depression. He argued that large Federal Reserve purchases of "long-dated [Treasury] issues" might "be effective in a few months" in revitalizing the economy. Indeed, Keynes – in his own words – attached "great importance to it." Might a similar move on the Fed's part during 2009 have delivered an early and welcome fall in American unemployment?

FIGURE 17.5

VOLATILITY OF M2 AND M3 GROWTH

Graph shows standard deviation of annualized 6-month growth rate
of M2 and M3 over previous two years; final date is April 2010.

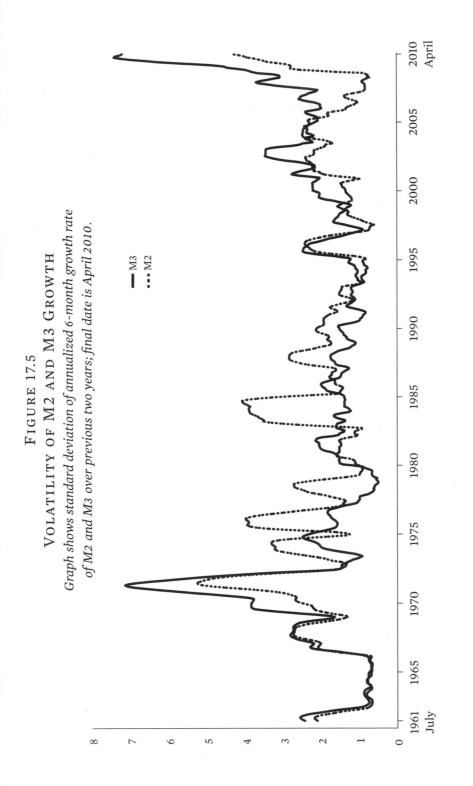

POSTSCRIPT: The bulk of this book was completed in August 2010, but revisions were made until the end of 2010. In early November the Federal Reserve announced that over the next six months it would purchase $600 billion of long-dated Treasuries in a set of operations called "QE2" – the second round of "quantitative easing." It remains to be seen whether these operations do in fact boost the growth rate of the quantity of money, broadly defined, but that does appear to have been their initial effect, and wider signs of economic improvement have started to appear.

Essay 18

The Role of Creditism in the Great Recession

KEYNES ONCE described a rival's work as "an extraordinary example of how, starting with a mistake, a remorseless logician can end up in Bedlam."[1] From September 2008 to spring 2009 the world economy was closer to Bedlam than at any other time since the end of the Second World War. Turmoil in stock exchanges and commodity markets was accompanied by almost constant public wrangling between politicians, financial regulators, and bankers. Even worse, output and employment were on a drastic downward slide, causing many comparisons to be drawn with the Great Depression of the early 1930s.

Was there an intellectual mistake which, by the remorseless logic of events, ended up in the international financial Bedlam of late 2008 and early 2009? Of course the crisis had many causes, and their interactions were complex and confusing. However, the argument here is that one particular line of thought had undue prominence in policy-making during the most traumatic period and must carry a large share of the blame for what went wrong. Only several months into the crisis did a rather different set of ideas begin to be heard. In the U.K. the articulation of these different ideas, which were derived from old-fashioned monetary theory, foreshadowed a radical move to better policies and a sharp improvement in the economic situation.

I.

Our starting point is a recondite article in the May 1988 issue of *The American Economic Review*, on "Credit, Money, and Aggregate Demand," by Ben Bernanke and Alan Blinder.[2] Both authors later became prominent in the Federal Reserve, with Bernanke receiving the ultimate accolade when he was appointed chairman of the board of governors in February 2006. The article's emphasis was on "the special nature of bank loans." Following the lead of the Harvard economist Professor Benjamin Friedman (not to be confused with the redoubtable Milton Friedman of Chicago), Bernanke and Blinder referred to "new interest in the credit-GNP relationship." By "credit" they meant bank lending to the private sector.

The 1988 article received numerous citations in other economists' journal articles, a key metric of academic stardom. In 1995 Bernanke was encouraged by this success to write a further article, with Mark Gertler, on "the credit channel of monetary policy transmission."[3] The heart of their argument was that "informational frictions in credit markets worsen during tight-money periods," with the difference in cost between internal and external funds to companies enhancing "the effects of monetary policy on the real economy."[4] The remarks on "informational frictions" were an allusion to Joseph Stiglitz, awarded the Nobel Prize for economics in 2001, who had written on "asymmetric information" as a cause of imperfections in financial markets. Bernanke and Gertler further differentiated between so-called "balance sheet" and "bank lending" channels "to explain the facts," although – curiously – they added a warning that comparisons of actual credit aggregates with other macroeconomic variables were not "valid tests" of the theory. (We shall return to this later.)

Bernanke, Blinder, Gertler, Benjamin Friedman, and Stiglitz are American, and all of them have had teaching spells in the great East Coast universities (Harvard, Columbia, Princeton, Yale). They are a motley crew, and are far from sharing the same politics or agreeing about everything. However, in economics as in other walks of life, branding makes a big difference to the marketability of what is produced. To non-economists – and indeed to most economists – the intellectual output of the East Coast universities more or less defines the latest and best in the subject. With all these distinguished names writing about credit and its importance, isn't it a fair deduction that credit – and, more specifically, bank lending to the private sector – must be vital to the health of an economy?

Such is the influence of the top East Coast universities that, when
the financial crisis first broke in the autumn of 2007, a universally held
view among policy-makers was that everything possible must be done to
sustain the flow of new bank lending to the private sector. The lending-
determines-spending doctrine was accepted without question. Few
clearer statements can be found than those from the U.K.'s own prime
minister and Treasury ministers. As the crisis escalated in September and
October 2008, Gordon Brown emphasized that official action was
needed to sustain extra bank lending and that his government's approach
went "to the heart of the problem." In his view, banks had a "responsibility" to maintain credit lines to small companies and family businesses.

But there is a problem with bank lending to the private sector.
Because borrowers may not be able to repay, lending is risky. Banks
must therefore have capital to absorb possible losses in their loan portfolios. So, the remorseless logician proceeds, not only is bank credit
central to the nation's economic well-being, but public policy must
concern itself with the quantity and quality of the banking system's
capital. Because bank lending to the private sector matters so basically
to the economy, the government is entitled to interfere with the banks,
and to tell them how much capital they should have and what form it
should take. If the reports and accounts prepared by tens of thousands
of internal and external auditors are to be believed, in the first half of
2008 Britain's banks were profitable and solvent. Indeed, not only was
their capital in positive territory, but also it was sufficiently positive to
comply with regulations agreed upon with the Financial Services
Authority. However, in late September and early October a number of
officials at the Treasury, the Bank of England, and the FSA got it into
their heads that the economy was in deep trouble and that the banks
were at risk of failure.[5]

It was certainly true that the closing of the international wholesale
money markets in August 2007 had cut off the flow of funds for some
banks, notably RBS and HBOS. With these markets shut down, the
banks were having difficulty rolling over their inter-bank borrowings
and so were restricting new credit. However, the problem could have
been tackled easily enough, either by loans (at a penalty rate) from the
Bank of England or by state guarantees on inter-bank borrowing (with
an appropriately high fee for the guarantee). A large body of precedent

from earlier crises suggested that answers on these lines ought to have been made available and would have worked.[6]

The package put together by U.K. officialdom did include guarantees on inter-bank borrowing. But that was only one element. The lending-determines-spending doctrine was so strongly and widely held that the authorities added a major qualification: the guarantees would be available only if banks had sufficient capital to continue lending during the downturn. Whereas two banks (RBS and Barclays) issued press releases saying they were not seeking extra capital, officialdom insisted that large amounts of new capital had to be raised. Further, if private shareholders would not cough up the money, the government would subscribe the money instead. Over the banks' protests that macroeconomic conditions were not too bad and a recovery could be envisaged in a few quarters, the Bank of England put together a planning scenario based on the assumption of a deep, long-lasting recession. This scenario implied that large amounts of extra bank capital were essential and had to be made obligatory.

In days (and often nights) of ferocious bargaining in October 2008, some of the world's largest financial organizations – organizations that have been household names in Britain for decades, and had long been widely admired around the world for their efficiency and expertise – were bullied into raising capital that they themselves did not think was necessary. The British government brushed aside such niceties of market capitalism as shareholders' rights and management independence. The East Coast economists applauded Brown's effort. The Nobel Prize–winner Paul Krugman of Princeton said in his *New York Times* column (entitled "Gordon Does Good") that Britain was "playing a leadership role," with Brown's bank-recapitalization program being superior to the U.S. Treasury's plans to buy up toxic assets from the banks.[7] Backed by Krugman's endorsement, Brown claimed that he was "rescuing the world." Press reports suggested that Bernanke at the Fed was instrumental in persuading the U.S. Treasury secretary, Hank Paulson, that American policy should move in the British direction.[8]

A few months later, at the World Economic Forum in Davos, the chancellor of the exchequer, Alistair Darling, described the underlying rationale for the official policy in two sentences. "We have got to recapitalize first. You've got to get the expansion of lending."[9] It was the imperative

of "more lending" – motivated by the theories of the East Coast economists – that justified the intimidation of the banks and the undermining
of property rights. As Marcus Agius, chairman of Barclays, told his
shareholders, the banks had faced "an existential threat."[10]

II.

Two questions have to be asked: Was the British government right in its
views on the economic outlook? and, Has the case for large-scale and
rapid capital-raising in the banking industry been validated? On the face
of it, the shocking deterioration in economic conditions in late 2008 and
the announcement of large losses in banks' loan portfolios in 2009 vindicated the stance taken by the government and its regulatory agencies. But
that conclusion is too hasty. Banks are unique and rather odd institutions
which occupy such a central position in a modern market economy that
their behavior can interact with the business cycle in unexpected and perverse ways. They can be caught in a Catch-22 double bind. The solvency of
the banks undoubtedly depends on the general level of asset prices and
the cyclical buoyancy of demand. But – because of the role of banks' balance-sheet size and deposit liabilities (i.e., money) in the determination
of macroeconomic variables – the general level of asset prices and the
cyclical buoyancy of demand also depend on the solvency of the banks.
The condition and behavior of the banking system are interdependent
with the condition and behavior of the whole economy. A well-known
characteristic of mathematical models is that, when variables are interdependent, the risk of instability increases. An argument can be made
that, if the banks and the economy had been handled more circumspectly
in the autumn of 2008, neither the slump in very late 2008 and at the
start of 2009 nor the severe loan losses in 2009 would have occurred.

In a 1933 academic article in *Econometrica*, one of the United States'
most influential economists, Irving Fisher, proposed "the debt deflation
theory of great depressions." Starting from a boom in which people had
borrowed heavily, he suggested that an unforeseen deterioration in
business conditions might cause large repayment of bank debt. The
repayment of bank debt would reduce the amount of money in the
economy (which he called "deposit currency"), which in turn would
cause a fall in prices, with a disproportionate effect on profits, the value

of businesses, and asset prices, leading to further repayments of debt, another round of reductions in bank deposits, a further fall in prices, and so on. The disaster was rather like the capsizing of a ship. In Fisher's words, under "normal conditions" a ship is always near "a stable equilibrium," but "after being tipped beyond a certain angle" it "no longer has this tendency to return to equilibrium, but, instead, a tendency to depart further from it."[11] The ship is no longer stable; it is so far from normal that its behavior becomes self-destructive; it capsizes and sinks.

The problem with October 2008's bank-recapitalization exercise was that it capsized the British economy. (The same comment is true of similar exercises in other economies. For further discussion of the situation in the U.S., see essay 17.) The warnings of a big recession were particularly foolish and counterproductive, since they caused an abrupt step downwards in business expectations. The shock to the banks was so sudden and severe that they reacted not by increasing the availability of credit, as officialdom had intended, but by restricting it further. The Bank of England publishes a monthly series for "sterling unused credit facilities." It had started falling in mid-2007, but the pace of decline accelerated in the immediate aftermath of the bank-recapitalization exercise. (See figure 18.1. The Federal Reserve has a similar series, although only on a quarterly basis, which was published in the last two annual surveys of bank profitability in the *Federal Reserve Bulletin*. It also plunged in late 2008 and 2009, for much the same reason, namely officialdom's demands for large increases in banks' capital/asset ratios. See figure 18.2.)

Just as Irving Fisher warned nearly eighty years ago, a restriction of bank credit stops the growth of households' and companies' deposits. The lack of money in the economy hits spending, profits, and asset prices, while asset-price falls lead to an unexpectedly high level of losses on bank's loan assets. The result is a self-feeding and unstable downward spiral of retrenchment. In the 1933 article, Fisher emphasized the sometimes paradoxical nature of this downward spiral. People repay bank debt in order to improve their financial circumstances, but, if everyone does so at the same time, the resulting fall in bank deposits (i.e., in the quantity of money) causes a drop in prices and possibly an increase in the *real* value of the remaining debts. To quote from him again, "the mass effort to get out of debt sinks us more deeply into debt."[12]

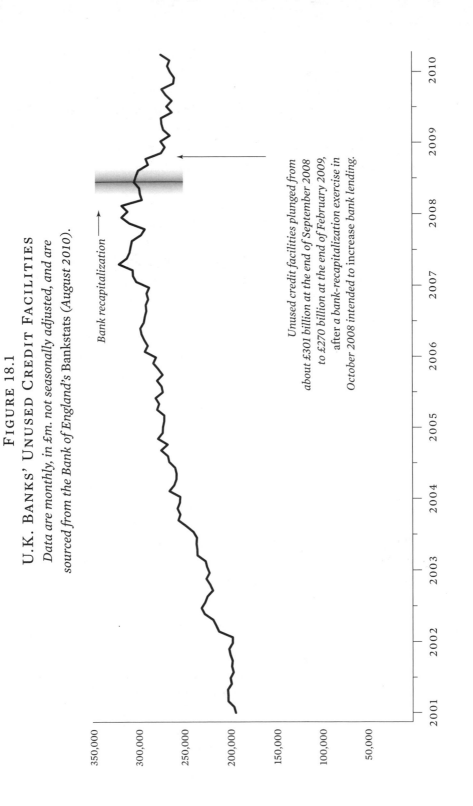

FIGURE 18.1
U.K. BANKS' UNUSED CREDIT FACILITIES
Data are monthly, in £m. not seasonally adjusted, and are sourced from the Bank of England's Bankstats (August 2010).

Bank recapitalization →

Unused credit facilities plunged from
about £301 billion at the end of September 2008
to £270 billion at the end of February 2009,
after a bank-recapitalization exercise in
October 2008 intended to increase bank lending.

The October 2008 bank-recapitalization package did not protect the economy against a deep recession. On the contrary, it accelerated the onset of recessionary forces and intensified them. By February 2009 Britain's policy-makers were desperate.[13] The previous October they had put together a package which they regarded as clever in conception, and appropriate and proportionate in its implementation. Indeed, their efforts had been praised by trend-setters of international opinion, including the *Financial Times*, which judged that the U.K.'s measures created "a global template."[14] In a world that places a premium on instant opinion, whether well informed or not, politicians and commentators parroted the *Financial Times* line. Many leading economists – including the American economists who had theorized about credit and its role in business – recommended programs similar to the U.K.'s for their own countries. But demand, output, and employment were deteriorating more rapidly after bank recapitalization than before. Although interest rates had been slashed almost to zero, banks were still cutting back on credit lines, and stock markets continued to decline; 2009 would be the worst year for the U.K. economy since the early 1980s. Similar macroeconomic trends were seen across the globe, with even nations that reportedly had robust and well-capitalized banks being hit by plunging demand and exports.

III.

As usual in cyclical downturns, Keynesian economists urged fiscal reflation – higher government spending unmatched by extra taxes, or indeed accompanied by outright tax cuts – in order to "boost demand." This is an ancient tribal custom, with the Keynesians apparently believing that the mere invocation of their hero's name can overwhelm experience and logic. Careful tests of the effectiveness of fiscal policy are needed, comparing changes in the cyclically adjusted budget deficit with concurrent or subsequent changes in total demand. The results of such tests are disappointing and show, quite simply, that fiscal policy does not work. (The International Monetary Fund website provides a database with values of both the structural, cyclically adjusted budget balance and the output gap for most of the world's economies since 1980. This database is mentioned on two other occasions in this volume, on p. 195 and pp. 242–243. An appendix to this essay shows the

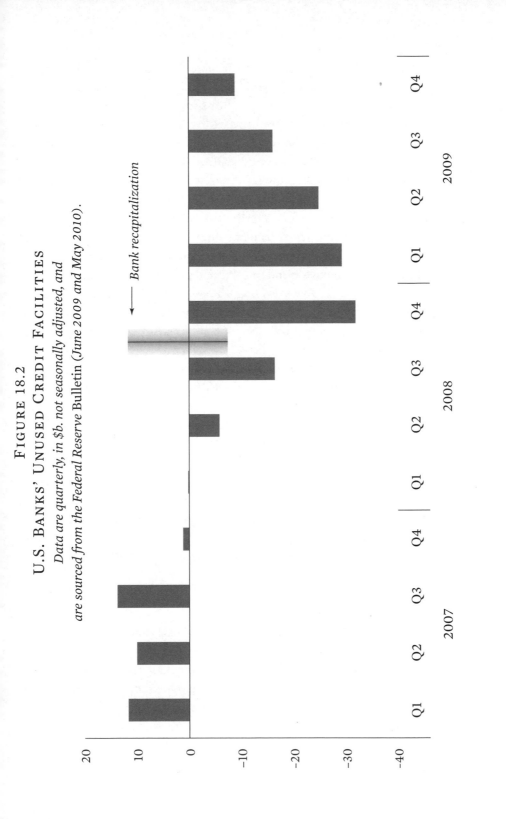

FIGURE 18.2
U.S. BANKS' UNUSED CREDIT FACILITIES
Data are quarterly, in $b. not seasonally adjusted, and
are sourced from the Federal Reserve Bulletin (June 2009 and May 2010).

results of a simple statistical regression of the change in the output gap on the change in the structural budget balance for the G7 economies from 1981 to 2008. The change in the budget balance did not have a statistically significant impact on changes in the output gap in any of them.)

Japan exemplifies the wider argument. Since the early 1990s it has been the target of constant criticism from foreign economists, particularly Krugman, who assert that the answer to its chronic demand weakness is fiscal expansion. In fact, over the last twenty years Japan has had prolonged phases in which the structural budget deficit has increased and demand has grown at a beneath-trend rate or fallen, and prolonged phases in which the structural budget deficit has decreased and demand has grown at an above-trend rate. Although Darling mentioned Keynes at the time of the 2008 Pre-Budget Report, the idea of a discretionary fiscal boost in the U.K. had been forgotten when the Budget itself was announced in March 2009. True enough, the Brown government was spendthrift, while throughout 2009 the advocates of fiscal activism were vocal in the public debate both in the U.K. and in other countries. They even took heart from analyses at the IMF which claimed that, once the money-market rate controlled by the central bank had dropped close to zero, monetary policy was "exhausted," and extra public spending and enlarged budget deficits were the only remaining means of revitalizing demand.[15] But the credibility of these analyses was dented by medium- and long-term extrapolations of fiscal sustainability in the nations running big budget deficits. The surge in the yield on Greece's government debt in early 2010, which added to its debt-servicing costs and exacerbated its fiscal woes, emphasized that financial markets do – eventually – impose a constraint on excessive budget deficits and public debt.

IV.

At the bleakest moments of the crisis, in January and February 2009, a major policy rethink seems to have started at the Bank of England. (If public statements are to be taken at face value, nothing comparable occurred at the Treasury, although the Bank had to consult the Treasury throughout.) In Bernanke's 1988 paper, the lending-determines-spending doctrine had been proposed as an alternative to "standard models of aggregate demand" (as he termed them), which paid more attention to money than to loans. In fact, Bernanke saw the "money-only framework" as "traditional" and regarded his own work as an innovation. He even coined the word "creditist" to describe a central bank with a special alertness to credit developments. Implicitly he was contrasting "creditism" with "monetarism," where monetarism is understood as the claim that the quantity of money – nowadays dominated by bank deposits – is crucial in the determination of national income. Bernanke said in forthright terms that in some circumstances "a credit-based policy" would be "superior" to "a money-based policy."[16]

Throughout the financial crisis of late 2007 and 2008, the monetary alternative to the lending-determines-spending doctrine had always been there. For many years the Bank of England had been agnostic over major theoretical issues. It may have veered towards the creditist side in the creditist/monetarist debate, but it had not made a final commitment.[17] With base rates down to a mere ½ percent, further significant cuts in the *price* of money were out of the question. The Bank decided to refocus on the *quantity* of money. On March 5, 2009, it announced a program of so-called "quantitative easing," in which purchases of gilt-edged securities to the tune of £150 billion, mostly from non-banks, would deliberately add to the level of bank deposits (i.e., the quantity of money).[18]

Credit and money are often confused, and confusions in a subject as arcane as banking theory are understandable enough. However, credit and money are distinct. Lending to the private sector is a totally different entry on a bank balance sheet from the figure for deposits. Increases in banks' loan portfolios add to assets and require extra capital to anticipate the risk of default; increases in bank deposits expand liabilities and may not need any more capital at all. The point is that banks can grow their deposit liabilities by acquiring assets with a negligible risk of default. These assets are of two main kinds, claims on the government (Treasury bills and gilt-edged securities) and claims on the central bank (their so-called "cash reserves"). When the quantity of money increases as a result of banks' acquisition of such assets, no new bank capital is required.

Reports in the media about quantitative easing were muddled. Many journalists remained imprisoned in the lending-determines-spending box and believed that the purpose of quantitative easing was to stimulate more lending.[19] Again, the mistake is understandable, as the phrases "the quantity of money" and "the money supply" are used interchangeably, and the second of these gives the impression that banks are "supplying money" (that is, making loans). However, it must be emphasized that "the money supply" consists of deposits, not loans. The money supply and bank lending are different things.

The intention of the Bank of England's program of quantitative easing was – explicitly – to increase the quantity of money by direct transactions between it and non-banks. Strange though it may sound, monetary expansion could occur even if bank lending to the private sector were contracting. In its essence, the mechanism at work was very simple: the Bank of England added money to the bank accounts of holders of government securities, as it bought these securities from them. (The details were more complex. See essay 4 for the distinction between money-market operations and debt-market operations, which is fundamental to the topic.) Roughly speaking, the quantity of money in the U.K. in early 2009 was about £2,000 billion. Gilt purchases of £150 billion over a six-month period would therefore lead by themselves – with everything else being held constant – to monetary growth of about 7½ percent. This would be equivalent, at an annual rate, to slightly more than 15 percent, which is a very stimulatory rate of monetary expansion.[20]

Some observers raised the objection that the major holders of gilts were pension funds and insurance companies, and that they could not "spend" the extra money in the shops. But the big long-term savings institutions were (and always are) reluctant to hold large amounts of money in their portfolios, relative to the total value of assets under management. In the long run, cash is an asset with negligible real returns. At the end of 2008, U.K. savings institutions had total bank deposits of about £130 billion compared with total assets of over £3,000 billion. They were reluctant to let the former number double, but, if the £150 billion were allowed to pile up uselessly, that would be the result. All being well, the money would circulate from the financial institutions to companies to households, and then circulate in part back to financial institutions to companies, and so on. Money would not stay idle in pension-fund and insurance-company bank accounts, but would spread around the economy.

What – more precisely – was the likely sequence of events? First, pension funds, insurance companies, hedge funds, and gilt-edged market-makers (i.e., the initial recipients of QE money) would try to get rid of their excess money by purchasing more securities. Let us, for the sake of argument, say that they would want to acquire more equities. To a large extent they would be buying from other pension funds, insurance companies, and so on, and the efforts of all market participants taken together to rid themselves of the excess money might seem self-canceling and unavailing. It is indeed true that, to the extent that buyers and sellers are in a closed circuit, they cannot get rid of money by transactions between themselves. However, there would be a way out. Since they would all have an excess supply of money and an excess demand for equities, upward pressure on equity prices would emerge. If equity prices were then to rise sharply, the ratio of the institutions' money holdings to total assets would drop back to the desired level. Indeed, on the face of it, a doubling of the stock market would mean (more or less) that the £150 billion of extra cash could be added to portfolios (so that cash holdings would be £150 billion plus the original £130 billion), and yet U.K. financial institutions' money-to-total-assets ratio would be unchanged from the original level. Second, once the stock market started to rise because of the process just described, companies would find it easier to raise money by issuing new shares and bonds. At first only strong companies might have the credibility to embark on large-scale fund-raising, but they could use their extra money to pay bills owed to weaker companies that were threatened with bankruptcy (and also perhaps to purchase land and subsidiaries from them). In the end, share prices would not double, as only a small proportion of the £150 billion QE injection would stay bottled up in the financial sector. (The processes described in the last two paragraphs are the same as those set out more elaborately on pp. 338–344 in essay 15 above and on pp. 37–55 of the author's 2005 monograph, *Money and Asset Prices in Boom and Bust*.[21])

In short, although the money injected into the economy by the Bank of England's QE operations might in the first instance be held by pension funds, insurance companies, and other financial institutions, it would soon pass to profitable companies with strong balance sheets and then to marginal businesses with weak balance sheets, and so on. The cash strains throughout the economy would be eliminated, asset prices would recover, and demand, output, and employment would all revive. Emphasis must be placed on one key point: this revival would be due to the additions to agents' bank deposits, and the circulation of these deposits from bank account to bank account. The extra expenditure would eventuate regardless of whether the banks' extra cash were lent out or not. Far too many newspaper reports said that the success of QE depended on the resumption of lending by banks, particularly lending to companies by banks. This was plain wrong: spending depends on money balances, not on bank credit.[22]

To summarize, the monetary (or monetarist) view of banking policy is in sharp contrast to the credit (or creditist, to recall Bernanke's term) view. Contrary to a plethora of misguided academic papers, the monetary view contained – and of course still contains – a clear account of how money affects spending and jobs. As proponents of QE correctly foresaw, the revival in spending after a large and patently exogenous boost to money holdings would occur because agents had to rebalance their portfolios and spending patterns, in order to restore desired ratios of money to wealth and income.[23] It would occur *even if bank lending were static or falling.*

In the event, the six months following the announcement of QE saw a dramatic surge in U.K. equities, while the Confederation of British Industry's monthly survey reported the sharpest favorable turnaround in companies' output plans in its history (which dated back to the early 1960s). The important variable for policy-makers is not bank lending to the private sector, but the level of bank deposits. (Remember Irving Fisher's reference to "deposit currency.") Indeed, because companies are the principal employers and the representative type of productive unit in a modern economy, bank deposits in company hands need to be monitored very closely. One contemporary advocate of QE suggested that, once these deposits started to rise strongly relative to companies' bank debt, the Bank of England's operation would have worked and the recession would be over.[24] In due course – by spring 2010 or so – it was obvious that this was indeed what had happened. QE had stopped the U.K.'s recession from turning into a depression.

V.

The debate about quantitative easing, and the larger debate between creditism and monetarism to which it is related, will rage for many years to come. Much will depend on events and personalities, as well as on ideas and journal articles. But there is at least an argument that Bernanke's creditism was the mistaken theory which, by a remorseless logic of citation, repetition, and emulation, spread around the world's universities, think tanks, finance ministries, and central banks, and led to the Bedlam of late 2008. The monetary approach – which Bernanke himself saw as standard and traditional – argued that measures such as quantitative easing, rather than bank recapitalization, were appropriate in September and October 2008. Why were large-scale expansionary open-market operations – operations targeted directly at increasing bank deposits – not adopted at that stage? Would not hundreds of thousands of jobs, and thousands of businesses, have been saved in the U.K. if the Treasury and the Bank of England had bought back vast quantities of gilts at that point instead of bullying the banks? (This is not to propose that the banks are perfect and angelic. They had been silly, naughty, and greedy in the years leading up to the crisis of 2008. But they tend to be silly, naughty, and greedy in the years leading up to most crises, and recessions as severe as this one are not normally visited on innocent bystanders.)

The academic prestige attached to the lending-determines-spending doctrine and other credit-based macroeconomic theories is puzzling. As noted earlier, Bernanke and Gertler included in their 1995 article the observation that comparison of actual credit magnitudes with macroeconomic variables was not a valid test of their theory. One has to wonder why. They claimed that bank lending was determined within the economy and so was "not a primitive driving force." (In jargon, bank lending was endogenous and determined by the economy, not exogenous.) Bernanke and Gertler must have known that the relationships between credit flows and other macroeconomic variables were weak or non-existent, casting doubt on their whole approach.

In the event, their reservations about the predictive power of credit aggregates were neither here nor there. In late 2008 policy-makers were bossy and crude in their demands that the banks lend more and have enough capital to support the new loans. More bank lending was deemed to be good, without ifs or buts. To repeat Darling's words, "We have got to recapitalize first. You've got to get the expansion of lending." Bluntly, the statistics justified neither the official policy nor

Darling's hectoring and aggressive tone, while Brown's claims to be "rescuing the world" and Krugman's praise of British policy-making later looked ridiculous. In no economy are there reliable relationships between bank lending to a particular sector and activity in that sector or in the wider economy. In that sense the bank recapitalization exercises were sold on a totally false prospectus. Another enigma here is that the alternative view – that over the long run national income is a function of the quantity of money – has clear and overwhelming substantiating evidence from all economies at all times. Both evidence and standard theory argue that the expansionary open-market operations that are the hallmark of quantitative easing, not bank recapitalization, should have been policy-makers' first priority in autumn 2008. In the next crisis they must accept that money, not bank credit by itself, is the variable that matters to macroeconomic outcomes.

Statistical Appendix: Is Fiscal Policy Effective?

The equations below are of change in output gap regressed on change in structural (i.e., cyclically adjusted) budget balance, using annual data, both concepts as a percentage of potential GDP over the period 1981–2008. Note that the budget concept is "the balance," i.e., it is negative when a deficit is recorded.

According to standard Keynesian theory, output should grow at an above-trend rate when the deficit increases, i.e., when the fiscal balance becomes more negative. So the Keynesian view on the effectiveness of fiscal policy would be validated if

1.   *the regression coefficients in the equations were negative,*

2.   *the regression coefficients were statistically significant, with a t statistic of at least 2,*

3.   *the regression coefficients took a value of over 1, consistent with the idea that the multiplier was a valid concept, and*

4.   *the equations had a good fit with the data (i.e., r^2 of, say, over 0.5, so that fiscal policy was "explaining" at least half the variation in the change in output relative to trend).*

1. The U.S.

Change in output gap = 0.04 + 0.20 change in general government structural balance

    t statistic on regression coefficient   0.9

    r^2 of equation   0.03

2. Japan

Change in output gap = −0.04 + 0.36 change in general government structural balance

    t statistic on regression coefficient   1.83

    r^2 of equation   0.114

3. Germany

Change in output gap = −0.01 − 0.19 change in general government structural balance

    t statistic on regression coefficient   −0.79

    r^2 of equation   0.023

4. France

Change in output gap = −0.02 − 0.28 change in general government structural balance

    t statistic on regression coefficient   −1.07

    r^2 of equation   0.042

5. The U.K.

Change in output gap = 0.01 + 0.19 change in general government structural balance

    t statistic on regression coefficient   1.23

    r^2 of equation   0.055

6. ITALY

Change in output gap = −0.06 − 0.22 change in general government structural balance

  t statistic on regression coefficient −1.26
  r^2 of equation   0.057

7. CANADA

Change in output gap = −0.06 + 0.06 change in general government structural balance

  t statistic on regression coefficient 0.22
  r^2 of equation   0.002

WHAT IS THE VERDICT?

1. The regression coefficients were positive in four of the seven equations.

2. None of the regression coefficients were statistically significant, according to the usual tests.

3. None of the regression coefficients took a value of above 0.4, casting doubt on the empirical relevance of the multiplier concept. (In any case, in the nation in which the value of the regression coefficient was almost 0.4, Japan, the coefficient had the wrong sign.)

4. The hypothesis did not fit the data at all, with an r^2 above 0.1 only in Japan, where – as already noted – the regression coefficient took the wrong sign.

CONCLUSION

Contrary to hundreds of textbooks, an increase in the budget deficit does not stimulate demand and output. Naïve Keynesianism – the supposed theory of fiscal stimulus – is not supported by the facts.

Notes

Introduction

1 Keynes was heavily involved in the early 1940s in the negotiations with the United States for the loans that enabled Britain to finance its military effort in the Second World War. I used the phrase "the Churchill of economics" on p. 14 of my 2007 book, *Keynes, the Keynesians, and Monetarism* (Cheltenham, U.K., and Northampton, Mass.: Edward Elgar). The third volume of Skidelsky's celebrated biography of Keynes is entitled *Fighting for Britain*.

2 Robert Skidelsky, *John Maynard Keynes: The Economist as Saviour, 1920–37* (London: Macmillan, 1992), pp. 460–461; Donald E. Moggridge, *Maynard Keynes: An Economist's Biography* (London and New York: Routledge, 1992), p. 562.

3 Milton Friedman and Anna Jacobson Schwartz, *A Monetary History of the United States, 1867–1960* (Princeton: Princeton University Press, 1963), particularly chapter 7, "The Great Contraction, 1929–33," pp. 299–419.

4 Friedman once suggested in an interview that his political affiliations alienated other economists, so that his scientific contribution was not appreciated. See Brian Snowdon and Howard Vane, *Modern Macroeconomics* (Cheltenham, U.K., and Northampton, Mass.: Edward Elgar, 2005), p. 206. In his words, "I was known as a close adviser to Reagan. The academic community was almost wholly anti-Reagan. . . . [T]he fact that I was connected with the Reagan administration had something to do with the desire on the part of the economics profession to separate themselves from my work."

5 See p. 60 of Joseph Stiglitz, *Freefall* (London and New York: Allen Lane, 2010). To quote, "On average the short-run multiplier for the U.S. economy is around 1.5. If the government spends a billion dollars now, GDP this year will go up by $1.5 billion."

6 Ibid., p. 262.

7 Friedman, like many others, thought that Keynesian fiscal activism had been dropped across the advanced world in the 1980s. But an episode of apparent fiscal "reflation" was attempted under the second President Bush in late 2001. According to a footnote in Skidelsky's *The Return of the Master*, Friedman complained, "Crude Keynesianism has risen from the dead." Robert Skidelsky, *Keynes: The Return of the Master* (London and New York: Allen Lane, 2009), p. 19.

8   I protested against the "Keynes" element in the "New Keynesian" label on p. 13 of *Keynes, the Keynesians, and Monetarism*.

9   The three-equation system was set out in Richard H. Clarida, Jordi Gali, and Mark Gertler, "The Science of Monetary Policy: A New Keynesian Perspective," *Journal of Economic Literature*, vol. 37 (December 1999), pp. 1661–1707.

10   For an example of this sort of thing, see Michael Woodford, "Monetary Policy in a World without Money," *International Finance*, vol. 3, no. 2 (2000), pp. 229–260.

11   Skidelsky, *Keynes: The Return of the Master*, p. 34.

12   Eugene Fama, "Banking in a Theory of Finance," *Journal of Monetary Economics*, vol. 6 (1980), pp. 39–57.

13   I have discussed Minford's views on monetary economics and policy in several places. See, for example, pp. 126–127 of Tim Congdon, *Reflections on Monetarism* (Aldershot, U.K., and Brookfield, Vt.: Edward Elgar, 1992) and pp. 304–307 of Congdon, *Keynes, the Keynesians, and Monetarism*.

14   See p. 195 of Geoffrey R. Gerdes and Jack K. Walton II, "Trends in the Use of Payment Instruments in the United States," *Federal Reserve Bulletin* (Spring 2005).

15   See, for example, Patrick Minford, "Optimal Monetary Policy with Endogenous Contracts," pp. 64–80, in Kent Matthews and Philip Booth, eds., *Issues in Monetary Policy* (Chichester: John Wiley & Sons, 2006). Minford argues that the stability of the economy is affected by unexpected shocks to the money supply, where the money supply is "M0, the monetary base" (p. 63).

16   In his work Robert Lucas, generally regarded as the leader of New Classical Economics, equates money with either the monetary base or the narrow money measure, M1. I argue in essays 15 to 18 that reliance on these money measures is wrong, not least because they cannot sensibly be regarded as having any role in asset-price determination. In a 1997 interview, Lucas said that ". . . econometrically it seems hard to account for more than a quarter or a third of U.S. real variability in the post-war period [by] monetary forces." Snowdon and Vane, *Modern Macroeconomics*, p. 278.

17   The terms "freshwater" and "saltwater" were first used, in the context of American academic economics, by Robert E. Hall in 1976. See Robert J. Gordon, *Productivity Growth, Inflation, and Unemployment* (Cambridge: Cambridge University Press, 2003), pp. 226–227.

18   In the 1996 Snowdon and Vane interview, Friedman said, ". . . economics has become increasingly an arcane branch of mathematics rather than dealing with real economic problems." (*Modern Macroeconomics*, p. 211.) Keynes protested against the over-formalization of economics in *The General Theory*, pp. 297–298.

19   Friedman made the remark in a paper published in a 1966 book edited by Bob Aliber. See Edward Nelson, "Milton Friedman and U.S. Monetary History: 1961–2006," in *Federal Reserve Bank of St. Louis Review*, vol. 89, no. 3 (2007), pp. 153–182, but particularly p. 172.

PART ONE
PREFACE

1   Moggridge, *Maynard Keynes: An Economist's Biography,* p. 82.

2   See, particularly, chapter XII on "Statistics of Recent Years" in Irving Fisher, *The Purchasing Power of Money* (New York: Macmillan, 1911). The latest edition is William J. Barber, ed., *The Works of Irving Fisher,* vol. 4, *The Purchasing Power of Money* (London: Pickering & Chatto, 1997).

3   Fisher, *Purchasing Power,* p. 329.

4   The possibility that the multiplier might be as high as five was mentioned on p. 121 of *The General Theory.*

5   He took eighty-seven pages of notes on it! See Alan O. Ebenstein, *Milton Friedman: A Biography* (New York and Basingstoke, U.K.: Palgrave Macmillan, 2007), p. 24. Friedman's copious note-taking is also mentioned in essay 8, on p. 189.

ESSAY 1

1   The best-known Keynesians in the U.K. in the 1960s and 1970s were Sir Roy Harrod, Lord Kahn, Lord Kaldor, and Joan Robinson. Kahn, Kaldor, and Mrs Robinson stayed at Cambridge, but Sir Roy Harrod taught at Oxford for most of his academic career. Although Cambridge was the home of Keynesianism, many economists in universities throughout England professed Keynesian affiliations, and it is, perhaps, misleading to locate Keynesianism too precisely in geographical terms. Throughout this essay, "Keynesianism" is used to mean the body of beliefs of this group of economists, and "the Keynesians" were these economists. A distinction is therefore being drawn between Keynesian economics and Keynes's economics. A similar distinction was made in Axel Leijonhufvud's *On Keynesian Economics and the Economics of Keynes* (New York: Oxford University Press, 1968), although Leijonhufvud was concerned with the whole body of Keynes's economics, whereas in this context I am interested only in his work on inflation. In the United States, the leading Keynesians – including John Kenneth Galbraith, Paul Samuelson, and Robert Solow – tended to congregate at Harvard, whereas Chicago remained committed to more traditional monetary economics. (See p. 580 of Skidelsky, *The Economist as Saviour.*)

2   Roger Opie, "The Political Consequences of Lord Keynes," in Donald E. Moggridge, ed., *Keynes: Aspects of the Man and His Work* (London and Basingstoke: Macmillan Press, 1974), p. 87.

3   Joan Robinson, *Economic Philosophy* (Harmondsworth: Penguin Books, 1962), p. 131.

4   In 1990 the Institute of Economic Affairs published *British Economic Opinion: A Survey of a Thousand Economists,* by Martin Ricketts and Edward Shoesmith. When asked for their views on the proposition "Wage-price controls should be used to control inflation," 5.4 percent of respondents "agreed strongly" and 28.3 percent agreed "with reservations," while 14.4 percent neither agreed nor disagreed. However, attitudes towards wage and price controls

would undoubtedly have been more positive fifteen or twenty years earlier.

5 Sir Roy Harrod, "Keynes's Theory and Its Applications," in Moggridge, ed., *Keynes: Aspects*, pp. 9–10, and Opie, p. 86. The 1970s saw suggestions that there was such a thing as a "just price" and that "social considerations" should enter into price determination. See Aubrey Jones, *The New Inflation* (London: André Deutsch, 1973), particularly chapters 5 and 6.

6 Harrod in Moggridge, ed., *Keynes: Aspects*, p. 9.

7 J. M. Keynes, *The General Theory of Employment, Interest, and Money* (London: Macmillan, Papermac edition, 1964), pp. 41–43. See, particularly, the footnote on pp. 42–43.

8 Sir John Hicks, *The Crisis in Keynesian Economics* (Oxford: Blackwell, 1974), pp. 59–60.

9 Harrod in Moggridge, ed., *Keynes: Aspects*, p. 9. Other examples: "It would be most inappropriate for me to stand up here and tell you what Keynes would have thought. Goodness knows he would have thought of something much cleverer than I can think of" (pp. 8–9); and "I do not think we can tackle it without direct interference. They do seem to be doing this rather more effectively in America now than here, having tribunals, boards, call them what you will, responsible for fixing maximum price increases. I am sure we have got to come to that, and, as our Chairman very kindly hinted, I had a letter in *The Times* on this very subject yesterday."

10 J. M. Keynes, *How to Pay for the War* (London: Macmillan, 1940), of which pp. 61–70 are reprinted in R. James Ball and Peter Doyle, eds., *Inflation* (Harmondsworth: Penguin, 1969), pp. 21–27.

11 J. M. Keynes, "Liberalism and Labour" (1926), reprinted in Keynes, *Essays in Persuasion* (London: Macmillan, 1931), p. 341.

12 An amusing footnote on this theme appeared on pp. 70–71 of Moggridge, ed., *Keynes: Aspects*. It was at Joan Robinson's expense. She had supported the notion that "Maynard had never spent the 20 minutes necessary to understand the theory of value," sublimely unaware that as a matter of fact (as is clear from one of the notes to her publisher) he had acted as referee on her very book on the subject.

13 Elizabeth Johnson and Donald E. Moggridge, eds., *The Collected Writings of John Maynard Keynes*, vol. II, *The Economic Consequences of the Peace* (London and Basingstoke: Macmillan for the Royal Economic Society, 1971), pp. 151–152.

14 Keynes, *Essays in Persuasion*, p. 284. The alternative of import restrictions was the one preferred in the context of the passage quoted, but Keynes was in favor of a devaluation if it was politically possible.

15 Keynes, *General Theory*, p. 296.

16 Ibid., p. 301.

17 The frailty of institutions in the face of economic imperatives was one theme of Gerald Allen Dorfman, *Wage Politics in Britain* (London: Charles Knight, 1974). See, particularly, chapter 2, on the inter-war period.

18   Keynes, *Essays in Persuasion*, p. 60.

19   There is a fascinating discussion of the notion of liquidity preference, and its connection with investment flexibility, in the second part of Hicks, *The Crisis in Keynesian Economics*.

20   Johnson and Moggridge, eds., *The Collected Writings*, vol. VI, *A Treatise on Money: 2. The Applied Theory of Money*, pp. 132–186.

21   Ibid., vol. IV, *A Tract on Monetary Reform*, pp. 141–148.

22   Ibid., vol. VI, *Treatise*, pp. 155–161 and pp. 170–175.

23   Keynes himself put "direct" in italics in the *Treatise* (p. 189), presumably because he thought that a rise in the price of money would cause people to economize on its use, and, therefore, the authorities could indirectly control the money supply. The belief that a central bank should not hold down the money supply directly, because it has the lender-of-last-resort function, is a very typical banker's attitude. Incidentally, it is one reason why Friedmanite economists and central bankers often do not see eye to eye.

24   Susan Howson, "'A Dear-Money Man'?: Keynes on Monetary Policy, 1920," in *The Economic Journal* (June 1973), p. 458.

25   Ibid., p. 461.

ESSAY 2

1   Skidelsky, *The Economist as Saviour*, p. 337.

2   Samuelson's remarks appeared in his contribution to Seymour Harris, ed., *The New Economics* (New York: Alfred A. Knopf, 1948). They were quoted by Murray Rothbard in his contribution to Mark Skousen, ed., *Dissent on Keynes* (New York: Praeger, 1992). See p. 184 of Skousen.

3   According to Harry Johnson, *The General Theory* gave "old concepts new and confusing names" and emphasized "as crucial analytical steps that" had "previously been taken as platitudinous." Elizabeth S. Johnson and Harry G. Johnson, eds., *The Shadow of Keynes* (Oxford: Basil Blackwell, 1978), p. 188.

4   Sir John Hicks, *Critical Essays in Monetary Theory* (Oxford: Clarendon Press, 1967), p. 189.

5   Ibid.

6   As Patinkin noted, the money holders' choice in *A Treatise on Money* was between bank deposits and "securities," whereas in *The General Theory* it was between money and bonds. Don Patinkin, *Keynes's Monetary Thought* (Durham, N.C.: Duke University Press, 1976), pp. 38–39.

7   The restriction of wealth to money and bonds continues to affect textbook writers to the present day. A standard text – *Macroeconomics*, by Dornbusch and Fischer – says, in a discussion of the demand for money, "The wealth budget constraint in the assets market states that the demand for real [money] balances . . . plus the demand for real bond holdings . . . must add up to the real financial wealth of the individual." So, "the decision to hold real money balances is also a decision to hold less real wealth in the form of bonds." Rudiger

Dornbusch and Stanley Fischer, *Macroeconomics* (New York: McGraw-Hill, 6th edition, 1994), p. 103. Surprisingly, the adoption of the limited definition of wealth follows shortly after an excellent account of real-world assets, which refers at length to equities and houses. Keynes's awareness that he spoke of "the rate of interest" in a dangerous way is evident in a footnote on p. 151 of *The General Theory*, in which he said that high stock-market valuations had the same stimulatory effect on investment as a low rate of interest.

8   The argument that an increase in "the quantity of money" reduces "the rate of interest" begs many questions, not least the meaning of the phrases "the quantity of money" and "the rate of interest." Keynes's analysis related to "the short period" (i.e., with the capital stock fixed) and assumed an economy in which the only non-money assets were bonds. But, as soon as one thinks of an economy with several types of assets, including equities, houses, and other forms of real estate, and in which agents look ahead over many periods, it is possible – as explained in the text – for an increase in the quantity of money to lead to *higher* inflation expectations, a *fall* in bond prices, and a *rise* in the rate of interest. Keynes's theory of the monetary determination of the rate of interest would then disintegrate. The point was also elaborated on pp. 47–51 of the author's *Money and Asset Prices in Boom and Bust* (London: Institute of Economic Affairs, 2005).

9   Leijonhufvud, *On Keynesian Economics*, p. 152.

10   Otmar Issing, *The Birth of the Euro* (Cambridge: Cambridge University Press, 2008), passim.

11   The quotation appeared in Don Bellante's contribution to Skousen, ed., *Dissent on Keynes*, p. 119.

ESSAY 3

1   Johnson and Moggridge, eds., *The Collected Writings*, vol. VII: *The General Theory of Employment, Interest, and Money*, p. 383.

2   V. H. Hewitt and J. M. Keyworth, *As Good as Gold: 300 Years of British Bank Note Design* (London: British Museum Publications, in association with the Bank of England, 1987), p. 27.

3   Charles A. E. Goodhart, *The Business of Banking, 1891–1914* (London: Weidenfeld and Nicolson, 1972), pp. 195–208.

4   Joseph A. Schumpeter, *History of Economic Analysis* (London: George Allen & Unwin, 1954), p. 256.

5   Henry Thornton, *An Inquiry into the Nature and Effects of the Paper Credit of Great Britain* (Fairfield, N.J.: Augustus M. Kelley, 1978; reprint of a 1939 edition published by George Allen & Unwin in London), p. 259.

6   I am not suggesting that Thornton was opposed to the gold standard. In fact, his 1811 contributions to two House of Commons debates show that he was strongly in favor of it. See *Paper Credit*, p. 346. I am claiming only that his writings hinted at the possibility of a different approach.

7   Johnson and Moggridge, eds., *The Collected Writings*, vol. IV, *A Tract on Monetary Reform*, p. 136.

8   Ibid., pp. 126–127 and p. 140.

9   Ibid., pp. 141–142.

10   Ibid., pp. 142–145.

11   I discussed some of the definitional problems in my contribution, "British and American Monetarism Compared," pp. 38–72, in Roger Hill, ed., *Keynes, Money, and Monetarism* (London and Basingstoke: Macmillan, 1989). (That paper is reprinted in this volume as essay 13.)

12   Lord Kahn, *On Re-reading Keynes* (London: Oxford University Press for the British Academy, 1975), pp. 22–23.

13   Johnson and Moggridge, eds., *The Collected Writings*, vol. VII, *The General Theory*, p. 378.

14   Wilfred Beckerman, ed., *The Labour Government's Economic Record: 1964–70* (London: Duckworth, 1972), pp. 340–341.

15   Francis Cripps and M. Fetherston, "The Role of Monetary Policy in Economic Management," in *Economic Policy Review* (Cambridge: University of Cambridge, Department of Applied Economics, March 1977), p. 54. The Department of Applied Economics lost its separate identity and was merged into the Faculty of Economics in 2003.

16   Tim Congdon, *Monetarism: An Essay in Definition* (London: Centre for Policy Studies, 1978), pp. 11–13. See also chapter 6, "How Friedman Came to Britain," pp. 172–202, of Wayne Parsons, *The Power of the Financial Press* (Aldershot: Edward Elgar, 1989).

17   See my pamphlet *Monetarism Lost* (London: Centre for Policy Studies, 1989), for a more detailed description of the evolution of monetary policy in the 1980s.

18   Johnson and Moggridge, eds., *The Collected Writings*, vol. IV, *Tract*, pp. 145–146.

19   Ibid., pp. 153–154. The Bank of England stopped preparing the M0 data in May 2006, on the grounds that reforms to its money-market management – notably the payment of interest on banks' reserve balances held with it – would render the M0 aggregate difficult to interpret. Data continue to be published on the components of M0, including the note holdings of the non-bank public, to which some economists once attached great macroeconomic significance. (See footnote 44 to essay 16 on the importance of the monetary base in the work of the Chicago economist Eugene Fama, and the role this had in Patrick Minford's thinking.) Whatever the reputed importance of the M0 aggregate, interest in narrow money has evaporated in the U.K. since the Bank's discontinuance of the numbers.

20   Alan Walters, *Britain's Economic Renaissance* (New York: Oxford University Press, 1986), pp. 116–117.

21   This is a reference to Sir John Hicks's famous paper "A Suggestion for Simplifying the Theory of Money," written before Keynes's *General Theory*.

22   Milton Friedman's "The Quantity Theory of Money: A Restatement," a paper originally published in 1956, said that "the demand for money is a special topic in the theory of capital." It was the theoretical launching-pad of the so-called "monetarist counterrevolution."

23   Professor Patrick Minford of Liverpool University argued late into the boom that the slow growth of M0 presaged an early return to 3 percent inflation. This was not the first time that Minford had been disastrously wrong by using M0 for forecasting purposes. He warned in late 1985 that, because of slow M0 growth, "we now have the tightest monetary policy we have ever had," and he maintained that "a stalling in the growth rate, unless immediate action is taken to reduce interest rates, is now increasingly likely." See p. 45 of Jock Bruce-Gardyne et al., *Whither Monetarism?* (London: Centre for Policy Studies, 1985). These remarks were made on the eve of the strongest boom in fifteen years.

24   According to one former civil servant, even Mr. Denis Healey, who as chancellor of the exchequer had made the announcement that introduced broad-money targets, did not really believe in them. "To ascribe paternity for the MTFS to Denis Healey seems to me to be going too far. He was described at the time as an unbelieving monetarist, meaning that he adopted monetary targets only with a view to inspiring confidence in the financial world, which did believe in them." Leo Pliatzky, *The Treasury under Mrs. Thatcher* (Oxford: Basil Blackwell, 1989), p. 122.

25   In any case, other European countries did not suffer the illusion that full membership in the EMS specified a complete anti-inflationary policy. They also used domestic financial targets stated in terms of credit and/or broad money. It was British economic policy-makers and their advisers who, in their regard for narrow money, had become idiosyncratic. As noted above in footnote 19, the Bank of England stopped publishing data on M0 in early 2006.

ESSAY 4

1   Paul Krugman, *The Return of Depression Economics* (London: Allen Lane, The Penguin Press, 1999), p. 73.

2   The quotation is from the second edition, titled "Deflation: Its Causes and Effects," of a paper titled "Remarks by Governor Ben S. Bernanke: Deflation: Making Sure 'It' Doesn't Happen Here," given on November 21, 2002, before the National Economists Club in Washington, D.C.

3   Johan van Overtveldt, *Bernanke's Test* (Chicago: Agate, 2009), p. 152.

4   Bernanke proposed the notion of "creditism" in a joint article with Alan Blinder in 1988. Ben S. Bernanke and Alan S. Blinder, "Credit, Money, and Aggregate Demand," *The American Economic Review*, vol. 78, no. 2, pp. 435–439.

5   Paul Krugman, *The Return of Depression Economics and the Crisis of 2008* (New York: W. W. Norton & Company, 2009), p. 180.

6   In the real world the boundary between short- and long-dated debt is a matter of convention and varies among countries, but the position of the boundary has

no fundamental bearing on the analysis. In the U.K. long-dated debt has a residual maturity of over fifteen years. In most other countries the boundary is much lower than this; in some countries, it is five years.

7   Central-bank payments of interest on banks' cash reserves have become more common in recent years. For example, the European Central Bank has paid interest on member banks' cash reserves from the start of the single European currency. But in the past, central banks did not pay banks interest on their deposits, just as they did not pay interest on their note liabilities.

8   One reason that governments do not have large deposits with commercial banks is that they would normally receive a lower rate of interest on such deposits than they pay on their debt. Debt-interest costs are minimized by consolidating the government's money flows into one account at the central bank.

9   Commercial banks' operational deposits with the Bank of England were included in the U.K.'s M0 measure of money when it was instituted in the 1980s. To say that operational deposits *by themselves* have no effect on the expenditure behavior of either banks or non-banks is not to deny that the operational deposits have some effect on banks' attitude towards expanding (or contracting) their earning assets. Of course, expansions or contractions of banks' earning assets do alter the quantity of money, as normally defined. But the further (and macroeconomically interesting) effects of any resulting changes in the quantity of money on expenditure stem from non-banks' response to the quantity of money itself. It is therefore sufficient and correct to focus on the quantity of money as normally defined (i.e., non-banks' deposits with the banks), and to exclude banks' operational deposits with the central bank from any money measure. The U.K.'s practice with M0 was eccentric by international standards.

10 Tobin distinguished fiscal policy from monetary policy and debt management in his paper "The Principles of Debt Management," prepared for the Commission on Credit and Money in 1963. "To summarize, changes in the size of the debt are the province of fiscal policy. They have two effects on demand. One, the fiscal effect, is temporary. The other, the monetary effect, is permanent. The strength of the monetary effect depends on the composition of the change in debt. This is the province of the authorities in charge of monetary policy and debt management. Indeed, their province is wider. They are not confined to deciding the form of marginal changes in the debt. They can alter the composition of the whole debt whether it is changing in size or not." (James Tobin, *Essays in Economics*, vol. 1: *Macroeconomics* [Amsterdam and Oxford: North-Holland Publishing Company, 1971], p. 382. The quotation is from the paper "The Principles of Debt Management," pp. 378–455, originally published in 1963 as evidence to the Commission on Credit and Money.) Tobin evidently believed that changes in the composition of the national debt could alter macroeconomic outcomes. This view was widely abandoned after Robert J. Barro's neo-Ricardian critique of fiscal-policy activism in his article "Are

Government Bonds Net Wealth?' in the *Journal of Political Economy* (Chicago: University of Chicago), vol. 82, no. 6 (1974), pp. 1095–1117. If macroeconomic outcomes could not be affected by the *size* of the national debt (as Barro was thought to have demonstrated), then how could the *composition* of that debt affect them? The difficulty with the Barro article – and the related 1980 claim by Fama that banks' behavior is of no significance for the economy's general equilibrium – is that they rest on certain assumptions and rely on the empirical validity of these assumption for their cogency in real-world policy discussions. (Eugene Fama, "Banking in a Theory of Finance," *Journal of Monetary Economics*, vol. 6, no. 1 (1980), pp. 39–57.) At least two of these assumptions – the so-called "transversality condition" and the absence of transactions costs – are violated in real-world economies. The government does more or less meet the transversality condition – that over a broad range (say, from a public-debt-to-GDP ratio of zero to 100 percent) its creditworthiness is not affected by the scale of its debt – but no other agent does. Indeed, it may be the uniqueness of the government's compliance with the transversality condition that explains the important asymmetry noted in the text, i.e., that the size of the government's money holding does not affect its spending decisions, whereas the size of private-sector non-banks' money holdings does affect their spending decisions. The author owes this point to discussions with Charles Goodhart of the London School of Economics' Financial Markets Group.

11 Data from Bank of Japan's *Financial and Economic Statistics Monthly*, various issues.

12 Data from Federal Reserve website, as of March 24, 2003.

13 In the real world of early 2009 the most extreme exercise in money creation – the U.K.'s quantitative-easing program – was in fact carried out by the central bank, the Bank of England. Milton Friedman's key criticism of the original version of this paper was that it had overlooked that debt-market operations could be carried out by the central bank as well as the government. Friedman's point was correct, but the author continues to prefer that debt-market operations be the government's work, precisely because of the cleanness of the outcome. Large central-bank balance sheets are politically controversial and a nuisance.

14 The proposition that an increase in the quantity of money leads to (or, more mildly, is associated with) an increase in the equilibrium level of national income is not argued here. Except in the discussion of the liquidity trap, the proposition is assumed to be correct, in accordance with traditional macroeconomic theory. Traditional macroeconomic theory needs to be distinguished from modern neoclassical macroeconomics, in which changes in the composition of wealth and balance sheets can have no effect on behavior. (Modern neoclassical macroeconomics is associated with such names as Barro, Fama, Robert Lucas, and the Modigliani and Miller of the "MM theorem.") Implicitly, a "real balance effect" is assumed to be at work with a broad measure of money. Note that this real balance effect *cannot* in the context be a wealth effect. The

validity of the real balance effect must depend on an asymmetry of some sort. See footnote 10 above.

15   In the late 1980s the author criticized the British government for failing to neutralize, by the appropriate debt-market operations, the monetary effects of a boom in bank credit to the private sector. In his final Mansion House speech as chancellor of the exchequer in 1989, Mr. Nigel (now Lord) Lawson claimed that "any money drained out of the system by selling gilts over and above the Government's funding requirements, or by buying in fewer gilts than these requirements dictate, would simply have to be injected elsewhere." As explained by the author in the November 1989 issue of Gerrard & National's *Monthly Economic Review*, this statement was ambiguous. (It was probably wrong, but the issue depended on what exactly Lawson meant.)

16   In the U.K.'s quantitative-easing program, central-bank purchases of £200 billion of medium- and long-dated government bonds were associated with a small fall in the quantity of money, partly because banks simultaneously continued to shed risk assets (such as loans to the private sector) and partly because they also issued huge quantities of equity and bond capital in order to raise capital/asset ratios. The effect of the capital raising was that non-banks' deposit claims on the banks (i.e., money) became non-deposit claims on the banks instead. Nevertheless, the QE exercise saw a dramatic rebound in the economy, perhaps because key private-sector agents had confidence that the authorities had a powerful enough weapon to stop a deep recession.

17   The original version of this paper appeared in Lombard Street Research's *Monthly Economic Review*s for March and April 2003. In the original version I wrongly suggested – or rather proposed as part of a definition – that debt-market operations could be conducted only by the government. I therefore went on to say that the Bank of Japan was not alone responsible for Japan's macroeconomic doldrums. In separate comments, Milton Friedman and Allan Meltzer objected that the central bank could purchase assets *from non-banks*. (See also footnote 13 above.) If such purchases were financed by the issue of cash reserves to the banks, the effect on the quantity of money would be the same as that of government asset purchases financed from the central bank. The author is most grateful to Friedman and Meltzer for this correction, which necessitated rewriting the paper. He would also like to mention that his distinction between two types of liquidity trap is far from exhausting the ambiguity of this notion, with a brilliant 1968 paper by Brunner and Meltzer identifying traps that are "said to affect interest rates, the banks' demand for excess reserves, the public's supply of loans to commercial banks, and the public's demand for money." (Karl Brunner and Allan Meltzer, "Liquidity Traps for Money, Bank Credit, and Interest Rates," *Journal of Political Economy*, vol. 76 [Chicago: University of Chicago Press, 1968], pp. 1–37. The quotation is from p. 2.) My "narrow liquidity trap" has some similarities to Hawtrey's "credit deadlock," which developed in debates between Hawtrey and Keynes in the 1930s. For further

discussion, see Roger Sandilands, "Hawtreyan 'Credit Deadlock' or Keynesian 'Liquidity Trap'?: Lessons for Japan from the Great Depression," in Robert Leeson, ed., *Scholarship and Stability: Essays in Honour of David Laidler's Contribution to Macroeconomics* (London: Palgrave Macmillan, 2010), pp. 329–365.

18   This policy was advocated by the author in an article titled "What Is to Be Done about Japan's Financial Crisis?" in the May 2002 issue of *Central Banking* (London: Central Banking Publications), pp. 67–72. Much the same proposal was made by Keynes in a letter to "Mr. President" (i.e., Roosevelt) in *The New York Times* on December 31, 1933, although Keynes saw the key transactions as being registered on the central bank's balance sheet. In Keynes's words, "The turn of the tide in Great Britain is largely attributable to the reduction in the long-term rate of interest which ensued on the success of the conversion of the War Loan gilt issue. This was deliberately engineered by the open-market policy of the Bank of England. I see no reason why you should not reduce the rate of interest on your long-term government bonds to 2½ percent or less, with favourable repercussions on the whole bond market, if only the Federal Reserve would replace its present holdings of short-dated Treasury issues by purchasing long-dated issues in exchange. Such a policy might be effective in a few months, and I attach great importance to it." Johnson and Moggridge, eds., *The Collected Writings*, vol. XXI, *Activities 1931–39*, p. 297. See also the same sentiment (on p. 303 of the same volume of Keynes's *Collected Writings*) in an article in *The Times* of London a few days later.

19   Governments often establish debt-management agencies whose officials become concerned that a particularly large national debt may increase "refinancing risk" if it is financed to a considerable extent at the short end. Refinancing may have to be at a higher real interest rate, with effects on the tax burden. An implication is that the maturity profile, as well the total quantity, of public debt is important for public policy. (See pp. 151–154 of Alessandro Missale, *Public Debt Management* [Oxford: Oxford University Press, 1999].) But interest payments on public debt are to a considerable extent transfers among the citizens of the same nation. The larger issue here is the extent to which the minimization of debt interest (a valid objective of public policy) conflicts with monetary stability (also a valid objective of public policy). Note also that the comment in the text – that debt-market operations *by the government* do not affect the size of the public debt and hence the government's creditworthiness – would be less persuasive if such operations were carried out *by the central bank*. The central bank could be left with large holdings of long-dated government securities after purchasing them and could incur accounting losses if yields rose subsequently.

20   Krugman has favored deliberate inflation in Japan, in order to reduce the real return on financial assets and so to encourage demand for goods and services. (Krugman, *Return*, pp. 78–79.)

21 The realization that aggressive purchases of long-dated bonds by the central
    bank might lead to heavy losses is not new. As Leijonhufvud remarked in his
    On Keynesian Economics and the Economics of Keynes, a central bank following
    Keynes's principles "will have to engage in quite large operations, buying and
    selling low, in order to vanquish first the bears and then the bulls. Conse-
    quently, it will take large losses" (p. 349). Keynes mentioned in *A Treatise on
    Money* that a central bank acting in the way he recommended would have
    losses, but he did not develop the point. As noted in the text, members of any
    country's political elite might condemn a central bank for losses due to its
    excessive bond holdings, even though the nation has no resource loss from the
    relevant transactions. Before making large purchases of government securities
    in its so-called "quantitative easing experiment" from March 2009 to February
    2010, the Bank of England sought and obtained an indemnity from the Treas-
    ury for any accounting losses on the securities bought. Even when debt-market
    operations are conducted by the central bank, cooperation with the govern-
    ment seems essential. For the author's exchanges with Friedman and Meltzer
    on this subject, see footnotes 13 and 17 above.

22 *Report of the Committee on the Working of the Monetary System* (chaired by
    Lord Radcliffe), Cmnd. 827, para. 603, p. 224 (London: Her Majesty's Stationery
    Office, August 1959).

23 Tobin, *Essays in Economics*, vol. 1, p. 383.

24 For an example of a detailed policy prescription on these lines, see Lars E. O.
    Svensson, "Monetary Policy and Real Stabilization," National Bureau of Eco-
    nomic Research, Working Paper no. 9486 (Cambridge, Mass.: NBER, February
    2003). Monetary policy is taken to have only one instrument, which Svensson
    calls "the instrument rate," set by the central bank. This is said to be "the short
    nominal interest rate," which is linked to other interest rates because of market
    expectations. "Thus, the lowering of the instrument rate normally affects the
    short and longer real interest rates, which will affect economic activity" (p. 2).
    A number of effects follow, such as that of interest rates on the exchange rate
    and so on economic activity. But there is no role for money. The notion that
    changes in national income may be a response to agents' attempts to equilibrate
    the demand for and supply of money is simply not noticed, let alone discussed.
    Monetary policy is 100 percent about money-market operations and the setting
    of the very-short-term interest rate. By assumption, there is no room for debt-
    market operations. The *locus classicus* of the whole approach is Michael Wood-
    ford's *Interest and Prices* (Princeton and Oxford: Princeton University Press,
    2003). The Woodford-Svensson view of the subject is widely held in modern
    central-banking circles. In the author's judgment this mistaken set of ideas goes
    a long way to explain the policy inertia in Japan in the last fifteen years and the
    more general failure of macroeconomic policy to avert the Great Recession. See
    also Professor Goodhart's 2002 Wincott Lecture on "The Constitutional Posi-
    tion of the Central Bank," in Milton Friedman and Charles A. E. Goodhart,

Money, Inflation, and the Constitutional Position of the Central Bank (London: Institute of Economic Affairs, 2003), pp. 91–109. In the lecture, Goodhart discussed the case for an independent (i.e., non-political) agency for fiscal policy, analogous to the independent central bank responsible for monetary policy. He said nothing about the location of responsibility for debt management, which traditionally in the U.K. was a job for the central bank, but which was transferred to a Treasury agency, the Debt Management Office, in 1997. More recently, Goodhart has advocated the closure of the DMO and the return of responsibility for debt management to the Bank of England. The DMO has never had much expertise or interest in monetary policy issues.

25　Leijonhufvud, *On Keynesian Economics*, p. 142.

26　See, for example, Keynes's review of Hawtrey's *Currency and Credit* in 1920 and his exchange with Edwin Cannan in 1924. Johnson and Moggridge, eds., *The Collected Writings*, vol. XI, *Economic Articles and Correspondence: Academic*, pp. 411–414 and pp. 415–419.

27　Ibid., vol. V, *A Treatise on Money: 1. The Pure Theory of Money*, p. 5.

28　Ibid., vol. VII, *The General Theory*, p. 167.

29　Ibid., pp. 198–199. The sentence is quite difficult, but its meaning is clear. If the banking system were not prepared to change its holdings of bonds at all in response to a change in the price, its cash reserves could not be altered by the monetary authorities, and open-market operations would be impracticable.

30　If Keynes meant "the central bank" when he used the phrase "the banking system," then he did have a narrow liquidity trap in *The General Theory*. Keynes's use of words was unclear. He may have thought more exact phraseology was unnecessary because the central bank could be taken as representative of the whole banking system. If the ratio of the monetary base to bank deposits were stable, this attitude would indeed have been fairly harmless. In chapter 25 of *A Treatise on Money* Keynes reviewed the data on banks' cash-reserve ratios in the U.K., the U.S., and elsewhere. His general conclusion was that the ratios changed, but not very much, and that the central bank ought therefore to be able to control the level of "bank money," even if such money was a liability of the commercial banks rather than the central bank. In the Great Depression in the U.S. – as in modern Japan – the ratio of base money to the quantity of money rose sharply. So the behavior of the central bank's balance sheet was different from that of the commercial banks' balance sheets, and Keynes's assumption was not harmless.

31　Johnson and Moggridge, eds., *The Collected Writings*, vol. VII, *The General Theory*, pp. 266–268.

32　For a discussion of money transfers in a wider argument that broad money, not narrow money, has a causal role in portfolio-management and expenditure decisions, see Tim Congdon, "Broad Money vs. Narrow Money," in *The Review of Policy Issues*, vol. 1, no. 5 (Sheffield: Policy Research Centre, Sheffield Science Park, Autumn 1995), pp. 13–27.

33 Johnson and Moggridge, eds., *The Collected Writings*, vol. VI, *A Treatise on Money*, p. 347. Monetary policy *à outrance* was defined as, in addition to "a very low level of the short-term rate of interest," the purchase of "long-dated securities either against an expansion of central bank money or against the sale of short-dated securities." If the purchase of the long-dated securities was "against an expansion of central bank money," the transactions would be a money-market operation, according to the distinction introduced in this essay; if the purchase was "against the sale of short-dated securities" *by the government*, it would be a debt-management operation. But Keynes did not add the phrase "by the government." Conceivably, short-dated securities could be issued – in his day or now – *by the central bank*, in which case the transactions would again be a money-market operation.

34 Johnson and Moggridge, eds., *The Collected Writings*, vol. VII, *The General Theory*, p. 206.

35 Ibid.

36 Ibid., pp. 167–169.

37 Ibid., p. 201.

38 Krugman's website addresses were web.mit.edu/krugman/www/ and www.wws.princeton.edu/ispkrugman/. As of September 2009, Krugman's official website continued to be accessed via www.mit.edu, although it opened with a promise that in due course all files would be moved to the Princeton-based website.

39 Krugman, *Return of Depression Economics*, p. 78.

40 The quotation is from section 3 of the May 1998 paper on Krugman's MIT website. Krugman's comments were surprising in two respects. First, he envisaged "zero-interest bonds." But it is obvious that no such bonds have been, or ever would be, issued. Further, the value of a bond with an interest coupon of any kind, even a very-low-interest coupon, would rise towards infinity as the yield approached zero and would deliver massive capital gains. Second, the whole point about the liquidity trap is that, as the quantity of money increases, no substitution into bonds occurs. What Krugman must have meant is that, as the quantity of money increases, wealth holders restrict their investment purchases to very-short-dated securities, such as Treasury bills, the yield of which falls to negligible levels. There is some justification for this in Keynes's suggestion (on p. 167 of *The General Theory*) that Treasury bills might sometimes be included in measures of "money." (They could certainly be included in measures of "liquidity.")

41 See section 5 of the May 1998 paper.

42 See Allan Meltzer, "The Transmission Mechanism," Carnegie-Mellon University and American Enterprise Institute, mimeo. The paper was published in *The World Economy* and is available on the web at www.gsia.cmu.edu/afs/andrew/gsia/meltzer/transmission.pdf.

43 Krugman's argument was developed in the section "The Open Economy" in a November 1998 paper on the MIT website titled "Japan: Still Trapped." The

idea was also mentioned on pp. 80–81 of *The Return of Depression Economics*, but in the book he buttressed the argument by referring to the build-up of income on Japan's foreign assets.

44   In his essay "The Principles of Debt Management," Tobin complained that Keynes had not included equities in his economy. The essay was concerned about the relationship between debt management and bond yields, and then between bond and equity yields, in the belief that equity yields had an effect on investment. Tobin believed that stimulatory debt management – such as purchases of long-dated bonds by the government – would lower equity yields, and so boost corporate investment and demand. Again, the conclusions reached by an economic analysis depended on the structure of aggregation.

45   Johnson and Moggridge, eds., *The Collected Writings*, vol. VII, *The General Theory*, p. 207.

46   Bernanke co-authored an article with Mark Gertler describing the relationship between money and the economy as "a black box." Ben S. Bernanke and Mark L. Gertler, "Inside the Black Box: The Credit Channel of Monetary Policy Transmission," *The Journal of Economic Perspectives*, vol. 9, no. 4 (Autumn 1995), pp. 27–48.

47   Krugman, *Return of Depression Economics*, pp. 187–188.

48   See the section on "Curing Deflation" in Bernanke's "Remarks" of November 21, 2002.

49   The Federal Reserve is owned by its member banks, not by the U.S. government. It is nevertheless obliged to return profits above operating expenses to the U.S. Treasury. The possibility of losses on securities held by the Fed did exercise those responsible for its creation in 1913, although this had been more or less forgotten subsequently – until the Fed's huge asset purchases starting in 2008.

50   The author does not want to deny the potential efficiency of government transactions in real assets as a policy instrument. (In fact, in evidence to the Treasury Committee of the House of Commons in early 2000, he suggested that one kind of open-market operation would be for the government to offer everyone £1,000 for their scruffiest pair of shoes. This idea has slightly more empirical plausibility than Friedman's helicopter drop. The evidence was reprinted as a research paper in the February 2000 issue of Lombard Street Research's *Monthly Economic Review*.) The trouble with purchases of real assets is twofold. First, they lead to profits and losses, and so are liable to be politically controversial. Second, the transactions are bound to affect some groups favorably and others unfavorably, again causing controversy. Note that massive purchases of gold and silver *by the U.S. government* (not the Federal Reserve) in 1933 and 1934 were crucial to the United States' recovery from the Great Depression. In line with the terminology of this essay, they might be described as stimulatory *real-asset market operations*. The U.S. government sold debt, largely to the banks, to finance its purchases of gold and silver. So money was created to acquire real assets.

51 Is the trouble that a media hullabaloo starts up at the mere mention of "print-ing money"? The phrase "creating money" may be less objectionable. Of course in a fiat-money economy of the modern type no money has commodity backing.

52 In the nineteenth century economics students were warned about the infla-tionary risks of inconvertible paper currency by the story of the *assignats* in revolutionary France, told in chapter 13 of book III of John Stuart Mill's *Prin-ciples of Political Economy*.

53 See the opening two papers in Rudiger Dornbusch and Mario Draghi, eds., *Public Debt Management: Theory and History* (Cambridge: Cambridge Univer-sity Press, 1990) for an example of treatments of the subject that wholly neg-lect the monetary consequences of different patterns of public debt financing.

PART TWO

PREFACE

1 I have to admit that I owe the information in this paragraph to Wikipedia.

2 Herbert Stein, *The Fiscal Revolution in America* (Chicago and London: Univer-sity of Chicago Press, 1969), p. 298.

ESSAY 5

1 J. C. R. (Christopher) Dow, *The Management of the British Economy 1945–60* (Cambridge: Cambridge University Press, 1964), p. 178.

2 Stein, *Fiscal Revolution*, p. 165.

3 Part of the explanation for the differences between Keynes and the Keynesians is to be sought in the complexity and obscurity of *The General Theory*. (See essay 2.) For example, while there can be little doubt that Keynes wished to promote fiscal policy relative to monetary policy, *The General Theory* says almost nothing about how exactly fiscal policy should be conducted. The American economist Abba Lerner tried to formalize the fiscal prescriptions implicit in *The General Theory* in his idea of "functional finance" (that is, to run a deficit in a downturn and a surplus in a boom). But Keynes was critical of Lerner's proposals, asserting that functional finance "runs directly contrary to men's natural instincts . . . about what is sensible." Robert Skidelsky, *John May-nard Keynes*, vol. 3, *Fighting for Britain 1937–46*, p. 276.

4 E. E. B. (Lord) Bridges, *The Treasury* (London: George Allen & Unwin, and New York: Oxford University Press, 1964), p. 90.

5 "The Economy Report" and "The Economy Bill," in Johnson and Moggridge, eds., *The Collected Writings*, vol. IX, *Essays in Persuasion* (London and Basing -stoke: Macmillan, 1972, originally published in 1931), pp. 101–105 and pp. 145–149, originally based on articles published in *New Statesman and Nation* on August 15 and September 19, 1931.

6 B. E. V. Sabine, *British Budgets in Peace and War* (London: Allen & Unwin, 1970), p. 300.

7   Ibid.

8   Dow, *Management of the British Economy*, p. 198.

9   White Paper on Employment Policy (London: HMSO, 1944), pp. 25–26, paragraphs 77–79.

10   Bridges, *The Treasury*, pp. 93–94. The quotation is from p. 93.

11   Dow, *Management of the British Economy*, p. 198.

12   Ian M. D. Little, "Fiscal Policy," in G. David N. Worswick and Peta D. Ady, eds., *The British Economy in the Nineteen-Fifties* (Oxford: Oxford University Press, 1962), chapter 8, pp. 231–291. The quotation is from p. 251.

13   Dow, *Management of the British Economy*, p. 161.

14   Little in Worswick and Ady, eds,, *British Economy in the Nineteen-Fifties*, p. 275.

15   Dow, *Management of the British Economy*, pp. 183–188. The quotations are from p. 183 and p. 187 respectively.

16   Sir Herbert Brittain, *The British Budgetary System* (London: George Allen & Unwin, 1959), pp. 53–54. Brittain and Keynes clashed at meetings held in the Treasury in 1945 to prepare papers for the National Debt Enquiry. According to George C. Peden (citing James Meade's papers, collected by Mrs. Elizabeth Johnson and Donald Moggridge), Keynes told Brittain to his face that he was "intellectually contemptible." As Peden notes, the sinking fund for national debt – of which Brittain was apparently a defender – was not phased out until 1954, and the above-the-line/below-the-line distinction survived until the publication of an official paper titled *Reform of the Exchequer Accounts* (Cmnd. 21014) in 1962. (See George C. Peden, *Keynes and His Critics: Treasury Responses to the Keynesian Revolution 1925–46* [Oxford and New York: Oxford University Press for the British Academy, 2004], p. 12, p. 331, and pp. 349–350.) Peden also emphasizes in his book on the Treasury the durability of a doctrine introduced by Asquith in 1906 and 1907, that the only investments which should be financed by borrowing were those which were expected to produce a money return, and which would not rely on future taxation for the servicing of the borrowing involved. (George C. Peden, *The Treasury and British Public Policy 1906–59* [Oxford: Oxford University Press, 2000], p. 39.) Jim Tomlinson has said that in the 1950s "day-to-day discussion of economic issues in government departments" was "notable for extraordinary crudity." (Jim Tomlinson, *Public Policy and the Economy* [Oxford: Clarendon Press, 1990], p. 256.)

17   Brittain, *British Budgetary System*, p. 56.

18   Ibid., p. 43.

19   Robin C. O. Matthews, "Why Has Britain Had Full Employment since the War?" *Economic Journal*, vol. 78 (September 1968), pp. 555–569. The quotation is from p. 556.

20   B. Hansen, *Fiscal Policy in Seven Countries 1955–65* (Paris: Organization for Economic Cooperation and Development, 1969).

21   Samuel Brittan, *Steering the Economy* (Harmondsworth: Penguin, 1971), p. 455.

22   Dow, *Management of the British Economy*, p. 384.

23 Samuel Brittan, *The Price of Economic Freedom* (London: Macmillan, 1970).

24 Wilfred Beckerman, ed., *The Labour Government's Economic Record 1964-70* (London: Duckworth, 1972), p. 25.

25 Denis Healey, *The Time of My Life* (London: Michael Joseph, 1989), p. 380.

26 Ibid., p. 382.

27 Ibid., p. 383.

28 See the papers "Monetarism and the Budget Deficit" and "The Analytical Foundations of the Medium-Term Financial Strategy" in Tim Congdon, *Reflections on Monetarism* (Aldershot, U.K., and Brookfield, Vt.: Edward Elgar for the Institute of Economic Affairs, 1992), pp. 38–48 and pp. 65–77. A growing interest in a medium-term perspective can also be noticed in Alan Budd, "Economic Policy and the Medium Term," in G. David N. Worswick and Frank T. Blackaby, eds., *The Medium Term: Models of the British Economy* (London: Heinemann, 1974), pp. 133–142.

29 See "How Friedman Came to Britain," in D.W. Parsons, *The Power of the Financial Press* (Aldershot: Edward Elgar, 1989), chapter 6, pp. 172–202.

30 R.J. Ball, *Money and Employment* (London and Basingstoke: Macmillan, 1982), p. 209 and pp. 232–234.

31 See the paper "The Relationship between Fiscal and Monetary Policy in the London Business School Model," by Alan P. Budd and Terence Burns, in Michael J. Artis and Marcus H. Miller, eds., *Essays in Fiscal and Monetary Policy* (Oxford: Oxford University Press, 1981), pp. 136–163. The quotations are from p. 136.

32 See "Implementation and Results of the Strategy," in Geoffrey Maynard, *The Economy under Mrs. Thatcher* (Oxford: Basil Blackwell, 1988), chapter 4, pp. 58–92. But the claim on p. 65 that the MTFS had as its "stated objective" a "progressive . . . return to budget balance" is not correct. The balanced-budget goal surfaced in official statements much later, in 1988.

33 Maynard, *Economy under Mrs. Thatcher*, p. 66.

34 The quotation is from p. 56 of M. Friedman, "Response to Questionnaire on Monetary Policy," in the House of Commons Treasury and Civil Service Committee (Session 1979–80), *Memoranda on Monetary Policy* (London: HM Stationery Office, 1980), pp. 55–62. As explained in footnote 11 to the introduction to his 2007 book *Keynes, the Keynesians, and Monetarism*, the author disagrees with Friedman's views on public finance.

35 HM Treasury, *The Next Ten Years: Public Expenditure and Taxation into the 1990s*, Cmnd. 9189 (London: HMSO, 1984).

36 Nigel Lawson, *The View from No. 11* (London and elsewhere: Bantam Press, 1992), p. 812.

37 A. Budd and G. Dicks, "A Strategy for Stable Prices," *Economic Outlook* (Aldershot: Gower Publishing for the London Business School, July 1983), pp. 18–23.

38 Lawson, *View from No. 11*, p. 811.

39 Sir Terence Burns, *Managing the Nation's Economy – The Conduct of Monetary*

and Fiscal Policy, given as the South Bank Business School annual lecture (London: HM Treasury, 1996), p. 5. Burns's 1995 lecture – in which interest rates and fiscal policy were taken to be independent instruments – was a long way from his London Business School papers of the late 1970s, in which the interdependence of fiscal and monetary policies had been emphasized.

40 "[T]here are very few practitioners who would argue that fiscal policy has no role to play at all in influencing demand. . . ." Burns, *Managing the Nation's Economy*, p. 5.

41 See, for example, Susan Howson, ed., *The Collected Papers of James Meade*, vol. 1, *Employment and Inflation* (London: Unwin Hyman, 1988), pp. 6–25, "Public Works in Their International Aspect," originally published in 1933.

42 Andrew Britton, *Macroeconomic Policy in Britain* (Cambridge: Cambridge University Press for the National Institute of Economic and Social Research, 1991), p. 215. But note Britton's warning on p. 217 that the cyclically adjusted public-sector financial deficits "do not identify policy acts, that is deliberate choices by government as distinct from the passive response of the system to events."

43 Frank W. Paish, *Studies in an Inflationary Economy* (London: Macmillan, 1962), p. 327.

44 For the introduction of the concept of the output gap, see essay 6. In the late 1980s and early 1990s the Organization for Economic Cooperation and Development in Paris devoted some effort to preparing historical estimates of these gaps in its member nations. See Claude Giorno et al., "Potential Output, Output Gaps, and Structural Budget Balances," *Economic Studies*, no. 24 (Paris: OECD, 1995).

ESSAY 6

1 In chapter 20 of *The General Theory* Keynes discussed the responsiveness of employment to demand and, in particular, proposed the notion of elasticity of output with respect to the number of wage-units (i.e., employment, if wages per worker were constant). He said that "ordinarily" the elasticity of output in this sense "will have a value intermediate between zero and unity." (See Johnson and Moggridge, eds., *The Collected Writings*, vol. VII, *The General Theory*, p. 284.)

2 Paish, *Studies*, pp. 310–311.

3 Ibid., p. 312.

4 Ibid., p. 319.

5 Ibid., p. 327.

6 The "New Economics" of the early 1960s was motivated partly by a view that high demand pressure would boost the United States' trend growth rate as well as eliminate the cyclical waste of resources. According to Walter Heller, "Gone is the countercyclical syndrome of the 1950s. Policy now centers on gap closing and growth, on realizing and enlarging the nation's non-inflationary potential." (Walter Heller, *New Dimensions of Political Economy* [Cambridge, Mass.: Harvard University Press, 1966], pp. vii–viii.)

7   Arthur Okun's paper "Potential GNP: Its Measurement and Significance" appeared in the American Statistical Association's 1962 *Proceedings of the Business and Economics Statistics Section* (Washington, D.C.: American Statistical Association), pp. 98–103. It was reprinted in Joseph A. Pechman, ed., *Economics for Policymaking: Selected Essays of Arthur M. Okun* (Cambridge, Mass.: MIT Press, 1983), pp. 145–158. The two sections quoted in the text appeared on p. 146 and p. 147 of the Pechman volume.

8   Indeed, Okun himself noted the skimpiness of attempts to justify the 4 percent figure. Ibid., p. 146. The point may seem trivial, but it has some importance in the development of ideas and, in particular, in casting doubt on Perloff and Wachter's claims that their 1979 paper was in the Okun tradition.

9   See pp. 426–429 of Richard Parker, *John Kenneth Galbraith: His Life, His Politics, His Economics* (New York: Farrar, Straus and Giroux, 2005), for a discussion of how the "New Economists" saw their work in the 1960s. Apparently, in a retrospective appraisal of the effects of the 1964 tax cut, Okun was "troubled" by some of his earlier conclusions and "worried privately whether he'd accounted for the effect of monetary policy" (p. 428). Indeed, "Having assumed an invariant 1.5 percent inflation rate following the tax cut, Okun's model surprised him when inflation burst upward soon after" (p. 429).

10 The period under discussion in Okun's 1962 paper was from 1947 to 1962. The unemployment rate was beneath 4 percent in 1948 and for a subsequent period of almost two years, from January 1951 to November 1953. It recorded a trough of 2.5 percent in mid-1953. But Okun did *not* in his 1962 paper allow these periods of very low unemployment to justify a bi-directional gap concept, with negative values of the gap for "over-full employment."

11 Arthur Okun's paper "The Gap between Actual and Potential Output," in Arthur Okun, ed., *The Battle against Unemployment* (New York: W. W. Norton & Co., 1965), pp. 13–22, was based on his 1962 paper in the American Statistical Association's *Proceedings*. But – as shown by the quotation here, which is from p. 22 of the later paper – the 1965 version was more explicitly a charter for expansion. The Tobin quotation is from p. 154 of the same book, in his paper (pp. 153–159) on "The Tax-Cut Harvest."

12 Johnson and Moggridge, eds., *The Collected Writings*, vol. VII, *The General Theory*, p. 303.

13 Ibid., p. 291.

14 John A. Tatom, "Economic Growth and Unemployment: A Reappraisal of the Conventional View," *Federal Reserve Bank of St. Louis Review* (St. Louis: Federal Reserve Bank of St. Louis), October 1978, pp. 16–22. The phrase "output gap" is used on p. 19.

15 The two celebrated papers were Edmund S. Phelps, "Phillips Curves, Expectations of Inflation, and Optimal Unemployment over Time," *Economica*, vol. 34 (August 1967), and Milton Friedman, "The Role of Monetary Policy," *The American Economic Review*, vol. 58, no. 1 (March 1968). The Friedman article

was the presidential address to the 80th annual meeting of the AEA and was given on December 29, 1967.

16 George L. Perry, "Potential Output and Productivity," *Brookings Papers in Economic Activity* (Washington, D.C.: Brookings Institution, 1977), pp. 11–47. Wachter's comment appeared on p. 52 of this publication.

17 Arthur M. Okun and George L. Perry, *Curing Chronic Inflation* (Washington, D.C.: Brookings Institution, 1978). The main policy message of the papers in the book was that tax-based incomes policy should be used to reduce the non-accelerating inflation rate of unemployment.

18 Jeffrey M. Perloff and Michael L. Wachter, "A Production Function–Non-accelerating Inflation Approach to Potential Output: Is Measured Potential Output Too High?" in Karl Brunner and Allan Meltzer, eds., *Three Aspects of Policy and Policymaking* (Amsterdam and New York: North-Holland Publishing Company, 1979), pp. 115–160. The quotation is from p. 131.

19 Ibid., p. 147.

20 Robert Gordon, "A Comment on the Perloff and Wachter Paper," in Brunner and Meltzer, eds., *Three Aspects*, pp. 187–194. Most of the quotations in the paragraph are from p. 187, but Gordon adopted the phrase "the natural rate of output" on p. 188. To quote, "It is by now well understood that the word 'natural' means equilibrium, in the sense of an absence of pressures for an acceleration or deceleration of inflation. . . . I will apply the short and simple phrase 'natural rate of output' to the real GNP series derived from the procedures Perloff and Wachter adopt. . . ." Friedman used the phrase "natural rate of unemployment" in his 1967 presidential address, but not the phrase "natural rate of output." Lucas had used the phrase "a natural output rate" in a 1972 paper. (See "Econometric Testing of the Natural Rate Hypothesis," pp. 90–103, in Robert Lucas, *Studies in Business-Cycle Theory* [Oxford: Basil Blackwell, 1981], originally published in 1972 in a volume from the Federal Reserve. The quotation is from p. 98.)

21 Charles I. Plosser and G. W. Schwert, "Potential GNP: Its Measurement and Significance," in Brunner and Meltzer, eds., *Three Aspects*, pp. 179–186. In his last book-length work, Okun accepted that his law had broken down. (Arthur Okun, *Prices and Quantities: A Macroeconomic Analysis* [Oxford: Basil Blackwell, 1981], p. 228.)

22 Perloff and Wachter did refer to one of Friedman's contributions, the address delivered in Stockholm in 1976 when he received the Nobel Prize, which was republished as "Inflation and Unemployment: The New Dimension of Politics," in Milton Friedman, *Monetarist Economics* (London: Basil Blackwell for the Institute of Economic Affairs, 1991), pp. 87–112.

23 Charles Adams, P. R. Fenton, and Flemming Larsen, "Potential Output in Major Industrial Countries," *Staff Studies for the World Economic Outlook* (Washington, D.C.: International Monetary Fund), August 1987, pp. 1–36.

24 Charles Adams and David T. Coe, "A Systems Approach to Estimating the Natural Rate of Unemployment and Potential Output for the United States," *IMF*

Staff Papers (Washington, D.C.: International Monetary Fund), June 1990. The paper had appeared in the IMF Working Papers series in October 1989.

25 Adams, Fenton, and Larsen, "Potential Output," p. 11.

26 Raymond Torres and John P. Martin, "Measuring Potential Output in the Seven Major OECD Countries," OECD Working Papers, no. 66 (Paris: Organization of Economic Cooperation and Development), May 1989.

27 See p. A74 of *OECD Economic Outlook* (Paris: Organization of Economic Cooperation and Development), June 1995, with a discussion of the data on "Supply Potential and Output Gaps." The table of output-gap estimates appeared on p. A14. The NAWRU in the quotation was "the non-accelerating wage rate of unemployment," which had been referred to on p. 6 of the May 1989 OECD Working Paper. The NAWRU may not be precisely a synonym for "the natural rate of unemployment," since Friedman intended that the natural rate be associated with stability of the rate of increase in *real* wages rather than in *nominal* wages, but in practice it comes to much the same thing. Torres and Martin made no reference to Friedman and his 1967 presidential address, but they did mention Okun's 1962 "seminal work."

28 But its definition is not always adhered to. In the spring of 1996 the Treasury Panel of Independent Forecasters in the U.K. prepared a report entitled *How Fast Can the Economy Grow?: A Special Report on the Output Gap.* (It was published by the Treasury in London on June 4, 1996.) On p. 5, the report noted, "There is no universal convention about the sign of the output gap, which itself can be a source of confusion. Here we take the output gap as positive when output is below potential, and negative when output is above potential." In other words, they followed the Perloff and Wachter approach in their 1979 paper rather than that of the OECD and IMF in these organizations' estimates in the late 1980s and early 1990s.

29 The idea of using business-survey results to draw conclusions, on a systematic basis, about the economy's position in the cycle must have occurred to many people in the 1960s and 1970s, and it may be impossible to identify the pioneers of the method. According to Norman Record, in the U.K. the CBI survey could and should have been used for cross-checking the output gap from the 1970s onwards. (Norman Record, "Stability, Growth, and the Output Gap," *The Business Economist* [Harrow: Society of Business Economists], vol. 35, no. 3 (2004), pp. 10–25. See, in particular, pp. 18–19.)

30 Arthur Burns and Wesley C. Mitchell, *Measuring Business Cycles* (New York: National Bureau of Economic Research, 1946).

31 The author, who has spent most of his career as an analyst in the City of London, proposed in a magazine article in 1983 that Friedman's accelerationist hypothesis in a labor market characterized by excess demand (i.e., unemployment beneath the natural rate) implied a decelerationist hypothesis in a labor market suffering from excess supply (i.e., unemployment above the natural rate). (Tim Congdon, "Following Friedman," *The Spectator*, May 28, 1983.) In

a research note for his brokerage firm (L. Messel & Co., "The Economy in the 1980s: Medium-Term Prospects for Output and Inflation," May 1983) he used this idea to forecast, correctly, that in the mid-1980s the U.K. economy *as a whole* could enjoy above-trend growth with continued low inflation. The generalization of the accelerationist and decelerationist hypotheses from the labor market to the entire economy was obvious, and at some point in the late 1980s the author started to use the phrase "output gap," without really being aware of the contemporaneous academic developments.

32   Under the leadership of Gavyn Davies (the partner responsible for international economic research), Goldman Sachs in particular devoted large resources in the 1990s to the calculation of both the output gap and leading-indicator indices.

33   John B. Taylor, "Discretion versus Policy Rules in Practice," Carnegie-Rochester Conference Series on Public Policy (Amsterdam: Elsevier Science Publishers, 1993), pp. 195–214.

34   Ibid., p. 202. Curiously, Taylor had used the phrase "the output gap" in a 1979 paper, although without development: "Staggered Wage Setting in a Macro Model," *The American Economic Review*, vol. 69, no. 2 (May 1979), pp. 108–113. The phrase appears on p. 111. The author owes this reference to Mr. Edward Nelson of the Federal Reserve.

35   For these papers, see John B. Taylor, ed., *Monetary Policy Rules* (Chicago and London: University of Chicago Press, 1999). For McCallum and Nelson's adherence to the natural-rate hypothesis, see their paper, Bennett T. McCallum and Edward Nelson, "Performance of Operational Policy Rules in an Estimated Semiclassical Structural Model," pp. 15–56, and particularly pp. 26–28. In their paper, "Policy Rules for Inflation Targeting" (pp. 203–246), Glenn D. Rudebusch and Lars E. O. Svensson say on p. 204 that the natural-rate hypothesis "is assumed."

36   Andrew Levin, Volker Wieland, and John C. Williams, "Robustness of Simple Policy Rules under Model Uncertainty," in Taylor, *Monetary Policy Rules*, pp. 263–299. The quotation is from p. 294.

37   Richard Clarida, Jordi Gali, and Mark Gertler, "The Science of Monetary Policy: A New Keynesian Perspective," *Journal of Economic Literature*, vol. 37 (December 1999), pp. 1661–1707. The quotation is from p. 1662.

38   For a sympathetic introduction to so-called "New Keynesianism," see Guido Zimmermann, "Optimal Monetary Policy: A New Keynesian View," *The Quarterly Journal of Austrian Economics*, vol. 6, no. 4 (Winter 2003), pp. 61–72.

39   Wendy Cornwall, "New Keynesian Economics," in J. E. King, ed., *The Elgar Companion to Post-Keynesian Economics* (Cheltenham, U.K., and Northampton, Mass.: Edward Elgar, 2003), pp. 275–280. The quotation is from p. 279.

40   See the introduction, pp. 1–11, to Marc Lavoie and Mario Seccareccia, eds., *Central Banking in the Modern World* (Cheltenham, U.K., and Northampton, Mass.: Edward Elgar, 2004). The quotation is from p. 4.

41 A debate has developed between monetary economists from the U.S. and the European Central Bank about the relative usefulness of the output-gap and money-supply data in the conduct of an inflation-targeting monetary policy. (See, for example, a box on p. 43 of the February 2005 issue of the *Monthly Bulletin* [Frankfurt: ECB] for a critique of the reliability of output-gap estimates.) But this debate does not imply that the estimation of output gaps and the monitoring of money-supply data are necessarily rivals in monetary policy-making.

42 Richard Layard, Stephen Nickell, and Richard Jackman, *Unemployment: Macroeconomic Performance and the Labour Market* (Oxford: Oxford University Press, 2005; reissue of first edition, published in 1991), pp. 489–490.

43 Athanasios Orphanides, "Activist Stabilization Policy and Inflation: The Taylor Rule in the 1970s," Centre for Financial Studies, Working Paper no. 2002/15 (Frankfurt am Main: Centre for Financial Studies, 2002). For the late 1970s, Orphanides mentions contemporary estimates of potential output in the 1977, 1978, and 1979 issues of the *Economic Report of the President*. From today's perspective those numbers appear much too high. But the *Economic Report of the President* estimates – prepared under the auspices of the Council of Economic Advisers, on which Okun had served – were still based on the Okun approach in the late 1970s. Orphanides does not cite the Perloff and Wachter paper.

44 Edward Nelson, "The Great Inflation of the Seventies: What Really Happened?" The Federal Reserve Bank of St. Louis Working Paper Series, no. 2004/01 (St. Louis: Federal Reserve Bank of St. Louis, 2004).

Essay 7

1 Sir Alan Budd, "The Quest for Stability," Julian Hodge Institute of Applied Macroeconomics annual lecture, Cardiff, given on April 25, 2002. (Printed as a pamphlet jointly by Cardiff Business School and Julian Hodge Bank.) The lecture was republished in the autumn 2002 issue of *World Economics*.

2 An official series for quarterly GDP is available only from 1955. A series was constructed using the industrial-production figures, and assuming that the difference in the volatility of GDP and industrial production in the 1945–55 period was the same as in the rest of the stop-go period.

3 See pp. 174–175 and footnotes 5, 6, and 8, below, for the belief that the first twenty-five years after the Second World War were unusually stable because of Keynesian policies.

4 Budd's emphasis on the continuity of policy from 1992 contrasts with claims of a sharp discontinuity in 1997 in *Reforming Britain's Economic and Financial Policy*, a collection of Treasury papers and speeches edited by Ed Balls and Gus O'Donnell. In the foreword to this book, Mr. Gordon Brown, the chancellor of the exchequer, wrote, "My first words from the Treasury . . . were to reaffirm for this government our commitment to the goal set out in 1944 of high and stable levels of growth and employment, and to state that from 1997 onwards

the attainment of this goal would require a wholly new monetary and fiscal framework." A few sentences later Brown talked of "a new paradigm" in 1997. (Ed Balls and Gus O'Donnell, eds., *Reforming Britain's Economic and Financial Policy* [Basingstoke and New York: Palgrave, 2002], p. x.)

5   Shirley Williams, *Politics Is for People* (Harmondsworth: Penguin, 1981), p. 17.

6   Wynne Godley and Francis Cripps, *Macroeconomics* (Oxford: Oxford University Press, also in Fontana paperback, 1983), pp. 13–14.

7   John Maynard Keynes, *The General Theory* (London: Macmillan paperback edition, 1964), p. 378.

8   C. A. R. (Anthony) Crosland, *The Future of Socialism* (New York: Schocken paperback edition, 1963), p. 79.

9   See, for example, Frank Hahn's comment in the 1981 Mitsui lectures that "inflation as such is not an outstanding evil, nor do I believe it to be costly in the sense that economists use that term." (Frank Hahn, *Money and Inflation* [Oxford: Blackwell, 1982], p. 106.)

10   The September 2002 issue of *Euromoney* magazine included a quotation (p. 67) from Joseph Stiglitz, the Nobel Prize–winning economist, to the effect that "Gordon Brown is a new Keynesian." The September 2002 issue of *Institutional Investor* magazine carried an interview with Brown in which he said, "We've reduced [public] debt very substantially in Britain, from 44 percent of national income to 30 percent. . . . So we are fiscal disciplinarians." If Keynesianism is to be equated with fiscal discipline, then Picasso's *Guernica* was stimulated by T. S. Eliot's poetry and Maoism was heavily indebted to John Stuart Mill. Perhaps, by the phrase "New Keynesianism," Stiglitz meant the adjustment of interest rates according to the level of the output gap. But – as explained in the introduction to this volume – the label "New Keynesian" is misapplied to this policy prescription.

11   At its first meeting in early 1993, five of the seven members of the Treasury Panel did not want its reports to include a section on monetary developments. The author of this volume wrote two Open Letters to the other members of the Panel, urging that a section on money was needed. (See the March and April 1993 issues of the *Gerrard & National Monthly Economic Review*.) Thereafter, a section on monetary developments did become part of the Treasury Panel's agenda.

12   See the note on "The Transmission Mechanism of Monetary Policy" delivered to the Treasury Committee of the House of Commons and the House of Lords Select Committee in May 1999. The note is also discussed in footnote 9 to essay 15.

13   Andrew Hauser and Andrew Brigden, "Money and Credit in an Inflation-Targeting Regime," *Bank of England Quarterly Bulletin*, Autumn 2002, pp. 299–307. The quotation is from p. 299.

14   The address was republished in Milton Friedman, *The Optimum Quantity of Money* (London and Basingstoke: Macmillan, 1969), pp. 95–110.

15   In a 1952 essay, "The Methodology of Positive Economics," Friedman argued

that economic theory generated "a body of generalizations" whose validity stemmed from "the accuracy of their predictions." (*Essays in Positive Economics* [Chicago and London: University of Chicago Press, 1953], pp. 3–43.)

16 ". . . [A]bove-trend growth can be reconciled for several years with low inflation." (Submission by Professor Tim Congdon of Lombard Street Research in the February 1993 report of the Panel of Independent Forecasters [London: H.M.Treasury, 1993], p. 25.)

17 See also pp. 9–11 of the June 1999 issue of Lombard Street Research's *Monthly Economic Review*, with Lord Burns's lecture on Lombard Street Research's tenth birthday. (The lecture was called "The New Consensus on Macroeconomic Policy: Will It Prove Temporary or Permanent?")

18 Nigel Lawson, *The View from No. 11* (London and New York: Bantam Press, 1992), *passim*. (See also essay 3 in this collection for British economists' fondness for basing interest rates on the exchange rate.)

19 James H. Stock and Mark W. Watson, "Has the Business Cycle Changed and Why?" originally published as NBER Working Paper no. w9127; collected in Mark Gertler and Kenneth Rogoff, eds., *NBER Macroeconomics Annual 2002*, vol. 17 (Cambridge, Mass.: MIT Press, 2003), pp. 159–203.

PART THREE

PREFACE

1 "Interview with Milton Friedman," in Brian Snowdon and Howard R. Vane, *Modern Macroeconomics: Its Origins, Development, and Current State* (Cheltenham, U.K., and Northampton, Mass.: Edward Elgar, 2005), pp. 198–218.

2 The list of names is reproduced on pp. 124–132 of Philip Booth, ed., *Were 364 Economists All Wrong?* (London: Institute of Economic Affairs, 2006).

ESSAY 8

1 "What Would Keynes Say Now?," a dialogue between Robert Skidelsky and Tim Congdon, December 2009 issue of *Standpoint* (London: Social Affairs Unit Magazines), pp. 30–35. The quotation is from p. 32.

2 Alan O. Ebenstein, *Milton Friedman: A Biography* (New York and Basingstoke, U.K.: Palgrave Macmillan, 2007), pp. 13–25.

3 Ibid., p. 24. These notes still survive. One of Friedman's teachers at Chicago in 1932–33 was Lloyd Mints, who gave a lecture course labeled "Economics 330," which was organized around *A Treatise on Money*. The first words that Friedman wrote in his notes were "Econ 330 Keynes." He then wrote that Mints's judgment was: "General framework of Keynes likely to endure much longer than details." (Robert Leeson, "From Keynes to Friedman via Mints," in Robert Leeson, ed., *Keynes, Chicago, and Friedman*, vol. 2 [London: Pickering & Chatto, 2003], pp. 483–525. The quotation is from p. 485.)

4 Elizabeth Johnson and Donald E. Moggridge, eds., *The Collected Writings of*

John Maynard Keynes, vol. VI, *A Treatise on Money: 2. The Applied Theory of Money* (London and Basingstoke: Macmillan, 1971, originally published in 1930), p. 347.

5 The essay appeared originally in the June 1948 issue of *The American Economic Review*, vol. 38, pp. 245–264.

6 The argument was a theme throughout Simons's *Economic Policy in a Free Society* (London and Chicago: University of Chicago Press, 1948), which was published after its author's death. Simons followed Irving Fisher in believing that, if the quantity of money were limited to the cash reserves created by the central bank, macroeconomic instability could be sharply reduced. (See Irving Fisher, *100% Money* [New York: Adelphi, 1935] for more detail.) However, it is clear that banks which are forbidden to extend loans to the private sector (and so to make profits on such loans) will need to charge for the money-transmission services they provide to depositors. For the argument that the cost of banks' services to non-banks declines with falls in the ratio of banks' cash and capital to their assets, see pp. 39–84 of Tim Congdon, *Central Banking in a Free Society* (London: Institute of Economic Affairs, 2009). One point of *Central Banking in a Free Society* is to reject the 100 percent cash-reserve notion as illiberal and inefficient.

7 See Milton Friedman's essay "A Monetary and Fiscal Framework for Economic Stability," pp. 133–156, in his *Essays in Positive Economics* (Chicago and London: University of Chicago Press, 1953). The quotations are from p. 136 and p. 138 respectively.

8 When a private individual pays more in tax than he receives in government expenditure, his bank deposit falls. So there is less money in the economy. Of course the government's bank deposit rises, but the level of a government's deposit has no bearing on its behavior. See footnote 10 to essay 4 for more on this important asymmetry.

9 The quotation is from p. 140. A closer reading of the 1948 paper supports this interpretation. It included a section (pp. 144–148 of *Essays in Positive Economics*) on "lags in response" which devoted much more space to lags between fiscal changes and expenditure than to those between changes in the quantity of money and expenditure. The whole performance from Friedman, already in his mid-thirties, was – in a word – "fiscalist."

10 See "Interview with Milton Friedman" in Snowdon and Vane, *Modern Macroeconomics*. The quotation is from p. 213.

11 Ibid.

12 Ibid.

13 Friedman denied in his 1980 evidence to the Treasury and Civil Service Committee's inquiry on monetary policy that the level of the budget deficit was relevant to money growth. See pp. 287–288 in essay 13 and the related footnote 31.

14 The Treasury view is associated with Ralph Hawtrey, who was director of financial inquiries (in effect, chief economic adviser) at the Treasury from 1919

to 1945. The definitive statement is usually regarded as his 1925 article in *Economica*. (R. G. Hawtrey, "Public Expenditure and the Demand for Labour," *Economica*, vol. 5 [1925], pp. 38–48.) But as late as 1939 Hawtrey continued to object in internal Treasury memoranda to Keynes's neglect of the importance of a budget deficit's financing pattern to its macroeconomic effect. ". . . [T]he form in which money is raised [to finance a budget deficit] may make all the difference." (The quotation is from p. 183 of G. C. Peden, ed., *Keynes and His Critics: Treasury Responses to the Keynesian Revolution 1925–46* [Oxford and New York: Oxford University Press, for the British Academy, 2004].)

15   The underlying thought in the Ricardian equivalence theorem is that, if government spending is financed by debt issuance rather than taxation, people understand that they will have to service and repay public debt in due course. So debt issuance does not make them better off. As they are no wealthier, it does not matter to total expenditure whether public spending is financed by running a budget deficit rather than entirely by taxation. (Robert J. Barro, "Are Government Bonds Net Wealth?" *Journal of Political Economy*, vol. 82, issue 6 [Chicago: University of Chicago Press, 1974], pp. 1095–1117.)

16   The exchange with Tobin in Friedman's 1972 *Journal of Political Economy* article, "A Reply to the Critics," was partly neo-Ricardian in character, before the 1974 Barro paper usually cited as the beginning of the neo-Ricardian argument. (See Milton Friedman, "A Reply to the Critics," *Journal of Political Economy*, vol. 80, no. 5 [Sept.–Oct., 1972], pp. 906–950.) Edward Nelson of the Federal Reserve has also drawn my attention to two pieces of Friedman's journalism with a neo-Ricardian slant ("Closet Keynesianism," *Newsweek*, July 27, 1981, and an article in *The Wall Street Journal* of April 26, 1984). The author is most grateful to Nelson for these references.

17   Paul A. Samuelson and William A. Barnett, *Inside the Economist's Mind: Conversations with Eminent Economists* (Oxford: Blackwell, 2007), p. 130.

18   Friedman believed that economists had come to accept the important role of money in the economy as a result of a debate between himself and David Meiselman on the one side, and Albert Ando and Franco Modigliani on the other, which had taken place in the mid-1960s. This debate was nicknamed the "Battle of the Radio Stations" after the initials (AM and FM) of the protagonists. See Samuelson and Barnett, *Inside the Economist's Mind*, p. 131.

19   Milton Friedman, "A Natural Experiment in Monetary Policy Covering Three Episodes of Growth and Decline in the Economy and the Stock Market," *The Journal of Economic Perspectives*, vol. 19, no. 4 (Autumn 2005), pp. 145–150.

20   On the need to confront theories with evidence in order to obtain a serviceable body of generalizations, the opening essay ("The Methodology of Positive Economics," pp. 3–43) of Friedman's collection *Essays in Positive Economics* is central. For Friedman's cynicism about multiple regressions, see Snowdon and Vane, *Modern Macroeconomics*, p. 209, and Samuelson and Barnett, *Inside the Economist's Mind*, pp. 133–134.

ESSAY 9

1   This is of course the line of argument that culminates, under certain extreme assumptions, in "the liquidity trap." See pp. 82–85 in essay 4.

ESSAY 10

1   The articles are reproduced on pp. 41–51 of Johnson and Moggridge, eds., *The Collected Writings*, vol. XXII, *Activities 1939–45: Internal War Finance* (London and Basingstoke: Macmillan, for the Royal Economic Society, 1978).

2   R. J. Ball, *Money and Employment* (London and Basingstoke: Macmillan, 1982), p. 29.

3   J. C. R. (Christopher) Dow, *Major Recessions: Britain and the World 1920–95* (Oxford: Oxford University Press, 1998), p. 38. Dow has a high reputation in some circles. Peter Jay, the former economics editor of the BBC, has referred to "the learned Dow" and described *Major Recessions* as "magisterial." (Peter Jay, *The Wealth of Man* [New York: Public Affairs, 2000], p. 238.)

4   The other recognized source of demand injections and withdrawals was the rest of the world, via the balance of payments.

5   As usual in discussions of these concepts, the question of the timing of the receipt of "income" and the disbursal of "expenditure" is left a little vague. The income-expenditure story is most plausible if people have nothing (i.e., neither money nor assets) at the end of a period, and receive their income at the beginning of a period and have spent it all by the same period's end. In other words, the story is easiest to tell about an economy without private property of any kind.

6   Johnson and Moggridge, eds., *The Collected Writings*, vol. V, *A Treatise on Money: 1. The Pure Theory of Money*, p. 217.

7   Dow, *Major Recessions*, p. 39. Given the context, Dow must have meant "determinand," not "determinant."

8   Johnson and Moggridge, eds., *The Collected Writings*, vol. VII, *The General Theory*, pp. 84–85. Note that, in this quotation, the word "prices" referred to the prices of securities, not of goods and services.

9   These processes are discussed in more detail in the author's *Money and Asset Prices in Boom and Bust* (London: Institute of Economic Affairs, 2005). It seems that, after a big change in the amount of money, asset prices change with a shorter lag and by larger percentages than the prices of goods and services. The explanation for this undoubted pattern is important to the analysis of real-world business cycles.

10   Hahn made an attempt at self-justification by claiming that "the monetarists" deny that an injection of newly printed money can boost demand because inflation expectations would deteriorate and "nothing 'real' will be changed." But this is to equate "monetarism" with the New Classical Economics of Lucas, Barro, Sargent, and others. It is now widely recognized that these are distinct schools of economics. (See, for example, K. D. Hoover, "Two Types of Mone-

tarism," *Journal of Economic Literature*, vol. 22 [1984], pp. 58–76.) Hahn's letter ended with a sneer. "Mr. Congdon's understanding of either side of the argument [by which he presumably meant either the Keynesian or the monetarist side] seems very insecure."

11   "Elasticity pessimism," i.e., a belief that behavior did not respond to price signals, was common among British economists in the first twenty or thirty years after the Second World War. Investment was thought to be unresponsive to interest rates, while exports and imports were held to be impervious to changes in the exchange rate. Leijonhufvud has outlined one "familiar type of argument" as the claim that "The interest-elasticity of investment is for various reasons quite low. Hence, monetary policy is not a very useful stabilization instrument." Hahn and the 364 may have been thinking on these lines. Leijonhufvud says that "the dogma" of the interest inelasticity of investment originated in Oxford, with surveys of businessmen carried out in 1938, not in Cambridge. (Axel Leijonhufvud, *On Keynesian Economics and the Economics of Keynes* [New York: Oxford University Press, 1968], p. 405.) But it was still widely held in Cambridge and other British universities in the 1970s and even in the 1980s.

12   Before the July 1983 article in *The Times* the author had proposed the concept of "mortgage equity withdrawal" in a joint paper with Paul Turnbull. (See "Introducing the Concept of 'Equity Withdrawal,'" pp. 274–287, in Tim Congdon, *Reflections on Monetarism* [Aldershot, U.K., and Brookfield, Vt.: Edward Elgar, for the Institute of Economic Affairs, 1992], based on a paper of June 4, 1982, for the brokerage firm of L. Messel & Co., "The Coming Boom in Housing Credit.") Dozens of articles have subsequently been written about "mortgage equity withdrawal" and its influence on personal expenditure, and the Bank of England regularly prepares estimates of its size. To economists spoon fed at university on the circular flow of income and the income-expenditure model (in which, as explained, assets do not affect expenditure), mortgage equity withdrawal was a striking idea. It showed how people whose only significant asset was a house (which is of course rather illiquid) could tap into the equity (often boosted in the Britain of the early 1980s by house-price inflation) by borrowing.

13   Note that monetary equilibrium could refer to
    i.   the equivalence of the demand for base money with the supply of base money, or
    ii. the equivalence of the demand for narrow money with the supply of narrow money, or
    iii. the equivalence of the demand for a broad money measure with the supply of broad money, or
    iv. the simultaneous equivalence of the demand for all money measures with the supply of all such measures.

The "Which aggregate?" debate will not go away. The chaos in the subject helps to explain why so many economists have dropped money from their analytical purview.

14   Congdon, *Reflections*, p. 252. The author first used the phrases "vacuum in intellectual understanding" and "the revenge of the 364" in a lecture in 1990. See p. 54 in essay 3, above.

15   For example, the textbook *Principles of Macroeconomics*, 2nd edition (New York: Irwin/McGraw-Hill, 2003), by Ben Bernanke and Robert Frank, contains an account of national-income determination and the efficacy of fiscal action which could have been lifted, in its entirety, from a similar textbook of the 1950s. When the textbook was published, Bernanke was professor of economics at Princeton University, a university widely regarded as in the vanguard of macroeconomic thought. Now – as chairman of the board of governors of the United States' Federal Reserve – he holds the most important position in monetary policy-making in the world.

16   In the 1970s the Bank of England's *Quarterly Bulletin* did not include a single article on the housing market. In the three years up to the summer of 2005 the *Quarterly Bulletin* carried seven articles and two speeches by members of the Monetary Policy Committee that related specifically to the housing market.

17   But the majority of British economists do not think that the income-expenditure model has been discredited by the sequel to the 1981 Budget. For example, the Bank of England's macroeconometric model – which purportedly is the starting point in its forecasting exercises – remains a large-scale elaboration of an income-expenditure model in which money is, to use the phrase that Dow presumably intended, a "residuary determinand." See *The Bank of England Quarterly Model* (London: Bank of England, 2005), *passim*.

18   Tim Congdon, "The Futility of Deficit Financing as a Cure for Recession," *The Times*, October 23, 1975. Some economists had seen in the late 1970s that the impact of fiscal policy on the economy was not independent of how budget deficits were financed. According to R. J. Ball, in a book advocating "practical monetarism," ". . . if the money supply is chosen as a policy target, the stance of fiscal policy must be consistent with it. [Fiscal and monetary policies] cannot in practice be operated independently in the medium term. For this reason academic debates about the 'pure' effects of fiscal policy lose much of their *raison d'être*." (R. J. Ball, *Money and Employment* [London and Basingstoke: Macmillan], 1982, p. 184.) Ball worked closely with Mr. Terry (later Lord) Burns at the London Business School in the late 1960s and early 1970s, and Burns became the government's chief economic adviser in 1980.

19   The two instigators were Professor Robert Neild and Professor Frank Hahn. Neild's subsequent interests were in peace studies and corruption in public life. (He has also written a history of the oyster in England and France.) As far as the author can determine, he dropped macroeconomics at some point in the 1980s. Hahn's position is more interesting and, in the author's opinion, more puzzling. He has written numerous academic papers on money (and money-related issues) in general equilibrium theory, brought together in Frank Hahn, *Equilibrium and Macroeconomics* (Oxford: Basil Blackwell, 1984). Most of the

papers in the 1984 book were concerned with rarefied topics, such as the existence, stability, and optimality of differently specified general equilibria. However, four of the papers (numbered 12 to 15) were more or less directly polemical exercises whose target was "monetarism," or, at any rate, what Hahn took to be "monetarism." They cannot be summarized here for reasons of space, but a salient feature of all the papers was the lack of references to real-world institutions, behaviors, and magnitudes.

Following Keynes, the author has argued – in the current essay and elsewhere – that a discussion of the determination of national income must be, to a large extent, a discussion of the role of money in portfolios. In a 1980 paper, "Monetarism and Economic Theory," Hahn cited a number of recondite papers before seeing in "recent macroliterature" two elements "that Keynesians have for long ignored." One was the portfolio consequences of budget deficits and the other "wealth effects." (*Equilibrium and Macroeconomics*, p. 299.) Given that, might one ask why Hahn should have been so sarcastic about the author's 1983 article in *The Times*, and its concern with mortgage credit, houses, and wealth. And might one also ask whether he really believes (as apparently he did in 1980 and perhaps as he continued to do when he orchestrated the 1981 letter to *The Times*) that the government should make "the rate of change of the money stock proportional to the difference between actual unemployment and half a million unemployed" (*Equilibrium and Macroeconomics*, p. 305). Is that the sort of policy which – on a considered analysis – would have led to the macroeconomic stability the U.K. enjoyed in the fifteen years starting in 1992?

STATISTICAL APPENDIX

1   David Hendry and N. R. Ericsson, "Assertion without Empirical Basis: An Econometric Appraisal of *Monetary Trends in the United States and the United Kingdom*, by Milton Friedman and Anna Schwartz," Bank of England Panel of Economic Consultants, *Monetary Trends in the United Kingdom*, panel paper no. 22, October 1983, pp. 45–101.

2   In John Maloney, ed., *Debt and Deficits* (Cheltenham, U.K., and Northampton, Mass.: Edward Elgar, 1998), pp. 84–115.

3   Nicholas Kaldor, "The New Monetarism," *Lloyds Bank Review,* July 1970, pp. 1–17, reprinted in Sir Alan Walters, ed., *Money and Banking* (Harmondsworth: Penguin Books, 1973), pp. 261–278. See, in particular, p. 277. In the late 1970s Alan Budd and Terry Burns also argued that the fiscal position had a strong medium-term influence on the rate of monetary growth. See A. P. Budd and T. Burns, "The Relationship between Fiscal and Monetary Policy in the LBS Model," Discussion Paper no. 51 (Econometric Forecasting Unit: London Business School, June 1978).

4   The breakdown of "Kaldor's rule" was noted in J. H. B. Tew, "Monetary Policy," which appears as chapter 5 in F. T. Blackaby, ed., *British Economic Policy 1960-74* (Cambridge: Cambridge University Press, 1978), pp. 218–303. See,

particularly, pp. 277–278. Ironically, for those concerned that excessive money-supply growth would lead to inflation, Kaldor's rule justified official action to constrain the budget deficit, as incorporated in the Conservatives' Medium-Term Financial Strategy starting in 1980.

ESSAY 11

1   For a very standard textbook treatment, see p. 105 of Rudiger Dornbusch and Stanley Fischer, *Macroeconomics*, 6th edition (New York: McGraw-Hill, 1994). Other examples are legion. In the words of Dornbusch and Fischer on the IS/LM model, of which the monetary equilibrium condition is part, it is "the core of modern macroeconomics" (p. 87).

2   Friedman's 1956 paper "The Quantity Theory of Money: A Restatement," usually seen as the launching pad of the monetarist counterrevolution, was explicit on the importance of the money-demand function being both stable and defined by a small number of variables. (See pp. 62–63 of "The Quantity Theory of Money: A Restatement," in Milton Friedman, *The Optimum Quantity of Money* [London and Basingstoke: Macmillan, 1969], pp. 51–67.) Friedman disliked the distinction between microeconomics and macroeconomics. In an interview given in 2000 (when he was eighty-eight) Friedman said that his teachers at Chicago had taught him economics as a unity, both "what's now called micro and macro. I hate those words, I think it's price theory and it's monetary theory." (John B. Taylor, "An Interview with Milton Friedman," in Paul A. Samuelson and William A. Barnett, *Inside the Economist's Mind: Conversations with Eminent Economists* [Oxford: Blackwell, 2007], pp. 110–142. The quotation is from p. 122.)

3   The articles that Keynes wrote in 1937, in attempting to convey concisely the rather complex message of *The General Theory*, are full of references to money and banking, as noted by – for example – Peter Clarke on pp. 154–155 of his *Keynes: The Twentieth Century's Most Influential Economist* (London: Bloomsbury, 2009).

4   John Hicks, "Mr. Keynes and the Classics: A Suggested Interpretation," *Econometrica*, April 1937, pp. 147–159.

5   In the last chapter of *The General Theory*, before the flashy and meretricious final section on "Short Notes Suggested by the *General Theory*," Keynes endorsed a monetary theory of price-level movements over the medium and long runs. "If there is some tendency to a measure of long-run uniformity in the state of liquidity-preference, there may well be some sort of rough relationship between the national income and the quantity of money required to satisfy liquidity-preference, taken as a mean over periods of pessimism and optimism together." (See *The General Theory* [London: Macmillan, 1964, paperback reprint of 1936 edition], p. 306.)

6   Ibid., p. 167.

7   Milton Friedman and Anna Jacobson Schwartz, *A Monetary History of the*

United States 1867–1960 (Princeton: Princeton University Press, 1963, reprinted in 1993), p. 277.

8   An explanation for Keynes's reliance on broad money in his work was given above in essay 4. See p. 83.

9   The word "preponderantly" is used and not "wholly." As the banking system becomes more sophisticated in the course of economic development, this "monetary" variable affects "real" outcomes. The point is not trivial. When large changes in the ratio of money to income occur, a problem of interpretation invariably arises. Do they reflect excess or deficient real money balances, which will cause macroeconomic instability, or do they reflect long-run changes in the "technological" or "institutional" determinants of the equilibrium ratio of money to income? The answer is rarely clear-cut.

10   Tim Congdon, *Money and Asset Prices in Boom and Bust* (London: Institute of Economic Affairs, 2005), *passim*, but see particularly the final chapter, pp. 129–138.

11   At their peak in the third quarter of 2007, U.K. house prices in real terms were almost 32 percent above the level justified by their long-run trend behavior, according to an analysis by the Nationwide Building Society. The Nationwide has been compiling house-price data for the U.K. as a whole, and by region, since 1952.

12   In the early 1930s British banks did acquire substantial holdings of long-dated gilt-edged securities, partly as a by-product of the conversion of the War Loan gilts issue in 1932. (See, for example, Margaret Ackrill and Leslie Hannah, *Barclays: The Business of Banking 1690–1996* [Cambridge: Cambridge University Press, 2001], pp. 96–97.) However, when inflation rose in the 1950s, they suffered heavy losses on these holdings and had jettisoned all of them by the 1980s.

13   The closing months of 2008 did in fact see heavy issuance of Treasury bills and short-dated gilts. In the last quarter of 2008 the issuance of new short-dated gilts totaled £24.3 billion, the highest-ever figure. The banks' net holdings of gilts rose by over £18 billion, helping to prevent a collapse in the quantity of money, even before quantitative easing took effect in March 2009. See tables 1.2D and 4.3A in *Financial Statistics* (London: Palgrave Macmillan, for the Office for National Statistics), any issue in early 2009.

14   Tim Congdon, *How to Stop the Recession* (London: Council for the Study of Financial Innovation, February 2009).

15   It should be clear from the preceding paragraphs that the budget deficit is important to the macroeconomic outlook, to the extent that it is monetized. However, the incurrence of non-monetized budget deficits (that is, deficits financed outside the banking system) is of unclear and limited significance to demand and income.

16   Ralph Hawtrey, "Public Expenditure and the Demand for Labour," *Economica*, vol. 5 (1925), pp. 38–48.

17   Robert J. Barro, "Are Government Bonds Net Wealth?" *Journal of Political Economy*, vol. 82 (1974), pp. 1095–1117.

18   The author covered these risks in chapter 3, "Finding Out about Budget Deficits," in his *The Debt Threat* (Oxford and New York: Blackwell, 1988). The debt-unsustainability arguments had been widely forgotten when the Great Recession struck in late 2008, creating new opportunities for the advocacy of fiscal reflation by Krugman, Stiglitz, Koo, and many others.

19   For the U.K., see essays 5 and 10; for most European nations, the watershed was the signing of the Maastricht Treaty in 1992, which obliged them to curb budget deficits in order to qualify for the new European single currency. It is fair to say that the U.S. did not have a decisive, once-for-all event that constituted an abandonment of fiscal activism, but see pp. 41–55 of Joseph Stiglitz, *The Roaring Nineties* (London and New York: Penguin Books, 2004, originally published in 2003 by W. W. Norton & Co.) for a justification of deficit reduction under President Clinton by an avowed Keynesian economist.

20   Richard Koo, *The Holy Grail of Macroeconomics: Lessons from Japan's Great Recession* (Singapore: John Wiley & Sons, 2008), p. 43.

21   Ibid., p. 51.

22   The concept of "the velocity of circulation" is extremely ambiguous. Is it the velocity of money relative to payments or to income? The total value of payments and income are very different. Keynes recognized this ambiguity and discussed it in some detail in chapter 24, "The Velocities of Circulation," in vol. 2, *The Applied Theory of Money*, of his *A Treatise on Money* (London and Basingstoke: Macmillan for the Royal Economic Society, 1971; originally published in 1930). In *The General Theory*, money was held relative to either income or an asset portfolio, and the very high value of bank clearings relative to income was ignored. This aspect of monetary economics has subsequently been almost forgotten.

23   See, particularly, chapters 22–24 in vol. 2 of *A Treatise on Money*. The discussion in those three chapters was the clear precursor of chapter 15 of *The General Theory*, which introduced the three motives for money-holding, then regurgitated by dozens of textbooks in the 1950s and 1960s.

24   Another quasi-theory is that the pattern of company finance, and especially the ability of companies to finance expenditure above receipts, has an important bearing on aggregate demand. This quasi-theory – which is an associate of the wider claim that agents' ability to borrow is important to the determination of economic activity – is commonly seen in broker reports and suchlike, but it is invalid. (The approach is also related to the notion of "a credit channel" injected into the literature by Bernanke and Gertler.) There is no difficulty conceiving of an economy where companies are denied all forms of external finance, and yet where money-supply growth rates of 100 percent or more a month – due to monetary financing of budget deficits – are accompanied by hyperinflation. All the borrowing-determines-expenditure theories overlook

the centrality of money in any plausible description of macroeconomic equilibrium and are false.

25 The critical assumption is that labor costs per unit of output are constant, the so-called "wage-unit assumption." See essay 12 and, particularly, pp. 257–258 for a discussion of the pivotal role of this assumption in *The General Theory*.

26 This is not the place for an extended discussion of the tendency of so-called "intellectuals" to incline towards a socialist political philosophy and, as a result, to favor state action over action by the private sector and free individuals. One of the earliest writers on this tendency – Schumpeter in *Capitalism, Socialism, and Democracy*, originally published in 1943 – saw quickly after the appearance of *The General Theory* that its message could be corrupted to support the confiscation of private property, even though this was emphatically not Keynes's intention. (Joseph Schumpeter, *Capitalism, Socialism, and Democracy* [London: Unwin University Books, 1952, 5th edition], p. 390.)

27 See, for example, Ian Little's 1952 comments on the relation of fiscal to monetary policy in "Fiscal Policy," in I. M. D. Little, *Collection and Recollections* (Oxford: Clarendon Press, 1999), pp. 299–307. A generalized contempt for monetary policy was common among British economists in the 1950s and 1960s, a phenomenon discussed at more length in essay 12.

28 See footnote 9 above, for the qualification to this statement, that changes in banking technology are a form of "monetary" variable that alters the demand to hold real money.

29 As argued by the author in Tim Congdon, "What Is to Be Done about Japan's Financial Crisis?" *Central Banking* (May 2002), pp. 67–72. See, also, essay 4.

PART FOUR

PREFACE

1 Richard Parker, *John Kenneth Galbraith: His Life, His Politics, His Economics* (New York: Farrar, Straus and Giroux, 2005), p. 99 and p. 570.

2 "The Fed has specified targets for several [money] aggregates primarily . . . to obfuscate the issue and reduce accountability. In general, the different aggregates move together." (Milton Friedman, "The Case for Overhauling the Federal Reserve," *Challenge* [July–August 1985], pp. 4–12. The quotation is from p. 5.)

ESSAY 12

1 One example will suffice. "Monetarism, like Christianity, makes a comeback from time to time. When things get bad, even sceptics start paying lip service, just in case there is something in the doctrine which might conceivably save them from eternal damnation." Christopher Johnson, in a review of Gordon Pepper's *Money, Credit, and Inflation*, in *The Business Economist* (Watford: Society of Business Economists), vol. 22, no. 1 (Winter 1990), pp. 64–65.

2   Economists at provincial ("red-brick") universities and financial journalists were the main contributors to a pamphlet critical of the Radcliffe Report, *Not Unanimous*, which was published by the Institute of Economic Affairs in January 1960. Only one of the seven contributors (R. F. Henderson) was from Cambridge University. Henderson opened his chapter with a recognition of indebtedness to Dennis Robertson, but to no other Cambridge economists.

3   Gordon Fletcher, *Understanding Dennis Robertson* (Cheltenham, U.K., and Northampton, Mass.: Edward Elgar, 2000), p. 404.

4   The inclusion of *Indian Currency and Finance* in the list may seem surprising. But – arguably – this was the beginning of Keynes's interest in the place of gold in an international currency regime that continued until the Bretton Woods negotiations (and Keynes's House of Lords speeches on them) in the mid-1940s.

5   Keynes, *The General Theory* (London: Macmillan, 1936), p. 293.

6   Ibid., p. 296.

7   Money plays a crucial role in asset-price determination, and sharp changes in asset prices affect expenditure. For more on these themes, see essays 15 and 16.

8   The phrases in quotation marks are taken from Keynes's famous introduction to the *Cambridge Economic Handbooks*, which he edited until 1936.

9   Mrs. Joan Robinson – a left-wing economics don at Cambridge – used the phrase "bastardised Keynesianism" to characterize the textbook income-expenditure model.

10 Milton Friedman, *The Optimum Quantity of Money* (London: Macmillan, 1969), p. 84.

11 Friedrich A. von Hayek, *Law, Legislation, and Liberty*, vol. I (London: Routledge & Kegan Paul, 1973), p. 14.

12 Andrew Shonfield illustrated this sort of thinking in his well-regarded *British Economic Policy since the War*. To quote, "the success or failure of the trade unions in controlling their members will determine the level of prices – and nothing else." (*British Economic Policy since the War* [Harmondsworth: Penguin, 1958], p. 278.) Shonfield – who had been a Marxist as a young man – became the influential director of the Royal Institute of International Affairs in 1972.

13 Professor Maurice Dobb has made the distinction between the two types of theory particularly well in a number of books, notably in *Political Economy and Capitalism* (London: Routledge & Kegan Paul, 1970).

14 Elizabeth S. Johnson and Harry G. Johnson, *The Shadow of Keynes* (Oxford: Basil Blackwell, 1978), p. 137. See also Mark Skousen, ed., *Dissent on Keynes* (New York: Praeger, 1992), p. 196.

15 See Roger Opie, "The Political Consequences of Lord Keynes," in Donald E. Moggridge, *Keynes: Aspects of the Man and His Work* (London and Basingstoke: Macmillan, 1974), pp. 75–90. The quotation is from p. 79.

16 *Financial Statistics* (London: Her Majesty's Stationery Office), September 1977 issue, p. 51 and p. 74; *Financial Statistics* (London: HMSO), July 2006 issue, p. 58 and p. 78.

17 This was the point of the title of Keith Joseph's 1976 Stockton Lecture, "Monetarism Is Not Enough." The title did not mean that monetarism was inadequate; it meant that control of the money supply had to be accompanied by restraint over public expenditure. To quote from the speech itself, "Monetary contraction in a mixed economy strangles the private sector unless the state sector contracts with it and reduces its take in the national income." Morrison Halcrow, *Keith Joseph: A Single Mind* (London: Macmillan, 1989), p. 113. Perhaps unsurprisingly, the ambiguous title of the 1976 speech has allowed it to be misinterpreted. David Willetts, a Conservative politician who became universities minister in the Conservative–Liberal Democratic coalition government of 2010, gave a speech in 2005 to the Social Market Foundation on "A New Conservatism for a New Century." To quote the speech, "In the 1970s Keith Joseph talked of the common ground, meaning the shared values of the British people. He understood that a free market economy had to operate in a strong society: that's why he observed 'monetarism is not enough.'" This was not Joseph's meaning at all.

18 If this remark seems outlandish, see footnote 9 to essay 14 in this collection, where George Orwell is quoted as saying – in 1945 – that Communists keen "to advance Russian interests at all costs . . . abound in England today."

19 The case for money-supply targets was advocated in the public debate at about the same time as the thesis that "Britain had too few producers," because public-sector employment (financed by taxes) seemed – almost continuously – to be rising faster than private-sector employment (financed by sales revenue). The thesis was presented by Robert Bacon and Walter Eltis in an article in *The Sunday Times* in 1974, and in a book titled *Britain's Economic Problem: Too Few Producers* (London and Basingstoke: Macmillan, 1976). Between 1961 and 1979 public-sector employment climbed at an annual compound rate of 1.3 percent from 5.86 million to 7.45 million, while private-sector employment contracted from 18.60 million to 17.94 million. (The source for the data is *Economic Trends: Annual Supplement* [London: HMSO, 1988], p. 209.) During the 1979–1997 Conservative government these trends were reversed, partly because of the privatization of nationalized industries.

20 See Donald E. Moggridge, "Keynes: The Economist," in Moggridge, ed., *Keynes: Aspects*, pp. 53–74. The reference to "wild asides" is on p. 74.

21 Michael Joseph Oakeshott, *Rationalism in Politics* (London: Methuen, 1962), p. 45. The remark appears in a review of Henry Simons's *Economic Policy for a Free Society*.

22 Milton Friedman, "The Fragility of Freedom," *Encounter* (November 1976), pp. 8–14.

23 It should be noted that the ideas put forward by Friedman in this article owed much to work on the theory of public choice. See footnote 26 below.

24 The point may seem remote from the realities of Britain in the 1970s, when inflation was running at "only" 10 percent a year. However, even this rate of

price increases meant that the value of money over a five- or ten-year time span was highly uncertain and prohibitive of long-term contracts. The issue of long-term fixed-interest debentures and loan stocks on London financial markets practically ceased in these years. The general message is that, as inflation accelerates, the time horizon of the typical economic transactor shortens until finally it is no more than a few hours or even minutes. See an amusing footnote on p. 41 of Keynes's *A Tract on Monetary Reform*, vol. IV of Johnson and Moggridge, eds., *The Collected Writings*.

25 "Consider the newly arrived Harvard assistant professor.... [H]ere she is at Harvard no less – the pinnacle of world universities." George Akerlof and Robert Shiller, *Animal Spirits* (Princeton and Oxford: Princeton University Press, 2009), p. 121.

26 The theory of public choice – which argues that public servants may put their own private interests ahead of the "public interest" – was developed, mostly in the 1970s, by James Buchanan and Gordon Tullock. Its "headquarters" are usually considered to be the Center for the Study of Public Choice, which at the time was based at the Virginia Polytechnic Institute and State University. The public-choice perspective was largely adopted by Chicago economists.

Essay 13

1 H.M. Treasury press release, June 9, 1980, Statement by Nigel Lawson, MP, financial secretary to the Treasury, during his meeting with regional city editors.

2 Thomas Mayer, *The Structure of Monetarism* (New York and London: Norton, 1978). See, particularly, p. 2 for a list of twelve characteristic monetarist propositions.

3 *Monetary Control*, Cmnd. 7858 (London: HMSO, 1980), and "Memorandum on Monetary Policy," by H.M. Treasury, pp. 86–95, in vol. II, *Minutes of Evidence of Third Report from the House of Commons Treasury and Civil Service Committee*, Session 1980–1 (London: HMSO, 1981).

4 "Memorandum," by H.M. Treasury, p. 90.

5 Note by H.M. Treasury on "The stability of the income velocity of circulation of money supply," pp. 126–127, in *Third Report from the Treasury and Civil Service Committee*, Session 1980–1.

6 For an example of the approach, see the chapter titled "Bank Lending and Monetary Control" in Charles A.E. Goodhart, *Monetary Theory and Practice: The U.K. Experience* (London: Macmillan, 1984), pp. 122–145.

7 It should be added that interest-rate changes acted not only on bank lending, but also on the ability of the authorities to sell gilt-edged securities as part of the funding program.

8 *Monetary Control*, p. 1.

9 Ibid., p. 2.

10 "Memorandum," by H.M. Treasury, p. 89.

11 See, for example, John Burton, "Trade Unions' Role in the British Disease: 'An

interest in inflation,'" in Arthur Seldon, ed., *Is Monetarism Enough?* (London: Institute of Economic Affairs, 1980), pp. 99–111, particularly pp. 105–106; and Tim Congdon, "Why Has Monetarism Failed So Far?" in *The Banker* (April 1982), pp. 43–49. The subject was also discussed in Tim Congdon, *Monetarism: An Essay in Definition* (London: Centre for Policy Studies, 1978), particularly pp. 53–56.

12   Keynes, *A Tract on Monetary Reform* (1923), reprinted in Johnson and Moggridge, eds., *The Collected Writings*, vol. IV, p. 126, p. 132, and p. 138. See essay 3 above, pp. 40–42, for a more extended discussion of Keynes's proposal for a "managed currency."

13   H.M. Treasury press release, May 12, 1981. The Mais Lecture given by Sir Geoffrey Howe, QC, MP, chancellor of the exchequer, at the City University, p. 11. At about this time Howe's Treasury colleague, and future chancellor, Nigel Lawson, became convinced that an exchange-rate discipline in the form of the EMS was superior to "targets for domestic monetary aggregates" in monetary policy-making. On June 15, 1981, he sent Howe a long note on the virtues of joining the EMS. (Nigel Lawson, *The View from No. 11* [London: Bantam Press, 1992], p. 111.)

14   Mayer, *Monetarism*, p. 27.

15   Few economists would regard the monetary base by itself as constituting a measure of the money supply. The Treasury was therefore rather iconoclastic in its attitude towards M0, which it apparently regarded as the full-scale aggregate when M0 was introduced in 1983. In both the U.S. and the U.K. the value of transactions in cash is less than 1 percent of all transactions by non-bank agents.

16   The quotation comes from p. 71 of Paul Meek, "Comment on Papers Presented by Messrs. Fforde and Coleby," in Paul Meek, ed., *Central Bank Views on Monetary Targeting* (New York: Federal Reserve Bank of New York, 1983), pp. 70–71.

17   The quotations are from p. 57 of Milton Friedman, "Response to Questionnaire on Monetary Policy," in the House of Commons Treasury and Civil Service Committee (Session 1979–80), "Memorandum on Monetary Policy" (London: HMSO, 1980), pp. 55–62. The self-confidence and assertiveness of Friedman's criticism of the U.K. authorities in 1980 looks misplaced, to say the least, in retrospect. At the time of writing (late 2010) no central bank tries to target the quantity of money by controlling the monetary base. In the words of Goodhart, writing in 1995, "the debate over monetary base control appears historical." (The quotation is from C. A. E. Goodhart, *The Central Bank and the Financial System* [London and Basingstoke: Macmillan, 1995], p. 261.) See also pp. 235–236 of Bindseil's *Monetary Policy Implementation* for critical comments on Friedman's position in the early 1980s. (Ulrich Bindseil, *Monetary Policy Implementation: Theory, Past and Present* [Oxford: Oxford University Press, 2004].)

18   The arrangements are described in "The Role of the Bank of England in the Money Market," in Bank of England, *The Development and Operation of Monetary Policy 1960–83* (Oxford: Oxford University Press for the Bank of England,

1984), pp. 156–164. The easy-going nature of these arrangements, which had long historical roots, was shattered in August 2007 when the Bank of England refused to buy certain securities when the banks faced a cash shortage. The refusal is generally seen as a personal decision of the then governor, Mervyn King, which led to rows both with his colleague Paul Tucker, the executive director for markets, and with the U.K.'s leading banks. For further discussion, see Tim Congdon, *Central Banking in a Free Society* (London: Institute of Economic Affairs, 2009), pp. 122–144.

19   Econometric work may identify a contemporaneous link between the monetary base and one or another measure of the money supply, but that does not mean that the base "explains" money rather than the other way round. If one wanted to predict the growth of M3 over the next six to twelve months, the level of monetary base today would not be much help, but forecasts of bank lending and the PSBR would be.

20   Meek, "Comment," p. 70.

21   Friedman, "Response," p. 58.

22   Keynes, *A Treatise on Money: 2. The Applied Theory of Money* (1930) reprinted in Johnson and Moggridge, eds., *The Collected Writings*, vol. VI, p. 224 and p. 225.

23   Ibid., p. 231.

24   Ibid., p. 225.

25   Keynes, *The General Theory* (1936), reprinted in Johnson and Moggridge, eds., *The Collected Writings*, vol. VII, p. 327.

26   Keynes, *Treatise 2*, pp. 30–32 and pp. 217–230. These distinctions anticipate the more celebrated analysis of the motives for holding money in *The General Theory*.

27   H.M. Treasury press release, October 19, 1978. Speech by Denis Healey, MP, chancellor of the exchequer, to the lord mayor's dinner.

28   The quotation is from p. 97 of P. E. Middleton, "The Relationship between Fiscal and Monetary Policy," in M. J. Artis and M. H. Miller, eds., *Essays in Fiscal and Monetary Policy* (Oxford and New York: Oxford University Press, 1981), pp. 95–116.

29   See pp. 21–23 of Tim Congdon, "The Analytical Foundations of the Medium-Term Financial Strategy," in Michael Keen, ed., *The Economy and the 1984 Budget* (Oxford: Basil Blackwell for the Institute of Fiscal Studies, 1984), pp. 17–29.

30   Mentioned on p. 5 of Jerry L. Jordan, "The Andersen-Jordan Approach after Nearly 20 Years," in *Federal Reserve Bank of St Louis Review* (October 1986), pp. 5–8.

31   Friedman, "Response," p. 56.

32   The quotation is from p. 2 of Christopher J. Allsopp, "The Assessment: Monetary and Fiscal Policy in the 1980s," in *Oxford Review of Economic Policy*, vol. I, no. 1 (Spring 1985), pp. 1–19.

33 Friedman, "Response," p. 59.

34 Mayer, *Monetarism*, pp. 24–25.

35 Keynes, *The General Theory*, p. 306.

36 Thus, for example, Laidler's awareness of trade-union power may have been one reason for his advocacy of a "gradualist" approach to the elimination of inflation. See Laidler on the case for gradualism, in David E. W. Laidler, *Monetarist Perspectives* (Oxford: Philip Allan, 1982), pp. 176–177.

37 Milton Friedman, *Unemployment versus Inflation?* (London: Institute of Economic Affairs, 1975), pp. 30–35. The quotations are from p. 32 and p. 33.

38 A. Budd, S. Holly, A. Longbottom, and D. Smith, "Does Monetarism Fit the U.K. Facts?" in Brian Griffiths and Geoffrey E. Wood, eds., *Monetarism in the United Kingdom* (London: Macmillan, 1984), pp. 75–119.

39 Keynes, *Tract*, p. 126.

40 For an account of the 1976 crisis by a civil servant prominent in decision-making at the time, see Douglas Wass, *Decline to Fall* (Oxford: Oxford University Press, 2008), particularly pp. 22–23, which are dismissive towards monetarism.

41 See, for example, Michael Parkin and George Zis, eds., *Inflation in Open Economies* (Manchester, U.K., and Toronto: Manchester University Press and University of Toronto Press, 1976).

42 See R. J. Ball and T. Burns, "Long-Run Portfolio Equilibrium and Balance-of-Payments Adjustment in Econometric Models," in John A. Sawyer, ed., *Modelling the International Transmission Mechanism* (Amsterdam: North-Holland Publishing Company, 1979). It was Burns's position in the exchange-rate controversy of 1977–78, and his papers on the interrelationship between fiscal and monetary policy, that gave him a reputation as a monetary economist – or even as a monetarist – in the public debate and so led to his appointment as chief economic adviser in January 1980. (See Geoffrey Howe, *Conflict of Loyalty* [London and Basingstoke: Pan Books, 1994], p. 156.) In his paper on "Exchange Rate Policy in the United Kingdom," in S. Holly, ed., *Money, Inflation and Employment: Essays in Honour of James Ball* (Aldershot, U.K., and Brookfield, Vt.: Edward Elgar, 1994), pp. 26–38, Budd highlights Ball's role in the 1977 debate. The final two sentences of Budd's paper read, "The challenge was to incorporate the monetarist ideas into an empirical model of the U.K. economy. That is what Ball and his colleagues were able to do and that is why they played a major role in reshaping ideas and were able to contribute to a significant change in policy" (p. 37).

43 Reprinted in Milton Friedman, *Essays in Positive Economics* (Chicago and London: University of Chicago Press, 1953).

44 Friedman, "Response," p. 53.

45 Keynes, *Tract*, p. 126.

46 Ibid., pp. 159–160.

47 Geoffrey Maynard, The *Economy under Mrs. Thatcher* (Oxford: Basil Blackwell, 1988), p. 100.

48 Alan Walters, *Britain's Economic Renaissance* (New York and Oxford: Oxford University Press, 1986), p. 117 and p. 121. The description of M3 as a "credit aggregate" was surprising. M3 consists of notes, coin, and bank deposits. To say that its growth is driven by bank credit is *not* to say that bank deposits are the same thing as bank loans. (They evidently are not.) In any case, in the modern world, where no money is backed by a commodity, the growth of M1 – or, indeed, even of M0 – is also driven by credit. (See Tim Congdon, "Credit, Broad Money, and the Economy," in David Llewellyn, ed., *Reflections on Money* [London: Macmillan, for the Economic Research Council, 1989], pp. 59–82.) Walters mentioned in a footnote on p. 118 of *Britain's Economic Renaissance* that he had used "M3 statistics" to make an accurate prediction of 15 percent inflation in 1974. See the footnote on p. 84 of Tim Congdon, *Money and Asset Prices in Boom and Bust* (London: Institute of Economic Affairs, 2005) for more on Walters's shifting views on the money aggregates.

49 Liverpool Research Group in Macroeconomics, *Quarterly Economic Bulletin* (October 1987), p. 13. If this proposition were true, it would have drastic implications for economic theory and policy. But it overlooks the banks' liquidity-transformation role. Since checks can be written against bank deposits and there is no loss of check-writing ability because of the existence of bank loans, the simultaneous expansion of deposits and loans increases the economy's liquidity and can change behavior.

50 More direct damage to British monetarism came in other ways. For example, *The Observer* – which, following the lead of its economics editor, William Keegan, was strongly anti-monetarist – reprinted Friedman's 1980 evidence to the Treasury and Civil Service Committee. It correctly judged that this evidence would weaken the credibility of official policy. For the influence of the New Classical economist Eugene Fama on Minford's enthusiasm for M0, see footnote 44 to essay 16 on pp. 467–468.

51 Walters, *Renaissance*, p. 135.

52 Patrick Minford, "The Exchange Rate and Monetary Policy," in W. A. Eltis and P. J. N. Sinclair, eds., *The Money Supply and the Exchange Rate* (Oxford: Clarendon Press, 1981), pp. 120–142. The quotation is from p. 121.

53 Again, see the chapter on bank lending and monetary control in Goodhart, *Monetary Theory*. On p. 126 Goodhart noted that "official reactions in the gilts market to developments in the monetary aggregates . . . have been relatively successful in offsetting unforeseen variations" in bank lending and other influences on broad-money growth.

54 Walters, *Renaissance*, p. 128 and p. 131.

55 These worries, which were particularly serious in Italy, Ireland, and Belgium, are discussed in chapters 1–3 of Tim Congdon, *The Debt Threat* (Oxford: Basil Blackwell, 1988).

56 Perhaps it should not come as a surprise, after his remarks to the Treasury and Civil Service Committee in 1980, that Friedman should say in a letter to *The*

Wall Street Journal on September 4, 1984, that he did not regard the United States' budget deficit – then about 4 percent of GDP – as a major issue or a cause for concern.

57   Keynes, *Tract*, p. 147.

ESSAY 14

1   Michael J. Oliver, *Whatever Happened to Monetarism?* (Aldershot, U.K., and Brookfield, Vt.: Ashgate Publishing, 1997), pp. 151–152.

2   Thomas Mayer and Patrick Minford, "Monetarism: A Retrospective," *World Economics*, vol. 5, no. 2 (April–June 2004), pp. 147–185.

3   Martin Ricketts and Edward Shoesmith, *British Economic Opinion: A Survey of a Thousand Economists* (London: Institute of Economic Affairs, 1990). A large majority of survey respondents disagreed that the central bank should follow a money-supply rule, but agreed – if with reservations – to an incomes policy as a means of controlling inflation. See pp. 74–78.

4   The reference to "pulp forests" was made by Samuel Brittan. (See p. 173 of his paper "Inflation and Democracy," in Fred Hirsch and John H. Goldthorpe, eds., *The Political Economy of Inflation* [London: Martin Robertson, 1978], pp. 161–185.) Literally thousands of papers were written in the 1960s and 1970s about the influence of trade-union bargaining on inflation. See, for example, J. Johnston and M. Timbrell, "Empirical Tests of a Bargaining Theory of Wage Rate Determination," in David E. W. Laidler and David Purdy, eds., *Inflation in Labour Markets* (Manchester: Manchester University Press, 1974), pp. 79–108.

5   An example of strong emphasis on the income-expenditure model of national-income determination is provided by the opening pages of Christopher Dow's *Major Recessions: Britain and the World, 1920–1995* (Oxford: Oxford University Press, 1998), as discussed in essay 10.

6   Charles A. E. Goodhart, *Money Information and Uncertainty*, 1st edition (London: Macmillan, 1975), p. 242.

7   The word "corporatism" was used, for example, by Mr. Peter Jay in his Wincott Lecture, "A General Hypothesis of Employment, Inflation and Politics," reproduced in Peter Jay, *The Crisis of Western Political Economy* (London: André Deutsch, 1984), pp. 33–55. See p. 47.

8   Keynes, *The General Theory* (London: Macmillan, 1964 – paperback reprint of 1936 edition), p. 379.

9   The phrase "interventionist bias" may seem a little shrill, but opinion surveys of British university economists confirm that the great majority have been and remain supporters of planning and intervention with the price mechanism. See Ricketts and Shoesmith, *British Economic Opinion*, and Wilfred Beckerman, ed., *The Labour Government's Economic Record: 1964–70* (London: Duckworth, 1972), both *passim*. There can also be little doubt about the bias of elite opinion in the immediate aftermath of the Second World War. According to George Orwell, writing in 1945, "Among the intelligentsia, it hardly needs saying that

the dominant form of nationalism is Communism. . . . A Communist, for my purposes here, is one who looks upon the U.S.S.R. as his Fatherland and feels it his duty to justify Russian policy and advance Russian interests at all costs. Obviously, such people abound in England today, and their direct and indirect influence is very great." Sonia Orwell and Ian Angus, eds., *The Collected Essays, Journalism, and Letters of George Orwell*, vol. III (Harmondsworth: Penguin Books in association with Secker & Warburg, 1971 – paperback reprint of 1968 hardback original), p. 414.

10 James Tobin, *Policies for Prosperity* (Brighton: Wheatsheaf Books, 1987), pp. 265–266.

11 R. J. Ball and T. Burns, "The Inflationary Mechanism in the U.K. Economy," *The American Economic Review*, vol. 66 (September 1976).

12 Alan O. Ebenstein, *Milton Friedman: A Biography* (New York and Basingstoke: Palgrave Macmillan, 2007), p. 186.

13 In its *Quarterly Review* of May 1973 the National Institute opined – in the middle of the biggest boom in the post-war period – that "there is no reason why the present boom should either bust or have to be busted."

14 The alarm was expressed in the weekly columns of Peter Jay in *The Times*, Samuel Brittan in the *Financial Times*, and other commentators. On April 29, 1975, *The Wall Street Journal* carried a leading article entitled "Goodbye, Great Britain."

15 See Robert E. Lucas's paper "Some International Evidence on Output-Inflation Trade-Offs," *The American Economic Review*, vol. 63 (1973); reprinted in Robert E. Lucas, *Studies in Business-Cycle Theory* (Cambridge, Mass., and Oxford, U.K.: MIT Press and Basil Blackwell, 1981), pp. 131–145.

16 "Butskellite" is a conflation of the names of Rab Butler, Conservative chancellor of the exchequer from 1951 to 1955, and Hugh Gaitskell, leader of the Labour Party in the 1950s.

17 The first edition of Karl Popper's polemical *The Poverty of Historicism* (London: Routledge & Kegan Paul), written "in memory of the countless men and women of all creeds or nations or races who fell victims to the fascist and communist belief in Inexorable Laws of Historical Destiny," was published in 1957 and went through five additional printings in the 1960s.

18 Tony Benn, *Arguments for Socialism*, edited by Chris Mullin (Harmondsworth: Penguin, 1980 – originally published in 1979), p. 44.

19 Noel Annan, *Our Age: Portrait of a Generation* (London: Weidenfeld and Nicolson, 1990), *passim*, but especially chapter 26, "Our Vision of Life Rejected"; and Bryan Magee, *Confessions of a Philosopher* (London: Weidenfeld & Nicolson, 1997), pp. 413–415.

20 Wayne Parsons, *The Power of the Financial Press* (Aldershot: Edward Elgar, 1989), p. 173.

21 Thomas Mayer and Patrick Minford, "Monetarism: A Retrospective," *World Economics* (Henley-on-Thames: NTC Publishing), vol. 5, no. 3 (July–September

2004), p. 182. For the antecedents to the MTFS, see Gordon Pepper and Michael Oliver, *Monetarism under Thatcher: Lessons for the Future* (Cheltenham, U.K., and Northampton, Mass.: Edward Elgar, 2001), especially pp. 8–20.

22   A large part of the rationale for the references to "prudence" in Mr. Gordon Brown's speeches and to the more extended treatment in the 1998 Treasury paper *Stability and Investment for the Long Term* is to be sought in ideas of intergenerational equity developed in the last twenty years by the American economist Laurence Kotlikoff and others. These ideas have nothing whatever to do with Keynes or Keynesianism.

23   Tim Congdon, "The U.K.'s Achievement of Economic Stability: How and Why Did It Happen?" *World Economics*, vol. 3, no. 4 (October–December 2002), pp. 25–41, and reprinted here with extensive revisions as essay 7.

24   Mayer and Minford did indeed say that "some of its [monetarism's] basic ideas have become so widely accepted that they are no longer monetarist" (p. 183).

25   Quoted on p. 166 of Johan van Overtveldt, *The Chicago School* (Chicago: Agate Publishing, 2007). In the formula, M denotes the quantity of money, V its velocity of circulation, P the price level of goods and services, and T the volume of transactions.

26   The ending of exchange controls in October 1979 was vital to the long-run competitiveness of the City of London as an international financial center, but it encouraged the location in London of new types of financial institutions, and their money balances exploded in the 1980s and 1990s. Financial de-regulation – notably the liberalization of mortgage credit starting in 1982 – led to an intensification of competition and a narrowing of banks' profit margins. This made it less expensive for companies and financial institutions simultaneously to hold bank deposits and to have bank borrowings, and again that raised the desired ratio of money to expenditure. The de-nationalization of large utility companies after 1984 expanded the private sector, and, for the reasons given in essay 12, that increased the corporate demand to hold money. The demand to hold money is essentially a demand from agents of imperfect credit-worthiness, who may not be able to complete payments by borrowing. They must therefore hold money. Such agents are found in the private sector, whereas the government (and to some extent nationalized industries, which are its financial clones) is highly credit-worthy and does not need to hold money in the same way. (See pp. 265–266 in essay 12.) Finally, the leap in interest rates in late 1979 made it more attractive to keep wealth in the form of interest-bearing deposits (which formed a large part of broad money) than before. Whereas the 1970s were mostly a decade of negative real interest rates, the 1980s saw almost continuously positive real interest rates. All these changes caused the equilibrium ratio of money to income to rise substantially.

27   Keith Bain and Peter Howells, *Monetary Economics: Policy and Its Theoretical Basis* (Basingstoke: Palgrave Macmillan, 2003), p. 327.

28   In an important respect the demand for money remained stable throughout the

1980s and 1990s. Of the three non-bank, non-public sectors in the U.K. (the household, corporate, and financial sectors), the largest money holder from the early 1960s until today has been the household sector. A standard finding in all econometric work is that the household sector's demand-for-money function has remained stable, according to the usual significance tests. (See, for example, L. Drake and K. A. Crystal, "Personal Sector Money Demand in the U.K.," *Oxford Economic Papers* [Oxford: Clarendon Press], vol. 49, no. 2 [April 1997], pp. 188–206, and R. S. J. Thomas, "The Demand for M4: A Sectoral Analysis. Part I – The Personal Sector," *Bank of England Working Paper* [London: Bank of England], paper no. 61 [1997].)

29   Edward Nelson, "Milton Friedman and U.S. Monetary History: 1961–2006," in *Federal Reserve Bank of St. Louis Review*, vol. 89, no. 3 (2007), pp. 153–182. See, particularly, p. 163.

30   Michael J. Artis and Mervyn K. Lewis, "The Demand for Money: Stable or Unstable?" *The Bsnker*, vol. 124 (1974), pp. 239–247, and Artis and Lewis, "The Demand for Money in the U.K., 1963–73," *Manchester School*, vol. 44 (1976), pp. 147–181.

31   More precisely, a lower probability value would attach to a specific range of values around, say, the central value of the growth rate of income forecast for a particular value of the growth rate of money.

32   For the Loughborough speech, see "Financial Change and Broad Money," in the *Bank of England Quarterly Bulletin* (London: Bank of England), vol. 26, no. 4 (December 1986), pp. 499–507. It would be nice to think that Leigh-Pemberton – who had been Thatcher's personal appointee to the governorship – knew what he was talking about. He has written nothing of significance in his own name on monetary theory or policy since leaving the Bank of England. (In his entry in *People of Today*, he lists his recreations as "country pursuits.") According to Lawson in *The View from No. 11* (p. 635), the "principal author" of the Loughborough speech was Eddie (later Sir Edward) George, who became the governor of the Bank of England after Leigh-Pemberton.

33   See the three chapters on pp. 50–154 of Gordon Pepper, *Inside Thatcher's Monetarist Revolution* (London and Basingstoke: Macmillan, 1998), for a comparison of monetarist and non-monetarist forecasts. See also pp. 191–194 of the author's *Reflections on Monetarism*, based on an article in *The Spectator* of March 11, 1989, for an account of the role of monetary data in the largely correct forecast for 1988 made by his forecasting team at L. Messel & Co., and David Smith, *From Boom to Bust* (Harmondsworth: Penguin, 1992), pp. 69–70. According to Lawson, in the mid-1980s "nearly all the reputable monetarist gurus – with the exception of the City analyst Tim Congdon – so far from urging broad money targets on me criticized me for giving too much influence to broad money in general and £M3 in particular." (Lawson, *The View from No. 11*, p. 453.)

34   Most academic economists are left of center, with a majority voting for the

Labour Party. (In the 1987 general election, "43 percent [of the electorate] voted Conservative; even 25 percent of unemployed people voted Conservative; but only 17 percent of academics supported the Conservatives." [David Willetts, *Modern Conservatism* (Harmondsworth: Penguin, 1992), p. 21, citing a MORI poll in *The Times Higher Education Supplement* of June 5, 1987.])

35 David C. Colander and Harry Landreth, eds., *The Coming of Keynesianism to America* (Cheltenham, U.K., and Brookfield, Vt.: Edward Elgar, 1996), p. 183.

ESSAY 15

1 Elizabeth Johnson and Donald E. Moggridge, eds., *The Collected Writings of John Maynard Keynes*, vol. XI, *Economic Articles and Correspondence: Academic* (London and Basingstoke: Macmillan Press for the Royal Economic Society, 1983), p. 376.

2 William J. Barber, ed., *The Works of Irving Fisher*, vol. 4, *The Purchasing Power of Money* (London: Pickering & Chatto, 1997; originally published by Macmillan in New York in 1911), p. 27.

3 Barber, ed., *Works of Fisher*, vol. 5, *Elementary Principles of Economics* (London: Pickering & Chatto, 1997; originally published by Macmillan in New York in 1912), pp. 242–244.

4 The analysis on pp. 242–247 of *Elementary Principles* is different from that in chapter 4 of *Purchasing Power*, even though chapter 4 had ostensibly been on the same subject of "the transition period" (i.e., the passage of events in the transmission mechanism). Chapter 4 of *Purchasing Power* is highly Wicksellian, with much discussion of the relationship between interest rates and the rate of price change, and then between real interest rates and credit demands. This Wicksellian strand was dropped in pp. 242–247 of *Elementary Principles*.

5 See Milton Friedman, "Statement on Monetary Theory and Policy," given in congressional hearings in 1959, reprinted in R. James Ball and Peter Boyle, eds., *Inflation* (Harmondsworth: Penguin Books, 1969), pp. 136–145. The quotations are from p. 141.

6 Don Patinkin, *Money, Interest, and Prices*, 2nd edition (New York: Harper & Row, 1965), p. 21. Keynes is sometimes said to be the originator of the idea of "real balances," as he used the general idea in his 1923 book *A Tract on Monetary Reform*, in a discussion of inflation in revolutionary Russia in the early 1920s. Patinkin's view on the importance of the real-balance effect seems to have changed in his later years. In an entry on "Real Balances" in the 1987 *Palgrave*, he said, "the significance of the real-balance effect is in the realm of macroeconomic theory and not policy." (See John Eatwell et al., eds., *The New Palgrave: Money* [London and Basingstoke: Macmillan, 1989; based on the 1987 *New Palgrave*], p. 307.)

7 This claim is controversial. Patinkin regarded the real-balance effect as a kind of wealth effect. It was pointed out that, as the banking system's assets and liabilities must be equal, that part of the quantity of money represented by banks'

deposit liabilities (so-called "inside money," from a distinction proposed by Gurley and Shaw in their 1960 *Theory of Finance*) could not represent a nation's net wealth. A logical implication was that the real-balance effect related only to "outside money," often taken to be equivalent to monetary-base assets issued by the central bank. It was then shown that, since the monetary base is modest compared to other elements in a nation's wealth, the real-balance effect is small and cannot have a powerful influence on macroeconomic outcomes. (See, in particular, Thomas Mayer, "The Empirical Significance of the Real-Balance Effect," *The Quarterly Journal of Economics* [vol. 73, no. 2, 1959], pp. 275–291.) The emphasis in macroeconomic theory moved away from the real-balance effect towards "the Keynes effect," to be understood as the effect of changes in the quantity of money on interest rates and so on investment. However, an argument can be made that the only concept of money relevant to the real-balance effect is an all-inclusive measure, since agents can eliminate excesses or deficiencies of smaller, less-than-inclusive measures by transfers between money balances (i.e., they can switch between demand deposits and time deposits, or between notes and demand deposits). Such "money transfers" plainly have no effect on aggregate demand or asset dispositions. (This point is developed in the critique of Minford's views on money on pp. 304–307 of the author's *Keynes, the Keynesians, and Monetarism* [Cheltenham, U.K., and Northampton, Mass.: Edward Elgar, 2007].) By implication, if the real-balance effect is indeed the *sine qua non* of monetary theory, it must relate to inside money and cannot be exclusively a wealth effect. (For further discussion, see Tim Congdon, "Broad Money vs. Narrow Money," *The Review of Policy Issues* [Sheffield: Policy Research Centre], vol. 1, no. 5 [1995], pp. 13–27.) Laidler has also used the phrase "the real-balance effect" to mean something more than just a wealth effect; he claimed that, in the U.S. economy for the years 1954–78, "the adjustment of real balances towards the desired long-run values has a pervasive and systematic influence on the macroeconomy." (David E. W. Laidler, *Money and Macroeconomics* [Cheltenham: Edward Elgar, 1997], p. 172.) Note also that the claim that outside money, i.e., the central bank's liabilities, constitutes net wealth to the private sector of the economy is debatable. It would obviously be invalid if the central banks' assets were all claims on the private sector. But, even if all the central bank's assets were in the form of government securities, and – in accordance with Barro's doctrine of Ricardian equivalence – government debt were judged not to be net wealth to the private sector, then,

i. outside money also cannot be net wealth to the private sector, and
ii. the private sector's net wealth cannot be increased when the central bank expands its balance sheet.

Yet virtually all macroeconomists accept that something important happens when the central bank shifts the position of the supply curve of the monetary base and changes short-term interest rates. If this effect is not a net-wealth

effect, how does it change anything and why does it matter? And, if it matters
so much even though it is not a wealth effect, why is it that changes in inside
money do not matter at all? These are some of the issues to which the author
hopes ultimately to return in a book on how money influences macroeconomic
outcomes in a modern economy (i.e., an economy with a commercial banking
system *and a central bank*).

8   In the autumn of 1995 *The Journal of Economic Perspectives* published a number of papers on the transmission mechanism of monetary policy. Not one of
the papers focused on the real-balance effect as the heart of this mechanism.
Indeed, despite Fisher's and Friedman's clear statements many years earlier,
and Friedman's and many others' vast output on the empirical relationship
between money and the economy, Bernanke and Gertler opined that "empirical analysis of the effects of monetary policy has treated the monetary transmission mechanism as a 'black box.'" (Ben Bernanke and Mark Gertler, "Inside
the Black Box: The Credit Channel of Monetary Policy Transmission," *The
Journal of Economic Perspectives*, vol. 9, no. 4 [Minneapolis: American Economic Association, Autumn 1995], pp. 27–48. The quotation is from p. 27.)

9   The Monetary Policy Committee of the Bank of England, *The Transmission
Mechanism of Monetary Policy* (London: Bank of England, in response to suggestions by the Treasury Committee of the House of Commons, 1999), p. 10. The
note is believed to have been written by John Vickers, the Bank's chief economist at the time. See also Spencer Dale and Andrew G. Haldane, "Interest Rates
and the Channels of Monetary Transmission: Some Sectoral Estimates," Bank
of England, Working Paper Series no. 18 (1993), for a description of the transmission mechanism in which the quantity of money plays no motivating role.

10   Johnson and Moggridge, eds., *The Collected Writings*, vol. V, *A Treatise on
Money* (London and Basingstoke: Macmillan Press for the Royal Economic
Society, 1971; originally published in 1930), chapter 15, "The Industrial Circulation and the Financial Circulation," pp. 217–230. Keynes argued that "the
industrial circulation . . . will vary with . . . the aggregate of money incomes, i.e.,
with the volume and cost of production of current output" (p. 221), whereas
"the financial circulation is . . . determined by quite a different set of considerations" (p. 222). In his words, "the amount of business deposits . . . required to
look after financial business depends – apart from possible variations in the
velocity of these deposits – on the volume of trading × the average value of the
instruments traded" (also p. 222). Arguably, these remarks contained the germ
of the later distinction between the transactions and speculative motives for
holding money. In the discussion of the financial circulation in *A Treatise on
Money*, securities (i.e., equities and bonds) are the alternative to money; in the
discussion of the speculative demand to hold money in *The General Theory*,
bonds are the alternative to money.

11   Milton Friedman and David Meiselman, "The Relative Stability of Monetary
Velocity and the Investment Multiplier in the United States, 1897–1958," in

Stabilization Policies (Englewood Cliffs, N.J.: Prentice-Hall for the Commission on Money and Credit, 1963), pp. 165–268. See, in particular, p. 217.

12   Ted Doggett, "The 1989 Share Register Survey," *Economic Trends* (London: HMSO for the Central Statistical Office), January 1991 issue, pp. 116–121.

13   Ryland Thomas, "The Demand for M4: A Sectoral Analysis, Part I – The Personal Sector," Bank of England, Working Paper Series, no. 61, 1997; and K. Alec Chrystal and Leigh Drake, "Personal Sector Money Demand in the U.K.," *Oxford Economic Papers* (Oxford: Clarendon Press, 1967).

14   Ryland Thomas, "The Demand for M4: A Sectoral Analysis, Part II – The Company Sector," Bank of England, Working Paper Series, no. 62, 1997; and K. Alec Chrystal, "Company Sector Money Demand: New Evidence on the Existence of a Stable Long-Run Relationship for the U.K.," *Journal of Money, Credit and Banking*, vol. 26 (1994), pp. 479–494.

15   The author developed his ideas on U.K. financial institutions' money-holding behavior over many years as a brokerage economist and consultant, when such institutions were his principal clients.

16   Of course, every economy has international transactions. Such transactions represent another escape valve for an excess supply or demand for money balances, in accordance with the monetary approach to the balance of payments. But to discuss the possibilities would take this essay too far. In any case, the incorporation of an "overseas sector" in data sets on transactions in particular assets is conceptually straightforward. (See table 15.3.) The overseas sector's transactions become entries in the capital account of the balance of payments. Again, it is conceptually straightforward – although empirically very demanding – to expand the arena of payments, the closed circuit for transactions, so that it becomes the world economy. (The reader may wonder why the essay uses the data for 1994 rather than a later year. The answer is that the Office for National Statistics no longer publishes the data in this form.)

17   The idea that investment adjusts until the market value of a capital asset equals the replacement cost is associated with James Tobin and "the Q ratio," i.e., the ratio of the market value of a firm's capital to its replacement cost. See his article "A General Equilibrium Approach to Monetary Theory," *Journal of Money, Credit, and Banking*, vol. 1, no. 1 (February 1969), pp. 15–29. But similar remarks have been made by many other economists, including Friedman. See his "The Lag in Effect of Monetary Policy," in Milton Friedman, *The Optimum Quantity of Money* (London and Basingstoke: Macmillan, 1969), pp. 237–260, reprinted from a 1961 paper in the *Journal of Political Economy*; see, in particular, pp. 255–256. When an excess supply of money affects asset markets, the result is "to raise the prices of houses relative to the rents of dwelling units, or the cost of purchasing a car relative to the cost of renting one," and so on. In Friedman's view, "the process operates through the balance sheet, and it is plausible that balance-sheet adjustments are sluggish in the sense that individuals spread adjustments over a considerable period of time" (p. 256).

18   Numerous studies identify a relationship between wealth and consumption. See, for example, Joseph P. Byrne and E. Philip Davis, "Disaggregate Wealth and Aggregate Consumption: An Investigation of Empirical Relationships in the G7," National Institute of Economic and Social Research, Discussion Paper no. 180 (London: National Institute, 2001).

19   An implication is that the circular flow of funds – such a familiar part of undergraduate macroeconomic courses – is misleading and unrealistic when it is taken to imply that national income stays in line with national expenditure unless autonomous injections of demand come from the government or overseas. Any agent can sell any asset, obtain a money balance, and use the proceeds to buy a good or service that constitutes part of national output; the purchase thus leads to increased national income and expenditure. Similarly, any agent can run down a money balance and buy a good or service, with the same effects. Assets differ from money in that the nominal value of money is given, whereas the nominal value of assets can vary without limit. The transactions involved in "mortgage-equity withdrawal" from the housing market – at present the topic of much interest – illustrate the merging of asset markets and markets in current goods and services. Much research on this topic has been conducted at the Bank of England. See, for example, Melissa Davey, "Mortgage Equity Withdrawal and Consumption," *Bank of England Quarterly Bulletin* (Spring 2001), pp. 100–103. The author introduced the concept of equity withdrawal to the analysis of personal-sector spending in a paper written jointly with Paul Turnbull in 1982. (Tim Congdon and Paul Turnbull, "The Coming Boom in Housing Credit," L. Messel & Co. research paper, June 1982, reprinted in Tim Congdon, *Reflections on Monetarism* [Aldershot, U.K., and Brookfield, Vt.: Edward Elgar for the Institute of Economic Affairs, 1992], pp. 274–287.) The argument in this footnote is developed at greater length in essay 11.

ESSAY 16

1   Mish's *Global Economic Trend Analysis*, "A Different Take on M3," December 9, 2005.

2   John Williams' Shadow Government Statistics, "Fed Abandons M3 without an Honest Explanation," issue no. 13B, November 23, 2005.

3   The author has been unable to locate an official Federal Reserve rationale for ending the preparation of the "liquidity" aggregate. In the crisis of the last few years, a common remark has been that "the Fed has injected *liquidity* into *the system*." The words "liquidity" and "the system" have so many different valid definitions that the remark is virtually meaningless, and the notion of "liquidity" (i.e., extra monetary-base assets) here is quite different from that in the pre-1998 liquidity aggregate (i.e., holdings of money and near-money assets by non-banks).

4   Ben Bernanke, *Essays on the Great Depression* (Princeton: Princeton University Press, 2000), p. 7. The italics are in the original.

5   In his early years at the Fed, Bernanke was a strong advocate of inflation targeting, but he was not enthusiastic about money targets. See Ethan S. Harris, *Ben Bernanke's Fed: The Federal Reserve after Greenspan* (Boston: Harvard Business Press, 2008), pp. 95–109.

6   Otmar Issing, "Monetary Analysis Is Essential, Not Old-Fashioned," *Financial Times*, December 15, 2005.

7   The real levels of income and wealth are of course determined by real variables, such as technology and demography. These real forces are not analyzed here.

8   The alleged instability and inadequacy of the free-market capitalist system is captured even in the subtitle of *Freefall: America, Free Markets, and the Sinking of the Global Economy*, a 2010 book by the Keynesian economist Joseph E. Stiglitz (London and New York: Allen Lane, 2010).

9   George A. Akerlof and Robert J. Shiller, *Animal Spirits* (Princeton and Oxford: Princeton University Press, 2009), p. xi.

10 Ibid., p. 131.

11 Keynes, *The General Theory*, reprinted in Johnson and Moggridge, eds., *The Collected Writings*, vol. VII (1973), pp. 155–156.

12 Akerlof and Shiller, *Animal Spirits*, p. 74.

13 For an example of a paper claiming that the monetary base (i.e., cash in the public's hands plus banks' own cash reserves) is interesting and useful as a guide to the future of the economy, see Edward Nelson, "Direct Effects of Base Money on Aggregate Demand: Theory and Evidence," *Journal of Monetary Economics* (Elsevier), vol. 49, no. 4 (2002), pp. 687–708.

14 For example, a paper titled "One Year under 'Quantitative Easing,'" by Masaaki Shirakawa, was published by the Bank of Japan's Institute for Monetary and Economic Studies in 2002 (IMES Discussion Paper no. 2002-E-3, April 2002). On p. 35 it presented a figure on "The Standard Transmission Mechanism of Monetary Policy." Arrows connect a box labeled "Change in Reserves" to one labeled "Change in Short-Term Interest Rates" and to another, "Changes in the Prices of Financial Assets (i.e., Medium- and Long-Term Interest Rates, Foreign-Exchange Rates, Stock Prices, etc.)," and then, both directly and via a box labeled "Change in the Behavior of Financial Institutions," to the final box, "Change in the Behavior of Domestic Private Economic Agents, Such as Firms and Households, and Also Overseas Economic Agents." The approach was similar to that of the paper prepared in 1999 by the Monetary Policy Committee of the Bank of England for the attention of the Treasury Committee of the House of Commons. A vital attribute of macroeconomic equilibrium – that the quantity of money be willingly held at the prevailing levels of asset prices and national income – was ignored in both the Shirakawa paper and the Bank of England paper. Numerous other illustrations could be cited.

15 In the simple versions of the story, nothing material is affected if the change in the money supply is a reduction. The argument proceeds in the same way, but the eventual equilibrium outcome is a fall in the price level rather than an increase.

16 In most countries with modern capital markets and payment systems, the total value of transactions is nevertheless a very high multiple – often fifty or so times – the value of national income and expenditure.

17 See Milton Friedman, "Statement on Monetary Theory and Policy," given in congressional hearings in 1959, reprinted in R. J. Ball and Peter Boyle, eds., *Inflation* (Harmondsworth: Penguin, 1969), pp. 136–145. The quotations are from p. 141. Note the similarity of the account of "the real-balance effect" here to that on pp. 331–333 of essay 15 and pp. 356–360 of essay 16. The two accounts have the same basic ingredients and structure.

18 Alan Rabin, *Monetary Theory* (Cheltenham, U.K., and Northampton, Mass.: Edward Elgar, 2004), pp. 71–74.

19 James Tobin, *Essays in Economics*, vol. 1, *Macroeconomics* (Amsterdam and New York: North-Holland Publishing Company, 1971), p. 273. The original paper from which the quote was taken ("Commercial Banks as 'Creators' of Money") first appeared in Deane Carson, ed., *Banking and Monetary Studies* (Homewood, Ill.: Richard D. Irwin, 1963).

20 Papers were written in the 1970s and early 1980s on "disequilibrium" or "buffer-stock" money, notably by Charles Goodhart and David Laidler, almost as if the problem of eliminating imbalances between the demand for and supply of money were a new topic. (See, for example, "Disequilibrium Money: A Note," in Charles A. E. Goodhart, *Monetary Theory and Practice: The U.K. Experience* [London: Macmillan, 1984], pp. 254–276.) Yeager had earlier written in a similar vein, well aware that the topic was not new. See footnote 29 below. Indeed, it can be argued that – at least since Hume's reference, in his famous 1752 essay "Of Money," to "the intermediate situation" in which an increase in money has not had its full effect on prices – the working out of excess or deficient real balances (i.e., monetary disequilibrium) has been the core of the transmission mechanism in monetary economics. (Hume in fact mentioned a quantified real-balance effect in France in "the last year of Louis XIV," when "money was raised by three sevenths, but price augmented only by one," quoting Dutot in *Réflexions Politiques*. [David Hume, *Essays, Literary, Moral, and Political* (London: Ward, Lock & Co., n.d.), pp. 170–171.])

21 Early in the twentieth century Irving Fisher explained why banks' cash reserves should be excluded from the quantity of money. (See William J. Barber, ed., *The Works of Irving Fisher*, vol. 5, *Elementary Principles of Economics* [London: Pickering & Chatto, 1997; originally published by Macmillan in New York in 1912), p. 178.)

22 As far as the author is aware, the two related points – that money-into-money transactions can nullify the causal role in the transmission mechanism of a less-than-all-inclusive money aggregate, and that an all-inclusive money measure is therefore the important one in macroeconomic analysis – have not received much previous emphasis by other economists. However, Irving Fisher hinted at these ideas in 1912. If check payments are ignored, "we may classify

exchanges into three groups: the exchange of goods against goods, or barter; the exchange of money against money, or '*changing*' money; and the exchange of money against goods, or *purchase and sale*. Only the last-named species of exchange involves what we call the *circulation* of money." (Ibid., p. 151. Italics are in the original.) See also p. 178 of *Elementary Principles* on the same theme. The point is repeated on p. 34 of Fisher's 1914 *Why Is the Dollar Shrinking?* (New York: Macmillan, 1914).

23   A 1998 Bank of England working paper contained a pie chart on "Sources of Cash in 1997." It showed that automated-teller machines, withdrawals from bank or building-society deposits, and cash-backs represented 66 percent of all such sources, with the rest being "state benefits" (presumably mostly from post offices at that time) and employers. In other words, most cash arose from money-into-money transactions. The value of "cash turnover for individuals" was put at £238 billion in 1997. This may sound substantial relative to gross domestic product in that year, which was just over £810 billion at current market prices. However, both cash turnover and GDP paled into insignificance compared with the value of bank clearings, which was over £36,000 billion in 1997. In other words, payments made via bank accounts had a value about 150 times that of payments made with cash. (See Norbert Janssen, "The Demand for M0 in the U.K. Reconsidered: Some Specification Issues," Bank of England Working Paper no. 83, pp. 14–15, and any issue of *The Annual Abstract of Banking Statistics* [London: British Bankers' Association], for the value of clearings.) The situation in the U.S. and other countries is similar.

24   See pp. 83–84 of Nicholas Kaldor, "The New Monetarism," in Christopher Johnson, ed., *Monetarism and the Keynesians* (London and New York: Pinter Publishers, 1991), pp. 79–100. Kaldor's paper originally appeared in *Lloyds Bank Review* in 1970.

25   See Tim Congdon, "Broad Money vs. Narrow Money," *The Review of Policy Issues* (Sheffield: Sheffield Hallam University), vol. 1, no. 5 (Autumn 1995), pp. 13–27. The quotation is from p. 21.

26   Of course the sequence of transactions, with money passing to and fro between different agents, takes time. This is the source of the famous "lags" in the transmission mechanism from money to the economy. Note also that the value of transactions involved in the equilibration of money demand and supply is many times higher than the value of national income. See footnotes 16 and 23 above.

27   An objection to the money-transfers argument – made with particular emphasis in the U.K.'s Radcliffe Report of 1959 – arises at this point. Why stop at the broadest possible measure of money? What about near-money liquid assets? Surely, if the causal role of narrow money in expenditure determination can be nullified by money transfers, the macroeconomic significance of an all-inclusive money measure can be similarly nullified by transfers between it and an aggregate including near-money liquid assets (i.e., by money-into-near-monies

transactions). There are two answers here. The first is to note, by analogy with the earlier discussion about M1, that – in an economy with money, near-monies, and goods – disequilibrium between the demand to hold broad money and the money supply can be eliminated in two ways, either by transactions involving money, goods, and/or non-money assets, or by transactions between money and near-monies. The macroeconomic significance of the all-inclusive money measure is undermined only if money-into-near-monies transactions are large relative to the macroeconomically much more important money-into-goods transactions. A reasonable conjecture is that in most economies money-into-near-monies transactions are small compared with economically significant transactions. Second, even if it were true that money-into-near-monies transactions were enormous relative to other types of transaction, frequent and large divergences in the rate of change of liquidity and M3 would need to be observed to justify a major switch of policy-makers' attention towards liquidity. If liquidity and M3 grow at much the same rate, a central bank should have sufficient guidance from tracking M3. But there is no harm in collecting data on liquid assets, and, from time to time, the differences between liquidity and money growth rates may be important in policy-making.

28 The notion of "a given nominal value" is more difficult than it seems. The point that the nominal value of money does not change in the course of transactions – unlike the nominal value (i.e., the price) of goods and assets – is definite enough. But in normal times "the nominal value" of most bank deposits does increase over time nowadays because of the addition of interest. (Obviously this has not been true in the last few years of virtually zero short-term interest rates.) The view that the payment of interest reduces the "money"-ness of a deposit has been attributed to Pesek and Saving. But interest-bearing demand deposits have now become common. Monetary economics is not an easy subject.

29 Two references to the literature may be apposite here. First, what is the bearing of the analysis in this essay on the notion of "Divisia money" (i.e., a so-called "monetary-quantity index" in which notes and coin are taken to be the most "money-like" form of money and so are given a higher weight than demand deposits, which in turn are given a higher weight than time deposits) compared with simple-sum money aggregates? The answer depends on the analyst's prior beliefs. In classic works from the 1930s to the 1960s, Keynes, Hicks, and Friedman insisted that the demand for money needs to be analyzed within asset portfolios. If that work is regarded as progress (and the author of this essay does regard it as progress), Divisia indices seem to lose a key insight into the subject. Second, proponents of the "disequilibrium money" school associated with Yeager (and, further back, Clark Warburton) might be expected to be sympathetic to the money-transfers argument in this essay, since that argument is intended to put the real-balance effect (or "the Wicksell process," or "the hot-potato argument," or whatever one wants to call it) once again at the heart of monetary economics. (For this tradition of thought, see in

particular Leland B. Yeager, *The Fluttering Veil: Essays on Monetary Disequilibrium* [Indianapolis: Liberty Fund, 1997].) However, their preference is for narrow money over broad money, although they sometimes claim that the "Which money?" debate is not particularly important. (Rabin, *Monetary Theory*, p. 122.) Rabin has even claimed – following Yeager – that "If money broadly defined is in excess demand, money narrowly defined must be in excess demand also." (Rabin, *Monetary Theory*, p. 103, and Yeager, *Fluttering Veil*, p. 218.) The preference for narrow money (i.e., M1) arises because of the belief that M1 is a stable multiple of the monetary base, which is under the control of the Federal Reserve (in the American context), and it is often accompanied by critiques of the use of the credit-money identity in central banking. (See Robert Greenfield and Leland B. Yeager, "Money and Credit Confused," in Yeager, *Fluttering Veil*, pp. 179–195.) To repeat, in the author's view the preference for narrow money is a mistake because of the ease of making money transfers between different types of money balance. The process of money-supply determination is a large and much-debated subject, although – again unlike Yeager and Rabin – the author does not believe that the quantity of money is usefully interpreted nowadays as a multiple of the base. (In this respect he agrees with chapter 10 of Peter Bofinger, *Monetary Policy* [Oxford: Oxford University Press, 2001], pp. 321–368. Bofinger's argument is in a tradition of research associated particularly with Professor Charles Goodhart of the London School of Economics.) It is possible to believe *both* that the quantity of money is not usefully interpreted as a multiple of the base (but is instead better seen as a relatively stable multiple of banks' capital) *and* that, when the demand for money differs from the quantity of money, asset prices and national income change (via the Wicksell process) as agents try to restore monetary equilibrium.

30 Alan Walters, *Britain's Economic Renaissance* (Oxford: Oxford University Press, 1986), pp. 116–117.

31 The data on the relationship between, on the one hand, life-insurance companies' and pension funds' holdings of money and liquid assets, and, on the other, their total assets, was regularly tracked at Lombard Street Research, the research company founded by the author in 1989. The data appeared in the official publication *Financial Statistics*, which had first been published in the early 1960s. See the author's *Money and Asset Prices in Boom and Bust* (London: Institute of Economic Affairs, 2005), *passim*, but particularly chapter 3, for further discussion.

32 However, the data are not altogether satisfactory. The exact amount of the different forms of money *held by the financial sector in aggregate* cannot be readily identified from published sources, in contrast to the ready availability of similar information in other industrial countries. In the United States' flow-of-funds data, figures are given for banks' total liabilities in the form of large time deposits and institutional money funds, but a split of these types of money *by holder* is not given. Further, data are not presented consistently for all types of

financial institution. As the methods of asset categorization vary so much from one table to the next, it is not easy to make comparisons between the money-holding behaviors of different types of institution. Open-market paper, such as one-month and three-month commercial paper, illustrates the problem. Data for holdings of such paper by state- and local-government pension funds are included, but comparable data for the holdings of the more important private pension funds are not. Sometimes the omissions are very frustrating for the analyst. For example, no information is given on mutual funds' holdings of bank deposits at all, even though they undoubtedly do have bank accounts, and mutual funds are now the largest type of long-term savings institution.

33 In a simple ordinary-least-square regression of the change in total assets on money assets, using the data in figure 16.2, the t statistic on the regression coefficient was over 10. (The r^2 was a perhaps rather disappointing 0.34.)

34 Large differences in the long-run behavior of the money/assets ratios and liquidity/assets ratios were observed for different types of financial institution. The ratio of liquid assets to total assets in the property and casualty (i.e., non-life, general) insurance sector was almost 10 percent in 1953, but little more than 2 percent at the end of 2005. By contrast, the money/assets ratio of life-insurance companies was about 1½ percent in 1953, but over 6 percent in the early years of the current century. Skeptics might say that large swings in the money/assets and liquidity/assets ratios invalidate the approach. However, the changes in money/assets and liquidity/assets ratios can often be attributed to institutional innovation and various special influences, implying that the underlying demand to hold money bore a stable relationship to total assets.

35 A 2005 book titled *Asset Price Bubbles* had several papers on the "credit determines asset prices" theme. (William C. Hunter, George F. Kaufman, and Michael Pomerleano, eds., *Asset Price Bubbles* [Cambridge, Mass., and London: MIT Press, 2005].) Santiago Herrera and Guillermo Perry, "Tropical Bubbles: Asset Prices in Latin America, 1980–2001," pp. 127–162, contains regressions of the relationship between domestic credit and real-estate prices in Latin American countries; Claudio Borio and Philip Lowe, "Imbalances or 'Bubbles'? Implications for Monetary and Financial Stability," pp. 247–270, contains a more wide-ranging discussion, including a reference to the United States' experiences in the 1925–30 period, without any mention of money.

36 The largest one-year increase in U.S. share prices in the twentieth century was in the year up to the first quarter of 1934. An "index of common stocks" increased by 70.0 percent. (Robert J. Gordon, ed., *The American Business Cycle* [Chicago and London: University of Chicago Press, 1986], p. 804.) In the same period the "loans and discounts" held by member banks of the U.S. Federal Reserve system were falling. In the four years up to mid-1936, their loans and discounts declined by 24.4 percent, from $16,587 million to $12,542 million, whereas the index of common stocks (1941–43 = 100) climbed from 5.08 to 13.58, or by 167.3 percent. (Ray B. Westerfield, *Money, Credit, and Banking*

[New York: Ronald Press Company, 1947], p. 906, and Gordon, *American Business Cycle*, p. 804.) The mid-1930s saw high money-supply growth in the United States, as the banks purchased government bonds issued to finance both the budget deficit and the U.S. government's purchases of gold and silver. The favorable effect of debt-management operations on asset prices – working via the quantity of money – was obvious. Again, in the Second World War, in both the U.S. and the U.K., the banks' lending to the private sector fell, but the quantity of money increased (as banks acquired more claims on the government), and both share prices and house prices rose.

37   "According to several studies, upward of 90 percent of paper money in New York, Miami, and London, and, it is suspected, other major cities, contains trace elements of drugs." Raymond W. Baker, *Capitalism's Achilles' Heel* (Hoboken, N.J.: John Wiley & Sons, 2005), p. 23.

38   See p. A15 of Brian K. Bucks, Arthur B. Kennickell, and Kevin B. Moore, "Recent Changes in U.S. Family Finances: Evidence from the 2001 and 2004 Survey of Consumer Finances," *Federal Reserve Bulletin* (Washington, D.C.: U.S. Federal Reserve, February 2006).

39   Geoffrey R. Gerdes, "Recent Payment Trends in the United States," *Federal Reserve Bulletin* (Washington, D.C.: U.S. Federal Reserve, October 2008), pp. A75–A106. The section on cash payments is on pp. A85–A87. The average debit to transaction accounts with a value under $100,000 was $492 in 2007, again inconsistent with the apparent value of currency per head.

40   Whether it has relevance because of its bearing on the size of banks' deposit liabilities – because, in other words, the monetary base affects the quantity of money – is a different subject.

41   The M1 measure of money is favored, for example, by Allan Meltzer in his *History of the Federal Reserve*. See Allan H. Meltzer, *A History of the Federal Reserve*, vol. I, 1913–51 (Chicago and London: University of Chicago Press, 2003). On p. 577, "money growth" is equated with growth of M1.

42   See table 2.5 in any issue of the ECB's *Monthly Bulletin*, as currently laid out.

43   Wicksell did not endorse a definition of money including all bank deposits, but his discussion of "the cumulative process" in *Lectures on Political Economy* would be incomprehensible if it were not implicitly assumed throughout that the banking system's behavior could affect the price level, and he explicitly rejected a quantity-theory approach in which money consisted only of metallic money (p. 154 and pp. 190–208 of vol. II, *Money*, of Knut Wicksell, *Lectures on Political Economy* [London: George Routledge and Sons, 1935]); Fisher explicitly included bank deposits in his "equation of exchange" and noted the effect of "deposit money" on the price level (p. 179 and pp. 186–187 of Fisher, *Elementary Principles of Economics*); Keynes's approval for broad-money measures in a footnote on p. 267 of *The General Theory* was forthright ("As a rule, I shall, as in my *Treatise on Money*, assume that money is co-extensive with deposits."); Robertson was relatively pragmatic, but clearly leaned towards an

all-inclusive measure in the *Lectures on Economic Principles* published towards
the end of his life: "I am in favour of casting [the net of definition] fairly
widely. . . . [F]or the kind of community in which we are most interested, we
must include deposits with a bank drawable on by cheque (and therefore
exclude coins etc. held by banks, i.e., our M is money in the hands of 'the public'); and I doubt whether it is convenient to try, as is sometimes done, to draw
the line at 'current accounts' [U.K.] or 'demand deposits' [U.S.A.]" (Dennis H.
Robertson, *Lectures on Economic Principles*, vol. III, *Money* [London: Staples
Press, 1959, p. 13]); Hawtrey's early work was written before concepts of
"money" had stabilized, but he proposed a concept of "the unspent margin"
which "could be arrived at by adding up the liabilities of all the banks, or by
adding up all the credits held by all their customers, whether depositors or
note-holders," and observed that it was the banks' "action, not the [central-
bank] note issue, which directly affects the value of the monetary unit" (Ralph
Hawtrey, *Currency and Credit* [London: Longmans, 1923], p. 34 and p. 50);
Friedman and Schwartz said in their *Monetary History* that "currency held by
the public and sight *and time deposits* . . . in commercial banks" (author's italics) is "our concept of money" (Milton Friedman and Anna Jacobson Schwartz,
A Monetary History of the United States, 1867–1960 [Princeton: Princeton University Press, 1963], p. 630); and Johnson remarked that "in a modern economy" money is "created by the banking system" (Harry G. Johnson, *Money,
Trade, and Economic Growth* [London: Allen & Unwin, 1962], p. 121). Numerous other references could be given for all these authors. To summarize, the
quantity of money in traditional monetary economics was a broadly defined
measure dominated by bank deposits.

44   The key paper here is Eugene Fama's "Banking in a Theory of Finance," *Journal
of Monetary Economics* (North-Holland Publishing Company), vol. 6 (1980),
pp. 39–57, with its claim that, if certain assumptions are met, "banks remain
passive intermediaries, with no control over any of the details of a general
equilibrium." Fama did not discuss the realism of the assumptions needed for
his conclusions, but some economists have taken his work as justifying a focus
on the monetary base (or "outside money") in real-world situations. For example,
Minford regards the M0 measure of the base as the same thing as "the money
supply." (See p. 63 of Patrick Minford, "Optimal Monetary Policy with Endogenous Contracts," in Kent Matthews and Philip Book, eds., *Issues in Monetary
Policy* [Chichester: John Wiley & Sons, 2006], pp. 63–80.) As shown in footnotes 16, 23, and 39 above, transactions in notes and coin account for less than
1 percent of all transactions in the U.S. and the U.K. nowadays. (Fama's argument is an application of the Modigliani-Miller theorem to banking, but it follows an earlier tendency – notably, by Patinkin – to say that only changes in
outside money [i.e., the monetary base] constituted changes in net private-sector wealth and were relevant to the real-balance effect.) If economists – on the
advice of eminent authorities – come to believe that the relevant money aggre-

gate is the one that is used in less than 1 percent of transactions, it is perhaps excusable that they should deem the monetary transmission mechanism "a black box." (Ben Bernanke and Mark Gertler, "Inside the Black Box: The Credit Channel of Monetary Policy Transmission," *The Journal of Economic Perspectives*, vol. 9, no. 4 [Minneapolis: American Economic Association, Autumn 1995], pp. 27–48.)

ESSAY 17

1   Milton Friedman and Anna Jacobson Schwartz, *A Monetary History of the United States, 1867–1960* (Princeton: Princeton University Press for the National Bureau of Economic Research, 1963).

2   *Foreign Policy* (Washington: Washington Post), December 2009 issue, pp. 26–27.

3   In Friedman's words, "The stock of money [should be] increased at a fixed rate year in and year out without any variation in the rate of increase to meet cyclical needs." See, in particular, Milton Friedman, *A Program for Monetary Stability* (New York: Fordham University Press, 1960).

4   Federal Reserve Board website (as of June 2010), 2002 speeches, Remarks by Governor Ben Bernanke on November 8 at University of Chicago, "On Milton Friedman's Ninetieth Birthday." The speech is not paginated.

5   Friedman and Schwartz, *A Monetary History*, pp. 712–714.

6   For a challenging discussion of Friedman's shifting allegiances towards the money aggregates, see Ed Nelson, "Milton Friedman and U.S. Monetary History, 1961–2006," *Federal Reserve Bank of St. Louis Review* (May–June 2007), pp. 153–182. The Nelson paper is also discussed in essay 14, on p. 317.

7   The main reference here is Richard Anderson and Kenneth Kavajecz, "A Historical Perspective on the Federal Reserve's Monetary Aggregates: Definition, Construction and Targeting," *Federal Reserve Bank of St. Louis Review* (March–April 1994), pp. 1–31.

8   The M3 value in December 2009 is an estimate prepared by the research company Shadow Government Statistics; the other values are from the statistical section of the website of the Federal Reserve Bank of St. Louis.

9   Johan van Overtveldt, *Bernanke's Test* (Chicago: Agate Publishing, 2009), p. 105.

10   Paul Krugman's *The Return of Depression Economics and the Crisis of 2008* (New York and London: W. W. Norton & Co., 2009) has a good discussion of the "shadow banking system" on pp. 153–164. In early 2008 the "auction rate security system" collapsed. At its peak it had liabilities of $400 billion and enabled financial institutions to deposit funds at highly attractive interest rates in a vehicle just outside the regulated banking system. At the time, $400 billion was almost 3 percent of the M3 money measure. See pp. 158–159 of Krugman, *Return of Depression Economics.*

11   Milton Friedman and Anna J. Schwartz, *Monetary Trends in the United States and the United Kingdom* (Chicago and London: University of Chicago Press, 1982), p. 31.

12 "Credit spreads" are the excess of the yields on bonds of risk-taking issuers over yields on very safe government paper.

ESSAY 18

1 Keynes's remark was in a highly critical review, which originally appeared in 1931, of Hayek's *Prices and Production*. See Johnson and Moggridge, *The Collected Writings*, vol. XII, *Economic Articles and Correspondence: Investment and Editorial* (London and Basingstoke: Macmillan for the Royal Economic Society, 1973), p. 252.

2 Ben S. Bernanke and Alan S. Blinder, "Credit, Money, and Aggregate Demand," The *American Economic Review*, vol. 78 (1988), pp. 435–439.

3 Ben S. Bernanke and Mark Gertler, "Inside the Black Box: The Credit Channel of Monetary Policy Transmission," *The Journal of Economic Perspectives*, vol. 9, no. 4 (Autumn 1995), pp. 27–48.

4 Almost immediately there is a problem, in that the reference to internal and external costs of finance makes sense only in the context of lending *to companies*. But in all countries, bank lending to companies is only part (usually much less than half) of total bank lending, and bank lending to *small* companies, where the informational frictions are meant to be most severe (and hence most significant for the cycle), is invariably a tiny fraction of total bank lending. In the real world, bank lending is dominated by lending on mortgages to help borrowers acquire real estate of various kinds (residential, commercial, and agricultural). Lending to small businesses – about which Bernanke and Gertler had written so extensively in their academic articles – was *not* prominent in the banking crisis of 2007–09, whereas the securitization of mortgages was.

5 See the October 2008 issue (no. 24) of the Bank of England's *Financial Stability Report* for a description and attempted rationalization of official policy. Perhaps the key claim appeared on p. 42: that "Recent events have illustrated that banks can now incur losses much faster than they can recapitalise themselves in stressed conditions." The report contained numerous references to "liquidity" and "credit," but at no point were the phrases "the quantity of money" or "the money supply" used.

6 In 1974, after the Heath-Barber boom of 1971–73, a large part of the U.K. banking system – the so-called "secondary banks" – was not just illiquid, but insolvent. The Bank of England orchestrated a massive program of inter-bank lending ("the lifeboat"), with the negotiations taking place as far as possible behind closed doors. Although the secondary banks' shareholders lost most of their investments, every deposit in a British bank paid back in full. The lifeboat program is usually seen as an outstanding example of central banking. Relative to GDP, much larger sums were at stake than in late 2008. The definitive account is Margaret Reid, *The Secondary Banking Crisis 1973–5* (London and Basingstoke: Macmillan, 1982).

7 Paul Krugman, "Gordon Does Good," October 12, 2008, column in *The New*

York Times. According to Krugman, ". . . we do know . . . that Mr. Brown and Alistair Darling . . . have defined the character of the worldwide rescue effort, with other wealthy nations playing catch-up."

8   The reports were corroborated in Andrew Sorkin, *Too Big to Fail* (London: Allen Lane, 2009), p. 439.

9   "U.K. Weighs 'Bad Banks,'" *The Wall Street Journal*, February 4, 2009.

10   See the report in the *Financial Times* on Barclays' annual general meeting on April 23, 2009. Also the author's "Central Banking, Financial Regulation, and Property Rights," in Eugenio A. Bruno, ed., *Global Financial Crisis* (London: Globe Business Publishing, 2009), pp. 29–39, and his "Expropriation of the British Banking Sector," "In the City" column, *Economic Affairs* (London: Institute of Economic Affairs), June 2009, p. 87.

11   Irving Fisher, "The Debt Deflation Theory of Great Depressions," *Econometrica*, vol. 1 (1933), pp. 337–357. The evocative image of a capsizing boat – used to show how a stable equilibrium could beyond a certain point be destabilized – is on p. 339.

12   "Then we have the great paradox which, I submit, is the chief secret of most, if not all, great depressions. *The more the debtors pay, the more they owe.* [Fisher's italics.] The more the economic boat tips, the more it tends to tip. It is not tending to right itself, but is capsizing." (Ibid., p. 344.)

13   The February 16, 2009, issue of the *New Statesman* carried a 2,500-word article on "The New Depression" by Martin Jacques. A quote appeared on the front page: "The political and business elite are [*sic*] flying blind. This crisis has barely started and remains completely out of control." The author understands that, at meetings held in the Treasury at this time, both officials and politicians were in utter despair and could see no end to the deterioration in macroeconomic prospects.

14   The *Financial Times* retained this view for many months after the crisis, despite the cataclysmic macroeconomic conditions that came in the immediate aftermath of the bank recapitalization. In the *Financial Times* of November 4, 2009, Andrew Hill wrote that U.K. officialdom's actions in October 2008 were a "Dunkirk rescue" of the U.K.'s banks and a "tactical masterstroke."

15   International Monetary Fund, *World Economic Outlook: Crisis and Recovery*, April 2009 (Washington: IMF), p. 42. The IMF discussion did contain a section on "Monetary Policy – Turning to Unconventional Approaches," but – as usual in this period – the text contained not one reference to "the quantity of money" or "the money supply."

16   See the last three pages of the Bernanke and Blinder article, which include both the word "creditist" and the phrase "the credit channel," with this latter phrase appearing seven years before the 1995 Bernanke and Gertler article, for which it was part of the title.

17   For an example of a purely creditist paper, see Glenn Hogarth and Joe Thomas, "Will Bank Recapitalization Boost Domestic Demand in Japan?" *Financial Sta-*

bility Review (London: Bank of England, 1999), pp. 85–93. The very title of the paper hints at the notion that bank recapitalization is positive for demand, helping to explain subsequent events in the U.K. Bank of England officials were among those involved, in late 2008, in dealing with a banking problem which they thought was like Japan's some years earlier. But other Bank of England research papers did refer to money and its important macroeconomic effects, perhaps implying an active internal debate about the role of money in the economy.

18   The Bank of England website contained an interview between the governor, Mervyn King, and the BBC journalist Stephanie Flanders, in which King made clear that the intention of quantitative easing was to increase the quantity of money on a broad definition (i.e., the quantity of bank deposits, in effect).

19   To quote – for an example of almost pure creditism – from Samuel Brittan, "Simple Truths about the Economy" (*Financial Times*, November 13, 2009), the QE cash is "being injected into the banks that have a thousand and one excuses for not passing it on in loans to businesses and households. Stimulative monetary policy is not black magic. It works by encouraging business investment and personal borrowing."

20   The course of events in practice was rather different. In early 2009, U.K. broad money was about to collapse, because banks were under regulatory pressure to shrink assets and raise capital/asset ratios. This would have led to a depression, if nothing had been done. In the first instance, the official gilt purchases under QE boosted the financial institutions' money holdings. The banks then raised enormous amounts of extra capital, by issuing more equity and bond capital. This converted money claims on the banks into non-monetary claims, but it also reduced the pressure on them to shrink assets and so to reduce the quantity of money. Meanwhile – with short-term interest rates almost down to zero – economic agents wanted to reduce the ratio of interest-bearing money to income. Measured correctly, the quantity of money was more or less unchanged in the year starting in March 2009, but this was compatible with a spectacular recovery in asset prices and demand.

21   Tim Congdon, *Money and Asset Prices in Boom and Bust* (London: Institute of Economic Affairs, 2005), particularly pp. 37–55.

22   A majority of U.K. households have no significant debt at all, while the number of people who have debt and no assets is a small minority. In 2005, of 18,678,000 individuals for whom Her Majesty's Revenue & Customs were able to estimate "identifiable wealth" data, 5,319,000 had mortgages and 8,630,000 had other debt, but many of the people with mortgages also had other debt. The total of "other debt," as measured by HMRC's approach, was £126.8 billion, compared to gross assets of all individuals of almost £4,000 billion and net wealth of £3,434 billion. Meanwhile, 1,668,000 individuals had no or negative wealth, with their total negative wealth estimated to be slightly under £6.8 billion, a fleabite compared with the assets owned by the overwhelming

majority of people who had positive wealth. (H.M. Revenue & Customs section of the National Statistics website, as of June 2010, table 13.1.) Almost by definition, companies must have positive net worth (i.e., assets in excess of debt) or be insolvent. Most long-term financial institutions have no debt at all. What is this nonsense that spending depends on lending? The U.K. pattern is replicated in similar countries. An overwhelming majority of agents in all economies have no significant debt and do not borrow any sizeable amount in the course of a particular year. How, then, can their spending depend on lending? And, given their dominance of total spending, how can aggregate spending depend on the level of bank lending?

23   Critics of the monetary account of national-income determination sometimes claim that the quantity of money is endogenous (i.e., that it is determined by the levels of national expenditure and income, rather than the other way round). This is obviously daft in hyperinflationary conditions. Does anyone believe that the German hyperinflation of 1923 was the cause of the many-million-fold increases in the reichsmark money supply? The Bank of England's purchases of gilts in 2009 were – undoubtedly, irrefutably – an exogenous event as far as private-sector money holders were concerned.

24   Tim Congdon, *How to Stop the Recession* (London: Centre for the Study of Financial Innovation, 2009). This pamphlet was published in February 2009, just before the Bank of England's announcement of QE in early March. On p. 35 of *How to Stop the Recession* the policy of central-bank purchases of assets from non-banks is described as "the most stimulatory monetary policy weapon imaginable." This was in fact the policy that the Bank of England adopted.

INDEX

Page numbers followed by *f* or *t* indicate figures or tables.

73–77f, 80–81t; money-market operations and, 67–71, 68f, 80t
Northern Rock, 236, 283

Oakeshott, Michael, 261, 269, 271
Obama administration, 271, 374; Old Keynesianism and, xx, xxii, xxiii, xxxi
Okun, Arthur, 108–109, 144–145, 147; output gap and, 142–153. 151t, 158–159t, 160–163
Old Keynesianism, xxi–xxiii
Oliver, Michael, 304
open-market operations: debt-market operations, 60, 66, 72–75, 73–77f, 80–81t, 96–101; generally, 60–67, 66f, 71; money-market operations, 60, 66, 67–71, 76–79, 80t, 81; zero-bound issue, xi, 57–60, 70–71, 92, 95t
Opie, Roger, 10, 11, 264
Organization for Economic Cooperation and Development (OECD), 134, 152–156, 159t
Orphanides, Athanasios, 162
output gap, xxiv–xxv, 108–110, 131–132, 142–164, 177–179, 195, 196t, 197t, 222, 224, 242, 243t, 303, 336, 338; monetarist and Keynesian concepts contrasted, 151t, 158–159t; monetarist concept, Great Moderation and, 162–164; monetarist concept, used by academics, 156–157; monetarist concept, used by central banks, 156, 157, 160; monetarist concept, used by economists, 152–156; monetary policy, technicians versus politicians, 160–162; Okun/Keynesian concept, 142–147; Okun/Keynesian concept, criticisms of and evolution to monetarist concept, 148–152; Okun/Keynesian concept, used by economists, 148–149, 152; in statistical analysis of Keynesian-revolution hypothesis, 131–132,

134–141; statistical analysis of fiscal policy and, 404–406
output volatility, in post-war periods: United Kingdom, 167–172, 169t; United States, 179–180, 180t
overfunding, 50, 53
Overtveldt, Johan van, 379

Paish, Frank, 143–144, 18, 158t
paper credit, evolution of, 4, 34–39
Parkin, Michael, 292
Patinkin, Don, 326, 333, 356
Paulson, Henry (Hank), 392
"Paying for the War" (Keynes), 113, 206–207, 224
Perloff, Jeffrey, 149–150, 152, 153, 162–163
Perry, George, 149
Phelps, Edmund, 148
Phillips, A. W., 143, 158t
Phillips curve, 46, 143–144, 147, 148, 160, 161
Pigou, Arthur Cecil, 254
Plaza Accord, 297
Plosser, Charles, 150
PMI (purchase managers' index), 155
portfolio balance, in The General Theory, 29–30
portfolios. See money-in-portfolios argument
"Potential GNP: Its Measurement and Significance" (Okun), 145
pound sterling: deutschemark and, 53, 293, 298–299, 303; exchange rate fixed to U.S. dollar, 42–43, 46–47; exchange rate fixed to U.S. dollar, Keynes's objections, 40–41; Exchange Rate Mechanism and, 4–5, 55–56, 165, 167, 172, 177, 178, 299; inflation controlled by avoiding devaluation of, 46
price levels, 37–38; Keynes sees as target of monetary policy, 41–42, 54–55